W9-BHO-455

THE WORLD HEAVYWEIGHT BOXING CHAMPIONSHIP

A HISTORY

Books by John D. McCallum

The World Heavyweight Boxing Championship: A History
College Football, U.S.A.
Boxing Fans' Almanac
Everest Diary
Going Their Way
Dumb Dan
The Tiger Wore Spikes
That Kelly Family
Six Roads From Abilene
The Story of Dan Lyons, S.J.
Not By Bread Alone
This Was Football
Scooper
The Gladiators
How You Can Play Little League Baseball
and other books...

THE WORLD HEAVYWEIGHT BOXING CHAMPIONSHIP

A HISTORY

JOHN D. McCALLUM

FOREWORD BY DR. CHARLES P. LARSON
FORMER PRESIDENT, WORLD BOXING ASSOCIATION

CHILTON BOOK COMPANY

RADNOR, PENNSYLVANIA

Published in Radnor, Pa., by Chilton Book Company
and simultaneously in Ontario, Canada,
by Thomas Nelson & Sons, Ltd.
Designed by Warren Infield
Manufactured in the United States of America

Library of Congress Cataloging in Publication Data

McCallum, John Dennis, 1924-
The world heavyweight boxing championship.

1. Boxing–History. 2. Boxing–Biography.
I. Title.
GV1121.M32 796.9'62'0922 [B] 74-1462
ISBN 0-8019-5951-9

TO

THE MEMORY OF

DAN MORGAN

AND

HARRY GRAYSON–

A

COUPLE OF CHAMPS

WHO

SHOWED ME

THE BEST SIDE

OF THE PRIZE RING

FOREWORD. THIS WAS BOXING!

BY DR. CHARLES P. LARSON
FORMER PRESIDENT, WORLD BOXING ASSOCIATION

THE survival of prize fighting down through the centuries is one of the minor miracles of athletic competition. This oldest of human sports has virtually disappeared from the public eye from time to time, a victim of reformers or lawmakers or ineptitude in its own management.

But just when it seemed doomed to permanent obscurity it would bounce back for another era of prosperity, leaving new names etched on the roster of ring greats.

The reason for this durability is quite simple: Boxing appeals to the primitive instincts of man. Beneath this veneer is the cave man, the man of violence and aggression. These basic instincts may be hidden by a cloak of timidity, or by inhibitions developed during a lifetime. But they are there. The boxer himself has a physical outlet for the urge to violence, while the spectator gets his thrill vicariously, surrendering to an empathy involving one of the combatants he is cheering for.

Few sports rely so heavily on personalities as boxing. Baseball and football, for example, have the mass appeal of the team as well as the individual. In the prize ring it is the supremacy of one man over another, and if the sport is universally great today it is because the men who wore the gloves in the past made it so.

There never has been a standardized type among fighters, either physically or in style. The diversity among them has added tremendous spice and drama to the sport. From the swashbuckling John L. Sullivan to the quiet Joe Louis, boxing idols have built up the game by dint of their own personalities. There was the sullen Jim Jeffries, the intemperate Stanley Ketchel, the twisted Sonny Liston whom I knew well, the phlegmatic Jess Willard, the tempestuous Jack Dempsey, the placid Gene Tunney, the fumbling Primo Carnera, the masterful Joe Gans, the clowning Max Baer, the fantastic Young Griffo, the business-like

Jim Braddock, the wily Sugar Ray Robinson, the tenacious Rocky Marciano, the garrulous Muhammad Ali—all contributing in their own special way to the lore of the prize ring. You will meet most of them intimately in this volume.

The fact that a fist-fighter is strictly on his own once he gets into the ring also has something to do with the sport's popularity, for boxing is the great leveler. The public has come to realize that wealth, education, inherited privilege and superficial cleverness are unimportant. The man who can combine brute force, muscular prowess, nervelessness and sharp thinking is the man who usually wins wealth and adulation. Many of our most compelling champions rose from abject poverty, fought their first battles in such sordid surroundings as smoke-filled rooms, frontier boom towns, musty barns, in gambling houses, aboard barges, in a circus sideshow, in the shadow of a slum tenement. Victory offered the only escape route from such environments.

Author John McCallum has spent 25 years in boxing research. Some of his findings have been printed in *The Encyclopaedia Britannica.* He learned, for example, that prize fighting traces back to 1750 B.C., when the young men of Mesopotamia—an ancient nation located where Baghdad is today—fought with their fists wrapped in leather. Some 850 years later, in Greece, the battles were for total victory, with the contestants wearing spiked metal gloves and continuing to punch each other until one was fatally injured. When the leaders saw what such bloody competition was doing to their manpower, they banned the so-called sport and it remained dormant for several centuries.

Then, in the twenty-third Olympiad of 688 B.C., the first boxing match in recorded history was held and a young warrior by the name of Onomastos fought his way to the championship. He was the first boxing champion we know of.

Boxing reappeared in England in the seventeenth century as men started to settle grudges with their fists, or just for the sport of it. At first, there were few rules or regulations. The day of the scorecard was a long way off yet. The fighters just slugged it out until it was clear who was the winner. This was the sort of decision-making that the late, great Grantland Rice argued was the only solution to picking winners. Granny always felt that choosing a winner on the basis of which fighter scored the greater number of points in the greater number of rounds was a stupid arrangement. He said that you could get more competent decisions by bringing a nine-year-old boy down to ringside in the last round and, when the bell rings, asking him, "Who won?" Unhesitating, the kid would point to one corner. "Him," he would say. Granny said, "Kids don't know anything about scoring methods; they only know that the guy who beats the other guy wins a fight."

Maybe Grantland Rice was right. Over the years, a good many different methods have been tried for arriving at equitable decisions.

Probably the most satisfactory would be the simplest, if it were possible always to have one thoroughly honest, unbiased and competent official. With such a man as referee, you let the boys fight and when they are done you ask the referee, "Who won?" The referee points. "He did." You don't need anything more than that.

However, there always have been and always will be officials who are venal or prejudiced or incompetent or all three. That's why systems of checks and balances have been created, with three officials scoring the match according to prescribed standards, so that there may be a written record of how they arrived at a decision.

Historically, the great Jack Broughton framed the first recognized rules for the prize ring. That was in 1743. For almost a hundred years thereafter his rules were in force, until they were replaced by the much more detailed London Prize-Ring Rules, designed for the British Pugilistic Association and promptly accepted as official on both sides of the Atlantic. The London Prize-Ring Rules were still in force when John L. Sullivan started his career, though the recently published Marquis of Queensberry rules were gaining favor. John L. preferred the Marquis of Queensberry rules.

In the days of the London Prize-Ring Rules, a fist fight could become an interminable and inexpressably dreary affair, with the adversaries clutching, wrestling and going to earth without a blow. That's how an Englishman named Tug Wilson earned $1,000 by staying four rounds with Sullivan in 1882.

Wilson had come to the United States shouting his intention of "chastising the presumptuous American puppy," but when the pair got on the stage of a New York theater, the Englishman confined himself to holding and crawling. He cashed in on Sullivan's standing offer of $1,000 to any man who could last four rounds, went home and opened a pub with his profits, and lived out his days as a hero of practically legendary valor.

Sports columnist Red Smith pointed out that there was an erroneous notion that the Marquis of Queensberry was seeking to refine the brutal business when he drafted a new set of rules in 1867, dividing a fight into three-minute rounds with one-minute rest periods.

He wasn't. He was trying to set up regulations that would insure three minutes of real fighting between rest periods. Under the Queensberry code, a man who sought a respite by dropping to the floor without being hit was disqualified. In the view of the Marquis, a fight was a contest to be continued to a finish, until one man was beaten helpless. It wasn't until later that bouts were scheduled for a limited number of rounds, removing the certainty of a knockout and creating the need for decisions.

In this vein, during my terms as President of the National Boxing Association (NBA) in 1961, and the World Boxing Association (WBA) in 1962, we adopted several good safety regulations. These resulted from many studies and investigations conducted by Dr. Leon H. Feldman and myself. We introduced such requirements as padding of ring posts, padding of ropes, banning metal or wire rope strands, better floor padding (including composition-type floor padding such as Ensolite®), checking glove weights and using non-absorbable material, more thorough examinations, with the addition of electroencephalographic tracings for all boxers who had been knocked out in the ring (either in training or in a bout), and automatic suspensions for boxers who had been kayoed. These suspensions following a knockout were for either 30 or 60 days, depending on the severity of the injury. Other innovations included suturing of accidental cuts and lacerations between rounds during a match. This is particularly vital in the case of where a good boxer is ahead on points and suffers a head butt, causing him to bleed profusely from a deep laceration. Prior to between-the-round suturing, this man would have been automatically disqualified under the old rule. His injury was serious only to the extent to which he was losing blood. Our suturing rule has since become quite practical and has been adopted by many state boxing commissions.

All of these safety measures have cut down on prize-ring fatalities considerably. Before they were adopted, prize-fighting suffered 20 or more deaths a year. That number has since dropped to less than 10 a year.

Over the years, I have examined numerous autopsy reports relating to boxing fatalities. My exhaustive research has included a large number of reports from the New York Medical Examiner's Office, as well as many other state medical examiners' and coroners' offices in the United States; a similar number came from foreign countries, principally European. Analysis of these autopsy studies indicates that the main cause of death in almost all cases was subarachnoid hemorrhage. This is the result of a contra-coup type of injury which is caused by the head striking an immovable object, such as a ring post, a metal object, or the floor. When the object is resilient and movable, head injuries and contra-coup subarachnoid hemorrhages seldom occur. I know of no instance where death occurred from a punch on the head if the head was moving. A straight punch to the head while the head is in motion is incapable of causing serious injury or subarachnoid hemorrhage because the contra-coup tearing of blood vessels does not occur unless the head is up against an immovable object.

During my medical research I read a great many articles regarding so-called "punch drunk" fighters. In my opinion, the term "punch drunk" is a misnomer. I don't think I have ever really seen an individual, who has gone into professional boxing with normal intelligence, who wound up suffering from the so-called "punch drunk" syndrome. Most fist-fighters who were classified as such really had only low-level intelligence to begin with. Boxing had little to do with their mental deterioration. Of course, this is not to say that boxers have not received injuries which produced neurological symptoms, because the records are saturated with such cases.

I love the story Lou Nova tells. It concerns the time he was sitting at ringside at a fight in California when a man came along with a small boy and said: "Lou, why didn't you show up at the house for dinner the other night?" Lou looked at him and knew he'd never seen the fellow before, but he got the pitch right away. The man wanted to make a big impression on his son, and Lou had once fought the great Joe Louis for the heavyweight championship of the world. So Lou said: "Oh, yes, I'm sorry. I wasn't able to make it. But the next time you invite me, I'll be there for sure."

Lou then turned to the little boy. "So this is the little fellow you were telling me about?" The man said yes, that was his son. "He's a fine, strapping boy," Lou said. "Now you take care of yourself, sonny, and drink a lot of milk and eat your vegetables and get plenty of sleep, and some day you'll be a great football player or a heavyweight champion."

"Well," the man said, "so long, Lou. Go ahead and watch the fight and I'll see you later."

"Right," Lou said, and as he turned away he heard the man speak to the boy. "See?" the man was saying. "Didn't I tell you he was *punch drunk?*"

In the days of the old Madison Square Garden you could find plenty of characters hanging around "Jacobs Beach," so nicknamed by Damon Runyon after the one-time ticket hustler, Mike Jacobs. That was where the fight mob congregated. When John McCallum wrote boxing for NEA, the Scripps-Howard Syndicate, he found many a hilarious story there. John told me that The Beach—promoters, matchmakers, managers, seconds, trainers and hangers-on—fell into roughly two classes: the Solvents and the Insolvents. The latter group heavily out-numbered the former and was perpetually tortured by the conflicting desire to make enough money to become a Solvent and the wish to remain an Insolvent for the sheer joy of being able to hate the Solvents. The Insolvents or apprentice Insolvents were happier and a lot more colorful. McCallum's heart was with the Insolvents.

Among John's prize Insolvents were "The Finger," a character who rented himself out as a hexer, and performed his magic by pointing at the doomed fighter from the time the poor guy climbed into the ring until he was carried out; Big Dick, a cane-carrying man of regal bearing, whose chief claim to fame was that he once rubbed up against President Roosevelt; Joe Jacobs, coiner of such winsome classics as "I shouldda stood in bed"; two famed dialecticians named Musky Jackson and Mushky McGee, the last of whom had the added distinction of resembling an unfrocked turtle; Evil Eye Finkle, who put the "curse" on this or that fighter by sitting at the ringside and staring at the fighter he had been hired to jinx; "Razor Phil" Lewis, who looked like a wicked old canary and who annually tendered himself a testimonial dinner at five dollars a plate; and Beezy Thomas, The Beach's official bootblack, who sometimes startled innocent passers-by by mounting his shine box and delivering a loud and abusive lecture in Senegalese.

For years, The Beach's elite had an active competition to fix the champion screwball of the area. The search started one night when Eddie Walker and the late Eddie Borden, a couple of Insolvent managers, got into a ringing argument over which was the daffiest. The dialogue, McCallum tells me, went something as follows:

Walker: "Aw, you're sca-rewy."

Borden: "An' you're punchy, daffy, loco, eggscentrik."

Walker: "Yeah—well, you're nuttier than me."

Borden, after thinking it over a moment: "Gimme a concrete example."

Walker, rubbing his chin for inspiration: "Well—lemme see. I got it. In the dead of winter once I seen you walking down Eighth Avenue in the snow, without no hat or coat, reading the *Racing Form.*"

Borden, laughing unpleasantly: "You call that nuts? How about you—devoting a lifetime to thinking up bad stories about Al Weill and—"

George Smith, a ticket man, interrupting: "You're both cracked."

This was too much for either of the accused to bear.

Walker: "Coming from you, that's great. You're the guy what gets out a calendar every year—with a pitcher of yourself on it, and giving a list of people who you don't speak to. And you call *us* nuts."

Suddenly, the debate had taken a sharp detour in complexion which might have confounded any eavesdroppers except paid-up members of The Fraternity, who reason intricately. Borden, Walker and Smith had veered into a sharp reverse. Borden was yelling that he himself was clearly nuttier than Walker; Walker was pointing out several irregularities from his own crazy-quilt life which, he claimed, made him more of a zany than Borden; Smith was probing ponderously back into his own jumbled past, baring indisputable evidence of mental rockiness. Borden finally settled it.

"We'll put up a hundred bucks apiece," he said, "and then we'll go to the Doc and let him decide which is the craziest. The nuttiest takes the three hundred."

Borden mentioned the name of a doctor who had been making a study of the behavior of Jacobs Beach. He had become particularly interested in the street's occupational disease of so-called "punch drunkeness."

The money was thus raised and the trio set off the next morning for the critical test. They were met at the doctor's office by a harried nurse.

"Where's the doc?" Borden asked.

The nurse started to cry suddenly.

"They just took him away to the insane asylum," she said.

Fortunately, not all medical men who work with the boxing fraternity end up that way. I retired from the WBA while I still had all my marbles.

It is good to see all the world's heavyweight champions back together again between one set of book covers. When I was a young man growing up in Spokane, Washington, my heroes were Dempsey and Tunney and Schmeling and the like. I was so crazy about the prize ring that I even hitchhiked to Shelby, Montana, to watch Dempsey and Tommy Gibbons go 15 rounds. I crawled under the fence to see the fight.

I remember still the gloom hanging over Spokane like dense fog the morning after Tunney beat Dempsey in '26. I was then in my first year of college at Gonzaga University and had a part-time job in the insurance department of the *Spokesman-Review,* the morning paper. The only form of radio we had to follow the fight at that time was a rustic crystal set with earphones. I didn't get to hear the fight. Newspapers were still the No. 1 way for Americans to get their news and I arranged with the fellows in the pressroom to give me the first bundles of the early edition, banner-lining the story of the bout on the front page. I hired about 15 kids to sell papers for me, and we raced up and down the main streets of Spokane hawking the early edition. The customers gobbled up those papers like hot cakes, eager to read the round-by-round account of Tunney's shocking upset of Dempsey. They were so anxious to get the details that some of them shelled out a dollar a copy—and didn't even wait for their change. We made a small fortune, selling more than 3,000 papers within the first hour!

I'll always be grateful to Dempsey and Tunney for helping me earn money for my schooling.

Perhaps you can understand why I have had such a soft spot for prize fighting.

I once wanted to be a prize fighter. I had my first amateur bout when I was only eleven. Later I turned pro. I had one professional fight. When I was seventeen, I fought under the assumed name of "Kid Phillip." Phillip is my middle name. My share of the welterweight purse was $100.

The opponent was a thirty-two-year-old black, a veteran fighter. But his experience didn't dim my self-confidence one bit. At the bell, I waded into him with leather flying in all directions and whaled the tar out of him. In the clinches he kept advising me to slow down... slow down. "Take it easy, Kid. You're going to run out of steam." The match was scheduled for six rounds.

Midway of the fourth round, he said, "Well, Kid, I'm going to have to put you to sleep. I hope I don't hurt you."

Suddenly, all the lights went out. The next thing I remembered I was lying on a bench in the dressing room, staring blankly at the ceiling.

That ended my professional boxing aspirations.

I had opened and closed in one.

That personal experience reminds me of another McCallum story. It involved John's old friend, the late Dan Morgan, one of the great boxing figures in prize-ring history. When Dan was a kid living on Manhattan's lower east side, he ran up a string of 14 amateur victories in a row and decided to turn pro. The promoter matched him at Brooklyn's old Pelican Club against a veteran named Phil Kelly. Kelly outweighed Morgan plenty and could hit like a trip-hammer. But Morgan out-boxed him for 14 rounds, until he got careless and ran smack into a right cross. He went down, dead to the world. He was out cold. They hauled him back to the dressing room, and for the next three days no one could understand what Dan was talking about. His words were mumbo-jumbo. Finally, they brought in a Chinaman from a nearby neighborhood laundry. He was supposed to be something of a language expert. He listened to Dan jabber a blue streak for a few minutes, then started to chuckle. They asked him what he was laughing about.

The Chinaman said, "This velly, velly funny. That language has been dead for two thousand years!"

When Dan realized what fist-fighting could do to a man's mind, he quit. He decided to limit himself to telling others how to do it. So he became a fight manager.

Good old Dan Morgan.

Because prize fighting was so disorganized and the records so vague, no attempt has been made in this book to trace the various championships back beyond the ascension of John L. Sullivan to a clear-cut claim to the World Heavyweight Championship. He won the crown in a bare-knuckle battle, in 1882, and lost it wearing gloves ten years later.

So this volume concerns itself primarily with the heavyweight champions of the glove era, the men who did their fighting under Queensberry rules. It begins where the record books leave off, breaking away from cold statistics to paint character and personality portraits of the champions, most of whose names are as familiar to ring buffs as are the names of the Presidents of the United States.

There goes the bell...

"Shake hands now and come out fighting."

CONTENTS

THE FIGHTERS

1. John L. Sullivan

PRIZE fighting lives by its heavyweight champion. Veteran ring buffs still talk of the golden days when a good club fight could be found every night in almost every city and aficionados will always admire the skill of fine boxers in any weight class. But to the public—the casual fans who pay to see fights on closed-circuit television—the fight game is wrapped up in the man at the top. The sport is a dormant giant that explodes into life only a few times a year with that magical phrase: Heavyweight Championship Bout.

The fact is that boxing draws its vitality from talented and colorful heavyweight champions. In theory, at least, a good big man can beat a good little man, so it can be assumed therefore that the king of the big men is the best fighter in all boxing. When a man such as John L. Sullivan or Jack Dempsey or Joe Louis or Muhammad Ali is on top it is no accident that interest in fist-fighting seeps down to the lesser divisions.

The Marquis of Queensberry introduced his rules in 1867, but it was not until 1892 that a heavyweight championship match was fought under conditions as we recognize them today, with padded gloves, three-minute rounds, etc. That was the contest in which James J. Corbett defeated John L. Sullivan to become the first man to win the title wearing gloves.

The great John L. might be called the true link between the bare-knuckle and the glove eras. He won championship recognition in a bare-knuckle battle with Paddy Ryan, in 1882, and lost it 10 years later in his gloved match with Corbett. Ryan had established undisputed claim to the bare-knuckle title in 1880, ending confusion dating back 150 years to the retirement of James Figg, of England. Figg, after defeating all comers, opened a boxing school on Tottenham Court Road, London, in 1719, and 11 years later retired from competition. As generally is the case in such circumstances, there were numerous title claimants and the continuity of the championship became obscure, but Paddy Ryan ended the chaos by establishing his clear claim to the world heavyweight crown.

The late Billy Roche, famous referee, often lamented that great fighters are too frequently remembered as they were in the sere and yellow of their careers, often as they appeared in tragic last stands. This was particularly true of John L. Sullivan, the Boston Strong Boy, who is remembered today as the over-stuffed, slowed-down, beer-soaked remnant of a great fighter who fell before the much younger, better trained and faster James J. Corbett. Roche saw Sullivan fight many times while he, John L., was still the renowned and invincible Boston Strong Boy. He rated Sullivan as the greatest of all heavyweights.

"John L. was well-built, standing 5 ft. 10½ in. and fighting best at about 190 pounds," Roche told me back in 1950, shortly before his death at eighty-seven. "He wore a little black mustache, had high cheek bones and sunken cheeks. He was taught to box by Mike Donaldson. John L. was a fine stand-up fighter. He was as clever a heavyweight as you would want to see. He knew how to feint and had the best one-two punch I ever saw."

John L. Sullivan, despite the fact that he was the hero of America's youth back in the not-so-Gay Nineties, did not quite fit the All-American Boy prototype. He smoked cigars, great quantities of big black ones, and puffed away on them even as he trained. It was also his opinion that liquor and the prize ring went hand in hand. His favorite hangout was not the gymnasium but Jimmy Wakely's, a bar in mid-Manhattan frequented by the sports mob. He would swagger into the saloon, dump a hundred dollars on the counter, and tell everybody standing at the bar to drink up. He amassed a million dollars—and did not save a penny of it! He was an easy touch for anyone.

Some historians saw John L. as a dull, quarrelsome, bragging bully when he was drunk. Others saw him only as the hero of the Gaslight Era. The press hung on his words, he packed the local theatres, and people followed him up the street, much as small boys trailed the circus when it came to town.

Sullivan said frequently and profanely, drunk or sober, that he could lick any so-and-so in the world. Others have made the same boast down the years, but John L. was different from most of the others—he was always ready to try it, and usually he could do it, and when he couldn't he did not go to the reporters with an alibi.

The late John Barrymore, the famous actor, remembered the first time he met John L. Barrymore was strolling along Broadway with his father, brother Lionel, and sister Ethel. He was seven. Each afternoon a parade of great names moved along Broadway. On this day, they

John L. Sullivan was the true link between the bare-knuckle and the glove eras. He is shown here in his prime, 190 pounds of muscle.

glimpsed their Papa's friend, the great John L. He had on a dark blue pea-jacket, tight trousers of robin's egg blue, and a high silk hat, which he tipped to little ten-year-old Ethel and bellowed, "Hello, sis! Happy to meet you!"

When John L. lifted his silk tile to Ethel and she saw the close-cropped skull, the child naturally believed him to be Genghis Khan. She fled behind her father's coat tails. John L. turned to Lionel. "And what's your name, lad?"

"Lionel," said the boy, eleven, panting with hero worship.

John L. grunted. "It is, eh? *Lionel!* Huh!" He looked at Maurice Barrymore accusingly, grunted again, then squinted at John and said cryptically, "Well, well, well!"

Little John Barrymore at this time was less than prepossessing. He seemed as slim and pale as a church candle, wore black bangs, and looked like a Siamese office boy. He had nothing about him to indicate that he would grow up to be a new Apollo.

John L. poked John gently with his walking stick, merely knocking the boy's wind out, then said to Maurice in parting, "Fine family, Barry! Fine family!"

Many years later, I was working on a biography of the John B. Kellys, of Philadelphia, family of Princess Grace. While poking around in the basement of their home, looking for old scrapbooks and family albums, I found a musty manuscript, written by Grace's uncle, Walter Kelly, famous in vaudeville for his "The Virginia Judge" role. Walter was a sports buff. He rubbed shoulders with the great and near-great of the athletic world. The manuscript told of his friendship with John L. It read, in part:

> Strolling northward on Broadway one night, the first thing to invite my attention and suggest a welcome was the cafe of the old Morton House at Fourteenth Street. Entering the bar, I suddenly stopped, rooted to the spot, for there, in a mellow and talkative mood, surrounded by half a dozen admirers, stood the idol of the decade, John L. Sullivan. He had noted my entrance and barked a friendly command for me to join the party. For the next two hours I reveled in the glory of his company. Generous commitments of liquid refreshments, coupled with stories of politics, the theatre, and the prize ring, made it a most joyous and eventful evening, only marred and finally broken up entirely by the suddenly announced determination of John L. to sing his favorite ballad, "Kathleen Mavourneen." From this night, and on through many years thereafter, I had frequent proof that the rendition of this ballad was his one besetting sin. No matter what the time or place, and heedless of the fact that his voice at its best resembled that of an ancient frog, he would burst forth with this classic, to the dismay of the guests and disgust of the proprietor and staff. On this occasion I found myself, in company with the rest of the patrons, out on Fourteenth Street by the time John L. had reached the first chorus.
>
> I met the mighty John L. many times after the Morton House songfest. Hour after hour, in a small private room at the end of Denny Kelliher's bar, I

listened to John L. tell stories of his boyhood battles in South Boston. Now and then, in demonstrating how he had ducked or swung in some earlier fracas, he would accidentally upset the table and drench four or five eager listeners with highballs and beer. But to his credit let it be said, he could tell a good story.

On another occasion, at Moana Springs, Reno, Nevada, the training camp of Jim Jeffries, whose guest I was at the time, I recall sitting on the front porch on a very hot afternoon, three days before the Jeffries-Johnson fight. With me were several famous sports writers, including author Jack London, who was there to cover the fight for the Hearst papers. Jim Corbett was also there.

Jeffries was sleeping in a hammock under a large dogwood tree. Suddenly a hired car pulled up in front of the house, and out stepped John L. First to see him was Corbett. As John L. approached the gate, Jim rose and walked rapidly toward him. Sullivan made no move to enter until Corbett had reached the gate. You could feel the tension in the air. We on the porch, knowing how cordially these two former champions hated each other, waited nervously for the explosion.

Corbett was the first to speak.

He said, "What the hell do you want?"

John L. stiffened. There was belligerence in his voice as he replied, "I want to interview Jeff."

Corbett said, "You can't talk to him. You can't even see him. Go on back to Johnson's camp. You'll be more at home there," in reference to an Associated Press dispatch in which John L. predicted Jeff's defeat.

John L. stared at Corbett coldly. We were all down at the gate by this time. "If you're running the camp," John L. said to Corbett, "I don't want to see him." He got back into his car and sped away.

That was the last time John L. and Corbett ever spoke to each other. I felt a lump in my throat as I watched John L. drive away. He was leaving the camp of a heavyweight champion without even the tribute of a handshake or a good-bye. For some reason, it just didn't seem right.

John L. was born on October 15, 1858, in a house on Harrison Avenue, Boston, almost opposite what was then Boston College. He was walking at ten months of age, and talking at fourteen months, his mother once recalled. Physically he was precocious. He was always strong, always healthy. His parents were Irish: she from Athlone, County Westmeath; he from Tralee, County Kerry. They had met in America.

Mrs. Sullivan stood 5 ft. 10½ in., exactly the height of John Lawrence Sullivan himself at his peak, and she weighed 180 pounds. The father, Mike, stood 5 ft. 3 in., and weighed scarcely 125 pounds. He was a fierce little man, ready to fight at the drop of a hat, and always contemptuous of his son's achievements. And he loved Ireland, fanatically, belligerently, with a fierce conviction.

Young John L. did not share this conviction. It may be that he loved Ireland, but if he did, it was romantically; whereas his love for America was noisily, patriotically real, immediate, and practical. He was the flag-waving type. He always wanted everybody to *know* that he loved the "good old USA." This was no hypocrisy, no play for publicity. He was totally obsessed by patriotism. Proud American that he was, John L. looked upon anybody who had not been born in this country as a "foreigner."

Almost from the beginning, except to his closest friends, who called him simply John, people called him John L., or Mr. Sullivan. He was never known as Jack, never as Sully. It was "John L.!" that the crowds shouted in the streets and at railroad stations. Few of his admirers even knew or cared what the "L." stood for.

The Sullivans lived on Harrison Avenue until John L. was ten. Then they moved to Parnell and Lenox streets and later still to Boston Highlands. John L. went to a public school on Concord Street, later to the Dwight Grammar School on Springfield Street, then to a night school at the old Bath House on Cabon Street, and for a little while to Boston College. He sometimes liked to refer to his days in "college," though in fact the grandly named Boston College of that time was what today would be called a high school; in any event, John L. was not there long.

His mother wanted him to become a priest, but he didn't have the disciplined temperament for it, and, besides, the priesthood meant too much study. Yet he was a good son and gave his parents little trouble. He worked six months as a plumber's apprentice, at four dollars a week, until he had an argument with his boss and quit. He then worked a year and a half as a tinsmith's apprentice; this job, too, terminated in a dispute with the boss. After that he worked as a hod carrier like his dad. Once again there was a clash with the boss.

John L. always was very fond of baseball, and in his late teens he played semi-pro ball for various teams around Boston. He once said, "I played mostly first base and left field, though I could play any position." He got $25 a game, twice a week, Wednesdays and Saturdays. He was a good athlete. He was once offered $1,300 a season, a considerable sum in those days, to play for a Cincinnati team. He refused the offer, however, for "at the age of nineteen I drifted into the occupation of boxer."

That's about what it amounted to—drifted. At the outset boxing was nothing more than an occasional chance to pick up a little money on the side. There was a variety show at the old Dudley Street Opera House in Boston Highlands, for example, and in one of the acts was a brute named Scannel, who announced from the stage that with boxing gloves—to stay on the right side of the law—he would fight and beat anybody in the audience. John L. was there and he took up the challenge. Scannel was supposed to be pretty good. Young John L. hit him so hard that he knocked him clear over the footlights.

John L. was on his way. He mowed down Cocky Woods, Dan Dwyer and one Tommy Chandler routinely, but when he took on Professor Mike Donovan, at the Howard Athenaeum, he was meeting class.

Donovan, who later was to become famous as the boxing instructor at the New York Athletic Club and sparring partner of Teddy Roosevelt, was heralded even then as one of the smartest boxers in the country. A Civil War veteran, he weighed only a little more than 150 pounds, while John L. weighed nearly 200.

The bout was strictly an exhibition affair. Donovan traveled to Boston and the match took place, not in a ring, but on a stage of a theatre. The fighters wore gloves and were not supposed to try to knock each other out–indeed, it was illegal to hit hard–but only to demonstrate boxing. This, however, was not John L.'s idea. Slapping his open left glove against his left hip as he came out of his corner against Donovan–it was a lifelong habit–he had only one thought. "By golly," Donovan said later, "it wasn't boxing. It was like being hit by a runaway horse!"

Donovan was not only a boxer, he was a fighter. He knew that John L. was trying to knock him out, and, sore, he went right back at him. "I kept glaring at Sullivan, but he did not seem to be the least bit uneasy, as most young fellows would be under the circumstances"–for Donovan had a big reputation, well earned. "Sullivan was the strongest man I had ever fought, and I had boxed all the best of them up to that time." Donovan soon gave up his plan of standing toe to toe swapping punches. He needed all his skill to keep from being knocked flat. They went three rounds, and both were on their feet at the end of that time; but Donovan himself, no man to underestimate his own ability, freely confessed afterward that he was no match for young John L.

That was John L.'s first meeting with a man of national reputation. Soon afterward he boxed an exhibition with and easily defeated Jack Hogan of Providence.

On April 6, 1880, he fought Joe Goss, at the Music Hall in Boston. Once again it was supposed to be only a three-round exhibition. Though no longer a youth, Goss was the former champion of England and America and still was a brilliant boxer and dead game. He lasted out the three rounds against John L., but only because the Boston Strong Boy permitted it. They became warm friends, and Goss, who was about to retire, went around singing the praises of John L. wherever he went.

Sullivan's reputation was spreading by this time. Some sports in Cincinnati summoned him to that city to fight John Donaldson, called the "Champion of the West." John L. fought him twice, the first time with gloves, when he whipped him decisively, the second time with bare fists for 10 rounds. That was all Donaldson could last.

John L. was growing cocky by now. He had always known he was good, and now he was proving it to the world. But for all his roughness, Sullivan disliked the brutality of bare-knuckle fighting under London Prize Rules and inveighed against them.

"Fighting under Queensberry rules before gentlemen is a pleasure," he said. "To the other element it becomes a brawl."

John L.'s career went on to overlap the bare knuckles and gloves eras, bridging the gap between those contrasting styles. In 1882 he notched his name in history as the last bare-knuckle champion, by stopping Paddy Ryan in nine rounds. The match lasted only 10 minutes and 30 seconds and was held in a ring pitched in front of a hotel in Mississippi City, Mississippi, for a purse and side bet totalling $5,000.

With the London Prize Ring heavyweight crown perched securely atop his jaunty head, John L. went around boasting in that Big Ben voice of his: "I can lick any man in the world in four rounds or less!" Most of the time he made good his boast, with one exception. Tug Wilson managed to stay four full rounds with John L. in 1882 by hugging and falling to the floor whenever the champion glared or cocked a menacing fist in his direction.

Sullivan was a natural showman, the sort of man about whom legends accumulate and traditions cluster. He was as cock-sure and confident out of the ring as he was in it. He would go from saloon to saloon, proclaiming flamboyantly, "I can whip any sonofabitch in the house!" He was not often called upon to back up his contention.

There was nothing lukewarm or halfway about John L.'s personality. People either hated him or looked upon him as the salt of the earth. One anti-John L. historian wrote: "He was a drunkard. He was a loudmouthed, oversized bully. He was a spoiled, irresponsible roughneck. A son of a bitch of the first water, if he ever drank any." On the pro-Sullivan side, another chronicler of the era described him in this manner: "He was not just a prize fighter. He was much more; a public hero, for a long time almost a myth, almost indeed a god. He was adored. He might have been a brute, if it pleases you; but a brute built on such a scale is as different from the rest of us as any prince of old reared in the serene belief that God had done something special to him and all his ancestors."

Anti-, pro- or neutral, the true John L. Sullivan could be found somewhere in between. One thing was certain, however; he had plenty of self-confidence. Never had he known, never was he to know, an instant of doubt concerning his ability to whip any man. "When going into the ring," he often said, "I have always had it in mind that I would be the conqueror. That has always been my disposition." With gloves or bare fists, he went instantly to work in the ring with one purpose in mind—to knock the other fellow down and to keep knocking him down until he stayed down. He didn't spar; he never felt an opponent out; in fact, though he learned to talk big about "science," he didn't even know how to box. He didn't need to. His attack—he had no defense—was very simple. Mike Donovan once explained, "He used his right as a blacksmith would use a sledge hammer pounding a piece of iron into shape: straight down, slamming away the other man's guard, for he was unbelievably strong, and then he knocked the man out either with a straight right to the jaw or a right hook to the side of the neck, his favorite punch. Not often did he have to do this more than once."

Through the haze of distance some folk mistakenly see John L. as a shambling, awkward giant. He was far from being muscle-bound. He was a "natural" puncher. His punches were perfectly timed, seldom wild, and fast. In the ring he was extraordinarily fast. His hands were large. His shoulders were enormous, his chest was remarkably deep. His nose was not broken, he had no cauliflower ear, and indeed his face was unmarked from fighting. He had beautiful, even teeth, a clear complexion. Given a chance to grow, as it was later, his hair was black, full, thick, slightly wavy; it grayed reluctantly, and he had all of it when he died.

John L. had a very deep voice. He unwittingly roared when he talked. While he fought he grunted, snarled, snorted, growled.

He was never known as a ladies' man, though he liked the birdies ("chickens" was a later word) well enough. He amazed everybody when he got married. The vows were done quietly, in a Catholic church at south Boston, and very little is known about his bride, Annie Bates, except that she was pretty, a Protestant, a chorus girl, a friend and neighbor of John L.'s from childhood days, and not the right wife for him. He never liked to talk about his marriage. Many people were unaware that he was married at all. When he did mention it he did so grimly, sometimes obscenely. It was, he would say, "strenuous in every way while it lasted." It did not last long. They lived together, off and on, for something like a year, and Annie bore him a child who died in infancy. They separated without any formal legal agreement.

Between his more important bouts John L. trouped around the country with a few sparring partners and a few vaudeville acts, giving nightly exhibitions, and offering first $50, later $100, $200, $500, and at last $1,000, to anybody who could stay four rounds with him. Prize-ring historians generally credit John L. with being the originator of this kind of barnstorming. There was never another fighter half as good at it as he was.

Some experts looked askance at John L.'s knockouts of comparative unknowns in those tank towns at times when he was as full of beer and bourbon as Irish fighting spirit. No less an authority than Billy McCarney, who saw the Boston Strong Boy in his prime, claimed he won many of those quick knockouts by chicanery and the application of a very simple gimmick.

"Those exhibition bouts were always held on the stages of theatres," Billy said. "There was always a backdrop upstage, behind the ring. Sullivan had a henchman with a sizeable bat behind the backdrop. If the sucker got too frisky and stayed around too long, or was giving John L. any trouble, the champion would maneuver his victim into the backdrop. Then the guy behind the curtain would clout the challenger lustily over the head with the bat—and Sullivan had himself another fast knockout."

Whether or not McCarney was right, the fact remains that Sullivan showed no mercy in the ring. There was no fancy sparring, no letting a local pug last a couple of rounds to please the crowd. John L. would go to work on each one immediately. He did not like to see an opponent until he saw him in the opposite corner, and by that time John L. would be scowling. He would shake hands, but there was nothing good-natured in the act; he was out to kill; he would release the hand immediately, looking aside and down.

Afterward he would be all affability. He would strip off his gloves, help to drag his fallen victim back to his corner, fuss over him until he saw he was going to recover, and then raise the great right arm for silence in order that he might make a few remarks, ending with, "Always on the level, yours very truly, John L. Sullivan." Most of the time he gave the victim a few dollars for his trouble.

"Don't you ever feel sorry for those men you beat up?" John L. was once asked.

"I do—after I've knocked them out!"

Sullivan was the first to discover that the point of the jaw was vulnerable. He had an old Irish physician show him in great detail that the real nerve center was on the left side of the nose just below the eye. Until his time, fighters aimed for a knockout at the temple or a point back of the ear. Sullivan shot straight for the nerve center, with usually sensational results.

He was the first to pioneer boxing gloves as we know them today, though James J. Corbett was the first to earn recognition as champion using what were then called "the big gloves."

By 1887, the Great John L. had grown into an international figure. He had cleaned up virtually all visible opposition in the United States, so he sailed for Europe, where he was lionized. He even gave a Command Performance, sparring privately before the Prince of Wales, who was destined to become King Edward VII. After the exhibition, John L., disregarding the instructions of the aides in swallow-tail coats as to proper protocol, marched up to Edward, grasped his hand and roared cheerily: "Hello, Prince. Howdy!" Sullivan then draped a muscular left arm over the shoulder of royalty and started to talk with unconcerned animation. "I'd like to box a couple more rounds for you, Prince, if you want me to show you more of my stuff." The Prince did, and John L. went back to work on his sparring partner, Jack Ashton. Edward was elated and applauded enthusiastically when it was all over. The two men became fast friends.

Sullivan was always completely John L. around notables. Several years earlier, he had met Grover Cleveland, who had just defeated James G. Blaine, the "Plumed Knight" of Maine, for the 1884 Presidency. The Great John L. had been one of Cleveland's staunchest supporters. For the first time in his life, Sullivan yearned for an introduction to a famous person. The meeting was arranged after the President's inauguration in 1885. Despite all he had been told about protocol and formality, John L. broke away from his guides as soon as he entered Cleveland's chambers, strode up to him, stuck out his huge hand and shouted: "How are you, Boss? Sure am glad to shake your hand." The champion pumped the astonished President's half-extended mitt so vigorously that the incident quickly became front-page news.

John L. showed signs of slipping in his two bare-knuckle bouts with Charley Mitchell and Jake Kilrain. On March 10, 1888, he battled Mitchell at Chantilly, France, and was held to a draw by his smaller opponent in 39 rounds. Five years earlier, Sullivan had stopped him in 3 rounds. It took him 75 rounds a year later to dispose of Kilrain, at Richburg, Mississippi.

The Sullivan-Kilrain fight remains one of boxing's classics. It went 75 rounds and 2 hours, 16 minutes before John L. won by a KO. Staged at Richburg, Mississippi, July 8, 1889, Kilrain was near death at the end—yet lived to be Sullivan's pall bearer in 1918.

Kilrain was not a slugger but he could go distance and he was a good wrestler, which was useful in bare-knuckle fighting, where a fall could be almost as punishing as a knockdown blow. "Sullivan is no wrestler," said the *New York World* on the day of the fight, and added with journalistic candor unknown today: "According to the history of all such drunkards as he, his legs ought to fail him after 20 minutes of fighting."

When the men came to scratch at 10 A.M., before a crowd of 3,000 fans, most of whom had come by train from New Orleans to the secret ring site—bare-fist fighting was illegal in all 38 states—the thermometer registered 100 degrees in the shade. It was a test between two champions for $10,000 a side, winner take all. Sullivan, resplendent in green breeches and flesh-colored stockings, was champion by popular acclaim; Kilrain, by decree of Richard K. Fox, publisher of the *Police Gazette*, who ignored Sullivan's claim and awarded the *Gazette's* championship belt to Kilrain. Snorted John L.: "I would not put Fox's belt around the neck of a bulldog."

In the quaint literary style of the day, the newspaper account of the fight picks up the details:

Kilrain won the toss for corners and the question of referee came up. Mike Donovan said his side wanted Pat Kendrick of New Orleans, an expert in pugilism. Charles Johnston said that, as one of the backers of Sullivan, they had only one gentleman to name for referee. He was an upright, honest and just man and one known all over Mississippi, John Fitzpatrick of New Orleans, the well-known politician. Mitchell proposed a toss-up for choice. The crowd seconded him, and this was done. Mr. Fitzpatrick was chosen.

The principals then divested themselves of their outer garments. Sullivan threw off his ulster, while the crowd, which was with him all during the battle, cheered lustily. His skin was pink and clear. All his muscles were prominent and he looked anxious for the fight. He had a pitch-pine plaster above the belt on the stomach. He wore a pair of bright green tights and white stockings. He wore his colors for a belt. Kilrain did not appear so favorably but was nimble and quick. He wore no colors and had on black tights and stockings. Cleary and Muldoon were Sullivan's seconds and Dan Murphy was his bottle holder. Mitchell and Donovan seconded Kilrain, with Johnny Murphy as bottle holder. Kilrain bet $1,000 with Sullivan.

At 10:15 principals and seconds shook hands all together in a double cross. The seconds climbed out of the ring and the fight began.

Sullivan smiled with confidence; Kilrain looked as if he felt that there was hard work before him. He rushed at Sullivan, clinched with him and threw him to the ground. This ended the first round, and all the interested ruffians at the ringside cheered lustily for Kilrain. In the next round, which lasted 30 seconds, Sullivan struck Kilrain heavily on the body and then threw him. They clinched in the third round and Kilrain struck several blows, which were hissed at as foul. Sullivan finally hit Kilrain a blow on the neck, and he fell.

In the next two rounds neither was hurt and Kilrain made Sullivan run around the ring after him, falling when he got too near him. Sullivan hit Kilrain powerfully on the jaw in the sixth round and, throwing him, fell upon him. Kilrain had to be carried from the middle of the ring; yet he was able, in the seventh round, to strike Sullivan on the right ear and make it bleed, which so enraged Sullivan that he broke down Kilrain's guard with a rush and ended the eighth round by knocking him clear off his feet with a heavy right-hand blow on the mouth.

After running about the ring for a while in the tenth round, Kilrain fell to avoid being hit. He pursued the same tactics in the next one, until Sullivan cried out: "Stand up and fight like a man; I'm no sprinter! I'm a fighter!"

Kilrain stood for a moment and struck Sullivan, but the latter rushed at him, held him against the ropes and then threw and fell on him. Sullivan struck him repeatedly and finally knocked him down with a terrible right-hand blow on the neck. The advantage continued for Sullivan.

Then Kilrain thrust a spike of one of his shoes into one of Sullivan's feet, causing it to bleed, and struck a blow which seemed intended to be a foul one. It failed, and he then fell to avoid the blows of his antagonist. This sort of procedure went on for a long time, Kilrain running and dodging and Sullivan calling on him continually to "fight like a man." But Kilrain insisted in fighting or, rather, running as Charlie Mitchell, his trainer, directed. In the 39th round Sullivan asked the referee to make his opponent "stand and fight," and made a claim of a foul, which the referee refused.

In the 44th round Sullivan became sick, but even then Kilrain was afraid to venture near him. He asked him to make the fight a draw, but Sullivan refused, and emphasized the refusal by knocking Kilrain down. He was angry now, and in the next round he not only knocked Kilrain down but he stamped upon him, which prompted a claim of foul from Kilrain's friends. This was not allowed, and it was repeated in the next round, after Sullivan had thrown Kilrain and fallen upon him. The crowd was now satisfied that only chance would enable Kilrain to win, and it jeered him for his Fabian tactics.

In the 67th, 68th, 69th and 71st rounds Sullivan managed to catch his fleeing antagonist and each time knocked him down. Each of the next four rounds ended by Kilrain falling to avoid being knocked down. At the end of the 75th the referee cautioned Kilrain not to repeat his tactics, but it was seen that Kilrain was in no condition to continue.

The English fighter, Mitchell, tried to play a trick upon Sullivan. He ran over to him and said: "Will you give Kilrain a present if he throws up the sponge?" Sullivan replied: "Of course I will." Mitchell's purpose was, apparently, to show that Sullivan was as willing to stop the fight as Kilrain, but before Sullivan answered, Donovan had already thrown up the sponge. Kilrain was frightfully bruised and bled profusely. Sullivan was but little marked.

The official time of the fight was 2 hours 16 minutes and 25 seconds. Sullivan was quickly placed in a carriage and taken to the train for the trip back to New Orleans. Kilrain was put in a gig and likewise driven rapidly to the train. He had to be supported in the vehicle and seemed indifferent to what became of him. He was crying like a child all the while and bewailed his unfortunate fate. On the train he refused to take any care of himself. "Yes, I know I can do better," he said. "I don't know what's the matter. Nobody but myself knows what this fight will do me," he continued almost incoherently. His friends tried to comfort him by saying he had made a plucky fight and would do better some other time.

"No, it's no use talking," he replied. "He whipped me. I ain't hurt. I'm exhausted. I ain't licked. I was told by the best doctors in England not to go into a fight, but I did it, because I couldn't get out of it."

He reluctantly put an undershirt on his still damp and badly-bruised body, and, resuming his lamentation, said: "I couldn't do my best; that is what makes me feel so mean."

He referred to the jeering of the crowd when he walked about the ring to avoid Sullivan. "I ran around. I did it for my friends. I was not strong at the start. I was not well trained. I could have fought ten pounds lighter, but I will fight again."

Kilrain's eyes were nearly closed. His nose was hurt and bleeding and both his upper and lower lip contained deep and ugly incisions and were badly swollen. On his left side, just above the belt, was a big red spot where he was struck in the third round and which was said to have done more than anything else to decide the battle. It was feared that several of Kilrain's ribs were broken by the blow.

The victory over Kilrain was followed by a tour of America in a melodrama called *Kind Hearts and Willing Hands.* The experience proved once and for all that John L. was a much better fighter than actor.

In 1891, after a trip around Australia, Sullivan came back to the United States and agreed to participate in a friendly exhibition sparring match with a spindly bank clerk, James J. Corbett, in San Francisco. The bout was advertised as a three-rounder and was arranged to give the fans of the Bay Area a chance to see the great John L. in action. Corbett was regarded only as a mere San Francisco boxing instructor at the Olympic Club.

John L. wanted to look good. He wanted to display his easy superiority over the young dancing master. It was supposed to be merely sham-battle action, but the champion couldn't touch the speedy Corbett. The bank clerk learned in those three play-acting rounds that he could beat Sullivan. He acquired the positive knowledge that the stocky John L., with his short arms, clumsy left and murderous right, fought the kind of fight that he, Corbett, would surely win. It was typical of Corbett that the biggest lesson he learned concerned defense–not getting hit. That was his state of mind–defensive.

Many years later, Gene Tunney and Jim Corbett became good friends. They had long talks about boxing and even though Corbett was by then in his mid-fifties, they sometimes sparred in the ring with each other.

"Corbett could talk better about boxing than any other man I've ever known," Tunney said. "He taught me a lot. He told me that in preparing for fights, he used to shadowbox for one whole hour every day–he called it shadowdancing, typical of Corbett, the dancing master. For that daily hour he would go stepping against a mythical opponent, and in Corbett's imagination that opponent was always hitting at him, Corbett blocking, ducking, side-stepping, schooling his mentality and his reflexes to defense. He told me he used to draw diagrams of defensive boxing problems, charting the position of feet and the movements of footwork. He'd diagram his position in a corner of the ring, and his opponent's position, and sketch the way he would feint and side-step, eluding a rush. It was something like a dancer charting foot positions of a new dance–always a defensive dance with Gentleman Jim."

Corbett, to his dying day, was always angry about the stories that John L. was no more than a bloated, whisky-soaked hulk by the time the two fought for the title at the New Orleans Olympic Club, on September 7, 1892, under Marquis of Queensberry rules.

The Sullivan-Corbett feature headed up what was perhaps the most spectacular boxing promotion in history. Billed as "The Tournament of the Three Jacks," the program called for three world championship bouts on successive nights for purses that were unheard of in those days. The Three Jacks, in order of their appearance, were Jack McAuliffe, Jack Skelly, and John L. (Jack) Sullivan.

On September 5, 1892, Jack McAuliffe successfully defended the lightweight championship by knocking out Billy Myer, the "Streater Cyclone," in the 15th round for a winner-take-all purse of $10,000 and a side bet of $5,000. The next night, Jack Skelly, challenger, was kayoed in the eighth round by featherweight champion George Dixon, the clever "Little Chocolate," for a purse of $17,500.

Now came John L. and Gentleman Jim, fighting for a $25,000 purse and a $20,000 side stake. For the actual eyewitness version we go back to the newspaper morgue again:

NEW ORLEANS, Sept. 7, 1892 (Special)–It was the old generation against the new. It was the gladiator against the boxer. Sullivan represented the first stage in the evolution of the American pugilist and swept away old methods and old traditions. The old style was severe training and bloody battles, fights under difficulties in secluded spots, which the contestants performed for little money before the most objectionable classes. Although Sullivan has thrice defended the title with bare knuckles, under London prize ring rules, he was the virtual inventor of the modern glove contest.

He did better with the gloves than all his predecessors with naked fists, and did as much execution with padded hands in four rounds as the old-time fighters with ungloved battering rams. He Americanized the manly art, deprived it of much of its brutality and made it possible to decide championships before athletic clubs under the best auspices before classes of people who formerly took little interest in the sport. Nature intended him for a gladiator, and although he abused nature to a considerable extent, not even the best trained rivals could defeat him. In England and America he defended the title of champion and he stood out a central figure in the history of pugilism and attracted to him a following from every corner of the country.

Wherever Sullivan fought people flocked to see him, and no matter what his condition, no matter who his rival, no matter what the odds, the crowd was for Sullivan. It was so in tonight's battle; the name of Sullivan contained the magic power.

All day long Tuesday special trains arrived, and even yesterday hundreds of people from almost every state, from California to New York and from Minnesota to Texas, came pouring into this city. Canal Street and St. Charles Street had a look of carnival season. Hotels, saloons, and all places of resort were crowded. Carriages, cabs, wagonettes, wagons turned into pleasure vehicles, and street cars began bearing spectators to the Olympic arena.

The betting was not very heavy. The champion of champions was a strong favorite in the pool rooms. The morning odds were 1 to 4 Sullivan and 3 to 1 Corbett. A rush of Corbett money in the morning forced a drop in the odds from 3 to 1 to 5 to 6.

Sullivan showed up in splendid shape, massive in proportions. Corbett, taller and slighter, looked equally well trained but not as strong. He appeared happy and confident while he waited for his five-ounce gloves to be adjusted. He was clotted with muscles. He was slight, but all the flesh on him was muscle. His stomach was covered with knots of sinew. His chest was hard but flexible. His back was hard, firm and deep with muscle. His large arms were a mass of sinew molded into ideal athletic form. His weight was 187 pounds. Sullivan came in at 212.

Corbett from the beginning was confident, and he showed his ability to stop Sullivan and avoid his blows. His tactics at first were purely defensive and he ducked, he sprang, he even ran out of Sullivan's reach; but it was by no means a walking-around match. Even at the beginning he faced his adversary, countered, stopped, and swung, and was away with lightning quickness before return could be administered. His early campaign was to tire and blow Sullivan. With this in view he kept bothering the big man into following him, swinging heavily at him and not finding him there. Then, when he drew blood in the fifth, he made a target of Sullivan's nose and mouth, jabbed him alternately in the stomach and the nose, and battered his man badly.

About this time Sullivan began to appreciate the fact that it was the next thing to impossible for him to reach the Californian. Nevertheless, he rushed at him and would only desist when his nose came up short against Corbett's left. In the tenth, Sullivan rushed the fighting in a vain attempt to finish the fight then.

When the end came it was unexpected. John L. had been bleeding from the nose, and his lips were swollen and sore, but even Corbett men expected him to stay in the ring twice as long as he did. But Corbett's finishing strokes in the 21st round were lightning in speed and force. Three times the left went into Sullivan's face. Four times the right smashed on the swollen nose and mouth. Then Sullivan collapsed. He went down hands first, then knees, then shoulders. He tried to push himself up, and did get his hands off the floor. The referee then began counting the ten seconds, but Sullivan had not really risen from the ground. The idol had fallen; the huzzas of the crowd greeted the new champion.

The battle commenced at 9:10. It started out rather slowly. But in the fifth round Sullivan landed his first heavy right and missed a fearful left hand. The champion seemed eager for hot work. First blood came from Sullivan's nose and he nearly fell on the ropes from left-hand jabs.

In the sixth Sullivan's nose was bleeding again. The champion was beginning to look tired. There was a heavy exchange of lefts on the head; Sullivan seemed to be angry and slapped his opponent with his left hand. It began to look like some of the fight was out of Sullivan.

Corbett in the seventh walked right up to Sullivan. The champion was trying his hardest for the right on the jaw, but the foxy Corbett was not there. He jabbed Sullivan continually on the nose in this round and blood flowed freely. Jim was cheered by the crowd for his skillful fighting.

In the eighth Jim was the aggressor. He sent his left in the champion's stomach, forcing him to the ropes, and landed a heavy left on the mouth, which brought blood and a smile from the champion. Sullivan looked very tired as the gong sent them to their corners.

In the ninth Jim landed a heavy left on the nose. Sullivan was missing many blows now. The Californian landed heavy on the stomach and went to his corner looking like the victor.

Sullivan in the tenth followed his opponent and both exchanged lefts. Corbett's right found the champion's head and his left got there a moment later, but the champion landed on the head in return. This was a great fight so far. Corbett was doing most of the hitting. When the round ended he was lustily cheered.

Both landed good blows in the eleventh. Corbett showed great ability, even at clinching his more bulky opponent. Sullivan was extremely cautious, though he got a crushing blow on the nose and a punch in the stomach from the left.

In the twelfth Sullivan got a left in the stomach. He got it again very heavily. Sullivan landed a fairly good blow with his right, though Jim landed another left in the stomach and ran away smiling. The champion's head was forced back twice from two heavy left-handers, and the round wound up with both Corbett's hands in Sullivan's stomach.

In round thirteen the men boxed scientifically for an opening. Sullivan could not draw Corbett on with left-hand feints and never attempted to land the right. Sullivan was now forcing matters, but carefully. In the fourteenth Corbett's stock was sky high. But both men landed good blows.

The start of the fifteenth found Sullivan making his famous rush and forcing his man all over the ring, though he was nearly knocked down with a right. The champion landed his left on Jim's nose, but his stomach was uncovered and he received a heavy blow.

Corbett looked very fresh as he punched the champion in the head and stomach in the sixteenth. In the seventeenth Sullivan was breathing hard and his face was very red.

In the eighteenth a fearful left-hand jab on the nose was presented to Sullivan and he got a hot one on the head for being too familiar. Jim's left found the champion's stomach and face, and also the head. John L. landed a right punch on the ribs that sounded all over the house, though he got a left swing in the stomach a moment later. This was all Corbett's round.

In the nineteenth they boxed cautiously. Corbett appeared too clever for Sullivan and laughed sarcastically at the champion. Corbett landed two quick lefts in the stomach and Sullivan lost his temper from a staggering right and rushed at his opponent, but he looked like a beaten man.

Sullivan appeared tired for the twentieth round, and his left was very short; he was blowing hard, but he was the same resolute, ferocious man of yore. Both exchanged rights, and Sullivan was beaten to the ropes with a right and left. The champion was nearly knocked down with a left on the stomach and a right on the head. Corbett was dead game and unhurt so far. Sullivan tried a right, and received five clips on the head and stomach. The champion's knees were shaking, and he seemed unable to defend himself. John L. was fought to the ropes with heavy rights and lefts, and the gong seemed his only safety.

The 21st round was the last. Sullivan's left lead was very weak and he seemed anxious to wait. His opponent was with him, however, saw the championship bee in his bonnet, and the champion received a left on the nose. Sullivan was trying for the right, though he made little attempt to drive it home. Sullivan was beaten down with heavy rights and lefts, falling to the ground. He attempted to rise and fight, but nature gave way and he fell and was counted out. Referee Duffy then proclaimed Corbett the new champion.

The ovation that Corbett received was something tremendous, and he walked around the ring kissing and hugging his friends. Sullivan afterward made a speech in the ring.

John L. went out like a champion. After being counted out, he rose to his feet, clutched a ring rope, and while swaying turned to the crowd and said:

"I fought once too often. But, thank God, I lost to an American."

A great era in the ring had ended. Most of the nation was stunned and bitter at the fall of their long-time idol. For years Corbett was condemned as "that dancing master," and "that lily-livered *boxer* who wouldn't stand still and fight the great John L."

Sullivan was the first man to lose the title under Marquis of Queensberry rules, but he carried his London Prize Ring championship with him to the grave, in 1918.

Following his last ring appearance in 1896 in an exhibition bout with Sailor Tom Sharkey, the man who had been a roistering, swaggering champion became a staunch advocate of temperance and lived out his life lecturing on the evils of drink.

John Lawrence Sullivan was the first truly glamorous figure in the modern prize ring. He electrified and intrigued the public. During his prime small boys tried to copy his stand-up fighting stance and for many years his fans went around saying, "Shake the hand that shook the hand of John L. Sullivan."

Sullivan fitted the times perfectly. He belonged in the rough, raw America of his day. He certainly did much to start the prize ring towards the eminence it was to reach.

Perhaps the best way to end this profile of John L. is to tell you another John Barrymore anecdote. Barrymore was in his early teens by this time, and had made a date to meet his father on Broadway. As the two Barrymores stood there a bulking man walked slowly past them. A quality of loneliness seemed upon him in this busy street. The elder Barrymore took a quick step toward the big man, calling out cordially, "Hello there, John!"

John L. Sullivan paused, turned his great head slowly, as if he suspected some kind of mischief. Suddenly his eye fired with recognition. "Aw, Barry! It's you. Guess I was just all wrapped up in myself too hard. Nice of you to speak to me."

The ex-hero resumed his gallant march down Broadway, the ghosts of former worshippers following his slow strides.

"Why did he say it was so nice of you to speak to him, Papa?" John asked.

Maurice Barrymore had been looking after John L., a sadness in his eye. He turned to his son. "This is Broadway, the longest street with the shortest memory in the world. I wonder if you remember the time I first introduced you to John L.?"

"Sure, I do," John said. "He knocked my wind out with his cane."

"Good God!" Maurice Barrymore said. "One of the greatest fighters that ever lived, and all you remember is that he poked you with his stick!"

On the morning of February 2, 1918, the end came swiftly. Sullivan's heart was none too good those days. He suffered from cirrhosis of the liver. He wore glasses. He had gout. He was very sensitive about his increasing deafness. The old bones were tired, he said. He had fainted, and when he regained consciousness he found his old friend, George Bush, rubbing ice on his head. Bush got him to bed. "I'm all right," John L. told him. "I'll be all right in a little while." Bush sent for the doctor, but before he could get there John L. was dead.

It was a bitterly cold day when they took John L. Sullivan to St. Paul's for a High Mass of requiem and later to Calvary Cemetery. They had set aside a plot of ground in the side of a little knoll for burial, and it was so cold that they had to use dynamite to break the frozen earth. Old Jake Kilrain watched the scene solemnly, and he was heard to whisper, "Just as John L. would have liked it."

2. Gentleman Jim Corbett

JAMES JOHN CORBETT is down in history as the most intelligent prize fighter the ring has ever known—the supreme master of defensive boxing.

Gentleman Jim started to run away from the first scuffle he ever had and kept moving swiftly thereafter—with usually disastrous consequences for the other fellow. He had his first fight with a much bigger kid named Fatty Carney at St. Ignatius School in San Francisco, in 1878. Jim was twelve, Fatty was fifteen. Corbett won by dancing out of reach of Fatty's wrathful swings and popping him in the eyes with counterpunches. Result of fight: both boys were suspended from school.

When he was seventeen, he was amateur heavyweight champion of the Pacific Coast. "And nine years after that," he said in an interview in 1928, "I won the heavyweight championship of the world. It only shows what a boy can do when he just takes care of himself."

Gentleman Jim brought class to the prize ring. He put pugilism in the parlor, and vice versa. A polished, cultured man, he proved to the world that good fighters did not necessarily have to be loutish ignoramuses or hoodlums to succeed. This is not to mean that all fighters before him had been ignorant or roughnecks, but no prize fighter preceding Corbett had his suave urbanity, his courtly manners and his good breeding.

As Corbett gained fame for his superb boxing skill and his impeccable deportment, more and more women were seen at the ringside, although their presence there didn't become commonplace until much later when Jack Dempsey reigned over the heavyweight division.

Jim's father operated a livery stable, an occupation comparable to running a garage today. It provided a comfortable living for Jim and his eleven brothers and sisters. Jim finished high school, then quite an accomplishment, especially for one destined to make his living in the

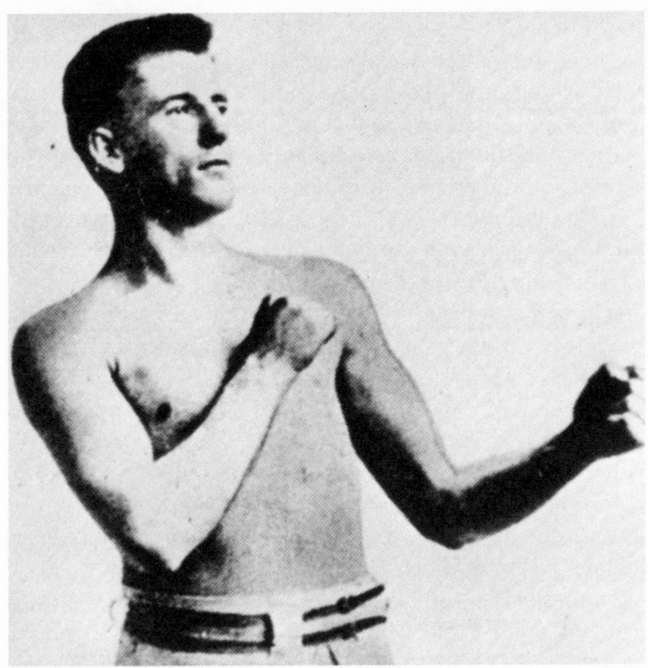

Gentleman Jim Corbett, in his typical stand-up stance, was a supreme master of defensive boxing.

prize ring. He worked around the San Francisco docks before taking a job in a bank, where his mastery of mathematics served him well.

Even as a boy, Corbett was obsessed with the urge to meet "important" people. To gratify this desire, he joined the famed Olympic Club in San Francisco. There he and Professor Walter Watson quickly discovered each other. The fifty-five-year-old Englishman was the club's boxing instructor and he saw in Corbett the makings of a great fighter.

After months of instructions, Watson decided Corbett was ready for his first ring test. He was matched with Dave Eiseman, middleweight champion of the club. Corbett boxed Eiseman's ears off in one round, then knocked him out of the ring with a right uppercut in the second.

Corbett continued to study his chosen trade, even spending long hours practicing in front of a full-length mirror so he could quickly spot any visible flaws.

Fighting only in and around San Francisco, Corbett built up a terrific reputation and a large following. Wearing his hair in a dashing pompadour, the erect, handsome, agile and intelligent youth soon had pretty well established his superiority over all fighters in the vicinity but one. The veteran Joe Choynski, a terrific puncher and good boxer, generally was considered the best heavyweight in the area.

Their first meeting, on May 30, 1889, in Fairfax, California, was broken up by police no sooner than it had started. Six days later they met again, this time on a barge just outside of Benecia, California. They fought on even terms for 26 rounds, but a broken nose suffered by Joe in the early rounds took its toll in the 27th. He became ill from large amounts of blood he had swallowed and his seconds tossed in the towel.

Jake Kilrain had just given the Mighty John L. Sullivan his hardest fight. Corbett, who was pointing for a title match like a bird dog, decided he could do no better than to fight Kilrain. They met in New Orleans and Corbett proved so superior to Kilrain as a boxer that the latter resigned the fight in disgust in the sixth round.

There still remained one big obstacle between Gentleman Jim and the heavyweight crown he hoped to slip on his pompadoured head. That barrier was Peter Jackson, an Australian who was known as the "Black Prince." Jackson had come to the United States with the idea of fighting Sullivan. John L., however, always had said he would never risk the title against a black, and he refused point-blank to meet him. "I will not fight Peter Jackson!" he snorted. "He's a *black* man!"

So Jackson decided to go to England. The journey across America from Nevada to New York became a leisurely procession in which heads rolled under the guillotine of his iron fists.

At Virginia City, he knocked out Shorty Kincaid in two rounds.

Sailor Brown was knocked out in Chicago.

Mike Lynch in Buffalo.

Paddy Brennan KO'd, Buffalo, one round.

Ginter McCormick went out like a light in the second round at Hoboken, New Jersey.

In England, Jackson gave exhibitions all over the Isles. The people flocked to see the Black Wonder as if he were royalty. Shortly before leaving, he wiped out the champion of England, Jem Smith, in two violent rounds. More or less as an afterthought, he was proclaimed champion of all the British Empire. Then, after an absence of three months, he returned to America.

Peter Jackson was now at the crest of his remarkable career. More than merely a superb fighter, he was a man of unusual intelligence and outstanding character. For the next 18 months the world was his stage and he bestrode it with an unassuming presence and dignity.

Meanwhile, Corbett had also proved himself a conqueror. Choynski, Jake Kilrain, Donovan and Dominick McCaffrey–four excellent fighters–he had destroyed them one after the other in a carefully thought-out campaign. Now only two men stood in his path to the world championship–Jackson and John L.

Unlike Sullivan, Corbett did not draw the color line, and he and the "Black Prince" met in an epic battle at the California Athletic Club, on May 21, 1891. Apart from the dramatic contrast of color, the two men were perfectly matched. Jackson, a heavy favorite, had the advantage in weight at 198 pounds. Both stood above 6-feet.

At the gong, Jackson moved into the center of the ring and crouched over his gloves. Corbett seemed to tower over him, orthodox, ice-cool, an illustration for a handbook on boxing. Then the photograph ripped into motion. A lightning left snaked out towards Peter. Peter moved stealthily and banged in with his right. The blow sped towards Corbett's ribs but was cleverly blocked. Corbett fought back with a flurry of short jabs to the heart. Jackson swung hard at the chin, a potentially killing blow if ever there was one. It was blocked.

As minute succeeded minute, the crowd began to realize that in Corbett a man had risen who was Jackson's equal. Though Jackson fought with every trick he knew and with a ferocity he had never transcended, Corbett parried, hit, ducked, danced away, hit true, hit hard. Here, indeed, was a master.

When two rounds had ended, Jackson realized he was facing the toughest opponent of his career. Sitting back in his corner, he watched the imperturbable face of the young Californian.

Once again the gong.

Out came Jackson, like a black flame, weaving to the attack with both fists. Corbett met him half-way and drove a crushing left hook to his stomach. Jackson countered with a hard right to the ribs. Was it mere imagination, or were Jackson's punches a shade less powerful than they used to be? There was a time when a blow like that would have made a man grunt with agony, but Corbett came on unchecked, his handsome face as imperturbable as antique marble.

The rounds flew by. In the whole history of boxing, had there ever been two such perfectly matched fighters? It was a contest of science, cunning and strength in which not a hair's difference could for a long time be discerned between the protagonists. Yet, clever and ferocious though Peter Jackson remained to the end, a certain splendor seemed to have gone from his style. Where was that flashing left that shot like a thunderbolt and crashed an opponent headlong into darkness? Where was that beautifully precise flick of a glove that jarred deep into the bone? Where, indeed, was that right jab travelling its few inches to hit like the slam of a door? The spectators waited, watched. An hour passed.

The pace seemed to be taking its toll on Jackson. His ferocity was petering out, the speed melting in his legs. On the other hand, Corbett seemed to be gaining confidence as the fight wore on. Now, for the first time, he dared sense victory. He tore across the ring as the gong sounded for the 29th round. Left, right, left! His fists smashed into Jackson's body and drove him reeling to the ropes. A savage left to the mouth jolted Peter's head so far back, it seemed the vertebrae were broken. Corbett moved in for the kill.

He slammed in the knockout punch: it disappeared harmlessly into space. For Peter Jackson was an incomparable master of ringcraft, too. He had snatched himself from defeat by the fraction of an inch. Now he showed one of the noblest qualities of a great fighter: the power to come back against all odds. He flew to the attack. A miracle was in possession of him. One moment he was a beaten man tottering on the edge of defeat, the next he was a machine jabbing a fist like a rod into Corbett's stomach.

Peter Jackson had saved himself. But it was a salvation without joy. At the end of the round, he walked back to his corner with a heavy heart. He seemed resigned that this long battle could not be won. He would fight on round after round, giving every atom of his skill and fighting instinct he had in him, but the referee might just as well have ended it then and there. For Peter felt that if he failed against Corbett, then he had failed against Sullivan, too. It was one and the same thing. Sullivan had drawn the color-line, and he, Peter Jackson, had dreamed and fought with only one object in mind–to cross that line in the end and make black men the equal of white men the whole world over.

Well, there was nothing to do but to fight on, and then still to fight on some more. The second hour passed. For round after round, with grimly sealed lips, Jackson forced the fight to Corbett, driving his collapsing muscles to their last ounce of performance. Corbett fought back with equal determination. They were both good men, each too good for the other, and not good enough. Saving an accident, neither could muster up that sudden starry explosion of energy that might have ended it once and for all.

Shortly after one o'clock in the morning, with the battle dripping, dripping, like a leaky water-tap, referee Hiram Cook claimed neither man had earned a decided advantage and he halted the match, calling it "no contest." It had lasted four hours and 61 rounds!

Gentleman Jim received only $3,000 for the fight and his followers decided to give him a benefit–a custom in those days–at the Grand Opera House. Sullivan was appearing in *Honest Hearts and Willing Hands* in San Francisco at the time and was invited to attend and spar with young Jim.

John L., even then past his peak, agreed but stipulated they appear in evening clothes. In that four-round exhibition, Corbett discovered he could outbox Sullivan.

One year later Corbett lifted the crown in New Orleans.

The general impression prevails that Corbett was a young usurper who had the temerity to face the most deadly hitter the ring had known. This is incorrect. Actually Gentleman Jim had seven years of active ring work behind him.

A tremendous Corbett build-up campaign won Gentleman Jim his big opportunity. As William A. Brady, his manager and boyhood friend, confessed, there was an element of chicanery in the whole promotion. Con McVey was sent ahead of the Corbett entourage and was used in town after town as Corbett offered to meet all comers. This won Corbett sufficient prominence to rate a crack at Sullivan.

Corbett was twenty-six years old when he fought Sullivan. John L. was thirty-four.

Gentleman Jim was the first "fancy Dan" to hold the heavyweight championship, and he did not meet with immediate public approval. At the outset he failed to draw at the gate. People resented the downfall of their idol, Sullivan. The mob wanted a man of brawn, not a boxing artist.

Corbett, in sweatshirt, is shown here training for his January, 1894, bout with Charlie Mitchell. That's Bill Brady, his manager, on the right.

After knocking out Sullivan, Corbett kayoed Charley Mitchell in three rounds in Jacksonville, Florida, January 25, 1894, to become undisputed heavyweight champion of the world under Marquis of Queensberry rules.

As the years went by, Corbett gained in stature. While the fight mob was apt to look at him with disdain, he succeeded in winning the general public. Corbett's unmarked face, his assurance and his engaging manner caught the fancy of those who had looked down on boxing.

Jim was handsome, pompadoured, blue-eyed and quick as a cat. Although he failed in several early stage ventures, including *Gentleman Jack* and *Naval Cadet,* he did enjoy a measure of success later in his career in musical comedies and vaudeville, where he was given supporting rather than leading roles.

Corbett was proud of his position in society. Once, when his father visited him in New York, Jim got a yen to show the old man how his son had come up in the world.

"Come on, Dad," he said, "I want to take you out on the town and show you the sights."

One of the sights was Steve Brodie's restaurant in the Bowery. Brodie was the Bowery character who had gained fame by jumping off the Brooklyn Bridge to collect a wager. The elite among sports gathered at Steve's. Naturally no sojourn in New York would be complete without a visit to the pub. Jim introduced his father to Brodie.

"Steve's the fellow who jumped off the Brooklyn Bridge," explained Jim to his dad. The elderly Corbett, who was quite deaf, didn't appear impressed, so Jim decided to go one step further.

"Come on, Dad," he said, "I'll show you the exact spot where he jumped."

The two men got into a hack and rode to the middle of the great span over the East River. There the rig stopped and the Corbetts got out.

"Here it is, the highest spot," said Jim. "Here's where Steve Brodie jumped off the bridge."

"Whatsay?" shouted his father.

"I SAID," repeated Jim, "THIS IS WHERE STEVE BRODIE JUMPED OFF THE BRIDGE!"

There was a moment of silence.

Finally the old man said, "Heck, Jim, any damn fool can jump off this bridge. I thought you said he jumped OVER it!"

Of all his ring achievements, Corbett was proudest of being called a "gentleman." He was obsessed with his own urbanity and it was for this reason that he detested any mention of one notable occasion when he forgot *éclat* and got into a street brawl. The target of his wrath was Bob Fitzsimmons, who had succeeded him as champion.

The incident happened in the barroom of Green's Hotel in Philadelphia, then the mecca for the theatrical and sporting set. Corbett was living in the hotel at the time and learned that Ruby Robert was at the bar enjoying a few drams of his beloved English ale. Corbett hastened to the bar and began to unmercifully berate Fitzsimmons. Fitz never turned his head but kept watching Corbett in the mirror hanging behind the bar. As Corbett grew angrier, Fitz grinned at him contemptuously. Several times it seemed as if Corbett would let go a punch, but he didn't. Finally he offered Fitz a flat challenge to put up his fists and face him, but Bob never turned his head. He just kept grinning at Jim in the mirror. Corbett so completely lost his head that he pulled Fitz around and spit in his face. The Cornishman turned away and snarled:

"When I fights, I fights like a gentleman–in the ring. And what's more, I gets paid for it."

It took the combined efforts of several employees to get Corbett out of the bar. The incident was played up in the newspapers, and it was, as Corbett said later, the one event in his life he regretted. It served its purpose in one respect, however; from that day on it was virtually impossible to provoke Jim into losing his temper outside the ring.

After two years of doubts and delays, Gentleman Jim finally put his heavyweight title on the line against Ruby Robert Fitzsimmons. The match was held at Carson City, Nevada, on the 17th of March, 1897. Corbett weighed 183, Fitzsimmons 167. They fought for a purse of $15,000, with a $5,000 side bet added.

The newspaper account follows:

CARSON CITY, NEV., March 17, 1897 (Special)–The heavyweight championship of the world was finally decided today when Robert Fitzsimmons sent James J. Corbett helpless to his knees with a left-hand blow under the heart after one minute and forty-five seconds in the fourteenth round.

The great contest was decided in the simplest manner and the "knockout" was the result of one unwary move on the part of Corbett. After the first minute of the fourteenth round had been spent in a few harmless clinches and counters Fitzsimmons made a "fake" lead with his right for the jaw. It was a simple ruse, but it caught the Californian napping. Instead of keeping his body inclined forward and throwing back his head just a trifle to allow the blow, which was of the very lightest kind, to slip by, Corbett contemptuously bent his head and chest backward and thus protruded his abdomen.

Fitzsimmons' small eyes flashed, and, like lightning, he saw and availed himself of his advantage. Drawing back his left, he brought it up with terrible force, the forearm rigid and at right angles to the upper arm. With the full power of his wonderful driving muscles brought into play, the Australian fairly ripped the blow up the pit of Corbett's stomach at a point just under the heart. Corbett was lifted clean off his feet, and as he pitched forward Fitzsimmons shot his right fist up and around, catching Corbett on the jaw and accelerating his downward fall.

Corbett sank on his left knee, and with his outstretched right hand grasped the ropes for support. His left arm worked convulsively up and down, while his face was twitching with an expression of the greatest agony.

Referee George Siler threw up his hands on the call of "ten" and left the ring. There were some cries of "Foul!" when the referee declared Corbett "out," but they were unheeded by anybody, as the battle was won fairly and squarely.

The defeat nearly drove Corbett wild. After his seconds had helped him to his corner, he broke away from them and rushed at Fitzsimmons, who had not yet left the ring. A scene of dreadful confusion ensued. The ring was crowded with an excited mob, but Corbett burst through them and struck at Fitzsimmons. The Australian kept his arms by his sides, and with a great deal of generosity made allowance for Corbett's half-demented condition. Fitzsimmons merely ducked under the blow, and when Corbett clinched with him and struck him a feeble blow on the ear the champion only smiled. It was with great difficulty that Billy Brady and the seconds succeeded in quieting Corbett down and getting him back to the dressing room.

The fight was clean and speedy. It demonstrated two facts—that Corbett is the cleverest boxer of his weight in the world, and that Fitzsimmons is able to hit him. The California boy smothered the Cornishman with left jabs in the face and right and left body blows. Fitzsimmons' most effective attack was a semifake left swing, followed with a quick half-arm hook. The first time he tried it, which was in the third round, Corbett threw back his head from the fake, coming forward for a counter when he thought Fitzsimmons' glove was comfortably past his jaw. Quick as a flash, Fitzsimmons doubled back and barely missed Corbett's jaw with the hook. Corbett's smile died away for an instant, and he took no more chances on countering on that particular form of lead afterward.

The battle was fought on purely scientific and almost new principles. Corbett made no attempt to bring around his right in breaking away, probably because Fitzsimmons held up his elbows too high. Corbett's only effort in the way of a parting shot was a full right uppercut, which he brought around very clumsily and failed to land by at least a foot every time he tried. He did get in one good uppercut in the fourth round, splitting Fitzsimmons' under lip and starting the blood in a thick stream. Several times the men clinched and parted with both hands up. Frequently Fitzsimmons worked Corbett into his corner and reached for him right and left with blows that would win any championship battle if they landed. Fitzsimmons himself admits that Corbett shuffled and sidestepped his way to safety in a manner which simply dazed him.

After the battle, W. A. Brady, Corbett's manager, expressed a willingness to back Corbett for $20,000 for another fight.

Fitzsimmons confessed that he never saw such a clever boxer in his life. He said, "Corbett got away from me time and again when I thought I had him dead to rights. I knew I could wear him out, and so I kept coming right along until my opportunity arrived. He was weak in that last round, and all his cleverness could not keep him away from that left punch under the heart. The only blow that really worried me was the one which split my lip. The others I hardly felt. He fought fair, and hereafter he may have my respect if he continues to merit it."

Corbett's version of the fight did not vary greatly from Ruby Robert's. "I made a mistake in not keeping away," he said. "I knew he was a terrific puncher, but I never thought he would be able to reach me. If the sixth round had lasted ten seconds longer I would have landed him. His nose was clogged with blood and his legs were wobbling. The gong sounded just as I was about to plug him with my right and end the battle. He recuperated wonderfully, and I stayed away from him until I thought he was about ripe for another drubbing at short range. My neglect in not standing off when he tapped me on the cheek in the fourteenth lost me the title. That heart punch simply choked me up. I could not breathe or move for fifteen seconds, and it was several minutes before I realized that I had committed a breach of etiquette in trying to follow up my opponent after he put me out. I meant it when I said I would be his friend hereafter. He whipped me fair and square.

But I don't think he is the best man yet, and we will have another go if money can bring him into the ring."

Gentleman Jim and Jim Jeffries dressed like a couple of prosperous businessmen in later years.

Gentleman Jim did fight for the crown again—but not against Fitzsimmons. He was the first ex-champion who twice fought a heavyweight champion in an attempt to regain the title. Each time he was knocked out by James J. Jeffries.

Corbett might have won back the championship the first time he fought Jeffries had he been less susceptible to the taunts of rival handlers and blood-thirsty spectators. The match was held at Coney Island, on May 11, 1900, and was limited to 25 rounds. Corbett had plainly won the first 22. Someone estimated that Big Jeff had started 156 left hooks in Jim's general direction, and not one of them touched the thirty-four-year-old dancing master.

"By the 20th round," Corbett said later, "I was completely sure of winning. Jeff couldn't hit me in a hundred rounds. I knew I had won back the championship, and I began thinking about the banners I'd hang out."

Gentleman Jim was very much of an actor, and to him regaining the heavyweight title meant great flaming banners of victory in front of the theatre where he was playing. Corbett, boxing beautifully all the time, became engrossed by the thought of the banners and the letters six-feet high. It was a brilliant exhibition of boxing skill, but the fans had come to see a fight. They resented Jim's cleverness. Big Jeff's handlers added flames to the fuel by calling Jim a sissy, a weakling who didn't dare stand up and fight the champion like a man. The jeering soon got under his skin.

"I'm going to mix with him this time," Corbett told his handlers while sitting in his corner waiting for the 23rd round to begin.

"No, Jim, no," they pleaded with him. "Don't change your pattern. You're winning. Stay away from him."

"I'll show them I can fight as well as box," he said.

Credit Gentleman Jim with the old college try. And credit James J. Jeffries with a knockout!

Years later, after he had plenty of time to think about the sudden ending, Corbett told about it. "I was in the corner, as I had been many times during the fight. He rushed me, just as he had rushed time and again. All I had to do was to sidestep and slip out, as I'd done a hundred times. He seemed to stagger toward me. He was really just throwing out his arms to get hold of me. In that desperate lunge, his left glove collided sidewise against my jaw. He was so powerful that the jolt knocked me out, banners and all. One punch and it was all over."

Jeffries gave Corbett a second chance to regain the title, on August 14, 1903. This time it took the defending champion only 10 rounds to flatten Gentleman Jim. By now Big Jeff had acquired the polish and skill which only experience could give him, while Corbett was feeling his thirty-six years.

Corbett, left, and Jeffries re-enacted their memorable championship battle for the benefit of photographers some years after their original 1903 fight.

Corbett had one weakness as a fighter. He lacked the killer instinct. He loved to box but there was nothing really brutal about him. He was fast physically and mentally, yet slow and deliberate in his speech. In and out of the prize ring he was always a great actor.

When promoters were doing their best to maintain interest in Gene Tunney in his final and unattractive match with the plodding Tom Heeney, in 1928, a boxing writer called on Billy Brady at his theatre in midtown Manhattan.

"I understand, Mr. Brady, that all old fighters are seen in the flattering light of distance, but can't you by some stretch of the imagination see Tunney as Corbett's equal as a boxer?"

A look of utter disgust came over Billy Brady's face.

"Young man," he said, "did you ever see Jim Corbett box?"

Such a comparison was interesting, because Corbett and Tunney became good friends later. They even fought in the ring once. You won't find the exhibition listed in any record book. Grantland Rice was the matchmaker and promoter. The year was 1925. Granny told me the story of that fight before he died, in 1954.

"I was in the business of making Sportlight films, and I finally sold Corbett on the idea of boxing three rounds, for pictures, with Tunney," Granny recalled. "Anxious to pick up any possible tips from the old stylist, Tunney was eager. We arranged a spot in midtown Manhattan, atop the Putnam Building, and Gene arrived at the appointed hour, ready to go and dressed in trunks. Corbett took one look at them and said, 'I'd like to wear long white trousers. I had a pair of good-looking legs in the old days but they don't look so good now. I'm nearly sixty and they are kinda shrivelled.'

"They boxed three 2-minute rounds. Tunney was on the defensive. Corbett was brilliant. He feinted with his left–then punched with his left. A left feint . . . a left hook; a right feint . . . a left jab; a right feint; a right cross. He still had bewildering speed! He mixed up his punches better than practically any fighter I've seen since–with the possible exception of Ray Robinson.

"After the exhibition, Tunney turned to me. He said, 'I honestly think he is better than Benny Leonard. It was the greatest thing I've ever seen in the ring. I learned plenty.'

"At fifty-nine, Gentleman Jim Corbett was still the master!"

James J. Corbett died on February 18, 1933, at Bayside, Long Island.

3. Ruby Robert Fitzsimmons

THE man who was to succeed James J. Corbett as heavyweight champion of the world was one of the quaintest personalities ever to hold any title. Yet for all of his eccentricities, Bob Fitzsimmons was one of the most devastating fighters and tremendous punchers of all times.

There always has been a dispute among the experts as to whether Fitz was really a very good boxer. Some declare he lacked grace, and was unscientific. But whatever his shortcomings as a stylist, there were few men better equipped to mix and give and take.

Ruby Robert moved with a shuffling, gangling gait. He stood flat-footed. His timing was perfect. He was a superb judge of distance. His punching, therefore, was deadly accurate.

Fitz stood 5 ft. 11¾ in. and weighed no more than 167 pounds at his peak. His appearance was outlandishly awkward. From the waist up he was a heavyweight. From his belt-line down, he was a featherweight. He was knock-kneed and had pipestem legs, a barrel chest and heavyweight arms that could deliver a blow as powerful as any the ring has known. From toenails to torso he was a guy who would evoke nothing but laughs in a bathing suit. From midriff to neck he resembled a Greek god. All that was topped off by a freckled face, garnished with sparse red hair which gained him the nickname, "Ruby Robert." The moniker stuck, although he was practically bald before he won the heavyweight championship of the world at thirty-five.

The Cornishman was the oldest boxer to win the title up to that time.

It is an axiom of the fight game that between two fairly evenly matched fighters, one must always pick the younger. Fitz was five years older than Corbett when he knocked out Gentleman Jim to take the crown.

Bob Fitzsimmons was one of the most devastating fighters and sharpest punchers of all times. He weighed no more than 160 pounds at his peak.

It is also a theory in the fight game that a good big man can always take a good little man. Fitz never in his life weighed more than 167 pounds. He was hardly more than a well-fed welterweight when he took boxing's highest honor.

Born in Cornwall, England, June 4, 1862, and raised in Timaru, New Zealand, where his father operated a blacksmith shop, Fitz developed his punching muscles in years spent at the smithy's anvil.

Ruby Robert came to the United States at an age when most fighters are ready to turn in their boxing gloves for slippers and pipe. He walloped Dempsey, the Nonpareil, to win the middleweight title, then looked around for bigger and better targets. He did not coin the expression, "The bigger they are, the harder they fall," but he acted on Joe Walcott's familiar epigram.

Fitz was the daddy of all middleweights. He was heavyweight champion at a time when he could still make 158 pounds.

He could punch at long range with lethal effect. The Fitzsimmons shift, which he popularized, was one of the most deadly maneuvers the ring has known. Bob would feint with his left or right, then shift with his feet, catching his opponent with a long left to the windbag that was paralyzing. He was a killer at short range, too. His defensive tactics were awkward, but effective because of his catlike reflexes and great sense of timing.

He had extraordinary recuperative powers and was a master of ring strategy. He would feign grogginess to set up an unsuspecting rival for an effective punch. Brittle hands were his Achilles Heel, to mix the dickens out of a metaphor.

Joe Howard, the eminent and venerable minstrel of the Gay Nineties who once claimed the bantamweight title himself, remembered Fitz vividly. He was closely associated with the champion, in fact refereed when Bob toured the country offering $250 to any man who could stay four rounds with him.

Before Fitz went into his act, it was the referee's job to sound out the contestants, as Howard used to tell it. If they wanted to be nice, he'd inform them they would be paid $100 for being jolted into slumber quite painlessly. If they wanted to take the whole thing seriously and risk their health trying for the $250 jackpot, that was perfectly alright, too.

"Sometimes they'd be obstinate," Joe recalled. "They'd really think they could stay with Fitz. Some even thought they could beat him. When I'd tell Fitz about these foolish fellows, he'd take off the big eight-ounce gloves and put on four-ounce 'smallies' that made only a tight covering around the knuckles. About midway of the second round, Fitz would run his right glove slowly across his face. That was the signal for me to take cover in the farthest corner. A second later, there'd be a smash to the solar plexus and we'd carry the stiff out."

The Fitzsimmons-Corbett bout at Carson City, March 17, 1897, always will be remembered as The Birth of the Solar Plexus Punch. Fitz, left, ended Corbett's title reign in the 14th round with the most famous single punch in boxing history.

Ruby Robert's first great battle in this country was that memorable contest against Dempsey, the Nonpareil, January 14, 1891, in New Orleans for the middleweight title. Fitz, weighing 150½ pounds, astounded the fistic world by knocking out Dempsey, 147¾ pounds, in the 13th round.

Bob's title bout with Corbett at Carson City, March 17, 1897, always will be remembered as The Birth of the Solar Plexus Punch. For 13½ rounds the pair fought evenly, though some ringsiders felt Gentleman Jim seemingly was more interested in self-preservation than protecting his crown. Then, late in the 14th round, the champion left his belly unprotected for a fraction of a second. Spotting the opening, Fitz shifted his weight and slammed a jarring left hook into Jim's solar plexus. That blow, ending the fight and Corbett's reign as champion, was the most famous single punch in the long history of boxing.

Most Americans were shocked by the Cornishman's victory, but those who had seen him against Dempsey had known all along that the grotesque Fitz was a superb fighter. Later, in his dressing room, Gentleman Jim told news reporters: "I came out of the ring today a defeated man. I think I fought as well as I've ever fought, but it wasn't good enough. The punch that won the fight was largely an accidental one. It was a left hook. It caught me directly under the heart. I dropped to my knees. My brain was clear and I could see everything going on around me, but I couldn't move a muscle and my breath came hard. My lips wouldn't move. It was almost a case of paralysis. Taking the fight from start to finish, it was the fastest fight I ever fought. My bout with Peter Jackson was faster in spots, but the speed in this one was more prolonged. We never took as much advantage of the free arm and breakaway hitting as people thought we would. Fitzsimmons is infernally clever, decidedly the best man I ever fought. He is better in the clinches than I thought he'd be and much stronger. He recuperates marvelously. I never expected him to get up after I knocked him down with a right to the jaw in an early round. I heard some of the men in my corner yell 'foul,' but there was no foul. It was a legitimate punch. Fitzsimmons can be proud of his victory. No one will ever hear me say that his wasn't a clear-cut victory."

Rumors circulated before the bout hinted that Fitz had accepted a bribe to lie down. Ruby Robert blamed the untrue stories on enemies.

"It is true that a San Francisco combination offered me $500,000 to throw the fight, and $250,000 by a New York gambler," admitted Fitzsimmons, "but I gave them my answer when I knocked out Corbett. I made up my mind I just had to win, that if they carried me out a loser it would be as a dead man."

Corbett asked Fitz for a return match, but Fitz announced he was retiring from the ring, that one of the reasons he had taken the fight was to prove to the world that a middleweight could beat a heavyweight.

"I have fought for the last time," Fitz told Corbett.

Gentleman Jim fumed, emphasizing his anger with some very ungentlemanly words. "If you don't give me another shot at the title I'll meet you on the street and beat you to death."

"If you do, Jim," Fitz replied calmly, "I'll kill you."

The subject was not brought up again.

An interesting sidelight to the Corbett-Fitzsimmons match was the appearance of Bob Davis in Ruby Robert's training camp two weeks before the fight. Young Davis (later to become a famous editor) was dispatched to Carson City on orders from Arthur Brisbane, William Randolph Hearst's New York editor. With preparations for the fight making front-page news all over America, Davis went to Fitzsimmons' training camp and for $10,000 got exclusive rights to any and all statements that came out of the camp. Then started a flood of inside news stories, written by Davis and signed by Fitz, in which the half-literate Cornishman was made to sound like a Rhodes scholar. The brilliant, succinct opinions under his by-line covered not only the upcoming fight, but also touched on national and international affairs. Davis, noting Fitz's ruddy complexion, dubbed him "Ruby Robert," a nickname destined to stick, and soon Fitz had a reputation for sagacity and intellect that made him tremendously popular with the American public.

During the fight, in which Fitz was floored in one of the early rounds, the twenty-eight-year-old Davis, short and overweight and wearing a turtleneck sweater, toiled in a minor seconding capacity in the challenger's corner.

Davis later admitted that it was the first prize fight he ever saw, but he gave *his* boy a lot of expert advice.

Fitzsimmons, as the years were to show, had a change of heart later and climbed back into the ring to continue fighting. As a matter of fact, he went on to fight another 17 years.

Ruby Robert's rivalry with Peter Maher was one of the strangest in ring history. Maher was the most pathetic of all contenders for the heavyweight title. The ring yielded him fame and hard knocks but little money.

Fitz was a jinx to the guileless Irishman who, on the advice of John L. Sullivan, came to the United States in the autumn of 1891.

Maher was born in Galway, Ireland, March 6, 1869.

Scarcely five months after he arrived in this country, Maher was matched with Fitz at the historic Olympic Club in New Orleans, March 2, 1892. Maher stood 5 ft. 11¾ in., weighed 180 pounds, and the fight proved to be a rousing one. Fitz knocked Maher down, drew first blood (important in those days) in the first round, but the Celt got up and weathered the storm.

Peter nailed Fitz late in the second round. The Cornishman dropped as if he had been hit with a sledge. Fitz was still on the floor when the gong came to his rescue. To his dying day Maher insisted that Joe Choynski, Fitz' chief second, had reached over and hit the bell with still another minute to go.

Fitz recovered and knocked Maher out in the 12th round to take the winner's purse of $9,000. Maher received $1,000.

Peter had even worse luck the second time he tangled with Fitz. A victory for Maher would have meant a crack at Corbett. The battle was originally scheduled to be fought in Dallas, but the Governor of Texas, in the midst of reform, convened the State Legislature and in 48 hours had boxing banned. Arkansas, Arizona and New Mexico, anticipating a move by Dan Stuart, the matchmaker, to hold the fight within their boundaries, acted quickly to block him. Mexico's President Diaz killed hopes of staging the bout there with a proclamation against prize fighting. But a last-hour telegram saved the match: INVITE YOU TO HOLD FIGHT IN LANGTRY. I AM LAW WEST OF PECOS AND GUARANTEE PROTECTION. It was signed by Judge Roy Bean. Judge Bean was an irrepressible opportunist who dispensed both justice and liquor from his saloon in Langtry. One heard incredible tales about him. He had named the Texas village in honor of his idol, actress Lily Langtry. A typical story told about him was that he had fined a dead man for the sum found on the corpse. Another said he let a known murderer go free. But whether or not he was an incorrigible scoundrel, the judge was the one man who could hold the outlawed fight. Promoter Dan Stuart assured everyone that the fight would take place on February 21.

Adjutant General Mabry, with his Texas Rangers, stalked into El Paso and told newspapermen that the Governor had ordered them to stop the bout, assuming it was held in Texas. Dan Stuart kept mysteriously mum about the site, and then put up a notice outside his office: PERSONS DESIROUS OF ATTENDING THE PRIZE FIGHT REPORT AT THESE HEADQUARTERS TONIGHT AT 9:45 P.M. ROUND TRIP FARE WILL NOT EXCEED $12.

By shortly after 9 o'clock, 300 excited fans had jammed the 10 extra coaches the Southern Pacific had added to its regular train. General Mabry and his rangers squeezed on board, to make sure that Stuart didn't hold the fight within the state. The fight special pulled out at midnight, and some 16 hours and 400 miles later it disgorged a disheveled crowd at the ramshackle town of Langtry. The judge, a ponderous man with a grizzled beard covering most of his face, sported his usual

The 1896 title match between Fitzsimmons and Peter Maher was outlawed in all states, so the promoters staged it 400 miles from El Paso, on an isolated sandbar in the Rio Grande River, separating the United States and Mexico. Some 300 people paid $20 apiece to see Fitz knock out Maher in 95 seconds.

battered Stetson. "This way to the fight of the century," he said, "and, gents, there's cold beer at ringside."

Between towering bluffs on each side of the Rio Grande along the United States-Mexico border was a cleared-out space on a river sandbar. This was "ringside." No seats, just a circle enclosed by a wall of canvas circus tenting.

High on the United States bluffs General Mabry shouted at his rangers: "Damn Roy Bean! He's holding the fight *outside* the United States!"

The sandbar was in Mexican territory and so remote there weren't any gendarmes around.

Finally Fitzsimmons appeared, then Maher. Fitz was confident, and Peter nervous. Referee George Siler gave the fighters their instructions, the crowd cheered, and the timekeeper banged the bottom of a tin bucket for round one. Fitz strode out of his corner and threw a left and, after a few blows, he clipped Peter on the jaw and the fight was finished—only 1 minute and 35 seconds after it had begun. Peter's handlers yelled at him to get up, he tried to rise, but couldn't make it.

Stunned at the quick ending, a spectator hollered at referee Siler as he was counting out Maher:

"Was it a fake, George?"

"If he lives," Siler replied, "it's a fake... nine... if he's killed, it's on the level... ten and out."

George raised Fitz' hand, and the disappointed crowd realized they had traveled 400 miles and paid $20 (plus the $12 round-trip fare) to see 95 dull seconds of fighting.

"Have some nice cold beer at my saloon while you wait for the train," comforted Judge Bean. He had thoughtfully provided an extra carload of beer and charged one dollar a bottle, a 100 percent markup. His profit from the fight was considerably higher than promoter Dan Stuart's. Stuart had lost his shirt, partly because many spectators had enjoyed a free view from the bluffs.

The promoter was not alone in his loss. Maher got exactly nothing for his part in the fiasco. He had to borrow carfare home. Fitz took the $9,000 purse, plus the $1,000 side bet. Maher's bad fortune was typical of him. Bad luck followed him all the way to the grave. When he died, in 1940, he was broke and working as a dock walloper.

Ruby Robert held the heavyweight championship until the night of June 9, 1899, when Jim Jeffries, the California boilermaker, relieved him of it. The fight was staged at the New Coney Island Sporting Club. The newspaper account left no doubt in anybody's mind as to how the match went:

> The long-heralded prize fight between Bob Fitzsimmons and Jim Jeffries resulted in an indisputable victory for the aspiring boilermaker from California last night in the eleventh round. The world now has a new champion pugilist

Jim Jeffries, left, and Fitzsimmons shake hands in ring center before their battle at Coney Island on June 9, 1899. Jeff won by a knockout in the 11th round. Referee George Siler is in background.

this morning and Fitzsimmons, who knocked out Corbett, who knocked out Sullivan, has taken his place in the long procession of fistic heroes known in ring circles as "back numbers" or "has beens."

The work of changing champions occupied a little less than 44 minutes. How much the two men gained in money nobody knows. On a rough estimate it is said that Fitzsimmons, whose dignity demanded large pecuniary inducements to display his prowess upon a comparatively unknown man, will receive about $25,000 of the gate receipts as his share, besides contingent profits from the vitascope, which took photographs of the fight.

Jeffries will do as well and is probably richer by a comfortable amount in side bets.

At 9 o'clock all the arena seats were occupied, and the tiers of seats banked at each side and the ends presented masses of white faces and shirt fronts. It was a well-dressed gathering. Many had traveled more than a thousand miles and spent hundreds of dollars to reach the ringside. Some of them had thousands and tens of thousands of dollars at stake.

There was a great cheer and a rattle of applause when Jeffries walked in. He looked huge and rather angry, and, with his red sweater under a sack coat, and a flimsy cap on the back of his head resting on his thick black hair, was the most carelessly dressed and the roughest-looking man in the building. There was a fainter cheer as Fitzsimmons was announced, and after his disappearance there were symptoms of impatience.

The rumor that there was a dispute over the rules had gone abroad. The uncertainty of Chief of Police Devery's intentions added to the uneasy feeling. Those in attendance had not come to see whether Fitzsimmons or Jeffries was the better boxer. They wanted to see which was the "best man," which could hit hardest, endure the most pain and fatigue, keep his head, and use his skill the better.

A cheer began at the eastern end of the great building. Moving through the throng was a gigantic horseshoe of pink, white and crimson roses, with American flags above it, and bearing the inscription, "Good Luck to the Champion."

Behind this aesthetic proclamation, Fitzsimmons stalked solemnly, like the chief figure in a classic spectacle. His bearing was solemn. He wore a bathrobe of pale blue. Jeffries was more on the rough-and-ready order. He moved briskly and swung his shoulders and wore a red sweater, with suspenders over it, and the breeches of ordinary, commonplace people. Then came the referee, George Siler, in blue-and-white-striped undershirt.

Mrs. Fitzsimmons got into the clubhouse and was in her husband's dressing room but she decided not to attempt to watch the fight. She saw William A. Brady, the manager of Jeffries, shook hands with him, and remarked:

"We will beat your man again tonight, as we did the other at Carson City."

Brady only smiled, and replied, "I hope not."

At 10:17, the two fighters met at the center of the ring, where they shook hands coldly. The contrast between the two was startling. Fitzsimmons looked little and white alongside the giant Jeffries, a dark man. The latter's eyes and hair are black and his skin almost a tan. Fitzsimmons is light-eyed and what hair he has is pale red. No woman has a skin whiter or smoother than his.

The word was given and the men rose from the stools to which they had returned. Neither looked cheerful. Jeffries swallowed hard; Fitzsimmons moistened his lips with his tongue, and as they slowly and cautiously circled about, feinting, advancing and retreating, never within arm's length, their eyes intently fastened on each other, he began to work his lips nervously.

If the crowd had been a crowd of dead men, the stillness could not have been deeper than it was. The fighters trod softly as cats. Nothing could be heard but the gentle thud, thud of their ever restless, shifting feet as they circled.

Then there was a sudden rush and the sharp slap of a glove landing, a gleaming of arms and twisting and violent motion of white bodies in the ring, a storm of cries, with applause and some roaring laughter from arena and encompassing seats.

Jeffries had led. He was not afraid to fight. That was one point settled.

Fitzsimmons' light blue eyes opened wide and blazed angrily. Jeffries crouched low, keeping his tremendous left arm well thrust out, his head down, looking from under his eyebrows.

In the second round the cheering and shouting began again. The crowd then felt that it would see what it had come to see–a fight with hard knocks. The two men in the ring smiled at each other as both missed and they came together in a clinch, but they did not relax their guards the fraction of a second.

The crowd was evidently with Jeffries, and when Fitzsimmons tumbled on his back, looking a much surprised man, joy was unrestrained. It was obvious then that the ideas of Chief of Police Devery on slugging were liberal, and that there would be no interference.

After the sixth round a new change came into Fitzsimmons' face. He had looked furious at times and amused at times. Now he looked old and worn and anxious. Wrinkles seemed to come into his cheeks. He was aggressive, crafty, watchful, always moving, his rather cruel lips working and working as if he would like to bite; but he seemed like a man who is hunted. Once or twice thereafter his lips broke into a smile. When he and Jeffries broke out of a clinch and separated at the end of the eighth round, their mutual grins were almost affable. But as he sat on his stool and breathed fast he looked worried.

When the end came it seemed very quick and easy. The blow that really did the work was given with Jeffries' left glove. After it was delivered Fitzsimmons stood an instant, his hands hanging by his sides, his knees bowed. The knockout with the right came swiftly. It was given from the hip, much like a quick slap. It was not like one of the long, hard swings Jeffries had aimed at him several times and which had gone over his head.

When it landed Fitzsimmons fell and turned on his right side. There was no need to count. His body was limp and doubled up. He passed the back of his hand wearily over his bald forehead and straightened out on his back, his lower lip hanging foolishly, his long upper lip scarlet.

Jeffries looked at him an instant and walked to his corner, breathing hard. A thousand men were storming and swirling about the ringside then. Hats were waving and the big hall was ringing with yells and cheers and exultant laughter.

Fitzsimmons was dragged to his stool, his heels trailing helplessly on the floor. It was all over. The time of the eleventh round was 1 minute and 32⅖ seconds.

After the knockout blow had been struck Chief of Police Devery jumped to the outer edge of the ring and waited for the referee to count the fatal tenth second. He stepped into the ring then and his men surrounded it. He was asked by a reporter whether he would arrest the principals, in accordance with his declaration of a few days ago. "Wait a few moments and we will see," he replied. And then, as he saw that Fitzsimmons had recovered sufficiently to sit up and answer the greeting and handshake Jeffries offered him, he added: "No, there will be no arrests. Fitzsimmons is all right now, and the law has not been violated. But I would have stopped the fight in a minute if I had seen anything that broke the law.

Not quite convinced, Fitz fought Jeffries again on July 25, 1902, in San Francisco. Big Jeff never dodged a return engagement. He was always ready to give a beaten opponent another chance and another beating. The encore was usually more decisive than the first. This time he knocked out Fitz in the eighth round.

Like Pudge Heffelfinger of Yale, who played tackle football for 50 years, Ruby Robert Fitzsimmons seemed to go on forever. He was forty-one years old when he defeated George Gardner in 20 rounds to win the light-heavyweight championship of the world, in San Francisco. The victory made him the first triple title-holder in the history of the prize ring. He fought his last prize fight when he was fifty-two, a no-decision match, with K.O. Sweeney, at Williamsport, Pennsylvania, on January 29, 1914. They simply couldn't get the old geezer out of there.

Fitz had a strange sense of humor as well as appearance. He wore a silk topper, like Sullivan and Corbett, but unlike John L. and Gentleman Jim he cocked it at a rakish angle. The talented cartoonist, T. A. (Tad) Dorgan, would laugh to himself while sitting at his drawing board portraying Fitz under the teetering bonnet.

Ruby Robert also loved practical jokes, the cruder the better. For a while he kept a lion around the house and delighted in frightening callers half to death with it. He personally often wrestled with the jungle beast. Those rough and tumbles finally got the better of the animal. He succumbed to his master and died. Fitz had him stuffed. Man or beast, the old champion knew no fear.

Even Fitz' personal life had an unusual twist. He divorced his first wife to marry Rose Julian, the wife of his manager, Martin Julian. Martin then married the former Mrs. Fitzsimmons.

4. James J. Jeffries

THE big, burly boilermaker who sat sullenly at the ringside in Carson City, on March 17, 1897, and watched James J. Corbett lose his title to Robert Fitzsimmons could hardly have been called a contender for anything—unless it was oblivion.

His name was James J. Jeffries and he was one of Corbett's sparring partners. He had looked so futile in the training camp that Billy Delaney, the famous trainer, wanted to fire him. Gentleman Jim, however, requested that Jeffries be retained. He found the oversized Jeff a good target on which to experiment and try out new punches. Corbett would throw them with everything he had, and Jeffries would take it without blinking an eye.

It is doubtful that the champion ever hurt Jeffries. He was a powerful young man originally out of Ohio. He was big, strong and hard as granite. Standing 6 ft. 1½ in. and weighing 215 pounds at his best, if the "California Grizzly" wasn't the greatest heavyweight who ever fought certainly he stands out as one of the more formidable.

Jeffries was born at Carroll, Ohio, April 15, 1875. At sixteen, he was a boilermaker and a tough one. His first fight is not in any record book. It was with Hank Griffin in Los Angeles. Jim won by a knockout in the 10th round. He was still only sixteen at the time, and his mother made him promise not to fight again until he was twenty-one.

Jeffries fought only one preliminary in his entire career, finishing Dan Long in the second round. That was on July 2, 1896. Ten bouts later he won the championship from Fitzsimmons.

This sounds like an easy march to fame, but actually it was a tortuous road. There were long hours of training as sparring partner to Corbett, of learning something new in every kind of fight, of the arduous plugging that doesn't show in record books.

Jeffries, the one-time boilermaker, weighed 220 pounds at the peak of his career, and had terrific power.

Jeffries was a stand-up fighter when he first started. One day while boxing in the gym with John Brink, the West Coast amateur champion, who had refereed Jeff's fight with Griffin, Jim was shaken by a left hook above the liver. The blow doubled him up. He could not straighten up but continued to fight from a crouch. He did so well that Brink was amazed. Later, DeWitt Van Court and Tommy Ryan helped him perfect the crouch and he was on his way. When he fought Fitzsimmons for the title, his stance nullified the short-arm punches of Ruby Robert, and while Fitz punished him unmercifully around the head, he could not reach Jim's jaw. So hard did Fitz hit, he broke both of his hands on Jeffries' head.

In 1940, Gene Tunney, who patterned his style more along the lines of Jim Corbett, the dancing master, was asked to appraise Jeffries as champion. Tunney was candid. He criticized the way Jeff had been managed and tutored.

"I know there are first-rate judges of boxing who pick the big fellow as the greatest of us all," Tunney said. "They will talk with persuasion and enthusiasm to prove it. But I am not one of them. Perhaps that is because of my lifelong preoccupation with championship as a state of mind. In thinking of Jeffries, I might say that sometimes championship can be a state of somebody else's mind. The ring strategy of Jeff was entirely the thinking of the man who trained him for the title fight with Fitz–Tommy Ryan, the great old-time middleweight champion, and one of the cagiest of them all. Tommy created the pattern of Jeffries' actions in the ring–taught him the famous crouch, body hunched away over and left hand stuck out. Had him just go plodding ahead like that, pushing the left out straight. It was one of the most uninteresting of ring styles, but it had its pertinent logic in the mind of Tommy Ryan.

"Jeffries' decisive quality was his tremendous physical toughness and endurance, the brawny giant who could hardly be hurt," Tunney said. "The Tommy Ryan system was for Jeffries to take all the beating the other fellow could give him, just go plodding on in a crouch and absorb all the punches that came his way, until his opponent wore himself out hitting him. It has been said that Jeffries, the ponderous giant, often displayed little love for battle, and sometimes wanted to quit. Well, you could hardly blame him, with that Tommy Ryan strategy of having Jeffries take all the beating the other fellow could hand out. The Ryan mentality was an incompatible thing for the Jeffries physique, even though it meant the championship."

In Jeff's favor, it can be said that he was unafraid. He gave every genuine contender two shots at his crown and thus made it official. As champion, he was taciturn to the point of surliness with strangers, but he was friendly and affable among friends. Unlike John L., he was not a dynamic aggressor, and, unless he was in there with an easy mark, preferred to bide his time and win deliberately.

After winning from Fitz, Jeffries won two highly satisfying decisions from his old boss, Corbett. He flattened Gentleman Jim in 23 and

10 rounds respectively. He fought all the tough contenders of the day: Joe Choynski, Peter Jackson, Tom Sharkey, and Fitz.

As a fighting man, Jeff had the acrobatic springiness of a tumbler in his massive although shapely legs. He was no lumbering "office safe," anchored to one spot, but a natural athlete, hardened by tramping through the Sierra Madre Mountains, a sprinter and broad jumper of considerable ability.

Jeffries' trademark was that extraordinary crouch. Lesser men could not imitate it with any degree of success. Tucking his chin behind his craglike shoulder, Jeff would extend his left arm after the fashion of a steamboat's walling beam, covering himself as by a Roman shield, and would crowd his opponents and counter their leads with right hooks. To get at Jeff you had to get by that massive left fist, and if you got by that barrier you were well stymied by his beetling shoulder. Even supposing you landed flush on his chin, you were apt to shatter your hands as Fitz did.

Deep in this vein, my old friend, the late George Trevor of the old *New York Sun,* once asked a tough-fibered Irish muleteer what he thought of Jeffries. The oldtimer knew his mules and his prize fighters. He took a reflective chew of tobacco as he weighed George's question. Then, with a judicial air, he replied: "Faith, man, I'd sooner have wan av thim mules lay his hoof to me jaw as have James J. Jeffries hit me with that divil av a left hand!"

On one of his taking-all-comers tours, the accepted practice for champions 70 years ago, Jeff almost lost his title. Clark Ball, a smart New York manager, had groomed Jack Monroe, a miner, to meet Jeff when he arrived in Butte, Montana. Jeff was in poor shape, and in the fourth round Monroe belted him in the belly and followed up with a jolt to the whiskers. A quick curtain saved the day and the title for Jeffries.

Clark Ball flooded the country with stories of the fight and labeled Monroe as "The Beaut from Butte." This ballyhoo paid off handsomely until the following year when Jeff, this time in A-1 condition and prepared for a stiff battle, flattened Monroe in two rounds at San Francisco.

Jeffries and Billy Brady, his manager, barnstormed through Europe after winning the crown. Midway of the tour, Brady was suddenly called back to the States, leaving his tiger in the hands of a close friend, Jack Barnes, a ring-wise operative.

Barnes took Jeffries to Paris, where a world's champion was a distinct novelty. Jeff attracted tremendous crowds. Parisians were awed by his size and would tag along after him as he strode up the boulevards.

A theatre manager suggested that Jeff fight the French champion, M. LaBlah, who fought *la savate* style. Jeff agreed. The champion also agreed to allow LaBlah to fight *la savate,* while he, Jeff, would box under regular rules. The American knew nothing of French ring tactics.

The bout was billed as a world championship match. Seat prices soared. A capacity house turned out. Thousands more were turned away.

Physically, LaBlah was no match for the champion. Short and frail, the Frenchman weighed only 140 pounds. But he showed no fear. At the opening bell, Jeff assumed his natural crouch. The little challenger folded his arms, rose to his toes like a ballet dancer, and began to spring lightly around the ring. Jeff tried a couple of feints with no response. Finally he dropped his hands and laughed. Immediately LaBlah bounded into the air and kicked Jeff in the left side of the face. His feet were covered with soft leather, fitting him as tightly as a glove. Jeff was plainly startled, and hurt. He set himself for the next assault, and when it came he caught the diminutive Frenchman on the rise with a smashing left hook on the chin. LaBlah sailed through the ropes with the greatest of ease. That was all. The fight was over. Jim Jeffries was champion of France.

Despite the defeat of a national hero, the French promoter was elated. He asked that Jack Scales, the champion of England, be imported so that Jeff could lay undisputed claim to the world title. A cable was dispatched to Scales, asking him to name his terms for a 20-round match. The Englishman wired back: "FOUR HUNDRED POUNDS AND ALL EXPENSES."

Jack Barnes agreed to the terms and the bout was scheduled. Jeff was to receive 65 percent of the gate and pay Scales' fee out of that. The admission price was doubled and again a capacity crowd was on hand.

The English champion compared favorably with Jeff in size but the resemblance ended there. Jeff, knowing he had a soft touch, felt around for the first three rounds, opened up in the fourth, and dropped Scales twice. After his second trip to the canvas, Scales got up slowly, raised his hand for attention and began to speak to the audience.

"Lydies and gents," he said, "E's absolutely too big and strengthy for me, so Hi bloody well 'ands over to 'im the champeen-ship of England."

Sailor Tom Sharkey, a rugged, sawed-off Pier-Sixer with a brass-bound sea chest of a torso and a rawhide constitution, gave Jeffries his hardest fights. Jeff won two decisions over this smaller edition of himself in 20 and 25 rounds, but he couldn't manage to rock the rugged sailor to sleep. Sharkey had a four-masted schooner tattooed on his deep chest, and it was his boast that he would "never give up the ship."

Sailor Tom was leading Jeff on points at the end of 15 rounds in their epic battle at Coney Island, November 3, 1899, but the champion's Big Bertha blows to the body told heavily during the last 10 rounds. Half the crowd booed when honest George Siler, the referee, awarded the decision to Jeffries. Siler was right, however. The bout's aftermath found Sharkey in the hospital for weeks, convalescing from the cruel body bludgeoning which caved in four of his ribs. Sailor Tom confessed to friends, "I couldn't have lasted 30 rounds."

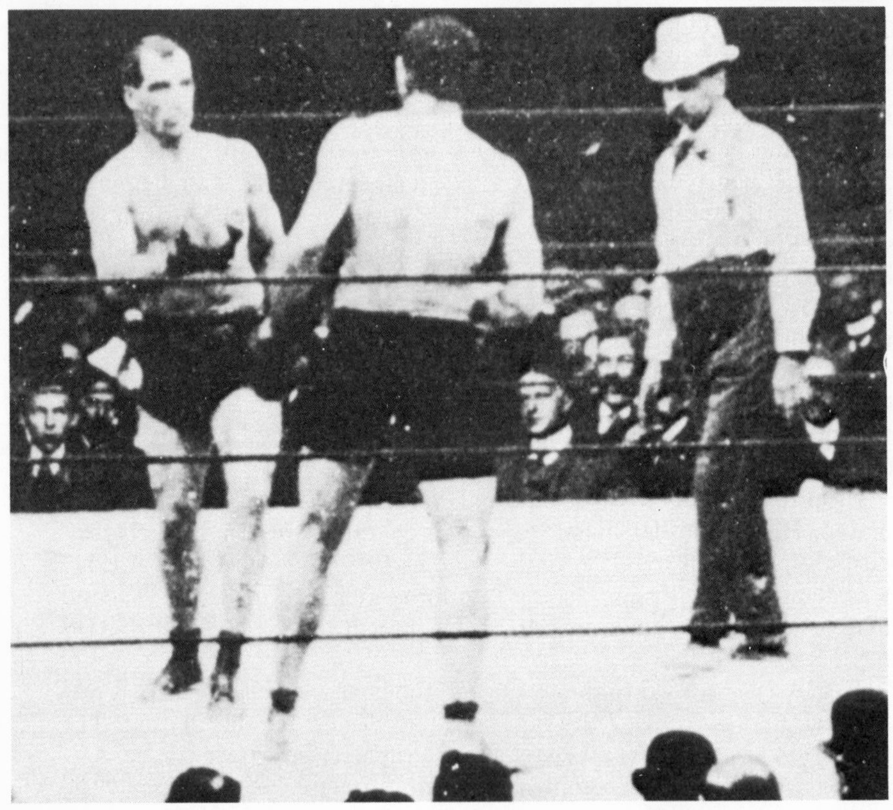

Jim Jeffries, back to camera, squares away with Sailor Tom Sharkey in defense of his title at Coney Island, November 3, 1899. Jeff retained his crown by winning on points in 25 rounds.

Sharkey was a topnotch heavyweight who came along at a time of great heavyweights. He probably would have been champion at any other time.

Colonel Harvey L. Miller, past President of the old National Boxing Association (now WBA), was closer to Sharkey than any other person. He told me that "Tom was plenty smart inside the ring but not so smart out of it." While Sailor Tom could neither read nor write, Heinie Miller said, it didn't keep him out of the Navy in the old days. He was a ship's corporal, a rating now obsolete.

"Tom was sort of a ship's policeman," Heinie said. "One pay day on the old U.S.S. Philadelphia, docked in Honolulu, the paymaster ordered Tom to line the men up alphabetically. Tom looked down at his men and sung out: 'If you blokes wanna git paid, line up alphabetically.' All would have been fine and dandy if he had left it at that, as all Adamses, Bakers, Conrads and such moved into position. But Tom had to show his authority. Nailing one meek-looking little guy, he snapped, 'Wot's yer name?'

" 'Phillips,' was the reply."

" 'Phillips is it?' roared Tom. 'Well, then git the hell up among the F's!' "

Heinie Miller recalled another instance when Sharkey was going ashore with a landing party. His leggings had been slipped on in reverse, the lacings on the inside. When challenged to explain, he did so in this manner: "Shure, an' I had me legs crossed when I laced 'em up."

Sharkey was a stickler for obeying orders—literally. One of his superior officers was getting married and the best man, another officer, summoned Tom and ordered him to go into town and buy a couple of two-pound sacks of rice. The instructions were explicit: "You and your boys hide under the gangway ladder and throw rice at the bride when she comes down the gangway." Tom obeyed. As the bridal procession came into view, Tom cocked his arm and let fly with a two-pound bag of rice. It hit the bride smack on the side of her head and knocked her stone cold. The officer had not thought to tell him to first take the rice *out* of the bag!

After he left the Navy, Sharkey was managed by Tim McGrath, of San Francisco. They got an offer to fight in Australia. Tom told Tim to accept it. "But, Tom, that's thousands of miles away," McGrath said. "You don't want to go there. There's nothing in Australia but a lot of kangaroos."

"I don't give a damn about nationality," Sharkey said. "A kangaroo's money is as good as anybody else's."

Sharkey retired from boxing in 1904 and opened a saloon on East 14th Street in Manhattan. Jim Corbett dropped in one day to give him a play. Corbett carefully inspected the premises and finally remarked, "Nice place you have here, Tom; except, of course, you should have a good chandelier."

Sharkey glared at his old rival suspiciously.

"Yeah," he said, finally, "but who the hell would play it?"

Then there was the day when Sailor Tom was standing in a Boston pub and the barkeeper twitted him for not being able to read.

"You're illiterate," the swipe said.

"I am not," Tom said. "I can read."

The mirror behind the bar was covered with a chalky mixture, that pasty stuff they coated 'em with in the old days, and the barkeeper wet his finger and wrote across the chalked glass: "THOMAS J. SHARKEY."

He turned back to Sailor Tom and said, "Okay, read that."

"That's easy," Sharkey said. "It says, NO SMOKIN'!"

May 11, 1900, remains a memorable date in the history of ring annals, for that was the night that Jeffries defended his crown against his old boss, Jim Corbett. Plenty of intrigue, maneuvering, shenanigans and the dear old double cross surrounded the championship match.

By 1900, Gentleman Jim was regarded by the experts as a has-been. He had been living a fast life. He ran a thriving saloon on Broadway, between 33rd and 34th streets on the site of what is now Saks department store. The intrigue began when he came to Billy Brady, his old manager who had since hitched himself to Jeff's star and made him champion, and told him a tale of debts and need and begged him to give him a match with his former sparring partner. Out of pity and for auld lang syne, Brady signed him on. What Billy didn't know was that Corbett had gone on the wagon and had been training secretly for the fight at Lakewood, New Jersey, for four months.

Jeffries, meanwhile, trained in equal privacy at Allenhurst, New Jersey, Brady's home, and in spite of the reports that Corbett was through, he took no chances. He still remembered how when he was Gentleman Jim's spar boy he never laid a glove on him. Jeffries did 10 to 15 miles of roadwork a day, 2,500 turns of rope skipping, boxed 8 to 10 rounds and morning and night washed his face and hands in beef brine and borax to toughen his skin.

The fight was staged at the Seaside Athletic Club off Surf Avenue, Coney Island. A ticket for the fight? Forget about the box office. There wasn't any in those days except the nearest bar, saloon or cafe. The fight game was in the hands of the Irish–politicians, theatrical men and saloon keepers. The saloon was its bank, matchmaking office, ticket office, stakeholder, betting commissioner, its beginning and its end.

Outside the Seaside AC a dark crush of men, and men only, sports in checked suits or dark, heavy fustian with the ubiquitous bowler or hard hat atop their heads, moved in a steady, steamy crush toward the entrances, breathing fight talk and alcohol fumes, to the brassy cries of the ticket speculators, leather-lunged scamps in high silk hats with greenbacks protruding from the fingers of both hands.

Inside the arena, a vast, gas-lit barn, you peered through a blue fog of smoke from 5-cent stogies. It seems as though every man of the 7,000 present had a cigar in his red face. Total capacity at Seaside AC was 10,000 so 7,000 was a small house. But then nobody knew, nobody believed that Corbett was in shape to fight. Men and men only. Women were not allowed into this purely masculine paradise. Every so often, some hussy would climb into breeches, stiff collar and coat, conceal her crowning glory beneath a go-to-hell cap or upcurved derby, to "take in" the "doings," but she was no lady. Decent folk didn't go to prize fights.

Very few decent people were present at this one. The guest list, had there been one, would have included every scoundrel within range. Beneath the choking haze of smoke, on bare plank benches held up by short scantlings, shoulder to shoulder, sat the crowd of sports, hard, tough, brutal men, saloon keepers, bartenders, burglars, pickpockets, second-story men, sluggers, bouncers, political bosses, big and small, ward heelers, con men, race track touts, jockeys, trainers, concessionaires, pimps, bawdy-house proprietors, gamblers, burlesque-house actors, managers, and a sprinkling of semi-respectable Broadway actors and rich young sports from Manhattan out for a night of thrill-slumming.

The ring was in the center beneath a battery of sputtering arc lights, installed because of those new-fangled motion picture cameras. The first fight movies had been made a year before when Jeff whipped Tom Sharkey in the same arena. The lights overhead cast a stifling heat as well as dazzling brilliance that lit up the red and sweating faces of the first rows of spectators. The ring was a raised platform with four posts, to the inside of which was affixed a thin layer of padding. There were three holes in the posts through which the ring ropes were threaded. The floor was covered with one layer of dirty gray canvas. There was no padding underneath.

The hall was quivering with lust and excitement. It would be hard for modern fight fans to picture how brutal, how mean and stone-hard was that Coney Island audience the night Jeff fought Corbett for the title. New York was yet a growing city, and its dregs went to a prize fight. One and all they were men who preyed on other men in one way or another. The roar of that mob echoed a coarseness and obscenity.

There they came at last, the two fighters followed by their entourages, managers, seconds, handlers, bucket-carriers, bottle-holders, towel-swingers, as big and burly and hard-bitten a crew as ever climbed out of the sinks of society. They were wearing their street clothes! Jeffries was clad in trousers, red sweater and cap pulled down over his big, surly head. Corbett was dressed more elegantly. In those days, they wore their knee-length, woolen fighting trunks fastened at the waist with an American flag beneath their street clothes and stripped in the ring before the eyes of the crowd.

A sigh went up as Corbett peeled down for action. By jingoes, he was in shape. A slender stripling compared to the brawny, hairy boilermaker, Jeffries, who was taller and 45 pounds heavier.

Attending Corbett were George Considine, Gus Ruhlin and Leo Pardello. Jeffries, as befitted the champion, had an even more imposing retinue headed by Billy Brady, his high choke collar neatly set off with a sporty bow tie, Tommy Ryan, the somewhat battered middleweight champion of the world who served as chief second, Jack Jeffries, Jim's brother, and a hippopotamus of a fellow, the 300-pound Ed Dunkhorst, a palooka known as the "Human Freight Car." Man for man there was a lot of fighting weight in the champion's gang, just in case.

There was a curious situation in Jeff's corner. The big boilermaker was suspicious of Brady because not only had Billy once managed Corbett, but also because the two had been boyhood friends and cronies. Jeff was afraid of a double cross, and Tommy Ryan had his confidence and the job of handling him. As if to show the big champion that he hadn't even slight grounds for doubts, Ryan protested when Corbett began to bandage his hands. Laughing, Corbett showed that he had no more than a yard of gauze and that there was nothing underneath but his knuckles.

How simple in those days. No boxing commission, no inspectors, no examining physicians, nothing but a set of powerful, tough guys, many of whom made up their rules as they went along.

The gloves were finally produced. They weighed four ounces. As soon as they were laced onto the hands of the fighters they began to break them, working the padding away from the knuckles so that after a round or two, when they got wet and soggy, they would be practically skintight and could cut like knives.

A hush fell on the house as Charley Harvey began the introductions with the classic opening, "In this corner...." Brady had plenty to worry about. The house was small. Corbett was lean and trim as a racehorse without an ounce of fat or flabby flesh on him. He looked like the Corbett of old. And if he was–goodbye championship.

The referee was Charley White, in shirt sleeves with armlets and braces, topped off by a handlebar mustache. There were no judges, no higher court to keep a wary eye out for skullduggery. Charley White had absolute power. He could award the fight to one or the other, call it a draw, call bets off on a foul or throw them both out of the ring. Nobody knew what he would do. The title was in his hands.

There were no instructions from the referee. The ring was cleared, the two fighters stood alone in their corners. The deep clang of the work bell was heard. Jeffries and Corbett moved toward the center of the ring, shook hands and the battle was on.

While details of the fight have been already given in the Corbett chapter, several incidents happened during the latter rounds that went generally unreported. Between the 19th and 20th rounds, Billy Brady climbed up into Jeff's corner. From below the ropes he had been trying to coach Jeff to bull his way in, and all he had got for his pains was a snarl from Jeff to shut up because Corbett could hear what he was saying. Jeff really believed that Brady was trying to make him lose.

Tommy Ryan picked up a bottle and said to Brady, "Get down, or I'll bust your head."

Undaunted, Billy quickly summoned two Coney Island cops, brass buttons, chamber-pot helmets and all and admonished Ryan sternly. "This is my fighter and I'm his manager. I'm just hiring you. If you don't get back there and keep still, I'll hand you to those cops and they'll rap you over the head and throw you out." Hungrily, the cops fingered their nightsticks. Ryan departed. Brady then won Jeff's confidence and sent him in to rush the more fragile and tiring Corbett with immediate results.

And the end of the fight? It was just crazy. While Charley White was swinging his arm up and down tolling the fatal seconds over the slumbering Corbett and the hall rocked in a pandemonium of hot savagery, George Considine, Corbett's chief second, came scuttling around the side of the ring with a bucket of water, intending to douse it over Gentleman Jim to try to arouse him in time to save the fight.

Nobody noticed him in the excitement, or made a move to stop him beyond a frantic shout or two. No one, that is, except Jeffries. Standing there panting, the drops of water glistening in the matting of hair that covered his powerful chest, his eyes glassy with battle fever, his face crimson from the cuts inflicted by Corbett's knifing left hand, big Jeff, the suspicious champion, was protecting his title and seeing everything.

With a snarl and a curse he moved over swiftly and from the height of the ring platform kicked Considine in the face, kicked him so hard and accurately that the handler flew backward, tail-over-teakettle, spilling his bucket of water over the toughs in the first row who screamed and cursed at him, and added further kicks when he was down—the good old Coney way.

So ended one of the great bouts of modern ring history.

In 1905, Jeffries retired undefeated. He had fought only twice in two years, both in defense of his title, and he was finding it harder and harder to get suitable opponents into the ring with him. So he induced Marvin Hart and Jack Root to battle it out for his vacated crown. Jeff refereed the match, July 3, 1905. Hart won and was dubbed the new champion by Jeffries.

After Australia's Tommy Burns beat Hart in 20 rounds in Los Angeles, February 23, 1906, to prove his right to the title, Jack Johnson shocked the world two years later by becoming the first black in history to win the heavyweight championship.

Five years after his retirement, friends coaxed Jeffries into trying to regain the title. The match was surrounded with racial overtones. Tex Rickard was the promoter and announced the fight would be held in San Francisco. Walter Kelly was in Jeff's training camp and told of all the confusion leading up to the bout.

"Rickard made plans for the ring to be built at Eighth and Market Streets," Kelly said. "It was now early in May, and Jack Johnson was to train at the roadhouse out at Seal Rocks several miles from San Francisco. Jeff was to train at Rowardenann, a beautiful spot up in the mountains 85 miles away. Jim invited me to spend some time at his camp with him.

"First, however, I loafed around San Francisco for ten days with Tex, who was busily fighting off the political buzzards of both city and state, all of whom wanted in on the action. Night after night I sat with him in his apartment at the St. Francis and listened to official racketeers make their claims on him. I can particularly remember one police official who blandly stated with a gesture of affability that he wanted no graft. All he asked was a hundred of the $50 ringside seats which he would dispose of himself.

"Another night, Tex advised me that he had just received word from an unknown source that he would be wise to send $50,000 to Sacramento, the state capital, which would effectively quiet the church-going legislators. Despite these problems, Tex went ahead with his plans to stage the fight in San Francisco.

"Jeff's camp was located in a grove of giant redwood trees well up in the Santa Cruz Mountains and along the narrow little San Lorenzo River. It was about nine miles from Santa Cruz. Jeff started his training program with great enthusiasm. Five A.M. found him up and ready for a five-mile jog over the mountain roads, then back to camp for a rubdown and shower, followed by an hour's nap. Then a tough routine of boxing, bag punching, wrestling, and calisthenics. At the personal request of his wife, a fine little lady, I always went with him on his afternoon trout fishing expedition or mountain hike. She asked me to go with him because she wanted him to get away from the grind of fight talk indulged in by trainers and sports writers. On these trips big, silent Jeff would grow as playful as a Newfoundland pup and then, all of a sudden, would settle into a brooding silence.

"Rickard drove up to Jeff's camp about twice a week, and on Sundays great crowds of sightseers stood outside the fence and stared for hours. Jim Corbett arrived from the East to work out with Jeff and serve as his adviser. Tad Dorgan, the famous cartoonist, was the next arrival. The camp was coming alive.

"A few weeks before the fight I drove down to San Francisco with Tex to watch Jack Johnson work out. He looked very good. When I returned to camp Jeff asked me to take a walk with him. We were strolling along the bank of the San Lorenzo when Jeff suddenly asked, 'How does Johnson look?'

" 'He looks ready to go, Jim.'

"Dropping his fishing rod, he set himself in his fighting stance. 'He'd better be ready,' he snarled. 'He may outbox me, but I'll show him up like I did Sharkey and Fitz.'

"That was the only time I heard him discuss the match.

"It was several more days before the news reached us. A small boy was the messenger. He came up the road on a cow pony to where Jeff and I were standing, hip deep, in a trout pool half a mile from camp. Jeff waded ashore and read the telegram, reeled in his line and called me. 'Read that!' he said. Pale and angry, he turned to me and waited for my reaction. The Governor had issued a telegraphic order stopping the fight in California. Jeff said, 'I should tell them all to go to hell and go back home. If it wasn't for Tex, that's just what I would do.'

"Deep gloom settled on the camp that night, and in my soul I believe that incident was the blow that whipped Jeff. A deluge of telegrams arrived and departed until midnight. I left the next morning by an early train to see Tex. He hadn't given up. He sent out telegrams to a dozen cities and towns in other states—places that wanted to stage the fight. Reno was the final choice.

"The turn of events left Jeff in a daze. He and his wife asked me to go along to Reno with them. The new camp was located at Moana Springs, a small resort a few miles from Reno. In his training here Jeff seemed like another man. He was listless and depressed. We were now only ten days from fight hour on July Fourth. Work on the stadium went on feverishly night and day. A few days before the fight dozens of Pullman cars were placed on side tracks to be used as hotels. Saturday and Sunday nights before the event thousands of fans arrived from the east and west, including an army of cowboys with their mounts, who slept in the open. The Golden, the Palace and Overland bars and gambling rooms were crowded to the rafters, and, in company with Jack London, Bat Masterson and George Considine, I spent most of the night wandering around town, sopping up the atmosphere.

"July Fourth finally arrived, with cloudless skies and a blistering Nevada sun. By noon the arena began to fill with cowboys and farmers, Mexicans and Indians, the wealthy and sporting fight fans from the North, East, South and West. Three or four movie cameras were planted on a 20-foot platform, and some thousand ladies gave a pleasant touch of color to the scene. Among those at ringside were John L. Sullivan, Tom Sharkey, Bob Fitzsimmons and Stanley Ketchel.

"Twenty minutes before the battle I went to Jeff's dressing room. I shook hands with him and wished him luck. I was shocked by his pallor and expression. He seemed to have aged ten years overnight. When I returned to my ringside seat I was doubtful and disturbed. Tex Rickard was already in the ring. He was to referee."

The Associated Press account of the fight told the story of Jim Jeffries, a broken man. It described him as the winner of 22 championship fights, a man who never had been brought to his knees before by a blow. "Now he's a broken idol," the story reported. "He met utter defeat at the hands of the black champion—John Arthur Johnson, a Texas negro, the son of an American slave."

For all the details, read on:

While Jeffries was not actually counted out, he was saved from this crowning shame only by his friends pleading with Johnson not to hit the fallen man again, and the towel was brought into the ring from his corner. At the end of the 15th round Referee Tex Rickard raised the black arm, and the great crowd filed out, glum and silent.

Jeffries was dragged to his corner, bleeding from nose and mouth and a dozen cuts on the face. He had a black, closed eye and swollen features, and he held his head in his hands, dazed and incoherent. Johnson walked out of the ring without a mark on his body except a slight cut on his lip.

Ring experts agree that it was not even a championship fight. Jeffries had a chance in the second round, perhaps, but after the sixth it was plain that the undefeated one was weakening and outclassed in every point, and after the eleventh round it was hopeless.

It was the greatest demonstration the ring has ever seen of the failure of a fighter to "come back" after years of retirement. The youth and science of the black man made Jeffries look like a green man.

The great Jeffries was like a log. The reviled Johnson was like a black panther, beautiful in his alertness and defensive tactics. Jeffries fought by instinct, it seemed, showing his gameness and his great fighting heart in every round, but he was only a shell of his old self. The old power to take a terrible beating and bore in until he landed the knockout blow was gone.

After the third round Johnson treated his opponent almost as a joke. He smiled and blocked playfully, warding off the rushes of Jeffries with a marvelous science, now tucking a blow under his arm, again plucking it out of the air as a man stops a baseball.

The battle was honestly fought. Of that there was no doubt after the first round. There was no evidence or hint of the famous "yellow streak" on the part of Johnson. Johnson proved himself so absolutely Jeffries' master that experts declared that Tommy Burns had put up a better fight against Johnson.

The end was swift and terrible. It looked as though Johnson had been holding himself under cover all the rest of the time, and now that he had measured Jeffries in all his weaknesses he had determined to stop it quick.

Jeffries had lost the power of defense. A series of right and left uppercuts, delivered at will, sent him staggering to the ropes. He turned and fought back by instinct and because he was dying hard.

With the exception of a few fast rounds, the fight was tame. Jeffries did not have the power in his punch to hurt Johnson after he had received blow after blow on the jaw, and his vital power was ebbing. But even before this stage came, Jeffries could not reach the black man effectively. The blows landed with nearly all the speed taken out of them. It was like hitting a punching bag. The Jeffries crouch was in evidence at times, but during most of the fight Jeffries fought standing straight and working with something of his old aggressiveness.

The fifteenth round started with a clinch. Johnson then tore loose and sent Jeffries down with a lightning-like left and right blows to the jaw. Jeffries fell half-way through the ropes. Those under him saw that he had lost his sense of surroundings and that the faces at the ringside were a blur to him. His time had come. He was feeling what he had caused others to feel in the days of his youth and power.

Johnson stood poised over Jeffries, ready for a left hook if the champion regained his feet.

Jim Corbett, who stood in Jeffries' corner all during this fight, telling Johnson what a fool he was and how he was in for the beating of his life, now ran forward with outstretched arms, crying, "Oh, don't, Jack; don't hit him!"

Jeffries painfully raised himself to his feet. His jaw had dropped. His eyes were nearly shut and his face was covered with blood. With trembling legs and shielding arms he tried to put up a defense, but he could not stop a terrific right smash on the jaw, followed by two left hooks. He went down again. Jeffries' physician and other friends jumped toward the ring.

"Stop it!" they cried. "Don't put the old fellow out!"

Sam Berger ran along the ring calling to Bob Armstrong, "Bring that towel–you know what I mean–don't let him get hit."

From Johnson's corner his seconds were calling to him to quit. Then the referee stopped the timekeeper, and it was all over.

Soothing lotions were applied to the fallen champion's bruised face, but his heart was something that could not be reached. He bowed his head in his hands and groaned: "I was too old to come back." Corbett, Choynski, Jack Jeffries and the others were ready to cry, but they united in trying to cheer the defeated man. "It's all off with you, Jim," said Corbett, "but you did the best you could."

In an instant the ring was stampeded by a wild throng. In the great mass of spectators there was a feeling of personal loss. Their idol had crumbled and this black man stood peerless. They could not help admire him, and there was little animosity shown toward him. Hundreds swallowed the bitter pill of heavy financial loss.

Less than an hour of fighting had served to bring to an end the career of the man hitherto believed invincible, and had solved the question that had been agitating the world since Johnson won the championship belt from Tommy Burns.

Among prominent journalists covering the fight for major metropolitan newspapers was Jack London, of the *New York Herald.* His story of the match ran 3,450 words–a superfluity of words by present-day standards–and it all boiled down to this:

"The fight today was great only in its significance," wrote the famous author. "In itself it wasn't great. The issue, after the fiddling of the opening rounds, was never in doubt. In the fiddling of those first rounds the honors lay with Johnson, and for the rounds after the seventh or eighth it was more Johnson, while for the closing rounds it was *all* Johnson. The greatest fight of the century was a monologue delivered to 20,000 spectators by a smiling negro who was never in doubt and who was never serious for more than a moment at a time. As a fighter Johnson did not show himself a wonder. He did not have to. Never once was he extended. There was no need. Jeffries could not make him extend. Jeffries never had him in trouble once. No blow Jeffries landed hurt his dusky opponent. Johnson came out of the fight practically undamaged. No one truly understands the new champion, this man who smiles. Well, the story of the fight is the story of a smile. If ever man won by nothing more fatiguing than a smile, Johnson won today. As for Jeffries, he disposed of one question. *He could not come back.*"

5. Tommy Burns

CHUNKY little Tommy Burns, 5 ft. 7 in., 180 pounds, was the shortest man ever to win the heavyweight championship of the world. The deep-chested French-Canadian was truly a chump among champs, and a champ among chumps.

Noah Brusso (Tommy's real name) made a little ability go a long way. He was boxing's original globetrotter and was highly adept at the game of tag. He led Jack Johnson on a merry chase around the world for a couple of years before Li'l Arthur finally caught up with him.

Tommy Burns, born at Hanover, Canada, June 17, 1881, flourished in an age when the heavyweight division was at extremely low ebb. Jim Jeffries retired after destroying all contention, leaving the title to Marvin Hart, at best a third rater. Burns' claim to the throne was based on his defeat of the Kentuckian and a triumph over light-heavyweight Philadelphia Jack O'Brien.

So as a prize fighter, Tommy Burns was a heavyweight champion of dubious authority.

On December 26, 1908, in Sydney, Australia, Jack Johnson toyed with Burns from the opening gong to the finish.

"Hit here, Tahmy," Jack would say, exposing the right side of his unprotected stomach, and when Burns struck, Johnson would neither wince nor cover up. He would absorb the blow with a happy, careless smile, directed at the spectators, turn to the left side of his unprotected belly and coax, "Now here, Tahmy," and while Burns did as directed, Johnson would grin again, flashing his golden smile. This went on for 39 minutes. The travesty finally bored Johnson and, in the fourteenth, he decided to end it. He knocked "Tahmy" out.

While there may be room for argument as to who was the greatest heavyweight champion up to the retirement of Gene Tunney in 1928,

Tommy Burns, 5 ft. 7 in. and 175 pounds, was the shortest man ever to hold the heavyweight championship. He was born in Canada.

there's no question that Burns was the worst. He nevertheless had a keen business sense and got a lot of mileage out of what he had. Not even The Wild Bull of the Pampas, Luis Firpo, could hold a candle to him when it came to extracting the last dollar out of bouts. In losing the title to Johnson, for example, Tommy got $30,000, while Johnson was paid only $5,000.

After his retirement from the ring in 1920, exactly two decades after he had started, Tommy Burns heard the "call." He entered the ministry and toiled diligently throughout the Pacific Northwest as an evangelist.

Burns succumbed to a heart attack in Vancouver, British Columbia, in 1955.

6. Jack Johnson

JOHN ARTHUR JOHNSON, the first black ever to win the world's heavyweight championship, fought for a full quarter century (1899 to 1924) and had himself a mardi gras. Great Jumping Jehosaphat, how that man loved this life! So much so that he could peacefully prophecy his own death in an auto accident in 1946.

Jack was invincible. But aside from such worthy black opponents as Langford, McVey and Jeannette, he encountered a fairly wretched lot. The few white heavies with talent drew the color line, and that Reno thing against Jeffries' ghost was a farce from beginning to end.

"Li'l Arthur" he called himself. Six feet, 200 pounds. Bullet head, wide face, gold-toothed grin. Magnificent physique. The fabulous strength that makes for tall tales and Bunyanesque whoppers.

Few heavies since Jeffries would have stood a chance against Jack. Yet he was a paradox in his prime. He was a great defensive fighter—maybe the greatest—but his colossal strength seemed wasted. Johnson gave the lasting impression of a fighter who was under wraps, who never extended himself to the limit. You always had the feeling that he could destroy his opponent whenever he wished. He could handle two-hundred pounders as nonchalantly as the flour sacks he used to toss into tramp steamers' holds. His jab was a pippin. His ferocious uppercut could have torn an opponent's head off. Did Jack know his own strength only too well? Whatever the answer, he was content to play the role of spoiler and defensive genius.

This happy man with the arms and torso of a gorilla could make almost any rival look bad. He had no equal at tying up a dangerous adversary and smothering blows at the source.

Smiling Jack Johnson was born in Galveston, Texas, on March 31, 1878. As he once confided to Dan Morgan, "My earliest days were the

Jack Johnson stood 6 ft., weighed 205 pounds, and was the first black man to win the world's heavyweight championship. He had a ball.

simplest. I was not yet in my teens when I hopped a freight and set out for New York to see Steve Brodie, my hero. After riding all night in the bumping boxcar, I unloaded the next morning. The place looked familiar to me. It should have. I discovered I'd been riding around the railroad yards all night as the train was being made up!"

When Jack finally located a freight that could straighten out and fly right, he ended up in New York's Bowery, where he achieved home town fame as "the boy who ran away from Galveston to see Steve Brodie."

Jack Johnson fought his first bout, a four-round knockout of Jim Rocks, back in Galveston in 1897, and wound up being knocked out by one Bill Hartwell in Kansas City in 1928. In 1945, at the age of sixty-seven, he fought two exhibition bouts in New York against Joe Jeannette and John Ballcort—the same night.

Ruby Robert Fitzsimmons was the only heavyweight to match Johnson's record for longevity in the prize ring, but Jack fought more often and fairly scouted the globe in search of fresh victims. He chased Tommy Burns for two years before Hugh D. McIntosh, the great Australian promoter, persuaded Burns to stand and take his beating for the lion's share of the gate. On December 26, 1908, in Sydney, Johnson administered said beating until police rescued the battered Burns in the 14th round.

This bout led to the famous Stanley Ketchel match of October 17, 1909. To fully appreciate the significance of the middleweight champion of the world challenging the heavyweight champion, you must understand Ketchel.

The "Michigan Assassin" lived a crowded life. He bunched more living into 24 years than most men can accomplish in a full span. Stanislaus jammed more action into one round of fighting than most boxers do in 15. And he brought more color and thrills to the prize ring than anyone before or since. There was something about him that set the crowd agog with excitement and anticipation of what was going to happen when he stood in his corner waiting for the bell.

Ketchel has been called the handsomest man ever in the ring and most oldtimers agree that, pound for pound, he was the greatest fighter in history. He had the *look* of a champion and the disposition—out of the ring—of a daring romantic college kid. He was a two-sided fighter, who could be gentle and tender, tough and implacable.

Only 5 ft. 9 in. and weighing a mere 154 pounds, he fought in all classes. He fought with such fury that he well deserved the title of "The Michigan Assassin," a nickname bestowed upon him by contemporary sports writers. But for the most part, he was just a hard-hitting, carefree youngster who grinned as he punched and never matured. He was the Peter Pan of the fight game. As a youth he worshipped such men as the James boys and would rather have been a great train robber than a champion fighter.

Although only a middleweight, such a knowledgeable observer as Billy Roche, who refereed several of Ketchel's fights, later told me: "I believe that Stanley would have knocked out as capable a heavyweight as Jack Dempsey." Coincidentally, Ketchel fought like Dempsey in the manner of style and attack, but he was the exact opposite of Dempsey in the matter of nerves. He never stopped attacking in the ring. He was innately cruel. In the gymnasium he had no mercy on his sparring partners, and would fairly slaughter them. He would knock out a tiny flyweight if they put a flyweight in there to spar with him, because his gloves knew no law. Unlike Dempsey, he had no nerves; at least he never displayed any signs of nerves, and when they have them they show them. They can't help it.

In his dressing room before a battle, Ketchel would be as cool and unconcerned as if he had no thought whatsoever of the business at hand. Fifteen minutes before his fight with Johnson, he was sitting in his dressing room smoking a cigarette and telling a story when one of his handlers bawled through the door: "Come on, Steve!" It was the summons to battle. Ketchel paid no attention. He quietly finished his story, and his cigarette, hurrying neither. When he finally got up, he remarked: "Well, let's go on out there and finish that skunk!"

Before another important fight, he sat in his dressing room trying to memorize the words of a song called "O'Brien Had No Place To Go," which he wanted to sing at a dinner to be given in his honor after the fight. He had not finished his task when the call to the ring came. So during the fight he continued mulling the song words over in his mind, and by the final round he had the lyrics down pat.

Ketchel was christened Stanislaus Kiecel. He was born at Grand Rapids, Michigan, on September 14, 1886, and spent most of his early life hobo-fashion. At one point he was a waiter in a Butte, Montana, honky-tonk. He became so adept at throwing out drunks that he was elevated to bouncer. From bouncing he turned to professional fighting in Butte. He finally landed in Sacramento, California, and knocked out a good fighter named George Brown, in 1907. This lead to a match with the champion, Joe Thomas. The match was fought in the small California town of Marysville and Sunny Jim Coffroth, famous California boxing promoter, took a party of friends to see Thomas "trim another sucker." Coffroth almost dropped dead as he watched Thomas barely escape with his life and a draw in 20 rounds. That was on July 4, 1907—and Stanley Ketchel was off like one of those old-fashioned rockets set off on Independence Day.

One of Ketchel's biggest fans was the famous old boxing manager, Dan Morgan, who later wrote a book with me *(Dumb Dan).* Dan told me, "Ketchel was an exception to the human race. He was a savage. He would pound and rip his opponent's eyes, nose and mouth in a clinch. He couldn't get *enough* blood. His nickname, 'The Assassin,' fit him like a glove."

Sunny Jim Coffroth was so impressed with Ketchel that he immediately rematched him with Thomas for a 45-round bout in September. It was one of the greatest fights on record. After both men were on the canvas for nine counts, Ketchel flattened Thomas in the 32nd round.

Yet, for all of his greatness in the ring, Ketchel will be remembered most vividly for first stating the famous rule, "Shake Hands And Come Out Fighting"–and he said it in the ring.

On June 4, 1908, in Milwaukee, Ketchel whipped Billy Papke, "The Illinois Thunderbolt," although he narrowly escaped defeat. As the opening bell rang, Ketchel sauntered to the center of the ring and was greeted by a vicious right-hand smash to the point of his chin. He went down as if struck by a bludgeon and got up at the count of nine, dazed and staggering. It was claimed at the time that the referee, Jack McGuigan of Philadelphia, gave Ketchel a slow count. McGuigan never denied this accusation, but later, in confidential talks, he implied that the blow had the earmarks of a foul since Ketchel was hit as he extended his hands for the traditional first-round handshake. Ketchel fought on by instinct, winning the decision in 10 rounds, but he didn't come out of that first-blow fog for more than an hour after he had reached his dressing room. It was Papke's first defeat and a stunning one.

Ketchel met Papke again that year in Los Angeles. At that time it was customary for fighters to tip gloves when they answered the work bell, and Stanley, a sincere lad, stuck out his hands. Apparently he failed to learn a lesson from Papke's first "sneak punch." WHAM! Billy floored him again. This time the punch broke Ketchel's nose and closed his eyes. Although he strove valiantly to battle back, Stanley couldn't recover from the paralyzing blow. He took a fearful beating before falling like a wounded dove in the 12th round.

Ketchel lost none of his confidence. The day following his defeat, he pleaded with Willis Britt, his manager, to make every effort to sign Papke for a third match. Britt, an astute gentleman, maneuvered Tom Jones, Papke's pilot, into making one of the most foolish moves in ring history. Jones signed his fighter for a third battle with Ketchel in San Francisco a little more than two months later.

This time Ketchel was ready. As the fighters met at the center of the ring for the referee's instructions, Ketchel said: "There'll be none of this hand-shaking business. Shake hands now–and come out fighting." They did and Ketchel knocked out Papke in the 11th round.

Stan the Assassin almost assassinated Willie Lewis one night. Lewis was a very fine welterweight. One afternoon Morgan was riding around New York with Dan McKetrick, Willie's manager, when suddenly McKetrick stopped the car in front of a little Catholic church. He said, "I'm going in and light a candle and make a wish." They entered the church, lit candles, said their prayers and left. Catholics are not supposed to talk about what they pray for or how much of a contribution they leave, but once the two Dans reached the sidewalk McKetrick turned to Morgan and said, "I dropped a quarter in the box and said a prayer that my Willie knocks Ketchel out." Morgan just looked at him and said nothing.

Morgan was working in Willie's corner on fight night. The bell rang, Ketchel moved in on Lewis and missed him repeatedly. Since it was only a six-round no-decision bout and Ketchel couldn't lose his title except by being knocked out, it was plain to see he was not trying too hard. Near the end of the first round, Lewis let go a terrific right for the chin. It missed Ketchel's chin, but landed flush on his nose, breaking it and covering Stanley with blood just at the bell.

Ketchel gave Lewis one look. Morgan didn't miss it. The Assassin stormed to his corner, kicked the stool out of the ring and refused to sit down at all. Morgan left Willie's corner and called to McKetrick, "He's all yours."

At the bell, Ketchel ran across the ring, put a paralyzing left into Willie's body, brought Lewis's head forward, then smashed him with a right to the chin. A hook to the mouth drove the upper part of Lewis's face in on his back teeth. That was all for Willie.

They carried Lewis to his dressing room where a doctor had to pry his jaws apart. Willie came around all right and Morgan turned to McKetrick.

"Where the hell do you get your nerve?", Morgan asked. "For a quarter you wanted the middleweight championship of the world!"

McKetrick looked at Morgan and answered:

"What do you mean? It would have been all right–only the saint didn't stand up!"

Dan Morgan believed there are three qualities which produce greatness in the prize ring and make a man like Ketchel a fighter for the ages. These are: ferocity, cold-bloodedness and gameness.

"Ketchel answered all the questions," Morgan said. "There's no place for pity in boxing, and Stanley never showed any. He was just a bloodthirsty fighter who always put winning above everything else–even his life!"

Ketchel's supreme self-confidence led to the match with Johnson.

The bout was obviously a mismatch even for so great a fighter as Ketchel and there was talk of an agreement on the part of Johnson to carry the smaller boxer. The talk was never confirmed or denied.

In the 12th and final round Ketchel went for Johnson the instant the gong sounded. Johnson greeted him with a left prod, and someone in Ketchel's corner yelled, "NOW THEN, STANLEY!" Ketchel reacted with a gigantic sweeping right fist that curved around Johnson's neck. Johnson tumbled awkwardly to the floor, a big grin on his face. But he jumped up like a Jack-in-the-box and met Ketchel's assault so effectively that Ketchel impaled himself on Johnson's fists. He went down with a dreadful thud and lay spread out on the canvas like a martyred eagle. Johnson peered down at him anxiously as the referee tolled the count. After it was all over, Jack tip-toed over to Ketchel's corner,

Heavyweight champion Jack Johnson is floored by a sneak punch from middleweight champion Stanley Ketchel in the 12th round of their title bout at Colma, California, on October 16, 1909.

The much bigger Johnson got back up and flattened Ketchel with one punch, ending the fight then and there.

where he slumbered still on his stool, and heaved a mighty sign of relief to see him still breathing. He thought he had killed him.

Johnson had a cute sense of humor. He loved to josh, and he liked his fun right in the ring. When one member of the press asked him why he had gone down grinning, Jack replied, "Oh, he hurt me, sure enough. He caught me flush on the bone behind the ear."

Actually, the fight had a strange ending. According to newspaper accounts, the climax was crowded into 34 seconds. The reporter for the *New York Times* wrote:

> At the beginning of what proved to be the last round there had been little preceeding on which to forecast the winner. The men in the center of the ring clinched and wrestled to Johnson's corner. Johnson suddenly broke away, and, poising himself, dashed at Ketchel, who sprang to meet him. Ketchel drove his right at the black's lowered head. Johnson ducked, and the blow landed behind his ear. He stumbled and fell, landing heavily.
>
> Ketchel backed toward the ropes with a faint smile on his battered, blood-streaked face. Johnson rose slowly as though dazed. As he straightened to his knees he looked at Ketchel and like a wild beast he leaped across the ten feet that separated them. His right fist shot to the white man's jaw. His left crashed to the stomach, and the right swung again with the speed of lightning, catching Ketchel's head as he reeled back from the onslaught.
>
> Ketchel dropped in a heap, and Johnson, unable to stop his rush, sprawled across his beaten rival's legs and fell full length himself.
>
> Johnson sprang to his feet with a bound, but Ketchel was out. Once, as the seconds were counted over him, he feebly moved his arms and rolled his head. He gave no other sign of life and his seconds picked him up from the floor barely conscious.
>
> Johnson was still dazed. He clung to the ropes and looked about him in a bewildered way. The crowd broke into murmurings and seemed unable to realize that the fight was over.
>
> Ketchel won many friends by his showing today. From the time he entered the ring until he was carried out, he was game to the core. Out-weighed, over-reached, and in every way the physical inferior of his gigantic opponent, he fought a cool, well-planned, gritty fight. His face was puffed and he was bleeding at the nose and mouth before three rounds had passed, but he kept following Johnson about the ring undaunted.
>
> Johnson appeared to be holding himself back all the time. Three times only did it look as though he went in to knock his man out—once when Ketchel landed a clean left hook on the jaw that broke the skin and raised a lump, once when a similar blow caught him from the other side, and the last time when he ended the fight.

In his dressing room after the fight Johnson said: "Ketchel is a good puncher and a strong man. I must say that he has given me a sorer chin than I ever had before," and he rubbed his swollen jaw reflectively. "He can take some heavy punches. See here," and he showed one of his gloves sodden with Ketchel's blood. There were several cuts on the leather. "That's where I uppercut him on the mouth."

The match drew more than 10,000 people, while another 3,000 were turned away. It grossed $40,000, considered a big gate in 1909.

Ketchel died as he had lived, excitingly and fast. He was shot in the back and killed under mysterious circumstances, in 1910, on Pete Dickerson's farm in the Ozarks where he had gone to get hold of himself following a spree in New York. Perhaps the greatest tribute paid to him was in the words of a close friend, Wilson Mizner. When informed by telephone that Ketchel was dead, the famous wit said: "Start counting—he will get up at nine."

Like his match with Ketchel, Jack Johnson's fight with Jim Jeffries was another pathetic mismatch in which Jack prolonged the agony only to give the crowd some measure of satisfaction. Had the old boilermaker been in his prime, Tex Rickard's shame would have indeed been the "Battle of the Century." Johnson's prodigious strength and

Jack Johnson checks over thousands of gold pieces—the total purse—for his fight with Jim Jeffries as Tex Rickard, left, looks on. The bout was promoter Rickard's first "Battle of the Century."

abnormal stamina was similar to Jeffries'. Certainly he would have given the real Jeffries a longer, harder fight than any other heavyweight contender past or present. But sooner or later Jeff's superior punching power would have told the story.

As it was, the dull-eyed flabby man who was once invincible stood with legs astraddle to keep from toppling over. Nine years later on another hot day in the desert another old man, Jess Willard, would face a similar situation.

It was the old, old story. Jeff, a sick man, needed the money. Watching him toughen up for the fight, old Mike Murphy, a famous trainer of the time, remarked, "He's not training properly."

Walter C. Kelly, famous for his "Virginia Judge" vaudeville act, conducts a Kangaroo Court at Jim Jeffries' training camp in 1910, all part of the program to relax Big Jeff before his match against Johnson. Shown here with Kelly, who was Princess Grace's uncle, are Jim Corbett, Jack Johnson, Jeffries, and Ned Brown (second from far left, back row), sports columnist for the old New York World *and later boss of author John McCallum.*

Jeffries worked out in the open but neglected to sharpen his timing and reflexes or perfect the tools of his trade. The lackeys who surrounded him gave him the old Madison Avenue business. But as the fatal day approached, Jeff became sullen, morose and apathetic. Crowds irked him, and he took off on fishing excursions. Ned Brown, the veteran New York writer, found Jeff fishing by himself in the turbulent Truckee River in California. He was talking to himself, so, as Brown said, "I made myself scarce without interrupting his conversation with himself."

Big Jack, on the other hand, was bursting with good health. Ever friendly and obliging, he loved the prefight hoopla, the crowds and the publicity. This was the first Rickard circus to be billed as the "Battle of the Century," and little old Reno was fairly jumping the night before the fight. Betting was rife at Tom Corbett's headquarters where Jeffries ruled the favorite.

The next day 15,760 fans paid $270,775 to witness the shambles of "what might have been." As soon as the telegraph offices began tapping the outcome, race riots erupted in various sections of the country. But joy was rampant in the black belts where Jack Johnson was the hero of his race.

This laughing giant was an irresponsible child of his time who loved to strum the banjo and drive flamboyant roadsters at breakneck speed.

He sported garish diamonds and a sophistication composed of sensual grace and the careless wisdom one derives from a free, untrammeled life. Jack went everywhere and did just about everything. Stevedore, sponge fisherman, ship's cook, stable boy and hostler, bullfighter, actor, promoter, even the manager of a Broadway flea circus.

Dan Morgan told me of the time when he dropped down to catch Johnson's itchy act at Broadway and 42nd Street. The huge man was an expert on fleas and could train them to do everything but close-order drill.

"Jack, what are you fooling around with those fleas for?" Dan joshed him. "Why don't you get yourself a heavyweight, train him and make a pile of dough?"

"Listen, Morgan," Jack replied, flashing that golden grin, "these fleas can think better than the heavyweights around today."

The scandal surrounding Johnson's personal life received the full rotogravure treatment. So they threw the book at him, including an indictment under the Mann Act, and he was forced to leave the country and grub out a living fighting in such places as Paris, Buenos Aires, Havana, Madrid, Barcelona, Mexico City, and Quebec.

Champion Jack Johnson infuriated a racist American public by marrying a white woman. The Johnsons are shown here at a Paris restaurant.

Age had already begun to sap his magnificent strength when he defended his title against Jess Willard under a merciless sun in Havana, on April 5, 1915. The "knockout," according to popular legend, had the odor that exudes from a decayed tooth. The camera shows Johnson reclining on the canvas in a comfortable position as he raises a gloved hand to shield his eyes from the sun's glare. Before that 26th round began, Jack signalled his Caucasian wife to leave the arena. One may assume that he was planning to call a halt and didn't want her to see him bow out to such an inexperienced fighter as Willard.

Years later, in his office in Times Square, Jack Curley, one of the greatest of all promoters, told Frank Graham, the dandy little sports columnist from the *New York Journal-American,* of the events leading up to the matching of Johnson and Willard. Curley promoted the fight.

"In 1914, we... my wife and two children and I... had an apartment on Riverside Drive," Curley said. "We had a chef, a French maid, a car—and chauffeur—and I didn't have a dime. The bills were mounting, but I lunched every day at the Astor for two reasons. I had to make a show of prosperity, and that was the place to be seen—and I had credit there. One day I met Lawrence Weber, the theatrical producer. I owed him $300 and was embarrassed on seeing him, because I had been unable to repay him. When he asked me to go to his office about three o'clock that afternoon, I thought he was going to ask for his money and I was feeling pretty low when I kept the engagement. A few minutes later, I was in the clouds.

" 'Jack,' he asked me, 'do you know where we can find a fellow to lick Jack Johnson?'

" 'I've already found him,' I said. 'Jess Willard.'

" 'Willard!' he said. 'That big bum? I saw him against Soldier Kearns two years ago and, although he knocked Kearns out finally, he looked terrible doing it.'

" 'He isn't a bum now,' I said. 'He's big and strong, he has a terrific punch, and I don't think there's anyone who can hurt him. Johnson hasn't had a real fight in more than two years and he's been carousing all over Europe. I'm sure he can't stand up to Willard for 35 or 40 rounds, even if Willard doesn't hit him.'

" 'All right,' he said. 'I'll take your word for it. Would you like to promote it? I thought you would. Starting now, draw on me for anything you need in the way of money.' "

Johnson, a fugitive from justice in the United States, was in Paris. Curley sailed that afternoon on the old S.S. St. Louis for Cherbourg. When he reached Paris, he proposed the match to Johnson.

"Weel-ard," Jack said, grinning. "It seems to me I have heard of him."

"Don't try to con me with that French accent," Curley said. "His name is Willard and you know it. And he can fight. Jack, sign with me and I'll put the fight on here or somewhere outside the United States and make a lot of money for all of us."

"Have you got Willard?" Johnson asked.

"Not yet," Curley admitted.

"Get him," Johnson said, "and you got me."

Curley returned to America. Willard was in California, and Curley wired him, asking for a meeting in Kansas City. It took place on a baggage truck on the railroad station platform. Jess quickly agreed to the match and promised that if his manager, Tom Jones, with whom Curley was not particularly friendly, had any objections, they would be overcome.

Now Curley had both fighters–but, overnight, World War I had erupted and Johnson had gone to Spain. Curley picked Juarez as the scene of the fight and directed Willard to train at El Paso. His problem now was to get Johnson to Mexico. He had been out of touch with Johnson for days–by now it was March of 1915–when he received a cable from the champion, who had reached Havana. It read:

"I'm here. So is everybody else. Bring the fight here."

And so Curley did, for Havana was jammed with Americans and South American seekers of pleasure who ordinarily would have been spending their money in Europe. The ring was pitched in the infield of the Oriental Park Race Track. The Associated Press version of the fight tells what happened:

> Jack Johnson, exile from his own country, today lost the heavyweight championship of the world to Jess Willard, the Kansas cowboy, the biggest man who ever entered the prize ring and a "White Hope" who at last has made good. The Negro was knocked out in the 26th round with a smashing swing to the point of the jaw.
>
> A crowd numbering between 15,000 and 20,000 wagered only small bets on the outcome. The odds varied from 8 to 5 to 6 to 5 on Johnson, who earned $30,000, while Willard got only a small share of the net receipts.
>
> For 20 rounds Johnson punched and pounded Willard at will, but his blows grew perceptibly less powerful as the fight progressed, until at last he seemed unable or unwilling to go on. Johnson stopped leading and for the next three or four rounds the battle was little more than a series of plastic poses. So it was until the 25th round, when Willard got one of his wildly swinging windmill right-hand smashes to Johnson's heart. This was the beginning of the end.
>
> When the round closed, Johnson sent word to his wife that he was all in, and told her to start for home. She was on the way out and was passing the ring in the 26th round when a cyclonic right to the jaw caused Johnson to crumple on the floor of the ring, where he lay, partly outside the ropes, until after the referee had counted 10 and held up Willard's hand in token of the cowboy's newly won laurels.
>
> Johnson was slow in responding to the gong for what proved to be the final round, while Willard seemed fresh. Willard delivered four blows in this round–a left to the face, a right to the stomach, a left to the body, and the final right swing to the jaw that stretched Johnson out for the count. Johnson seemed powerless to make any defense. He was shaky from the start of the round.

There is much discussion tonight as to whether Johnson really was knocked out. In the sense of being smashed into unconsciousness, he certainly was not put out. The consensus is that Johnson felt that there was no possibility of his winning and when knocked down chose to take the count rather than rise and stand further punishment. Johnson often has stated that fighting is a business, and that he would not foolishly submit to repeated knockdowns when he found he had met his master.

A second or two after Jack Welch, the referee, had counted 10 Johnson quickly got up....

A cry of "Fake!" instantly was raised. Johnson later said he had agreed to lose on condition that he be allowed to return to America and escape a year's jail sentence that had been passed upon him.

To the day he died, Curley denied that this was so.

Johnson lost his title to Jess Willard in 1915 under a scorching Havana sun. Li'l Arthur was KO'd in the 26th round but many people thought he threw the fight.

"I imported Jack Welch from California to referee," he said. "There had been so many rumors of a fake that I wanted him, an honest man, to protect me. Johnson lost because, as I had told Weber, he couldn't even walk around after he had passed the 25th round. He could have got up but, if he had, he would have been knocked down again, and, maybe, badly hurt. He knew Willard had killed Bull Young in California."

Willard, himself, had his own explanation as to what ended the fight. "The blow that actually brought the fight to a quick conclusion was a right-hand smash to Johnson's body early in the last round. I felt Johnson grow limp in the next clinch and knew I had the championship within my reach. A left to the body and a right smash to the jaw put Johnson down for the count."

Dan Morgan was one of the most colorful and beloved fight managers in the history of boxing. He managed four world champions and was adviser to 35 more. When Jack Johnson wanted to redeem himself with Americans, he joined Morgan's boxing troupe and went around the country entertaining at church benefits, hospitals and military posts. (Dan Morgan was the subject of author John McCallum's first book, Dumb Dan.*)*

Jack Johnson's escapades are old hat, yet the public never knew that he yearned for the good and useful life. Years after his retirement he came to Dan Morgan.

"Morgan," he said, "I'd like to make up for the wild life I've led. Do you have any ideas?"

Dan was then appearing at church benefits, hospitals and military posts, staging boxing programs.

"Why don't you join me?" he said.

"I'm at your service," Johnson replied.

"But you're a wanderer," Morgan said. "How do I get hold of you when I want you?"

"Just put a notice in the newspapers," Johnson said. "Get hold of me any way you can, and I'll be there."

Johnson lived up to his promise, too. He never missed a show. For 15 years he appeared with Morgan, bringing joy to the hearts of thousands. "He was a good speaker, too," Dan said. "Our audiences loved the way he told his stories."

Then, one day, Johnson failed to show up at a Morgan program. The date was June 10, 1946. The headlines on the sports pages that night cleared the mystery: "Ex-Champ Jack Johnson Killed In Auto Accident." He had been on his way from North Carolina to keep his appointment with Dan Morgan—and died exactly the way he always told Morgan he would die.

7. Jess Willard

JESS WILLARD was the rawest fighter ever to win the heavyweight championship of the world. He had about as much natural fighting inclination as Primo Carnera, who had less than a rabbit.

Cowboy Jess was twenty-six years old before he ever saw a boxing glove.

The "Pottawatomie Pounder" was a direct product of the White Hope frenzy following Jack Johnson's knockout of Jim Jeffries. He was a giant of a man, 6 ft. 6¼ in. and 250 pounds. Born on the edge of an Indian reservation in Pottawatomie County, on December 29, 1881, he rode wild horses as a youth, hunted, developed endurance, and became a plains teamster.

Willard was in his middle twenties when he drove a six-horse team into a small town in Oklahoma and discovered the citizens wildly excited about the downfall of Jim Jeffries. That was on Independence Day, 1910. When the owner of a local tavern saw Jess he pointed a challenging finger at him and asked, "Why don't you try fighting? You're big enough." Until that moment, Jess hadn't thought much about it. "Well," the pub owner said, "what about it?"

Suddenly the idea appealed to Jess.

"I'll do it," he said.

Soon Cowboy Jess Willard was in places like Sapulpa and El Reno and Elk City bowling over round-heels with names like Fink and Burke and Mendeno and Shiller. The build-up was on.

Of a peaceful disposition and embarrassed because of his size, Willard lacked fighting spirit. This was never more evident than the night he fought Joe Cox in Springfield, Missouri, on October 11, 1911. Jess had run up a string of seven straight victories, five by knockouts, and had Cox fairly well under control until the fifth round, when Joe

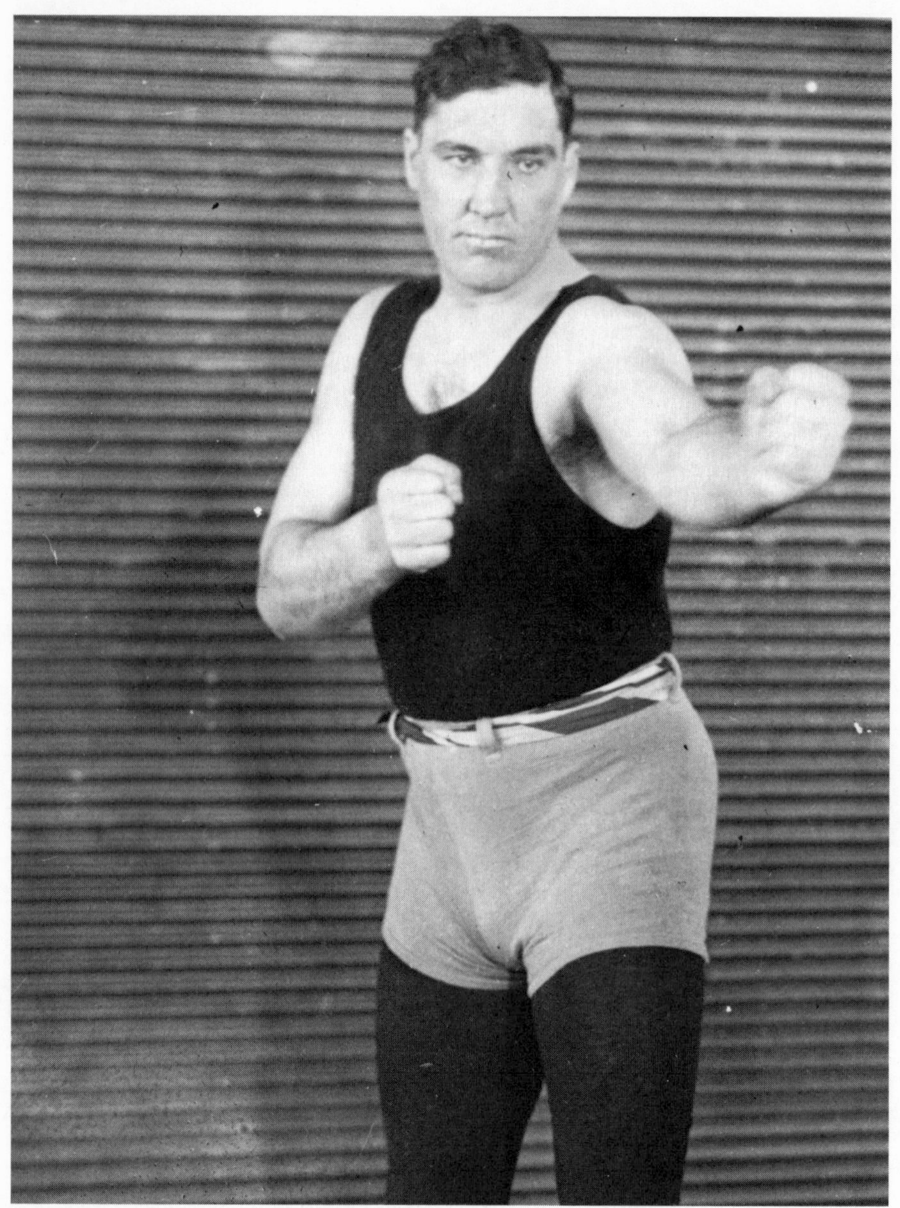

Cowboy Jess Willard was a giant of a man, 6 ft. 6¼ in. and 250 pounds, and was twenty-six years old before he ever saw a boxing glove.

smashed a solid left hook into his stomach. Jess turned white in the face. He grabbed Jimmy Bronson, the referee, and, using the little man as a shield, backed into the ropes and ducked out of the ring.

Billy McCarney was the promoter. He had been sitting at ringside and as Jess climbed down the steps he cried, "What are you quitting for? You're not hurt, you big oaf!"

"I know that, Mr. McCarney, but it's a wise man who quits before he is hurt."

Three and a half years later Jess Willard was heavyweight champion of the world.

On his way to knocking the crown off Jack Johnson's head, Willard showed enough improvement to keep busy. He had looked good in no-decision matches with Arthur Pelkey, Luther McCarty and Carl Morris. He dropped a 20-round decision to Gunboat Smith, and in another bout killed Bull Young.

Big Jess was the first of three modern heavyweight champions who killed opponents in the ring. Primo Carnera and Max Baer were the other two. Oddly enough, Willard and The Preem were always accused of lacking the killer instinct.

Years after Jess knocked him out, Jack Johnson went around claiming he had laid down. There were those who accepted a photograph of Li'l Arthur comfortably sprawled on the floor, shading his eyes from the sun, as something in the way of evidence that he was telling the truth, but Billy Roche was not one of them. "Jack hardly would have stuck around for 26 rounds in that scorching Havana sun before taking a dive," the old referee said. "His handlers worked over him five minutes before he was himself again."

There are still many versions as to what really happened in that final round. The Associated Press dispatch reported that Johnson was back on his feet as soon as the referee's count reached the fatal 10. Roche insisted that Jack was still groggy and had to be helped back to his corner. Take your pick.

Willard was idle most of his years as champion. Of course, World War I was on and most of the fighters had other things to do. Jess fought only five times during the war years. He successfully defended his title only once, against Frank Moran. The bout is listed as a 10-round no-decision affair and served as the great Tex Rickard's first promotion in New York.

In 1918, only a dozen months before young Jack Dempsey sailed into him, Willard got busy and warmed up in two 10-round exhibition matches.

On Independence Day, 1919, the stage was set. For four years the newspapers had been selling mud and mass carnage. The war was over, but the national pulse had been stepped up and was still beating to march time. Physically or vicariously, the nation had been living next-door neighbors to "Eat, drink and be merry; for tomorrow we die." The audience was ready. Circulation managers of newspapers were looking for an adequate substitute for AMERICANS ADVANCE ON THE

Jess Willard towers over Frank Moran before their 10-round, no-decision match in New York, March 25, 1916. It was the only time Willard put his title on the line before losing to Dempsey three years later.

SOMME; GERMANS IN FULL RETREAT, to stimulate sales. The publicity medium was ready. And the final coincidence: In the wings stood the scowling Manassa Mauler–Jack Dempsey–waiting to go on. Waiting to take Willard's heavyweight crown away from him.

Looking at post-World War I's first heavyweight championship fight, it was hard for some experts to give Dempsey much of a chance. He stood slightly over 6 feet and weighed 180. Willard, at 6 ft. 6¼ in., weighed 250 at least.

Big Jess regarded Dempsey as a little boy. The night before the fight in Toledo Granny Rice called on him. Jess said he thought the fight was a joke.

"...outweigh him 70 pounds," Willard said. "He'll come tearing into me... I'll have my left out... and then I'll hit him with a right uppercut. That'll be the end."

Next day, Dempsey sat on his stool waiting for the work gong to ring. His mind was on strategy, a fight plan. "I didn't know if I was going to be in a scrap or a footrace," he said, many years later. "I thought I could knock him out in the first round. But I looked over in his corner and saw how big he was and decided I had better fight for my life. I wondered if I was going to have enough of a punch to knock him out of the picture. He was in great shape and looking very confident. I made up my mind to keep away from him as much as possible and not let him hit me and do the punching myself."

When the first round opened, Dempsey circled Willard for some 25 or 30 seconds. He was a tiger circling an ox. Finally Willard couldn't wait any longer. He jabbed at Dempsey with his left, and the roof fell in. Jack ducked under Willard's left, threw a right to the body. At the

1919: A fierce Jack Dempsey, right, in his typical crouch, cut Willard to ribbons in three rounds at Toledo, Ohio. Big Jess always claimed Dempsey's gloves were "loaded," but his own handlers watched Jack wrap his hands before the fight and found nothing irregular.

same time he nailed Willard on the right side of the head with a smashing left.

"I knew it was all over then," Dempsey said later. "I saw his cheek bone cave in. Funny thing about this fight was that Jack Kearns, my manager, claimed he had bet $10,000 to $100,000 I'd knock out Willard in the first round. That's what I did. The referee had raised my right hand, awarding me the fight. Willard's head was hanging over the lower rope. He was practically unconscious from several knockdowns. I left the ring. The fight was over–or it should have been. I must have been 25 yards from the ring when they called me back. That was the biggest shock in my life...when I was told the bell had rung three seconds too soon. Suppose it had? My hand had been raised and I had been given the fight by the referee."

Even then Big Jess might have retained the title two rounds later had he elected to get out of his corner for the fourth round. Dempsey, by then, was that tired. But Willard, who had been down seven times and was bleeding like a half-butchered ox, was unable to answer the bell for the fourth round.

"I sure recall my end of that purse," recollected Dempsey. "For three rounds I got $27,500. It was my first big payday. Willard did all right, too. His share–win, lose or draw–was $100,000."

There were rumors after the fight that Dempsey's hands were "loaded." Willard was bitter. He spent years telling anyone who would listen that he had been the victim of foul play on that July 4, 1919, afternoon.

"I want the people to know how the gangsters *took* the title away from me over there in Toledo," he told one radio announcer. "They really gave me a rough time. I could beat fighters but nobody can beat gangsters. And that's exactly what I was up against. The truth should be known. You couldn't believe what they did to me."

I asked Dan Morgan if there was any truth in Willard's charges. Dan saw the fight and he talked to Walt Monoghan, the chief second and trainer for Jess.

"As Willard's chief second," Dan said, "he was authorized to enter Dempsey's dressing room when the tape was strapped on before the fight. Jack taped his own hands. Walter was with Dempsey all the time. When Dempsey climbed into the ring, Jess walked over to his corner and carefully examined his hands. Walter watched Kearns tie on Dempsey's gloves. At the same time, one of Dempsey's men watched every move made by Willard. There were no irregularities.

"Closer to the truth about what really happened, Willard was in no condition to fight that day. When he first entered the ring he showed not one trace of pink. His skin had a peculiar olive-drab tone. Dempsey was as brown as an Indian. Willard's idleness after winning the title from Johnson, his age (thirty-seven), and his lack of hard training for the bout were what really lost him the title. As one paper said later, the fight he made against Dempsey was pitiful for a world's champion."

The customers shelled out $452,522 to see nine minutes of fighting. The 45,000 onlookers included 500 women.

They witnessed one of boxing's all-time blood baths. Willard's face was a mass of gore. Dempsey was spattered all over his front and shoulders with blood—Willard's. Jess' right eye was completely closed, there was a freely bleeding cut beneath it, his mouth was bleeding, six teeth were missing, and the whole right side of his face was swollen to almost twice its normal size. Dempsey had not one mark.

Though outweighed by 70 pounds, Dempsey finished Willard in only nine minutes of bloody fighting. Jess lost six teeth and was a mass of gore.

One New York paper reported:

"So terrific was the punishment which Willard received, so weak was he, so incapable of defense, that during the third round shouts of 'Stop it! Stop it!' rose from many parts of the arena. It was one of the poorest fights in the history of boxing. It was unpleasant to watch. It gave no satisfaction to anyone except those who had bet on Dempsey. It was pugilistic murder."

Willard went broke after losing the title, but he became well-fixed again in 1923 with two more fights. He knocked out Floyd Johnson in 11 rounds and was flattened in 8 by Luis Angel Firpo.

Big Jess had height, reach and weight. He rarely cut loose except when he was hurt. Then he could be as dangerous as dynamite, especially with that right-hand uppercut.

The Kansas giant developed courage as he found his way around.

The day he finished Jack Johnson, Jess Willard was much more formidable than many people gave him credit for.

8. Jack Dempsey

TENNESSEE-born Grantland Rice started his career in sports journalism in 1901. At high noon on July 13, 1954, that marvelous career ended as he died suddenly while working on his nationally syndicated column, *The Sportlight.* Two months earlier, I sat with Granny at lunch in Toots Shor's talking about oldtime boxing champions.

I said, "Who was the greatest puncher you ever saw?"

"Dempsey," he said.

"Not Louis?"

"No, Dempsey," he repeated. "Jack Dempsey was the greatest attacking star in sports I've ever seen."

"Do you recall the first time you ever saw Dempsey?"

"I had been in France during 1917 and '18," he said, "so had seen no prize fights in two years. When I first met Dempsey, he was burnt purple. He'd trained down to 180 pounds in getting ready for Jess Willard. Jack was then twenty-four years old. He was keen and lithe and fast. It was his speed, speed of hand as well as foot, that made him such a dangerous opponent. He was the oddest mixture of humanity I have known. In the ring he was a killer—a superhuman wild man. His teeth were frequently bared and his complete intent was an opponent's destruction. He was a fighter. He was a fighter who used every trick possible to wreck the other fighter."

William Harrison Dempsey was the most spectacular prize fighter to hold the heavyweight championship. He was electric. He created excitement. For the first time the public poured millions into boxing because they knew they would get their money's worth in spine tingles any time Jack defended the title he cherished and fought so savagely to keep.

Jack Dempsey—the most spectacular prize fighter in the history of the heavyweight division—as he looked in his prime.

Dempsey was the first fighter to draw a million-dollar gate, a figure he exceeded five times. His last fight with Gene Tunney grossed $2,658,660. His great magnetism drew the general public to boxing for the first time in history. Before he exerted his mass appeal, the ring was, for the most part, a magnet only for the roughneck, the race tout, the sporting character. In Dempsey's heyday, with the help of the uncanny genius of Tex Rickard, boxing was made to appeal to the doctor, the lawyer, the merchant, the school teacher. In Dempsey's time, boxing finally achieved eminent respectability.

From 53 years' experience as one of America's most distinguished sports writers, Grantland Rice called Dempsey "the greatest attacking star in sports I've ever seen."

When Dempsey fought, things happened that never happened before. Granted not all of his title defenses were ring epics, but they were all enveloped in the greatest possible excitement and hysterical activity.

Jack's sensational fracas with Luis Angel Firpo at the Polo Grounds stands out as one of the most thrilling events in the history of sports. His second joust with Tunney remains the most controversial in boxing. His match with the smaller Georges Carpentier created perhaps the greatest prefight taking of sides of any prize fight. And his bout at Shelby, Montana, with Tommy Gibbons, a comparatively mild affair once it started, was preceded by enormous furor, which led to a bank failure, threats of lynching, and was a public disaster for the town in which it was staged. Even Dempsey's first fight against Tunney, in which he lost the title, while actually a mediocrity to watch, satisfied the customers.

Dempsey's great drawing power, as developed by Rickard, first was felt in his title defense against Carpentier, in 1920. Jack had twice defended his crown, against Billy Miske and Bill Brennan, but those were just two more heavyweight championship fights.

Not only was Dempsey *not* a good drawing card at this time, but he was still more or less despised by the general public who still remembered he had been tried on charges of being a slacker in World War I. The courts had officially cleared him of the charges, but the legal verdict had little effect on people at large. Dempsey had to fight his way into public favor.

Signing Georges Carpentier to fight Dempsey at Boyle's Thirty Acres, Jersey City, for July 2, 1921, was a shrewd piece of work by Tex

More than 75,000 overflowed the Jersey City arena on July 2, 1921, to watch Dempsey knock out Georges Carpentier of France in the first of boxing's million-dollar gates. It also marked the first fight to be broadcast.

Rickard. The Frenchman, with a gaudy if superficial war record, had returned to Paris in one piece—and hungry. He was a pretty fair light-heavyweight, but he was so light they trained him in secret, so that no one would find out that he was no match for the man who had routed

Willard. At any rate, Rickard, knowing the public's love of a hero *vs.* villain, cast Dempsey, the scowling, wire-bearded "draft dodger" as the bad guy, with apple-cheeked Carpentier, the amiable, personable soldier boy, as the good guy. Pictures of Dempsey, riveting battleships in patent leather shoes—all at his manager Jack Kearns' behest—flooded the sports pages, along with those of Carpentier, virtually winning the war single-handed.

The fight was the first to be broadcast, with Graham McNamee describing the action, and it had the whole nation taking sides for or against Dempsey. The bout itself was nothing. It was all over in four rounds. Most experts figured Dempsey could have nailed Carpentier in the first round had he been in a hurry to get home. From ringside, all

In the first of the great post-World War I organized ballyhoos, the Dempsey-Carpentier bout was nothing. Carpentier lasted only four rounds.

French ships at sea received this cabled flash: "Your Frog flattened in fourth"—for a new high in international diplomacy. A crowd of 75,000 paid $1,789,238 to watch Dempsey do his thing.

It marked the first of the great organized ballyhoos. Boxing was off on a mad, squanderous, money rampage which during the next nine years saw 1,488,900 customers contributing $14,247,313 for big fights around New York alone.

The Roaring Twenties were out for superlatives. The biggest gates, the biggest crowds and, certainly, the greatest rough-and-tumble brawl ever conducted outside a barroom or a lumber camp—the classic round-and-a-half fought by Dempsey and Firpo at the Polo Grounds, September 14, 1923, before a crowd of 85,800 hysterical people. Firpo, the bottle-washer from the Argentine, came to America, his bull neck encased in a celluloid collar and his belongings in a handkerchief. He fought abysmally and like a wounded animal. Of boxing he knew nothing except that one began fighting with the bell and stopped when it rang again. He ran at his opponents with his nostrils flaring, his black hair standing straight up, and his eyes gleaming with the pure lust of battle. He clubbed and battered them until they dropped.

His unquenchable pugnacity and flaming spirit completely captured the imagination of the American public. He was nicknamed "The Wild Bull of the Pampas," and he looked it. Guided by the wily Rickard, he was cleverly built up, clubbed his right hand until every opponent who barred his way to Dempsey quit or was counted out, and was matched for the heavyweight championship.

Granny Rice recalled he got his first glimpse of Firpo two weeks before the fight. "His training camp was at Atlantic City," Granny said. "When I arrived early one morning, Firpo was tackling a light breakfast: a huge steak smothered with lamb chops. After finishing, he walked over to a couch and lay there like a python who'd just swallowed a calf. He seemed dopey and indolent. I compared his camp to Dempsey's at Saratoga. There the order of the day was mayhem, with the massive George Godfrey as Jack's No. 1 sparring partner at $1,500 per week, and I wondered at the fight that was about to be perpetrated on the unsuspecting public. Fifty-dollar ringside seats were being gobbled up for a hundred dollars each. Firpo had a couple of two-bit sparring partners whom he outweighed by a ton and belabored at will. He sure didn't spend much on that camp, except for food."

Before the fight two men Dempsey knew casually called on him at his training quarters. After a few minutes of small talk they asked Jack what round he expected to finish Firpo in.

"I don't know," Dempsey said. "I'll take care of him just as quickly as I can."

"Pin it down," they said. "Which round are you going after him for a knockout?"

"Why?" Jack asked.

"Because a lot of money depends on the information."

"Get outta here!" roared Dempsey. "You're lucky you don't leave here with a broken jaw."

Gamblers weren't Dempsey's only headache. Tex Rickard bugged him, too.

"Tex asked me to carry Firpo for four or five rounds, to give the customers a run for their money," Dempsey confessed later. "I told him to go to hell. I told him that Firpo was too strong and hit too hard to play with. I told Tex I'd put Firpo away in the first round—if I could."

Actually, it was no match between the South American greenhorn and the greatest puncher developed in America since Sullivan. Because Dempsey could box, and had he elected to spar, it might have been no contest. But Dempsey was at that time very unpopular. He was anxious to reestablish himself in popular favor and regain some of the prestige he had lost in the Gibbons fight. He went in to slug it out, was knocked to one knee, and then clean out of the ring by the giant South American, himself blinded and stunned by blows.

There never was such a shambles in ring history. The lightning action in the ring projected itself among the spectators. Before the opening gong had faded, Dempsey had hurled himself at Firpo and battered him to the floor four times. Then Firpo electrified the screaming crowd by smashing Dempsey through the ropes and out of the ring. Dempsey

1923: Luis Angel Firpo, the "Wild Bull of the Pampas," sends Dempsey sailing out of the Polo Grounds ring in the greatest rough-and-tumble brawl in heavyweight history. Jack climbed back in to club and batter the South American until he dropped for good in the second round.

landed on the typewriter of Jack Lawrence, the boxing writer for the *New York Herald-Tribune*. Lawrence was very strong and helped Dempsey back into the ring. How Dempsey was half-pushed, how he half-crawled back has been told many different ways, but the fact remains that Lawrence gave him the greatest impetus. What happened after that took place quickly, and is history.

There was no attempt at science or skill; neither bothered with defense; it was a heart-stopping, brutal battle between two animals—one with the speed and aggressiveness and claws of a panther; the other, well-named, with the strength, the courage and the obstinancy of the water buffalo. No one who was there that sultry September night can ever forget the sound of 85,800 screaming people, the cracking of breaking benches, the hot, swift thud of the red leather gloves against bone and flesh, and the sight of the stung, semiconscious giant struggling to his feet for yet another thrust at his tormentor; or the last moment, when Firpo rolled helplessly on his back and stomach in the second round, his brain no longer functioning. It is still the classic hand-to-hand of all time.

Firpo in deep slumber after a round and a half of wild and woolly pounding. Dempsey's sensational victory marked his last successful title defense. It was also the last time his manager, Jack Kearns, worked in his corner. They split over financial matters.

The hysterical madness of the crowd probably will never be totally recorded. Mickey Walker, for example, found himself beating on a man sitting in front of him and shrieking crazily for Dempsey. Suddenly the big fellow in front of him turned around and smote Mickey, the welterweight champion of the world, on the chest, knocking him four rows back. When some semblance of sanity was returning to the arena the big man turned to Mickey and apologized. Mickey gasped.

"Gee, Babe," he said, "no wonder you hit me so hard. Honest, I didn't know it was you."

But that's who it was–Babe Ruth!

The battle inside the ring was wild and woolly, too. Listen to Dempsey's version:

"Before the fight I had been told by Granny Rice that Bill Brennan had said Firpo threw rocks at opponents... that he had a rubber arm... that he'd sock you from a good way off. Well, in that first round I got in a little too close and Firpo's first shot–a full right–caught me on the chin. I almost went down but kept punching. I was dazed. The sports writers wrote that I hit him when he was just getting up. At that time I wasn't fighting for any championship or any million dollars. I was fighting to keep from being killed. I would have hit him at any place I found him. The wallop that sent me through the ropes was a half punch and half shove. It was nothing like that opening right hand he nailed me with earlier. What was my first thought as I went flying through the ropes? To get back up and in as quickly as I could. I might say that no one at ringside tried to help me. They put up their hands to break my fall. It was all instinctive."

Firpo earned one consolation. He received a guarantee of 12½ percent of the gate receipts, amounting to $156,250. Dempsey's share was $468,750.

It was three years before Dempsey put his title on the line again. In other words, the Firpo fight marked his last successful title defense. It was also the last time Jack Kearns, his manager, worked in his corner. They fell out over financial matters.

"I was grateful for everything the guy did for me," Dempsey said, "but he sued me. I didn't sue him. He sued me for breach of contract, and we had no contract. He always got fifty percent of what I made, after expenses. I won the suit. If there was any trouble I didn't make it."

Dempsey was born in Manassa, Colorado–the ninth of the 11 children of Hiram and Celia Dempsey. Jack had five brothers and five sisters. His father was a poverty-driven Mormon sharecropper and itinerant railroad hand who shifted his family by covered wagon to Uncompahgre, then to Delta and Montrose, in Colorado, and eventually to Provo, Utah. At fourteen and fifteen, Jack was mucking in coal and copper mines. He vagabonded across the Rocky Mountain states as carnival fighter, fruit-picker, mule-driver, and professional pool-shark through his formative years. At eighteen, he was a bouncer in a Salt Lake City saloon. It was from there that Jack left to enter the ring.

Dempsey took seriously to fist-fighting in 1914. He fought for purses as low as $2.50. He made his debut as a promoter-fighter. That is, Jack and his pal Freddy Woods hired Moose Hall at Montrose, and announced they would fight for the gate receipts–if any. Jack knocked Freddy out in four rounds. The collection came to $40. He had been fighting under the name of "Kid Blackie." Now he was changing it back to Jack Dempsey.

Doc Kearns saw Dempsey for the first time in San Francisco. Dempsey was then working in a shipyard. Although he had been fighting professionally for several years and had fought in New York, he was still a nobody. He was discouraged, down on himself.

"I'm washed up," he groaned. "I can't fight. I'm going to quit."

This was Dempsey talking to Kearns when chance brought them together. Doc was inclined to agree, but he was broke and if he could get Dempsey for nothing, what could he lose? That's why Kearns induced Jack to return to the ring.

Dempsey was raw. He was right-hand daffy. There was one thing Kearns knew for sure and that was a fighter, to get any place, had to have a knowing left hand. So Doc lashed Dempsey's right arm to his side, forcing him to attack and defend with his left. To keep from getting hit, Dempsey started to bob and weave. Eventually he was a two-handed fighter.

It was one thing to get Dempsey back in the ring. It was another to develop him into a competent fighter. It was still another to sell him to matchmakers.

"Keep in mind that Fireman Jim Flynn, even then an old man, had stopped Dempsey in one round," the late Joe Williams, of the *New York World-Telegram and Sun,* told me. "Or rather, the desperate and disgusted Dempsey had done a half-gainer in a dry tank, for which he was paid $300. Later, he made it up with his conscience and his record by flattening Flynn in one round."

Kearns admitted once that matchmakers offered him only $20 for Dempsey when Jack was ready to resume his career. Fat Willie Meehan was Dempsey's first opponent under Kearns. That was on March 28, 1917, in Oakland, California. Slightly less than three years later, Kearns had Dempsey fighting for the championship in boxing's first million-dollar gate. While this was a head-spinning adventure in high finance for the pair, it also marked the first and last time that Doc Kearns ever failed to get all and more than was coming to him and Dempsey. Doc, you'll recall, refused to gamble on percentage with Tex Rickard. He insisted on a guarantee and missed out on an extra $200,000.

On the morning of the Jess Willard fight Kearns asked Dempsey: "Can you stop this bum in a round?"

"No," Jack said. "I'm weighing 183 and he's weighing around 250. But I'll knock him out."

"You'd better knock him out in the *first* round," Kearns said.

"Why?"

"Because I just bet $10,000 against $100,000 that you'll stop him in the first round."

"You must be crazy," Dempsey said. "We're only getting $17,500 for the fight. That means we'll only get $7,500."

"No, it doesn't," Doc said. "It means we will collect $117,500. You can punch his head off in a round."

Dempsey, who rarely clinched in the prize ring, is shown here rehearsing with actress Estelle Taylor for his stage role in The Big Fight, *under the direction of D. Belasco. In real life, Jack and Estelle were married.*

That was the spot Kearns had put Dempsey in when he stepped into the ring against Cowboy Jess.

While an incompetent group of officials cost Dempsey and Doc a hundred grand, Willard, who died in Los Angeles in 1968, never ceased to charge that Dempsey beat him with loaded gloves. In the opinion of most experts, however, the twenty-four-year-old, hard-as-nails, hungry Dempsey could have whipped Jess with pillows that steaming July afternoon.

"But for all of that Willard could still be right," Joe Williams told me. "Years ago when Dempsey was beginning his comeback to meet Gene Tunney I put the question to him cold and he laughingly side-stepped it. He said, 'Even if I did, you don't think I'd be foolish enough to admit it, do you?' Then one summer, for the first time, Kearns confessed to me he had treated the hand tape with a talcum substance that turned concrete-hard when wet; he said this explained why Willard's face cut each time Dempsey landed a blow. Further, it explained why Dempsey couldn't put Willard down again after the second round. He was having a tough time lifting his arms. The stuff had hardened and the gloves were like iron weights. Kearns' version could be true. The bitterness he held against Dempsey did not rule out truthfulness altogether, and since Doc's philosophy always was to protect yourself at all times, you can rest assured he overlooked no bets in moving Dempsey toward the championship."

The Dempsey who emerged as champion when he flattened Willard was an unshaven, unmannerly mass of muscles with but eighth-grade schooling, a dreadnought punch, and a lightweight sense of values.

"As champ, Jack was always in hot water," a friend pointed out. "While the country went nuts about him, he spent or gave away a half-million bucks. He was bled white by the leeches, had two divorces, got sued for things he did and didn't do. No wonder he was always scowling when he got inside that ring."

The late Colonel Eddie Eagen knew first-hand what it was like to be in there with Dempsey. This was the same Eddie Eagen who later became Chairman of the New York State Boxing Commission. In his youth, he had been the best amateur heavyweight boxer in America. Out of Denver and as a student in high school, he won a scholarship to Yale. At Yale, he won the intercollegiate heavyweight championship, the AAU championship and about all the amateur championships there were lying around loose. At Yale he won a Rhodes Scholarship to Oxford. There he quickly became a heavyweight champion, defeated the heavyweight champion of Cambridge and went on from there to become amateur heavyweight champion of England.

Eddie's achievements did not pass unnoticed by Tex Rickard, who knew a drawing card when he saw one or even heard of one. And so there was this day in London in the winter of 1923 when Eddie, down from Oxford for the Christmas holidays, received a cable from Tex offering him $20,000 to fight at the old Madison Square Garden, the opponent to be selected subsequent to his agreement to fight. Eddie sought out his old friend, Frank Graham, to ask his advice.

Dempsey and the one-time faro dealer, Tex Rickard, who promoted all five of his million-dollar gates.

"Twenty thousand dollars is a lot of money," he told Frankie, "and I've got nothing but my scholarships, my books and my clothes. Do you think I should take it?"

"Do you want to be a prize fighter?" Frankie asked.

"No," Eddie said.

"Then don't take it," Frankie told him. "If I thought you could beat Dempsey…"

Eddie shook his head.

"I can't," he said. "I tried it once. When I was a kid in Denver. Dempsey came in there to box for the Red Cross and I was nominated to box him. I didn't know it, but Otto Floto, the sports editor of the paper that was putting the show on, hated Jack Kearns and he said to me: 'Dempsey is a phony. I know this is supposed to be a three-round exhibition, but you go right out in the first round and hit him on the chin as hard as you can. You'll knock him out and that will fix this bum who thinks he is going to be heavyweight champion of the world some day.' So I went right out in the first round and hit Dempsey on the chin. Then he hit me on the chin with a left hook and everything got dark all of a sudden. When my eyes cleared, Dempsey was holding me upright by both elbows and he said: 'Listen, kid. Don't try that again or I'll knock your brains out.'

"So," Eddie said, "we boxed the next two rounds nice and easy."

"All right," Frankie Graham said, "don't take Rickard's $20,000. It's easy enough for me to say that because, right now, I would fight Dempsey for $20,000, and I can't lick you, even. Know what I mean?"

"Yes," Eddie said. "That's why I asked you in the first place, Frankie. I just wanted to hear you say what I've been thinking."

Three world champions got together for this picture. Left to right, Jack Kelly, Philadelphia's Olympic sculling champion (Princess Grace's father); turf champion Man o' War; and heavyweight champion Jack Dempsey.

In 1921, Paul Gallico, the prize-winning author, saved his job at the *New York Daily News* by putting on the gloves with Dempsey. He was fresh out of Columbia and was working as the paper's motion-picture critic. He lasted exactly 4 months and 29 days on the job. On the 30th day he was removed from the chair by Joseph Medill Patterson, founder of the fledgling tabloid, because his reviews were too smart-alecky. He was not fired from the *News;* this was not the custom of the publisher. Captain Patterson merely, in a fit of exasperation, told his managing editor, Phil Payne, to get "that man" out of the movie department. Payne hid young Gallico in the sports department as an anonymous and un-bylined sports reporter, odd-jobs and rewrite man.

"And here I give you a first-class lesson in how to begin a literary career from the prone or horizontal position," Gallico said. "Assigned to write some 'color' from the Dempsey training camp at Uncle Tom Luther's at Saratoga, myself a heavyweight still in good condition after four years as a galley slave on the Columbia varsity crew but with no experience of boxing, I asked Dempsey if he would let me into the ring with him in order that I might find out first-hand what it was like. As I have indicated, the results were drastic, since I was unknown and for all Dempsey and his camp knew might be a ringer sent to injure him or make him look bad. But at any rate, after one minute and 27 seconds I was flat on my back with a cut lip and a prize headache. But I also had a story. In an old-fashioned narrative one might say that in this manner my fortune was made. Certainly it was the beginning. There were other elements, but the fact was that the left hook Dempsey whistled to my unprotected chin changed the frown on the face of Captain Patterson to a smile. For the next eight years I applied myself to my new job as sports editor and columnist of the *Daily News.* I owed it all to Dempsey and a smack on the jaw."

In some ways, Dempsey's most demanding fight was the Tommy Gibbons title match at Shelby, Montana, on July 4, 1923. Granny Rice told how it came about.

"Mike Collins, a fight manager of sorts out of St. Paul, had a string of fighters barnstorming through Montana that year, working any town where there were a few bucks to be made," recalled Granny. "Collins met Loy Molumby, head of Montana's American Legion, and in a short time they were cruising all over the state in a flimsy old airplane, shooting off horse pistols and calling for wine. In the course of their wanderings they ran into a man named Johnson, who, among other things, was mayor of Shelby and president of the local bank. With the talk flaring around fights and fighters, somebody had the glorious idea of staging a heavyweight championship fight right there in Shelby! It would cause a land boom, make it a city overnight. Collins called his pal, Eddie Kane, Gibbons' manager back in St. Paul, and put the proposition to him.

"Kane replied, 'Listen, Mike. You get Dempsey out there and Gibbons will fight him for nothing. All you got to do is pay Dempsey. What do you think of that?'

"That, they liked. Next they wired Jack Kearns, offering him $300,000 to defend the title against Gibbons at Shelby on July 4th. Kearns wired back: 'Send $100,000 now...$100,000 in a month, and $100,000 before Dempsey steps into the ring and it's a deal.'

"The first hundred grand came easily enough and seeing they meant business Kearns and Dempsey headed West and set up training quarters at Great Falls, Montana, about 70 miles south of Shelby. Eddie Kane went direct to Shelby and set up Gibbons' training camp there."

Late in June, Granny boarded a Pullman in Chicago with a crowd of other writers and they were off by way of the Great Northern to the Wild West. Great Falls, they discovered, was a fair-sized town. Granny found Dempsey in high humor.

"I recall it was June 24th, his 28th birthday," Granny said. "His dad was there and so was his cousin, Don Chafin, a raw-boned kid from West Virginia. The camp mascot was a cub timber wolf. Dempsey was giving himself daily facials with some sort of bear grease that had toughened his face to the general texture of a boar's hide. It was Jack's first title defense since he fought Carpentier, in 1921, but he looked to be in great shape. Even walking, he seemed to slither along, snakelike, his muscles glinting in the sun."

Granny said he didn't know just what he expected from Shelby, the fight site, but he wasn't impressed. A town of perhaps 2,000, it was little more than a crossroad in the middle of a desert. There were few houses and a building or two that passed for hotels. The Pullman cars shoved over on a siding served as press headquarters and living accommodations.

Gibbons, meanwhile, was training hard. He was eager to get this crack at Dempsey. Most of the visiting sports writers felt he was heading for certain annihilation. Tommy's wife and two children were with him.

Granny recollected: "Shortly before the fight, Hughey Fullerton spotted a Blackfoot brave in war regalia, including paints and eagle feathers. In broken Indian dialect, Hughey asked him, 'Who Big Chief like? Dempsey or Gibbons?' Big Chief replied, in perfect English: 'Sir, I happen to like Dempsey. Gibbons has the skill as a boxer. Dempsey has the power. Power usually prevails over skill.' "

As the fight drew nearer, the city fathers of Shelby began to feel the pinch. They were having a hard time scraping up that second $100,000, with still a third installment to come. Kearns was adamant.

"You've got to pay us every cent, or you won't see Dempsey at all!" he warned. Mayor Johnson all but hocked his bank to come up with the second payment. Four days before the bell rang, Kearns' vacillations about the purse forced special trainloads from San Francisco and Chicago to cancel.

The eve of the fight was the most harrowing in Shelby's history. In the span of six hours Kearns "officially" called off the fight seven times. Visiting scribes were going nuts trying to keep up-to-the-minute.

At the last hour, Kearns again reversed his decision, decided to gamble on the gate receipts and declared the fight was on. Shelby's main street erupted into a madhouse. Everybody celebrated. Against a background of blaring bands, a snake dance down the center of town lasted clear through the night. Prohibition was supposed to be the order of the times, but that night in Shelby, Montana, everybody packed a bottle.

"And looking down on it all from his little family shack on a bare hill sat Tom Gibbons," Granny said. "I thought about him, a family man 34 years old, who was about to face Dempsey, the Killer, and for nary a thin dime! The fight was scaled at $50 ringside and the huge wooden bowl built for the match was erected to hold some 50,000 people. But the final paid ticket count was a trickle over 7,000 and so they opened up the gates and let in another 13,000 free! The fight was a financial bust. It broke all the banks in town."

July 4, 1923: The fight that busted a town. The Dempsey-Gibbons match was a financial fiasco for Shelby, Montana. Only a few more than 7,000 of this crowd of 21,000 actually paid; promoters had counted on paid attendance of 50,000. Somewhere in this photo is Dr. Charles P. Larson, then a teenager from Spokane, Washington, who sneaked into the arena. Dr. Larson grew up to become an internationally famous pathologist and President of both the NBA and WBA.

Dempsey and Gibbons went 15 rounds like two featherweights. It was the only one of Jack's championship battles to last the distance. Gibbons was well versed in the clever stuff.

"I've never witnessed as much sheer speed in a heavyweight bout," Granny said later. "At the finish, the decision was clearly Dempsey's, but Tommy, a wildcat that steaming afternoon, remained dangerous all the way. Dempsey couldn't nail him as Gibbons fought the fight of his life—for nothing."

Gibbons testified as to the power in Dempsey's punches.

"Lord," he said, "how that fellow can hit! In the first round I saw a right hand coming. It was too late to do anything else about it, so I dropped my head and took it on the forehead. I didn't know where I was for four rounds. It was a week before I could put on my hat because of the bumps Dempsey raised on my head. Don't let anybody ever tell you Dempsey can't box. He knows all the tricks."

Dempsey was at the peak of his career. Sports writers figured that he was earning $2,700 for every day of the year. He loved the good life. He paid $16,000 for a custom-made gas-buggy and drove it at 80 miles per hour until the radiator exploded. But there was lots more where that came from. He was well on his way to earning some $3,568,114 in the ring.

In the mid-Twenties, there was talk of matching Dempsey with Harry Wills, the hard-punching black star. Gene Tunney was another possibility. Dempsey was looking for another big payday. If he had a preference, Jack said he would take Tunney.

"He has a better chance of licking me than Wills," Dempsey said. And then he made this most prophetic observation: "In fact, I expect to see the next champion a young fellow like Tunney..."

Boxing writers were calling Tunney the "Greenwich Village Folly" and predicting that Dempsey would certainly maim, and might possibly kill, him. After the match was finally signed—for Philadelphia, September 23, 1926—the ballyhoo was on. If ever there was a "natural" fight, this was it. No promoter could have asked for anything more. The boxer *vs.* the slugger. Gentleman *vs.* roughneck. Ex-Marine *vs.* slacker. All the ingredients were there.

The smart money was on Dempsey. Out in the Far West, however, there was a brash young boxing writer named Harry Grayson who met Tunney in Los Angeles several months before the fight and asked him lightly what chance he thought he had against the champion. Tunney said he thought he could win.

"Win!" sneered Grayson. "With what?" It is not known how much Tunney knew about Grayson, a Marine lieutenant in World War I, but his answer was perfect. "With the spirit of the Marine Corps," he said.

Actually, the two factors which weighed most heavily in Grayson's eventual decision to pick Tunney in newsprint were his knowledge of Dempsey's poor condition and his astute realization that there would

Dempsey and Tom Gibbons went 15 rounds like two featherweights. It was the only one of Jack's title bouts to last the distance. Ringside seats sold for $50.

be no prestige for a young writer who picked the favored Dempsey. When Grayson arrived in Philadelphia to cover the fight, he made up his mind and filed his final prefight story:

Philadelphia, September 23, 1926: Boxer vs. *slugger. Gentleman* vs. *roughneck. Ex-Marine* vs. *"slacker." If ever there was a natural fight, Dempsey vs. Tunney was it. Gene won on points in 10 rounds in one of the biggest upsets of all time. Harry Grayson and Harry Keck were the only two sports writers of record to predict his victory.*

"Tunney will win every minute of the ten rounds," he wrote in the *San Francisco Bulletin.* "He may knock out Dempsey in the first. Dempsey's true condition is shockingly bad."

When the other metropolitan writers got word of Harry's prediction, they began to ask about this Grayson who was picking Tunney. "Seen Tunney?" one veteran writer asked him. "I don't have to see him," snapped Grayson. "I've seen Dempsey."

The *Bulletin*, not without misgivings, printed Harry's daily pieces, most of them long and effusive descriptions of the Tunney camp. The challenger, irked by the short shrift the press was according him, welcomed Grayson and spoke freely to him.

When Tunney defeated the champion in a startling upset, only two writers had correctly guessed the outcome—Grayson and Harry Keck of Pittsburgh. The *Bulletin* welcomed Grayson back to California with full-page ads and not a little fanfare.

About 120,757 people sat through a cloudburst that lasted 40 minutes in Philadelphia to see Tunney outbox Dempsey. They had paid $1,895,733 to witness the spectacle, and not one of them left the great Sesquicentennial arena as the skies opened just as the two men were lacing on their stuffed mittens. The two men fought a slow, careful fight, the rain fell in blinding sheets, there were no knockdowns. The crowd sat through the drenching, spellbound merely by the sight of the blond boxer holding the man-killer helpless, and finally in contempt. Clothing was ruined, health injured, but the boxing fever was in everyone's blood. No one cared to, or had sense enough to, come in out of the rain.

Many years later, Tunney made a confession.

"Little chance was given me against Dempsey," he said. "The odds were 4 or 5 to 1 against me. The best I could hope for was to avoid getting knocked out in a few rounds, or so they said. My obvious way of fighting Dempsey was to use boxing craft. Everyone advised me to stay away from him and box him.

"I pretended to accept that advice, and never gave the slightest hint of what I was up to, constantly practicing a straight right. Not in public training bouts. In these I put on exhibitions of sparring and footwork. But secretly, with the heavy and fast punching bags, I practiced a straight right, developing the knack of putting all I had into one shot. On the road, jogging along, I'd stop for a bit of shadowboxing, imagining Dempsey in front of me, rushing me, and then I'd lash out, nailing him in imagination with a straight right. But I never let on.

"That was part of what turned out to be a very peculiar psychological mix-up. I took a plane from my camp in Stroudsburg (Pennsylvania) to the fight because I didn't want the long automobile trip on slippery roads; it had been raining. I was cocky about flying, having been up once before—for a few minutes on a bright day in France. I was too cocky. I got airsick. It was a dim, dismal day, with rain threatening, ceiling not much more than zero. The great old pilot, Casey Jones, who flew me, lost his way in the clouds. It was one of the worst airplane rides anyone ever had, and I almost passed out airsick. When I got to Philadelphia, I was shaking and pale, green. And I had to go at once to weigh in. Boxing Commissioner Weiner saw how I looked—shaking, pale, green—and he drew his own conclusion. He told a group of friends that I was scared to death, quaking in my shoes.

"The illusion created by my airsickness put the finishing touch to the psychological background. The Dempsey camp believed more than ever that the champ needed only to go in for a quick kill. That Dempsey would rush me headlong became the surest of sure things. When the bell rang, he came charging. I fended him off and backed away, giving him still more impression that I was strictly on the defensive. He made a second rush, and I repeated the maneuver of elude and clinch to confirm the belief that it was a hoofing match. Then, when he rushed a third time, I waited for the inevitable opening, the wide left hook that he was throwing at me.

"I stepped in with the straight right I had so long been practicing for just that moment. I had learned to throw it with every ounce of power I had, and it landed. But it landed high. It landed, not on Dempsey's jaw but on his cheek. He fought with his head down and his chin on his chest, and the tendency was to hit him high.

"Dempsey was stopped in his tracks and his knees sagged. I could see he was hurt. Perhaps if the punch had landed on Jack's jaw, I might have knocked him out. As it was, that blow won the fight. Dempsey was dazed for the rest of the battle, and it was a certainty to outpoint him for the championship."

Just how thoroughly Tunney trounced Dempsey in their first fight was told by correspondent Jim Dawson, of the *New York Times*. Excerpts from the story he filed follow:

> Through every round of the 10, Tunney battered and pounded Dempsey. He rained rights on the tottering champion's jaw and he bewildered Dempsey with his speed and the accuracy of a whiplike left hand which Dempsey could not evade.
>
> The transfer of the title surprised the majority of those who witnessed the fight. It surprised almost everybody but Tunney. He was complete master, from first bell to last. He outboxed and he outfought Dempsey at every turn. Where it had been expected that Tunney would break and run before the vicious attack of Dempsey, the tiger man, Tunney, the fighting marine, not only failed to back up but he went forward all the time with the instinct of the true leatherneck and hammered Dempsey in a driving attack which brooked no restraining effort on the part of the champion.
>
> There was no question of the victor at the finish. There was no question even of the winner of each round as the battle progressed, and Dempsey, instead of flashing the fighting fury which was expected of him, instead of surging forward with tigerish, vicious rushes, proved himself instead a floundering, weakened, almost helpless fighting machine from which the spark had gone.
>
> All the evidence of the old Dempsey was merely thin; there were only faint flashes in a performance of futility, of helpless hopelessness, of utter ineffectiveness. At the finish Dempsey was a sorry, pitiful sight as he slumped in his corner. His mouth and nose spouted blood, his left eye, bruised and battered, was closed tight and bleeding. There was a cut under his left eye about an inch long. And he was all in, absolutely at the end of his tether.

Tunney's convincing victory over Dempsey marked the first time in history that the heavyweight championship of the world exchanged hands on a decision.

The late Joe Williams remembered being in Dempsey's hotel room the day after the fight when actress Estelle Taylor, then his wife, rushed dramatically in and asked:

"What happened, Ginsberg?"

And Dempsey, a beaten idol, both eyes closed, sitting alone in a room with all shades drawn, answered through split lips:

"I just forgot to duck, honey."

Williams said later, "You may have read several versions of this incident but this is a factual word-for-word account. I led Estelle to the darkened room in the suite where the humbled ex-champion sat. I had been helping Jerry the Greek, the trainer, relay hot towels from the bathroom. Dempsey was using them to reduce the swelling of his face and draw out the pain. 'Ginsberg' was Estelle's affectionate nickname for Dempsey. In a mad rush of vanity some months before, he had gone Hollywood and had his nose lifted."

In his prime, Jack Dempsey was one of the most savagely destructive punchers that boxing has ever seen. W. C. Heinz, boxing writer for the old *New York Sun*, once asked Dempsey what it was that a fighter lost first when he started downhill.

"Ambition," Dempsey said, honestly. "I'd say the average fighter loses his ambition."

"Before he starts to come apart physically?" Bill asked.

"The first thing you lose is courage and ambition to fight. You do that, you lose your speed, your timing, everything. Of course, the first thing that goes bad with a fighter physically is his legs. You get hit and you can't take a punch, and you don't know what happened."

Dempsey was not the old fighting machine when he fought Tunney for the first time; luxurious living and three years of idleness had done their work.

One year and one day later, they battled again. This time the match was held in Chicago. It drew 104,943 people who paid $2,658,660. Tunney's share was $990,000, while Dempsey got $447,500.

When Tunney was sounded out as to how confident he was of beating Dempsey again, Gene remarked in no uncertain terms: "A lot of people think the fight in Philadelphia was a fake. I want to prove to these persons it was not a fake and that I was then and am now Dempsey's master in the ring. I'd rather beat Dempsey than have all the money in the world. I have told all my friends to bet on me, and I am going to win for them, for my family and for myself. And you'd better have a good bet on me, too."

That was Tunney, all right.

Although Dempsey was better in the second fight, the bout was almost a repetition of the first fight for 6½ rounds. Then with a suddenness that blew everybody right out of their seats, the dramatic blow was struck. For a brief, tantalizing moment, fate rode in Dempsey's gloves once more. He landed a man-killing left hook to Tunney's jaw. As Gene's legs crumpled, Dempsey tore into him with both hands, battering the champion with lefts and rights as he sank to the floor. Just

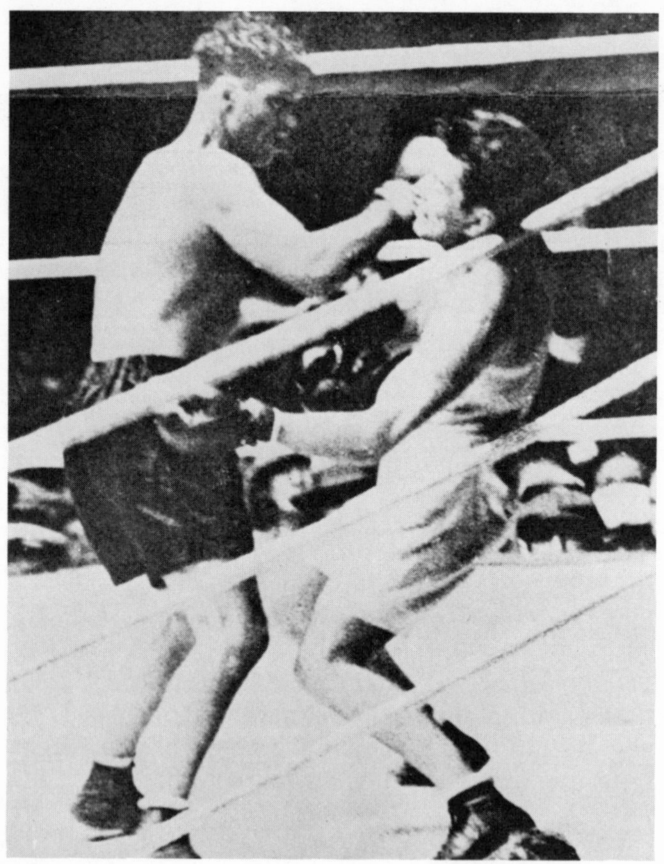

In the seventh round of the Battle of the Long Count, in Chicago, September 22, 1927, fate rode in Dempsey's gloves once more as he battered Tunney to floor with lefts and rights. Here Gene is sinking to the canvas.

how many times Dempsey hit Tunney on the way down is a moot point. They still argue about it, as they argue about almost everything else connected with this particular fight.

Both Tunney and Dempsey gave their versions of what happened. First, Tunney:

"Everybody saw Dempsey land that left hook to my jaw, but they never knew how much it surprised me. I never saw the punch. Not seeing it coming really injured my pride—I was always cocksure about my eyesight in the ring. The blow was the second in that series of seven that put me on the canvas for the first time in my life. I remember clearly Jack crossing a vicious right over my left lead for the first of the series. I scolded myself for being hit by such an obvious blow. What I actually said to myself was: 'Tunney, what a sucker you are to be nailed by that.' The next cerebration was that I'd been hit a fearful wallop on the right jaw. I hadn't seen the blow start or in flight, but I certainly felt it. It was the hardest of the seven blows and the one that prepared me for the five others, and incidentally, for a much-discussed but pleasant 14 seconds' rest on the floor.

"My blindness to the melodramatic punch was caused, I conscientiously believe, by a traumatic astigmatism due to a severe eye injury sustained in a training bout several days before the contest. A sparring partner hit me a blow in the eye with his thumb extended. It destroyed several small blood vessels and injured the retina. Those 30 or 40 seconds after the thumb was removed were the most painful seconds of my life. Two prominent eye specialists were rushed out from Chicago to my camp. After the first treatment—treatments continued until the day of the contest—when I began to see a little out of the injured right eye, I had one of the great moments of my life; I was not going to lose the sight. This is not to be construed as an alibi or an attempt to belittle a great fighter like Dempsey.

"I was oblivious of the long-count aspects, which caused so much debate. There has been plenty of myth and confusion about that. I first became aware of the count when I heard the referee say, 'Two.' Eight seconds to go, eight seconds in which to do the most critical thinking in my life. I had never been knocked down before, but had often thought about what I'd do if I were—what to do after getting up. It would be either of two things—clinch to gain a few more seconds, or put everything in a punch as my opponent came charging in for the kill. Which course depended on the type of opponent. But neither alternative would do against Dempsey. Trying to clinch with him, the way he was hitting, I might get knocked out then and there—particularly by a rabbit punch at the base of the skull. Trying to slam him with one desperate punch was not promising either. Jack's way of keeping his chin down on his chest made his jaw a difficult mark to shoot at. In 20 rounds in the ring with him, I don't think I ever hit him once fairly on the jaw—always high, on the cheeks and around the eyes and forehead. So I had to make a complete change of all I had planned, revise the strategy during those eight seconds on the floor.

"I had noted, earlier in the fight, that Dempsey at times would flounder toward me. That confirmation I had—that a new type of footwork had been taught him. I knew that in training, his handlers had put him through special road work to toughen his legs. But what about my own legs? It is no secret that when a boxer is badly hit, the first thing to be affected is his legs. Still, my legs felt all right. I had always based my ring technique on my speed and sureness of foot. And now it seemed to me that the best bet was to match my legs against Dempsey's legs, until I had completely recovered from the effects of the knock-down. That was my decision when, at the count of nine, I got onto one knee and then rose. I circled Dempsey to the right, to keep away from his left hook. My legs were better than his. They kept me out of danger until I was my normal self again, fighting my normal fight, stepping in and hitting. At the end of 10 rounds, I had Jack almost helpless."

Once Tunney was sprawled on the canvas in the seventh round, a controversy was really in the making. Both fighters had been instructed that in event of a knockdown the fighter scoring the knockdown would retire to the farthest neutral corner. Dempsey hovered over Tunney as he had over other fighters he had floored. Referee Dave Barry tugged and hauled at Dempsey for several seconds before he was able to tear him away from the kill and shoo him to the proper corner. Then Barry returned to the recumbent Tunney and started counting, "One...two ...three..." And there is the basis for the endless arguments.

Dempsey hovers over Tunney as referee Dave Barry tugs and hauls at him for several seconds to get him to go to a neutral corner before beginning the controversial count.

Here, Dempsey picks up the controversy:

"Personally, I didn't know nor care how long Gene was down. I was pretty doggoned tired myself. But Paul Beeler, the official timekeeper at the fight, later explained that he was leaning on the edge of the ring holding his counting stopwatch in his left hand. On his table were two more stopwatches, left running to record the time for the starting and stopping of the rounds.

"The round was just 50 seconds old when I started my attack. We were only a few feet from my own corner. Gene was a little careless as the round started and didn't seem to be carrying his hands as high as he should. Suddenly I exploded on his head and chin. Every punch connected. Beeler said he was on his feet immediately, ready to start the count when Gene went down. He said he started the watch and began tolling off the count the instant Tunney's hips touched the floor. As he reached the count of five, he said, he couldn't hear the referee's voice counting with him, and he glanced up to see what the trouble was. Here are his exact words:

" 'Two things flashed into my vision. Barry was facing me, swinging his right hand and yelling, *One.* I had a second in which to decide whether to go along with Barry's count or continue my own original count that started when Tunney was floored. I went along with Barry. He was in charge. When Barry had reached the count of *Nine* Tunney got to his feet and did a great job of back-pedaling for the rest of the round. I sat down and took a look at my counting watch, which I had started the instant Tunney hit the canvas, and stopped the instant he got off the floor. The watch read *seventeen* seconds! Tunney certainly had sufficient time to take a good rest. Why did the watch read seventeen seconds? Well, Referee Barry had inadvertently slowed down the cadence of the count from my five to his nine. Why the 14 count then? It was due to the sportswriters adding my five and Barry's nine. It is most difficult to count seconds accurately without using a stopwatch, the general tendency being to count them slower than they actually are, and that's what Barry did.' "

After their first fight in Philadelphia, Dempsey said he would have to try something different in Chicago.

"I knew Tunney would expect me to come barging wildly at him in an attempt to knock his block off with a flurry of wallops," Dempsey said. "I made up my mind I'd do just the opposite. I hit on the plan of starting one kind of attack and then shifting quickly. I knew Gene was an exceptionally good boxer, and that he did a lot of studying and planning in the ring. I also knew that these 'thinkers' frequently make the mistake of forgetting to figure that the other fellow might do a little thinking and planning himself.

"When I got into that ring, I had decided to box with Tunney, and to keep my attack aimed almost entirely for his body. I figured that after a few rounds of this Gene would reason that I hoped to wear him down, and that I would probably not cut loose until the ninth or tenth rounds. He would also think I was conserving my strength for a last-round rally.

"He was about right, except that I decided to make my bid in the seventh round. I figured that by then, if I started that round like all the rest and suddenly switched to an intense attack after about a minute, I would catch him unaware and get over the haymaker that would end the fight with a knockout.

"And that's the way I fought. When the bell started us on the seventh round, I went out with the old 'do-or-die' idea in mind. After nearly a minute of the routine body attack, I suddenly straightened and let go that right to the jaw. It landed, just as I planned and hoped, and it sure was a beaut. I had put plenty of 'hop' on it, and it staggered Gene back on his heels.

"Just how badly he was hurt, only Gene knows. At any rate, I tore into him and, forcing him to the ropes, I let loose that left hook he didn't see. Even if he had *three* good eyes, he couldn't have done anything about that particular clout, because he was in a position on the ropes where he couldn't very well do anything.

"I saw I had him. Then I let loose with everything I had and poured leather into him until he sank like an empty meal sack to the floor of the ring. I knew he was 'out.' And I was nearly so myself. But I felt that I'd finished the job, and, with everything all over, I let down and relaxed. I felt that, so far as I was concerned, I had carried out my plan exactly as I had mapped it. But I was wrong. Tunney got back up, recovered, and my luck ran out.

"Maybe I was the lucky one after all. I am perfectly willing, and have always been willing, to accept the official decision in the so-called Battle of the Long Count. I do know this. If there actually was a long count, it was a good thing for me. I know now that one more fight with Tunney might have caused me to go blind. I had absorbed a terrible beating around the eyes in both my fights with him. Had I been awarded the second fight with him on a knockout, I would have had to give him a return match—and I might not have been able to see today."

The things one remembers about that historic fight of long ago. When Dempsey had Tunney on the deck Paul Gallico was there at ringside. As Sports Editor of the *New York Daily News* he was writing it all down. He remembers the dazed expression that came into Tunney's face as Dempsey slugged him with both hands over on the ropes to the right of where Gallico was sitting and the glazing film that clouded Gene's eyes as he sank slowly to the ring floor, one leg crumpled beneath him.

"How could I forget it?" Gallico said. "We were trying something new that year, something that had never been tried before at a big prize fight—direct telephonic connection between the working-press section at ringside and the composing room of a great metropolitan tabloid newspaper.

"Of course," Gallico continued, "today you would use short-wave radio, or you could set up a television peer box right next to the linotype machine, with an assistant sports editor standing by to check it and give the word 'go' when the knockout seemed official. But in those dark, benighted and backward days there wasn't any television and radio was just a baby.

"We had broadcasting, all right, but it was kind of fuzzy and you couldn't rely on the darned thing, or the guy who was doing it, either, when it was a question of an important thing like a prize fight. When it came to getting the flash, you wanted to have your own sports editor at the other end of the wire. Nothing was quite so important to us as getting out on the street with the blow-by-blow detail and the flash on the winner before any other paper. Not only minutes but literally seconds counted.

"Up to that time, it was the custom to have a Western Union operator set up his instrument at ringside, with the other end in the newspaper office. The fight expert would dictate his punch-by-punch account of each round. The operator would tickety-tick it off on his bug. Another telegrapher would be sitting at his typewriter in the newspaper office, taking it off the receiving instrument. This copy would eventually find its way to the composing room.

"And so, for the Big Fight, we leased a telephone wire from ringside to composing room. Cost a pretty penny, too. In the working-press section, nose to canvas, wearing a chest set and earphones, was our eager hero, me. Glued to the receiving earphones in our composing room, prepared to take it down on the typewriter and whip it to the linotype operator sitting next to him was Nick Kenny, who was later to make such a name for himself as a song writer and columnist. Can't think for the life of me why it should have been Nick, since he didn't work in my sports department. But it was.

"When Tunney performed that slow el foldo to the floor in the seventh, I screamed into my telephone mouthpiece in a voice that had gone considerably falsetto from excitement: 'Tunney is down from a series of lefts and rights to the head, for a count of...'

"Whereupon Kenny shouted back, 'What?'

"Up to that moment the connection had been good. But when the excitement started, every telephone operator along the line opened her key to listen to the doings. Click, click, click, click. You could hear them cutting in—South Bend, Toledo, Sandusky, Cleveland, Buffalo, Rochester, Syracuse, Utica, Schenectady, Albany, Harmon and 125th Street, New York. That sweet ol' private line became filled with buzzes, ticks, pops, and the roar of that great crowd.

"I hollered into my mouthpiece: 'I said Tunney is down from a series of lefts and rights to the head. D'ya get it?'

Tunney rises at nine as Dempsey comes at him to finish the kill. But Tunney's legs were better than Jack's and he managed to weather the storm and go on to win another decision.

"Nick said, 'Who did you say was down? Dempsey?'

"I screamed, 'Get the wax out of your ears, you dumb turkey. Tunney is down. Can you hear me? Tunney, Tunney, Tunney!'

"Nick said, 'Get the mush out of your mouth. I can't hear you. Who did you say fell down?' "

When the round was over, someone tapped Gallico on the shoulder and he turned. There was a little man sitting there. He had graying hair, a gnarled ear and a seamy face. He was holding one of those large, split-second stop watches with a dial like Big Ben and looking at it with bewilderment. He said, "Hey, whadd'ya know about this? There's somethin' funny here. I hit it when he went down and stopped it when he got up."

The hand showed that 14.5 seconds had elapsed. The little man and Gallico stared at the stop watch. "It kind of hypnotized us," Gallico said, "because, as we both very well knew, if a stricken fighter isn't on his feet inside of 10 seconds he is presumed to be out, napoo, finished for the evening. I asked the little man who he was. He told me his name was Battling Nelson."

The notion for the big return match which was to draw the world-record gate was, of course, fermenting in Tex Rickard's mind a year earlier, right after Tunney battered the left side of Dempsey's face into a jelly and took his title away from him. But first there was the little matter of a Lithuanian sailor to be disposed of and the collection of another million-dollar gate in the process. Jack Sharkey of Boston had soundly whipped Dempsey's nemesis, Harry Wills, the year before and had knocked out or beaten every prominent heavyweight, including George Godfrey. A Dempsey-Sharkey match as a build-up for the second Dempsey-Tunney fight was a natural.

So the Battle of the Long Count wasn't officially on until that moment on the hot night of July 21 when sailor Sharkey, in the seventh round of an altercation he appeared to be winning on points, turned his countenance away from Dempsey to protest to the referee that more than a few of Dempsey's shots were dropping below the Taylor-Foulproof line.

The beautiful side view of the sailor's kisser, all nude, unguarded and inviting, was more than Dempsey could resist. He whipped over the old right hook, there was a *plock* followed by the usual thud and Sharkey entered dreamland. The referee counted from one to ten, and Tex Rickard had himself the biggest prize fight, from the point of view of the gate, ever held anywhere, anytime.

Warmth had not yet begun to return to the chilled body of Jack Sharkey when Dempsey began telling how he knocked him out.

"I had Leo P. Flynn in my corner," he said, "and he was a smart fella. He told me that Sharkey didn't take it too good to the body, so I kept hitting him there to bring his hands down. He knocked the hell out of me in the early rounds, but in the seventh I hit him on the belt line and he turned and complained to the referee. What was I supposed to do? Write him a letter? I hit him and knocked him out. He said I hit him low, and I said, 'The referee didn't think so, and he's the boss.' "

Which was how Dempsey, and not Sharkey, got the big fight with Tunney in Chicago.

Dempsey was in five fights that passed the million-dollar figure: his two bouts with Tunney, the second of which drew $2,658,660, and his matches with Carpentier (1921) and Firpo (1923) and Sharkey (1927).

Following the Battle of the Long Count, Dempsey went into semiretirement. Most of his prize fighting was limited to exhibition bouts. In 1936, he found himself up in New England, involved in politics and campaigning for the Democratic Party. The Presidential electioneering was heating up to fever pitch and Dempsey and a handful of professional wrestlers volunteered to get out and warm up some of the doubtful Democratic districts. Dempsey was the referee and after each grunt-and-groan show one of the members of the barnstorming party, sometimes Jack himself, would stand up and say some nice words in behalf of Mr. Roosevelt.

"We were probably the only political troupe ever to give the rassling buffs anything but an earache," Dempsey said.

One night they appeared in Rochester, which turned out to be an exceptionally high-class town. The literary rate was so high there that the city would have nothing to do with the rasslers. Ned Brown, who was working as Dempsey's publicity man, wandered around town a day in advance and found out that the natives were so dead-set against the shin-bending business that whenever a parent caught a kid tussling with another in a friendly spat on the lawn, he would whale the tar out of the youngster for using a half-Nelson instead of a left hook. This made Mr. Brown realize that if they put on their wrestling exhibition, they were liable to create a lot of Republicans, just out of protest.

So Ned did some thinking. Why not Dempsey? Ned went to the old champ and asked him if he would spar a few rounds in a friendly little exhibition.

"Sure, why not?" Jack said.

Ned found a guy who wanted to fight Dempsey, a fellow named Mike Conroy, a fine old ex-pug who was operating a pub. The pub wasn't doing much business and, anyway, Mike wanted a chance to fight the great Dempsey.

Two hours before the fight, Ned happened to stroll through Conroy's pub, and during the trip he picked up one of those muddlers, the little clubs used to grind up lump sugar in an "old fashioned." He was very glad he did. He was also very pleased that the only seat in the auditorium that night was located right next to the bell at ringside. Ned sat back to enjoy the fight, though it was a little disturbing to see Conroy dressed in full ring attire: tights, teeth-guard, seconds, everything. Dempsey had peeled down only to his slacks, T-shirt, and street shoes.

The gong rang and the action glided along nice as you please for the first two minutes, with the old champ boxing the way he did against Gibbons. Ned didn't see Conroy cranking up his Sunday punch. Neither did Dempsey—Jack must have been practicing his speech on what they'd do for the farmers. WHAM! Conroy spotted an opening and let one fly that would have beheaded a brass antelope. It hit Dempsey right over the heart. They said afterward that Jack's face went deathly white, but Ned didn't see that. He was too busy whacking the bell with his muddler. He made it sound like the anvil chorus. Conroy danced back to his corner. Dempsey tottered weakly back to his.

The timekeeper was sore. It seems that Mr. Brown did not have a timekeeper's license in the City of Rochester, or whatever was needed to beat those bells. It could have gotten much more personal had Ned not been waving the muddler dangerously in his duke. The timekeeper gave the bell the business again to start the second round. It was still only an exhibition for Dempsey, and he sparred around nice and proper, when Conroy saw another opening and shook Jack's bridgework again. That did it! Dempsey dropped his sparring pose like it was hot and tore after Conroy with the same weaving motion he used to scare opponents to death with. He clipped Conroy with a short left hook and split his nose from the bridge to the upper lip. Down went Conroy like a thatch hut in a hurricane.

Mr. Brown belted the bell again, when the referee got the count to eight. He wanted to see another round. They got Conroy out for the next round somehow, but two more jolts to the head finished him. He was in the hospital for two days, and he should have stayed longer, but he took off the bandages and hustled back to his pub.

You never saw a guy prouder of a busted beezer. People...customers...came from miles around to see the beautiful damage inflicted on him by the great Jack Dempsey, the old Manassa Mauler's last fight. It boosted Conroy's business plenty, and when Dempsey returned to New York, after making the world safe for Democracy, a letter was waiting for him.

> Hello, pal, old pal.
>
> Well, pal, just a line to let you know what a pal you were to beat me up, old pal. Pal, they have come into my place in droves since the night you belted me out, pal. The docs said I better put some bandages on those cuts, pal, to keep out infection. But not me, pal. I don't want those things to heal too soon, pal. It would be bad for business.
>
> Your old pal,
> Mike.

The late Max Waxman, who for many years was Dempsey's business partner, once told Bill Heinz about the last man Dempsey knocked out. He said that Jack never wanted to talk about it, but that it happened in World War II while Dempsey, nearly fifty, was on a transport in the Pacific.

It came about when Dempsey was refereeing a boxing program. He ruled a bout a draw, and one of the boxers got mad and challenged Dempsey to put on the gloves.

"I had no business fighting the man," Jack said, "because I was an officer and he was an enlisted man, but the boys started hollering, 'Come on! Come on! Take him on!' So I lost my head, which I never should have done. He was an ex-fighter, this boy—big, but not too much of a fighter. I had no right to do it. The first round went pretty good, and then the second round—I was in pretty good shape—he ran at me with his hands down, and I happened to get lucky and hit him a left hook and it was all over."

Outside the ring, Jack Dempsey always has had the reputation of being one of the gentlest men you would want to know. Granny Rice once wrote: "I've seen him in his Broadway restaurant at times when some customer, with more enthusiasm than good sense, would grab his vest or part of his shirt–strictly for a souvenir–with no kickback from Jack. I've known the man closely for more than 30 years and I've never seen him in a rough argument or as anything except courteous and considerate."

Inside the ring–well, that was something else again.

9. Gene Tunney

JACK DEMPSEY was on the spot. He had just been asked to crawl out on a limb and name the greatest fighter he had ever seen. The old champion hedged. He refused to be pinned down.

"Benny Leonard was a great fighter," he said. "Mickey Walker was a great fighter. Harry Greb was a great fighter. Gene Tunney was a good fighter."

He paused and smiled. "Of course," he said, "you have to bring Tunney in, because he beat me twice, but he was a good fighter. He was better than the public thought he was. At that time I was more or less of an idol, and Tunney licked me. He licked me good. He got no credit, but Tunney was a good fighter."

The old Manassa Mauler's hesitancy in labeling Gene Tunney a *great* fighter was understandable, for Tunney never entered the prize ring with the natural, instinctive fighting equipment of a Jeffries, a Johnson—or a Dempsey. He wasn't a natural-born puncher, his physique was not adapted to fighting, and although he did possess superb reflexes, they had to be adjusted to boxing. Through sheer will power and mental exertion, Gene converted ordinary equipment into one of the finest fighting machines the ring has ever known.

For this achievement alone—this dramatic example of the triumph of mind over matter—he deserves to be classified as *great*. Two oldtime experts, Dan Morgan and Billy Roche, both told me they rated Tunney as the sixth greatest heavyweight in history. They ranked Jeffries first, followed by Sullivan, Johnson, Fitzsimmons and Corbett. Dempsey was seventh.

Many people are under the delusion that Tunney fought very little before he knocked the crown off Dempsey's head. Actually, he had 65 bouts before he won the title. He was no glamor boy. He came up and learned the hard way.

Through sheer will power and mental exertion, Gene Tunney converted ordinary physical equipment into one of the finest fighting machines the ring has ever known.

Tunney said, "The impression always has been that I was basically a defensive fighter, the very reverse of a killer. The papers usually pictured me as the prize fighter who read books—even Shakespeare. The truth is that I started my ring career as a pretty good hitter, then my hands cracked up and I had to resort to boxing and strategy to win. To break a hand in the first or second round and get a decision at the end of 10 or 15 rounds requires and develops resourcefulness. So I was forced to become a boxer, relying on skill and speed. I could normally hit hard enough, as anyone who studied my fights might have known, but it was science and tricks that got the job done.

"I did six years of planning to beat Dempsey. I got my cue from a punch that proved futile—a blow that failed. I watched the Dempsey-Carpentier battle, when Jack was at his most devastating. I noted one thing: When Carpentier hit Dempsey—the only real thrill in the fight, the only hard punch that Carpentier landed—he hit Dempsey with a straight right. The Frenchman had a good punch, but was no dealer of paralyzing destruction. He hit Dempsey too high—on the cheekbone instead of the jaw. Yet Dempsey went back on his heels, and for an extended moment was dazed. I said to myself that he had his weakness, that Dempsey could be hit by a straight right and hurt. This was confirmed by what I saw in subsequent Dempsey battles—when the clumsy Firpo battered the champion with a right.

"The next pertinent factor was Dempsey's ring mentality. If you were to ask me, 'Who is the most intelligent fighter you have ever known?' I should reply: 'Jack Dempsey *out* of the ring.' In the business life, Jack always has handled himself with an amount of nimble wit and deftness that sometimes makes me envious. I have often thought, if circumstances had not made Jack a prize fighter, he might well have become a clever and able politician. But in the ring Jack was an instinctive fighter. I doubt if he ever planned anything in the ring, or thought about it much. But what a fighting instinct he had—the intuitive craft of doing the right thing subconsciously. I knew he could be hit with a straight right, but I might get killed while trying it. My best chance, I reckoned, was surprise. Get the champion to rush me, headlong and careless, and never expect what was coming—an attempt to knock him out with a right-hand smash to the jaw."

Tunney first caught the eye of Grantland Rice when he fought "Soldier" Jones, a tough trial horse in a supporting bout to the Dempsey-Carpentier fight at Jersey City. Tunney, known only as an ex-Marine who had won the light-heavyweight championship of the AEF in France, scored a seven-round knockout. However, he had not fought as a bona fide heavyweight and surely didn't look like one.

After the bout, Granny asked Gene, "What are your plans?"

"My plans are all Dempsey," he replied.

"Very interesting," Granny said. "But why not sharpen your artillery on Harry Greb, Carpentier or Tom Gibbons before you start hollering for Dempsey?"

The "Fighting Marine" gets a lift from fellow Marines as Tunney sets sights on Dempsey's crown.

"I suppose I'll have to beat them on the way up," Tunney said. "But Dempsey is the one I want."

Tunney was twenty-three years old at the time. Granny studied him. He decided this clean-cut, forthright young man would make a fine insurance salesman. Certainly he had no business inside a prize ring with Dempsey. That was in 1921.

Six months later, Tunney won a 12-round decision from Dan Morgan's Battling Levinsky and with it the light-heavyweight championship of the world. Once more Tunney was ready. His footwork was better, he was punching sharper than ever. He went to work smoothly, scientifically on the great Levinsky, lacing him soundly.

Tunney wasted no time cashing in on his new title. Three of his next four opponents were knocked out. His undefeated record was causing talk and Tunney was rewarded–if that is the word–with a match against the colorful Pittsburgh Windmill, Harry Greb.

Greb was a wonder. He stood only 5 ft. 8 in. and weighed 158, but he had the killer instinct of a jungle beast. He was a speed demon who operated from bell to bell like the change box in a five-and-dime. His style of fighting was as unique as the Charleston or the Turkey Trot, and he was a "spray hitter" who hurled more leather from more angles for more hits than possibly any puncher in the history of the ring. As one of Greb's opponents once said the day after he'd been creamed by Harry: "I thought somebody had opened up the ceiling and dumped a carload of boxing gloves on me!" He was appropriately nicknamed the "Human Windmill."

Greb ignored training rules. Between the ring and the dance floor he was too busy to train. He found that a saloon made a dandy gym. "All I need is a shine, shave and shampoo," he explained to those who thought he should train. "I keep in shape fighting." He hit the booze pretty hard. That was a good time to steer clear of him. Sometimes after a few boilermakers he would challenge every man in the house. Then he would start with the biggest guys–the heavyweights–and work right down to the roosters. That's what Harry always liked about a nice cozy saloon; a man could enjoy a quiet drink and beat hell out of his neighbor.

One night while he was speeding to a fight date with a carload of admiring females, Greb was temporarily halted by a "stalled" car and four stick-up men. Harry bailed out and flattened the quartet before racing on to his engagement. The cops picked up the futile foursome, and Greb made it five for the day with a two-round KO.

This was the man Tunney fought five times!

Tunney and Greb met for the first time, on May 23, 1922. It stands in the records as the one and only defeat of Tunney's entire career.

"I believe it was the bloodiest fight I ever covered," Granny Rice told me. "A great fighter–or brawler–Greb handled Tunney like a butcher hammering a Swiss steak. How Gene survived 15 rounds I'll never know–except that he always enjoyed more and better physical conditioning than anybody he ever fought. By the third round, Gene was literally wading in his own blood. I saw him a few days after the fight. His face looked as though he'd taken the wrong end of a razor fight. He told me he'd lost nearly two quarts of blood against Greb. Abe Attell, the old featherweight champion, probably saved Gene from bleeding to death. Abe was sitting near Tunney's corner, just a spectator, and when he saw the shape Gene was in after the second round, he ducked out to the nearest druggist and bought the entire supply of adrenalin chloride. Abe then hustled back and slipped the bottle to Doc Bagley. Between rounds Doc's long fingers flew. He was a superb 'cut' man and managed to stop the bleeding only to watch Greb bust Gene's face apart in the following round. It was discouraging.

"To me," Granny said, "that first fight with Greb convinced me that Tunney meant to stick with prize fighting. I tried to tell him that Greb was too fast for him, to go after a softer touch. The second day after defeat, however, Tunney was down at the boxing commission posting a $2,500 bond for a return match with Greb. Then he went to the country and slept for almost a week. When he got up he spent nearly a year perfecting his plans to whip Greb. He got his title back, too–in fact, they fought four more times and Tunney won them all."

Tunney did not hesitate in naming Harry Greb the dirtiest fighter he ever fought.

"I would say without qualification that of all the fighters I met," he said, in the understatement of the century, "Greb was the least interested in the rules." Then rubbing his classic face, he recalled: "Greb gave me a terrible whipping in the first fight. He broke my nose, maybe with a butt. He cut my eyes and ears, perhaps with his laces. But don't think he didn't hit me, either. My jaw was swollen from the right temple down the cheek, along under the chin and part way up the other side. The referee, the ring itself, was full of blood. It happened to be mine. But it was in that first fight, in which I lost my American light-heavyweight title, that I knew I had found a way to beat Harry eventually. I was fortunate, really. If boxing in those days had been afflicted with the Commission doctors we have today—who are always poking their noses into the ring and examining superficial wounds—the first fight with Greb would have been stopped before I learned how to beat him. It's possible, even probable, that if this had happened I never would have been heard of after that."

After knocking out Carpentier in 15 rounds in 1924 and disposing of Tommy Gibbons in 12 rounds in 1925—along with a string of other tough babies like Jimmy Delaney, Martin Burke, Chuck Wiggins, Tommy Loughran, and Johnny Risko—Tunney was once again hot on Dempsey's trail. He spent the next 10 months preparing only for the champion.

That winter in Florida Gene played a round of golf with Tommy Armour and Granny Rice. Gene would hit his drive, toss aside his club and run down the fairway throwing phantom punches—left and right hooks—and muttering, "Dempsey... Dempsey... Dempsey."

Armour, the old golf champion, looked at Granny and said, "He's obsessed. His brain knows nothing but Dempsey. I believe Jack could hit him with an axe and Gene wouldn't feel it. I don't know if Dempsey has slipped, but I'll have a good chunk down on Tunney when they fight."

Few Americans could imagine Tunney in the same ring with Dempsey, Tommy Armour notwithstanding. Some of the boxing writers called him the "Greenwich Village Folly." But Tunney wasn't afraid of the devil. He had so much confidence that when questioned by writers as to how he felt about the unanimity of opinion against him (not 1 out of every 50 prominent figures from all walks of life picked him to win), he blithely replied: "I wouldn't know what they say. I am content to eschew the newspapers until after the bout is terminated."

Tunney was the most intellectual of fighters. This characteristic amused the camp followers attached to his training quarters. One of Dempsey's trainers, Jerry (The Greek) Luvadis, made reference to the challenger's penchant for polysyllabic language at a prefight press meeting. "Tunney," he told reporters sardonically, "will have an edge over my man on account of them six-syllable words of his. Dempsey is strictly a two-syllable guy."

Golf served to keep Tunney in shape for his fights. He is pictured in Palm Beach here with, left to right, promoter Tex Rickard, cartoonist Rube Goldberg, Grantland Rice, and humorist Ring Lardner.

Harry Grayson had it figured out better than that. He told me he picked Tunney to win because he liked the way Gene was training.

Harry said, "Tunney had every movement figured out weeks in advance. He knew he was going to knock much of the will-to-win out of Dempsey with that first right-hand smash to the head. He must have worked on that punch a thousand times before he let it go for keeps in the first round of his bout with Dempsey. He had learned to throw it with every ounce of power he had, and it landed. Jack was stopped in his tracks and his knees sagged. You could see Jack was hurt, dazed for the rest of the fight. That one blow won the fight for Tunney."

Jack Dempsey once was asked if he was religious.

"Well," Jack said, "I was baptized in the Mormon church, and I believe in it. I think all churches are good, but I happened to be brought up in a Mormon church. Once in a while I attend services, but not very often. I do if I'm some place around a church, but I don't do like I should, and I don't keep the Word of Wisdom. I smoke and I drink a little bit, and I'm not a good Mormon, but I believe in the gospel. I believe–I believe in God–and I pray. I say my prayers every night. Sometimes in the morning, too."

The newspapers of the day usually pictured Tunney as the prize fighter who read books—even Shakespeare.

It was a side of the old Manassa Mauler the public seldom saw.

Gene Tunney also had a religious side. It played a big role in his first victory over Dempsey. Prefight fear had nearly cheated him out of the championship.

Years later, he made this confession:

"Dempsey was an overwhelming favorite to knock me out. The newspaper talk was that he would murder me. Being human I read the papers to find out what they were saying about me.

"One night, at the beginning of my long training period, I awakened suddenly and felt my bed shaking. It seemed fantastic. Ghosts or what? Then I understood. It was I who was shaking, trembling so hard that I made the bed tremble. I was that much afraid... afraid of what the great Dempsey would do to me. The fear was lurking in the back of my mind and had set me quaking in my sleep. I pictured myself being mauled and bloodied by Dempsey's shattering punches; helpless, sinking to the canvas and being counted out. I couldn't stop trembling. Sure, the newspaper gossip was getting to me. Right there I had already lost the Dempsey fight before it was even fought. That championship meant everything to me. I had lost it—unless I could regain it.

"I got up and took stock of myself. What could I do about this terror inside me? I could guess the cause. I had been thinking about the fight the wrong way. I had been reading the newspapers, and all they had said was how Tunney would lose. I was losing the battle in my own mind.

"Part of the solution was obvious. Stop reading the newspapers. Stop thinking of the Dempsey menace...his killing punch and ferocious attack. I simply had to close the doors of my mind to destructive thoughts and divert my thinking to other things. It took discipline.

"Here was where prayer and faith served as my pillars of strength.

"I can remember still getting down on my knees, alongside my bed, and praying as fervently and humbly as any man ever has. I prayed that in the Dempsey fight I might not be permanently injured. I didn't ask that I might win. I just asked that I might not embarrass myself. All I wanted was to make a good account of myself. Thus as I prayed I gained self-confidence. This took the edge off mad, irrational fear. If it hadn't been for this strength I gained from prayer, I imagine I'd gone into the ring against Dempsey inwardly shaking and quaking, thoroughly beaten in advance. As it was later, I climbed into the ring against Dempsey with enough courage to fight my normal fight. I suddenly realized how groundless my fears had been. Dempsey was no super-man...as I was to prove in both my fights with him."

Tunney remembered an incident when he was down on the floor during The Battle of the Long Count. Sitting near his corner was Father Francis Duffy, the beloved World War I chaplain of the famous Fighting 69th, and a close friend of Gene's. In the seat directly behind him was a very noisy young man. While Gene was lying dazed on the canvas, trying to get up, the young man was in a frenzy, wild with excitement. Then he noticed Father Duffy in his black garb and Roman collar.

FATHER, FOR CHRIST'S SAKE! JUST DON'T SIT THERE. PRAY—PRAY FOR TUNNEY TO GET UP!"

Father Duffy told Gene after the fight that he instinctively began to pray.

At the Yale Club in Manhattan during a father-and-son Christmas party, I got Tunney off in a corner and talked to him about the second Dempsey fight. What, I asked him, had referee Barry said to him and Dempsey when they were called together in the center of the ring for their final instructions?

"He explained the knockdown rule, slowly and clearly to us," Tunney said. "After he finished he looked at me and said, 'Do you understand, Champ?' I had never before been called champ. It felt good. Then he turned to Jack and asked, 'Do you understand, Jack?' We both nodded.

Barry then said, 'In the event the man scoring the knockdown does not go to the farthest neutral corner, I *will not* start counting until he does reach it. Do you understand that, Champ? Jack?' We both answered yes."

Tunney defended his championship only once more. That was on July 26, 1928, against a rugged but inept Tom Heeney in New York. Tunney knocked him out in the 11th round and then retired to the life of a country squire in Connecticut with a beautiful bride, Polly Lauder, daughter of a steel family. His end of the Heeney purse was $525,000. He had more than a million dollars in the bank when he hung up the gloves.

Tunney retired from the ring to marry Polly Lauder of Greenwich, Connecticut, Andrew Carnegie heiress, Social Registerite, blueblood and a darned sweet girl. They are shown here receiving a warm welcome in Turkey on their honeymoon.

After his marriage, Tunney began applying the same will power and concentration to his private life that had brought him fame and success in boxing. He became a country squire completely equipped with four children, one of whom grew up to become a Senator from the State of California. Gene has had a fabulously successful career in the business world, has lectured at Yale on "Troilus and Cressida" by invitation of the late Billy Phelps, renowned English Professor at Yale.

In 1932, Tunney campaigned for Governor Franklin D. Roosevelt of New York, the Democratic Presidential candidate. Seated next to Governor Roosevelt is Governor Wilbur Cross of Connecticut.

Tunney was commissioned a naval Lieutenant Commander in World War II, put in charge of a vast physical training program, and discharged as a full Captain. After the war, he became president of a number of companies, and was on the board of directors of many more.

The career of James Joseph Tunney paralleled that of his idol, Gentleman James J. Corbett, in many ways. He lived out a classic American success story. He was born in the rough-and-tumble section of New York's Greenwich Village, May 25, 1898. His parents were poor but proud. His father, a stevedore, was not a big man, but his mother was a husky. "I got my size from my mother, my spunk from my father," he said.

In the process of surviving in the rugged atmosphere of the Village, Gene had been pushed around plenty by the roughnecks who infested his neighborhood. He finally got tired of being shoved around, so he began frequenting a neighborhood gymnasium to learn to box. From the very beginning he concentrated on defensive tactics. He was tall, skinny (152 pounds) and lightning-fast and quickly developed rare boxing skill. He inevitably attracted the attention of Billy Roche, one of the leading managers of the day, and Billy convinced him to turn professional.

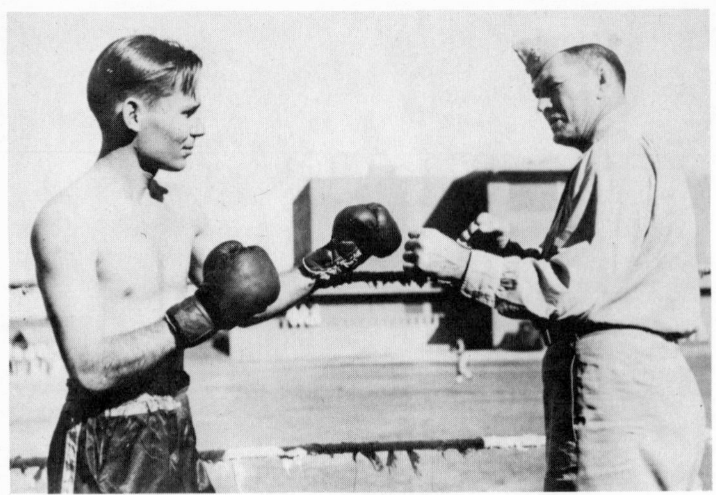

Commander Gene Tunney helped organize a physical fitness program for the Naval Air Corps in World War II.

In his first pro prize fight Tunney knocked out an experienced fighter named Bobby Dawson in seven rounds. With Roche guiding him, Tunney fought nine more times, none of which show in the record book. Came the war and Tunney enlisted in the United States Marines. Roche went overseas, too, staging boxing matches for the armed forces. Tunney continued to box in the service and wound up winning the light-heavyweight title of the AEF in a post-Armistice tournament in Paris.

Tunney returned to the United States a more seasoned fighter than when he had left. But he still wasn't satisfied with his ringmanship. Under the expert eye of Roche for a while, then with Doc Bagley as his manager, Tunney set about correcting his faults in a series of bouts against carefully selected opponents. The bouts were not screened because they were "soft touches" for Tunney. On the contrary, many of the opponents were the toughest possible men Tunney could have fought at that time. They were all chosen because they each had some particular way of fighting from which Tunney could learn something.

Tunney was ready for the first big break that came his way. There wasn't a great deal of money to be made in the semi-final spot Tex Rickard offered him on the Dempsey-Carpentier card in Jersey City, but there was a chance to show his ability before one of the largest fight crowds ever assembled. Tunney took the chance and belted out the highly regarded Soldier Jones.

After finishing Jones, Tunney accepted other matches which gave him a chance to improve his fighting finesse.

On his way to the heavyweight championship, Tunney was managed by several men, including Sam Kelly, Billy Roche, Frank (Doc) Bagley, and Billy Gibson, here shown talking to Gene about his retirement in 1928.

Opportunity knocked again—real loud this time—when he was matched with the great Battling Levinsky for the American light-heavyweight championship of the world.

The rest is history....

But as long as Tunney and Dempsey live, they will be asked to give their versions of the Battle of the Long Count. What were their thoughts while Tunney was down in that near-fatal seventh round?

Dempsey: "While he was sitting there, I kept hoping he'd never get up. Unfortunately for me he did—and more power to him. A great boy and a great champion."

Tunney: "It was the luckiest night of my life. I was down, heard the referee count two—and I knew I had to get up. But what to do after I got up was the important thing. I decided stay away from Jack. It was a very wise decision, as the final results showed."

Despite their rivalry in the ring, Tunney and Dempsey have remained lifetime friends. In 1965, they were in Washington, D.C., together to see Congressman John V. Tunney, Jr., center, of California, take his oath of office. Gene's son is a Democrat.

When, after he had been proclaimed "winnah and still champeen," Tunney spoke into the microphone held by Major J. Andrew White, who had broadcast the fight, the public heard him say, "...and regards to my friends in Greenwich." Few knew that it was the tip-off to one of the best happy-ending stories of all time. Those at ringside, the members of the press, thought he was greeting his pals in the old Greenwich Village section of New York, where he was born and raised.

He wasn't at all. He was speaking to someone in Greenwich, *Connecticut.* America found out *who* a couple of months later when Bill Corum, sports columnist for the old *New York Journal,* scooped the pants off the rest of the press by printing the exclusive story that Gene Tunney was retiring from the ring to marry Polly Lauder of Greenwich, Andrew Carnegie heiress, Social Registerite, blueblood and a darned sweet girl.

Poor boy wins heiress, the pug and the aristocrat, beauty and the beast—the fairy tale to end all fairy tales had come true. A lot of the oldtimers swear it could only have happened in those times and those days.

That's how it was in 1927.

10. Max Schmeling

MAX SCHMELING of Germany was the first Continental European to hold the world's heavyweight boxing championship. He won and lost the crown under distressing circumstances—and on each occasion the implausible Jack Sharkey was the antagonist.

The Black Uhlan from the Rhine backed into the title on a foul perpetrated by Sharkey in Yankee Stadium on June 12, 1930. This was an elimination match to determine a successor to Tunney, and until late in the fourth round, the mad Balt gave Schmeling an old-time going-over. Max had just driven Sharkey into the ropes with a great right to the jaw when the self-made Bostonian countered with the controversial punch—a wicked left hook to the groin. The dead-game German was counted out as his manager, Joe Jacobs, cried "Foul!" For the next three minutes, 79,222 customers champed and chafed as the ring officials haggled like merchants over the contested blow.

Referee Jimmy Crowley, one of football's famous Four Horsemen of Notre Dame, and Judge Charles Mathison had missed the punch. Judge Harold Barnes claimed he saw it, and on his testimony Crowley disqualified Sharkey. Six days later the Boxing Commission elected Schmeling champion of the world by a 2 to 1 vote, and Schmeling thus earned the dubious distinction of becoming the first and only heavyweight titlist to win by a foul.

Schmeling fought Sharkey again at Long Island on June 21, 1932, and the championship was returned to the USA by one of the worst decisions ever perpetrated on an incredulous public. Some critics suspected the conniving hand of old Pete Reilly, the late "Silver Fox" of the ring, who for some mysterious reason had soured on Max.

The punch that cost Jack Sharkey the title is shown here—the only time in history that the heavyweight championship has been awarded on a foul. With five seconds left in the fourth round, the blow floored Max Schmeling and left him writhing (see other picture). In the rules of 1930, a foul disqualified the offender, so Joe Jacobs, Schmeling's manager, jumped into the ring at the bell and insisted his man be declared the winner. When the bell rang for the next round Schmeling was still down and no decision had been made. Finally it was announced that Max was the winner on a foul.

Referee Jim Crowley, one of Notre Dame's famous football Four Horsemen, agreed that the blow was low, but with the title at stake he felt it was not the occasion for a bout to be won on a foul. He urged Schmeling to take a three-minute rest and then resume fighting. Schmeling and Jacobs refused. Then after much confusion at ringside, one of the two judges, Harold Barnes, signaled to Crowley he had seen the foul. "So I had to concur and award the fight to Schmeling," Crowley said. Barnes later said he didn't believe Schmeling was hurt. "But there was no doubt a foul punch had been struck," Barnes said. "I had seen it, and I had to say so."

The decision created so much confusion that the New York State Athletic Commission reviewed it. Although they declared Schmeling champion, they made the metal supporter required boxing equipment and they took steps to change the rules so that now a foul means only loss of the round. Sharkey got his revenge two years later when he took the title from Schmeling in a 15-round decision.

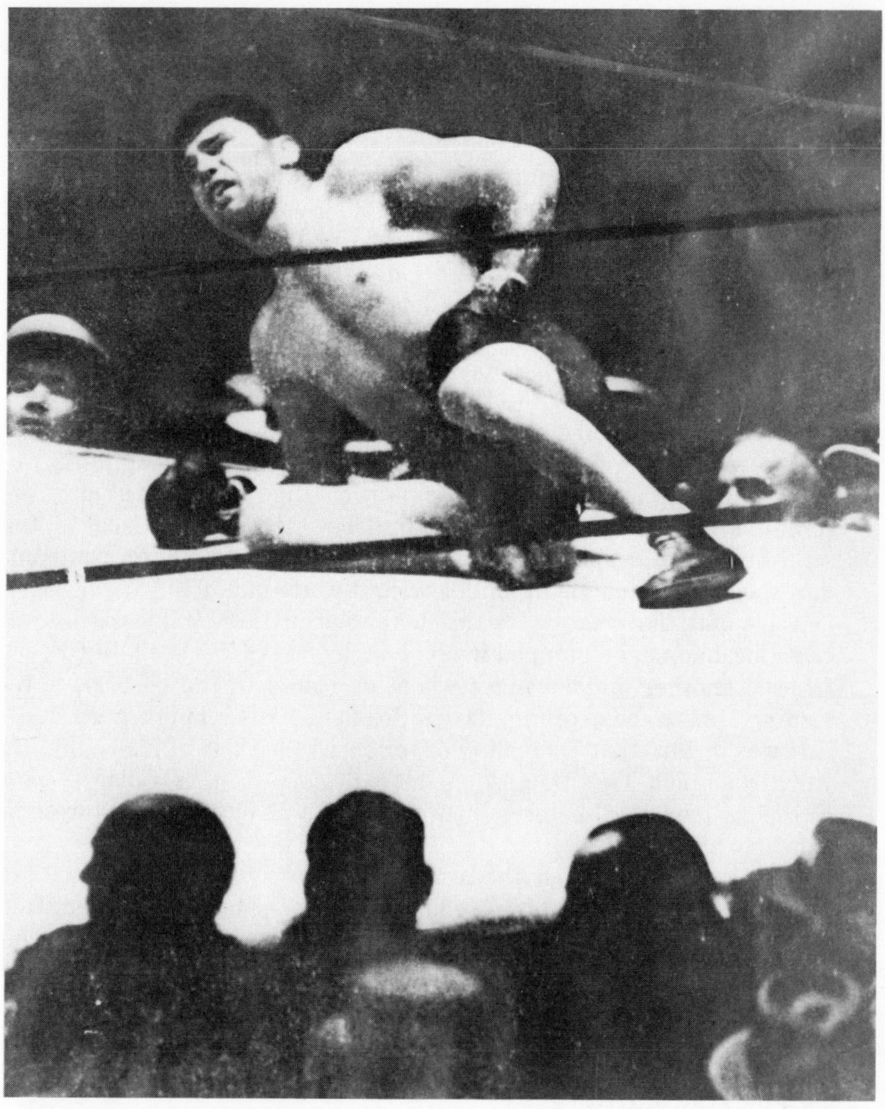

Was Max Schmeling descended from the savage Wends of the Black Forest? Whoever his dark progenitor, he showed a fortuitous combination of strength and cunning. Certain experts were inclined to write him off as a plodding, workmanlike heavyweight with a dangerous right-hand punch. Yet he was a genuinely great fighter the night he befuddled Joe Louis in one of the classic upsets of all time.

Young Schmeling grew up in the bitter, poverty-ridden Germany of the Versailles Treaty years. In 1919, he was forced to leave school at the age of fourteen and grub for worthless marks. He worked for three years as an apprentice in the advertising department of a Hamburg newspaper. In 1922, he hit the road, bumming his way from one job to another. The sturdy lad developed his barrel chest by toiling on farms and in foundries, open coal mines, railway shops, and garages.

When he was eighteen, Max blew into Cologne-Mulheim, where he became a pumper at the municiple waterworks and joined the Mulheimer Boxing Club and the Benrath Club. At the Benrath he became such an outstanding wrestler that he considered turning professional, but with his first taste of flying leather he decided in favor of prize fighting.

In his 1922 Benrath debut he didn't know what the bells were all about. When the gong rang, Max stood like a clod in the center of the ring, hands at his sides. His opponent immediately bloodied his nose, so Max chased him all over the ring and succeeded in knocking him out—long after the bell had ended the round.

Two years later, Schmeling had licked all the middleweights in Cologne-Mulheim, and a local boxing patron, Hugo Abels, wanted to become his manager. Max held out until he lost to Otto Nispul in the semi-finals of the Chemnitz amateur tournament. In his pro bouts under Abels, the rising young middleweight won 9 out of 10.

Abels quit the racket after his wife died in 1925. Willie Fuchs, another local manager, stepped in and handled Max for a spell. But Fuchs favored another middleweight whom he placed in the best spots, resigning Max to cheap preliminaries. Schmeling left him in a rage.

It was in 1925 that Schmeling experienced the thrill of his young life when champion Jack Dempsey, who had stopped off in Cologne on a European tour, told the press how struck he was by Max's close resemblance to himself.

Dempsey then invited the ecstatic Schmeling to step a few fast rounds, and this led to a bit of prophecy. Said the Manassa Mauler after their friendly exchange: "Listen, kid, don't let anyone tell you that you can't fight. Keep at it. Practice all you can, and some day you may be the world's heavyweight champion."

Horatio Alger hogwash? Perhaps. But back in the 1920s, when young men still harbored grand dreams, it was the kind of advice future champions ate up with gusto.

Unlike most prize fighters from abroad who arrive in the United States in the full panoply of ballyhoo, Max slipped in on his own, without fanfare, and quietly got lost in Bey's training camp at Summit, New Jersey. He remembered what had happened to Rudy Wagner and Franz Diener, the man he had whipped for the German heavyweight title. As all-conquering heroes, they were a complete bust. Therefore, aside from his manager, Art Beulow, the only person aboard the steamship *New York* who was aware of Max's mission in America was a pilot who happened to be his father.

Sports writers listen to promoter Jack Dempsey as he talks about his upcoming Schmeling-Max Baer bout in New York. Left to right, seated, were Dan Parker, Sports Editor of the New York Mirror; *Harry Grayson, Sports Editor of the NEA syndicate; Schmeling, Dempsey, and Tim Mara, of the New York Football Giants. Among the others shown here were Nat Fleischer, publisher of* Ring Magazine *(rear and left of Schmeling), and Ned Brown (whose bald head peers over Nat's left shoulder). Baer later won the June 8, 1933, bout at Yankee Stadium with a 10th-round knockout.*

In that dreary period following Gene Tunney's retirement there was more excitement behind the scenes than could be found in the ring, and the dire machinations involving Schmeling's contract were no exception. Joe Jacobs was just another hungry manager in search of a world-beater when he learned about Schmeling from Dempsey. Joe hastened out to the Jersey foothills, where Max was nursing a broken hand, a souvenir of his fight with Diener six months previously.

What happened after that has been told countless times. Max and Beulow were to receive a $3,000 guarantee for a 10-rounder when the contract was repudiated by Tom McArdle, who had succeeded Jess McMahon as matchmaker. The nimble Jacobs immediately stepped in and arranged a $1,000 guarantee for eight rounds against Joe Monte, a fairly good light-heavyweight from Boston. It was a shrewd move: Max showed his stuff as he won by a knockout in the eighth. And Beulow began to feel the squeeze.

Just how Jacobs and his partner, Billy McCarney, got rid of the indignant Beulow will always remain a mystery. In any event, the crafty pair, assisted by Pete Reilly, wound up owning every part of Max.

Jacobs made his first big move when he put Schmeling in with Johnny Risko, the Cleveland "Rubber Man." Risko was a great spoiler who had already upset Tex Rickard's plans for a successor to Tunney by whipping Jack Sharkey, Tex's favorite contender. It was a mighty gamble, but again Jacobs proved his matchmaking ability. Schmeling stopped Risko in nine rounds.

Then came Paulino Uzcudun, the last obstacle between Max and Sharkey. This was a tough decision for Jacobs. Though the Basque had little to offer in the way of an attack, he could make a solid hitter look bad by his crustacean-like defense. The wily manager conceived the brilliant idea of studying films of Paulino's previous fights—the first time motion pictures were ever used in a training camp.

Those films did the trick. When Uzcudun scuttled from his corner—this was at Yankee Stadium on June 27, 1929—he was dismayed to see that Schmeling could anticipate his every move. Whenever he bobbed, Max bobbed; when he weaved, Max did the same. The customers were bored by this exhibition of mimicry, but few realized that the Rhinelander was timing his opponent with short, jolting uppercuts to the forearms and biceps. By the 10th round it was apparent that Uzcudun could no longer keep his arms up, and by the 15th and final round he was out on his feet.

Meanwhile, the Beulow business returned to haunt Billy McCarney in the form of a practical joke that scared the daylights out of him. As Billy was working late one night in his Broadway office, a Germanic-looking character poked his head in the door and gutturalled, "You Villy McCarney, ya?"

McCarney took one look at the ominous stranger and said no.

"I vas friend of Artur Beulow," the stranger continued. "I vant Villy McCarney who steal Max Schmeling."

McCarney insisted that he was not there and wouldn't be in until morning.

"I ting you lie!" the big man menaced. Billy now realized he was hiding something behind his back. "I ting *you* Villy McCarney. You steal Artur's boy. I blow you hup!"

Whereupon, the fellow tossed a sputtering bomb at McCarney's feet and fled.

"Then I did the damndest thing," Billy said later. "My office was on the fifth floor, and the elevator wasn't running at that time of night.

Instead of chucking the bomb out the window, for some reason I picked it up, ran down five flights of stairs and placed it in the street. Then I backed away and began screaming bloody murder. Did I feel silly when the bomb squad arrived and discovered the thing was only a coconut with the hair shaved off and a Fourth of July sparkler attached!"

After several years of brooding, McCarney learned that Beulow's "friend" was an unemployed actor who had been hired by Pete Reilly to pull the elaborate prank.

That wasn't the only time that Schmeling's crowd was picked on by practical jokers. One of his German newspaperman companions, a thoroughly hated character, was another victim. The reporter had come over to cover the Schmeling-Sharkey match. He soon incurred the hearty wrath of the American sports journalists. One night this German was roused from deep sleep by a telephone caller who identified himself as the representative of the New York Telegraph Company. The Kaiser was dead, he said, and the correspondent's Berlin office wanted 1,000 words on Wilhelm's love of sports. The German labored until dawn and then, after filing his story by cable, he went back to bed, trusting that his sentimental output was satisfactory. That afternoon he was jarred by a sharp cable from Berlin. The Kaiser was *not* dead; they did *not* want any story; and they were fining him the cost of the cable. It was two years before the German learned that his original caller had been Harry Grayson, the colorful boxing writer of the *New York World-Telegram* (and later my boss at the NEA Syndicate).

Certainly the highlight of Schmeling's ring career came on the night of June 19, 1936, at Yankee Stadium, when he did what no other fighter had been able to do: He knocked out the seemingly impregnable Joe Louis.

Schmeling, a 1-to-10 underdog, fought the coolest and most carefully conceived fight of his life.

It was a fight that ranked high in any Yankee Stadium collection of pugilistic nostalgia. Before the bout Max studied films of Louis in action. He reviewed every round of every fight that the Brown Bomber had ever been in. Over and over again he would run those pictures, discovering minute flaws in the supposedly puncture-proof armor of the Detroit star. "Zop zee peeczure," he'd announce. "I zee somezings." One of the faults he saw was Joe's vulnerability to a right. He thus went into the bout with a definite fight plan. It was based on his observation that when Louis advanced to attack, he always carried his left hand low, ready for a smashing left hook. This left his left jaw wide open for a straight right. It was a right-hand punch that knocked out Louis in the 12th.

This is the way James P. Dawson, of the *New York Times*, described the action:

> Under a murderous fire of desperate rights to an unprotected jaw, Louis went down to be counted out by Referee Arthur Donovan. Exactly 2 minutes

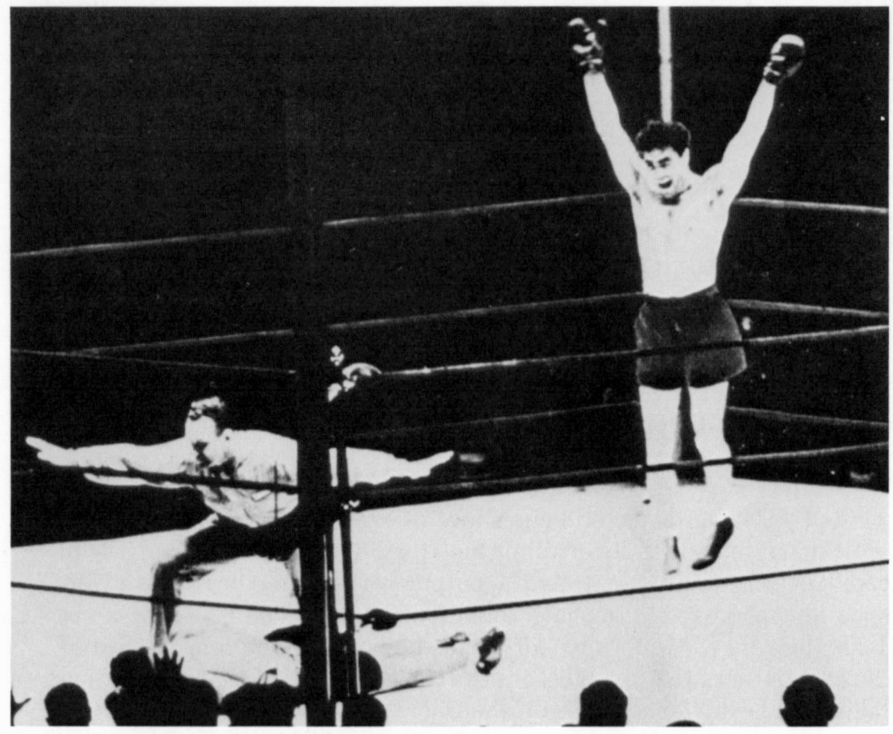

This is the highlight of Max Schmeling's ring career. Here referee Arthur Donovan counts out the seemingly impregnable Joe Louis in the 12th round at Yankee Stadium on June 19, 1936, as Max, a 1 to 10 underdog, does a victory dance.

29 seconds of the fatal 12th had gone into history when Louis, hailed as the king of fighters entering the ring, was counted out, his invincibility a shattered myth, his vulnerability convincingly established and his claims to heavyweight distinction temporarily, at least, knocked into the discard.

Louis had to be carried to his corner while the shouts of a crowd of 45,000 delirious fight fans rang in the ears of his battered, bruised and bleeding conqueror. Louis required several minutes of resuscitating before he was able to stagger on shaky legs out of the ring—unnoticed.

With the might of his right fist, his chief weapon of attack, Schmeling hammered his way into another chance at the heavyweight title he lost to Jack Sharkey. He ignored the contempt in which he was held as a foe for Louis, with the latter's unbroken string of 27 victories that held 23 knockouts, and fulfilled the promise he made that he would fight his way into another crack at the title.

The German is now undisputed challenger for the crown. None who saw last night's upset would contradict Schmeling's bold assertion that he will be the first man in all ring history ever to regain the heavyweight championship.

Overcoming not only the mental discouragement of the betting odds that held him so cheaply... Schmeling also withstood the shock of seeing a man die at his feet in his dressing room before the fight. A report reached the ringside early in the night that the veteran Tom O'Rourke, ex-manager, promoter and State Athletic Commission attache and judge, had dropped dead as he visited Schmeling to wish him luck. Schmeling, it was said, was upset by the sight of the stricken man toppling at his feet, although he was allowed to think it was merely a fainting spell.

But he came into the ring shortly after with one set purpose in mind and did not leave it until he had achieved his goal. He hammered Louis into defeat simply because he refused to believe that Louis was a superman of the ring, because he had plenty of courage, because he never let himself be swayed from a set line of battle and because he is, on the record, a greater puncher than the man whose hitting prowess hitherto struck fear to the hearts of opponents.

Schmeling's weapon of attack was his right hand. He seldom used his left. But with his resourcefulness, adaptability to different ring situations, and his crafty ring work, he had Louis beaten on points when the knockout occurred.

Louis had two years to mull over that beating; 24 months to correct his faults. The aging German never had a chance, really, for he was fighting *two* foes: Joe Louis and *hate.* Because of snide remarks he had made about Louis to the press, and his boastful references to himself as a member of the Super Race, Max incited Louis to mayhem.

A reporter in Cleveland asked Gene Tunney before the fight to pick the winner. The retired champion declined.

"I'm not going out on the limb for either one of them," Tunney said. "But just keep this in mind–Max Schmeling will go into that ring in New York with a *spiritual* edge that can't be laughed off. Don't think that is nonsense. He honestly believes the prestige of all Germany depends on his performance. That may seem silly to others, but it isn't to Max, and that's what counts. He'll have something plus when he goes against Joe Louis."

Louis was champion now, and one of the largest crowds in boxing history (80,000) paid nearly a million dollars to watch Schmeling try to become the first ex-heavyweight champion to win back the title. Ringside seats sold for $30 each!

The battle was short, but it was furious and savage while it lasted, packed with drama. For excitement, for pulse throbs, those who came from near and far felt themselves well repaid. They saw a fight that, though one of the shortest heavyweight championships on record, was surpassed by few for thrills.

One newspaper account described the highlights in this manner:

The exploding fists of Joe Louis crushed Max Schmeling last night in the ring at the Yankee Stadium and kept sacred the time-worn legend of boxing that no former heavyweight champion has ever regained the title.

The Brown Bomber from Detroit, with the most furious early assault he has ever exhibited here, knocked out Schmeling in the first round of what was to have been a 15-round battle, to retain the title he won last year from James J. Braddock.

Max Schmeling trains for the second Joe Louis fight in New York in June, 1938.

In exactly 2 minutes and 4 seconds of fighting Louis polished off the Black Uhlan from the Rhine. With the right hand that Schmeling held in contempt Louis knocked out his foe. Three times under its impact the German hit the ring floor.... On the third knockdown, Referee Arthur Donovan took one look at Schmeling's crumpled figure and signaled an end of the battle. The count had reached five. Further counting was useless. Donovan could have counted off a century and Max could not have regained his feet. He was thoroughly out. It was as if he had been poleaxed. His brain was awhirl, his body, his head, his jaws ached and pained, his senses were numbed from the furious, paralyzing punching he had taken.

Following the bout, Schmeling claimed he was fouled. He said that he was hit a kidney punch, a devastating right, which so shocked his nervous system that he was dazed and his vision was blurred. To ringsiders, however, the punches which dazed him were thundering blows to the head, jaw and body in bewildering succession.

Louis had something extra going for him last night. He wanted to erase the memory of that 1936 knockout. It was the one blot on his brilliant record.

He aimed to square the account.

He did.

Stressing the savagery with which Louis went after Schmeling was the German's feeble effort to defend himself. Max threw exactly *two* punches. That was how completely the Detroit Bomber established his mastery in this second struggle with the Black Uhlan.

Thus was exploded Hitler's superman myth.

Schmeling and Louis hold opposite views as to the political overtones surrounding their 1938 bout. Louis, today, still feels it represented the Free World against the Nazi World. In February, 1973, the sixty-five-year-old Schmeling, who now heads a soft-drink bottling firm in Hamburg, denied there were any social implications.

"Political events did not affect us," Max said. "That was just played up in the press. It was just publicity to sell tickets. There never was any criticism in Germany about Louis, neither political nor racial. I never viewed the fight as a contest between superior and inferior faces. In fact, Joe and I remain good friends."

Schmeling was 35 years late making his point. He should have told Louis this on that June night in 1938. The Brown Bomber might have gone a little easier on him.

How could Schmeling's performance have changed so much between June 20, 1936, and June 23, 1938? There were many reasons. In the first place, Louis was mad, enraged through and through. For the first time in his career he wanted to kill an opponent. He was eager to commit murder. That made him four or five times as dangerous as he had been in their first fight. At the same time, Schmeling had serious personal problems. His father-in-law back in Germany had been indulging in monkey business with foreign currency, putting him in hot water with Hitler's minions. The father-in-law mysteriously vanished.

To make matters worse, Schmeling's wife, a German movie actress named Annie Ondra, was placed under "protective custody." The SS had her confined to the family residence in Berlin. Schmeling was half out of his mind with worry.

That wasn't all. Several days before the fight, he was told by one of Hitler's special envoys that "Der Fuehrer *commands* you to win as a symbol of Aryan supremacy."

It was amazing that Schmeling even bothered to show up for the bout. Obviously he had other things on his mind.

The late Eddie Mead, who had been hired by Louis' managers to help train him for the second fight, had an interesting and most revealing experience in connection with the bout. Just a few minutes before it was time for the fighters to climb into the ring, a friend of his, one of the New York State Athletic Commission's inspectors assigned to the dressing rooms, told him quietly: "You'd better go take a look at Schmeling. I don't think he'll make it to the ring."

Eddie went immediately to Schmeling's dressing room, where he found Max a pitiful sight. He was in a cold sweat and trembling. The knowledge of the burden placed upon him by Hitler, fear for his wife's safety, and the knowledge of Louis' bitterness and determination apparently all had hit him at once and reduced the ordinarily phlegmatic fighter to a quivering jellyfish. Mead always said until his dying day that he was not sure Schmeling wasn't going to bolt right up to the opening bell.

Schmeling joined the German parachute troops in 1941 and saw much combat. Thereby hangs a strange tale. On May 29, 1942, headlines around the world blared: SCHMELING IS KILLED IN CRETE. Details of the incident told how the ex-champ had been wounded and captured in the Battle of Crete; how, while being taken to a field hospital by Allied ambulance corps, he grabbed a rifle from a guard and went into action like a wild bull. Before he did any damage, however, someone shot him down, and that was the end of Max. Or so the story went. The very next day the wire services carried a denial of the reports: SCHMELING NOT DEAD. It had been a clear case of mistaken identity. Max had been involved in the fighting at Crete, but had managed to escape, wandering half a day alone in the Crete wilderness before he was found by Nazi invasion forces.

Joe Jacobs was one of the last of the great fight managers. Joe had been trained in the fight game by my old friend, the late Dan Morgan. He will be remembered always not only for his role in making Schmeling champion, but for his two notable contributions to the American language. When Schmeling lost the title on a debatable decision to Sharkey, it was Jacobs who screamed over the radio:

"We wuz robbed!"

And it was Joe who, on a raw, bone-chilling day in Detroit during the 1935 World Series between the Tigers and the Cubs, exclaimed in the press box:

"I shoulda stood in bed!"

On the day Joe died, he had had lunch with Harry Mendel at an Italian restaurant at Summit, New Jersey. When they reached New York, Joe complained of indigestion and Harry took him to a doctor's office and there Joe died, not of indigestion, but of a heart attack.

Afterward Joe's girl friend asked Harry: "When Joe was dying, did he mention my name? Did he ask for me?"

Harry realized later that if he had been smart he would have replied, "Sure, he did." But he was upset and all he could say was the truth, which was that Joe's last words were:

"I knew I shouldn't have et so much of that veal scaloppini."

11. Jack Sharkey

A wave of good old-fashioned sentimentality swirled around Yankee Stadium in 1973, its golden anniversary year. It was natural that the sport that was most responsible for its construction—baseball—would get the lion's share of attention. Yet not all the stars who stalked across the center stage wore baseball gloves.

Some wore boxing gloves.

"For some peculiar reason that I've never been able to explain," recalled Arthur Daley, the *New York Times'* Pulitzer Prize-winning sports columnist, "I have always been intrigued by the Dempsey-Sharkey fight. It contained so many appealing aspects, including the fact that it was the only non-title bout ever to draw a million-dollar gate. Dempsey had just been dethroned by Gene Tunney while Sharkey was five years away from winning his heavyweight championship. This was in 1927 when fighters worked at their trade and didn't have to concern themselves with getting into higher brackets in the income tax structure. Despite his well-earned reputation as one of the greatest of all champions, Dempsey did not rate an automatic return match with Tunney. Tex Rickard, the gambling man from Klondike, was a superior boxing promoter and he ordained that the winner of the Dempsey-Sharkey match would face Tunney, thereby assuring himself of an extra million-dollar gate."

The old Manassa Mauler was beginning to show his age (thirty-two). Sharkey was a twenty-four-year-old heavyweight who had almost everything. He was a 196-pound, 6-footer who was fast of hand and foot. He boxed beautifully and he could punch.

"But he was also probably one of the most unstable characters to ever step into a ring," Arthur Daley added.

On that night of July 21, Sharkey stepped into the Yankee Stadium ring amid the raucous jeers of a gathering of 70,000. Dempsey was

When the spirit moved him, Jack Sharkey could be one of the most devastating hitters of all time. He was a natural-born fighter.

cheered to the last thunderous echo. Sharkey bristled and a resentful anger warped his judgment. It was typical of him.

In the first round he gave Dempsey a fearful pounding and left the old Mauler groggy on the ropes at the bell.

"I must have hit him five punches in quick succession," Sharkey later recalled. "What a sucker I was! Instead of charging across the ring at the opening gong, Dempsey uncustomarily held back and waited for me to make the first move. I did–and nearly decapitated him with lefts and rights. The old champ was staggering. All I needed was one more solid punch to finish him. But then I remembered how they cheered him and booed me when the ring announcer introduced us. So I turned to the mob and shouted, 'Here's your bum champion! How d'ya like him now?' When I got back to Dempsey, he had recovered enough to clinch and save himself. That's how I lost the fight."

It certainly appeared as though Sharkey would methodically chop Dempsey to bits and fling the pieces to the spectators whenever it suited his fancy.

"Sharkey gave me living hell for the first five rounds," acknowledged Dempsey afterward. "He was as good a fighter as I had ever seen. I thought he was going to knock me out."

In the sixth Dempsey began shifting his attack to the body and by the seventh all firepower was aimed there with reckless fury. Dempsey was tearing away at his tormentor with the careless abandon of a stevedore on a binge. If a punch was low it was low. Then came a right to the groin that was as plain a foul as ever was delivered. Sharkey went into his infamous act. He clutched his middle and turned his head to the referee to complain. "He's hitting me low," cried Sharkey. Jutting out at a perfect and inviting angle was the Sharkey chin. Dempsey took aim. Bull's eye!

"What was I going to do–write him a letter of apology?" said the unrepentant Dempsey. "I belted him."

The agate type in the record book reads, "KO...7." It means that Dempsey knocked out Sharkey in the seventh round.

Sharkey left the Yankee Stadium after the fight and he didn't even know it. He wasn't aware he had been in a fight, didn't know whether he was coming or going. He was oblivious to being knocked out by Dempsey. He stood on the sidewalk outside the ball park and kept gazing up at the clouds in the sky. He shook his head and turned to Johnny Buckley, his manager.

"John," he said, "I don't like the look of those clouds. I'd hate to have the fight postponed by rain."

"What fight?" Buckley said.

"My fight with Dempsey, of course."

"That fight ended an hour ago," said Buckley. "Dempsey knocked you out in the seventh round."

The end had been shrouded in controversy. Dempsey had opened the round with two sharp rights to the stomach. Both blows landed smack

In the only non-title bout ever to draw a million-dollar gate, Jack Dempsey stands over Jack Sharkey in Yankee Stadium ring after knocking him out in the seventh round, on July 21, 1927.

on the belt line. Stunned and hurt, Sharkey appealed to the referee, O'Sullivan, who warned Dempsey to keep his punches higher. Dempsey responded with two more low haymakers, and as Sharkey again turned to the referee–WHAM!–a left hook caught him flush on the jaw. Down he went, still nursing his groin as though he were suffering from an attack of green apples and milk. Referee O'Sullivan hesitated, unable to decide whether to start counting or award the fight to Sharkey on a foul. He counted, and at the toll of ten all hell broke loose. Shouts of "foul!" and "quitter!" and "yehhh, Dempsey!" rained down on the ring, but the decision stuck.

Dempsey later admitted that his victory over Jack Sharkey was his hardest.

"Sharkey, thy name is controversy"—though in all fairness to him he was indeed a victim of circumstance in his next questionable bout, this one against Jack Delaney. The Canadian heavyweight was so cockeyed drunk when he entered the ring that he could barely raise his gloves to defend himself. So Sharkey couldn't be blamed for knocking him out in the first round.

Following Tunney's abdication of the heavyweight throne, Sharkey and Schmeling met in an elimination bout on June 12, 1930, in New York. Max became the first heavyweight to win the title on a foul. When the disputed blow landed, neither the referee nor anyone else seemed to know what happened.

In a return championship match, June 29, 1933, Sharkey stole the crown in one of the worst decisions ever witnessed in New York.

Give or take a syllable, Joseph Paul Zukauskas or Cuckoshay was the most *exasperating* heavyweight champion of all time. A natural-born prize fighter, this man who took the fighting name of Jack Sharkey botched more opportunities for greatness than perhaps any other fist-fighter in history.

Oddly enough, he was the only champion who succeeded through repeated failure.

A volatile soul of Lithuanian lineage, Sharkey was too emotional for the ring. He fought as he lived—by extremes. For example, take his crusading streaks. He required a burning reason for winning a fight to become the most devastating hitter of all time. But when he didn't have a rooting interest, he boxed like an amateur.

Sharkey cried at the drop of a towel, and when he won, he pulled out all the stops. He would cavort around the ring, make fake passes at his retinue, bathe his upturned face in the glare of the overhead floodlights and pound his right fist into his left glove. There was more ham in him than in John Barrymore.

Everything Jack did was a production, and while he never endeared himself to the Irish of Boston, his adopted town, he maintained a kind of upsidedown popularity with fight fans in general. Equally admired and detested, he somehow managed to be all things to all men—fistic marvel, fourth-rate bum, hero of his time, unluckiest man alive, perpetrator of dark deeds and always Fortune's yo-yo.

They called him The Fighting Fool, a misnomer if there ever was one. It takes some fooling to gross a cool million. The unpredictable Sharkey, whose half namesakes were Jack Dempsey and Sailor Tom Sharkey, had everything it takes to be an all-time great except self-control. The great fighter moves in the eye of the hurricane.

A shame, really. Jack's repertoire of punches was something to behold. When he first started out, his only weakness was a looping right that he'd toss as though he were pegging an indoor baseball. After painstaking study, he developed the short lethal jolt that begins at the chest and travels only a foot.

There are no more than eight real blows in boxing—the left jab, left hook to the head, left rip to the body, right cross to the chin, straight right to the body and right uppercut. If you wish, you might ring in the left and right inside uppercuts. Few heavyweights past or present can use them all, and no one but Sharkey could deliver each one with devastating effect.

Jack's left jab was no flickering thing like Tommy Loughran's but a solid smash with the whole shoulder behind it. Tunney had it, but he never had Sharkey's whizzing left hook that could separate a man from his senses as quickly as his right. Sharkey would step in with his right under the heart just like Tunney, but then he'd risk a right cross to the chin, which was not for Gene. Tunney preferred to reach with the punch—it was safer.

Sharkey left Binghamton, New York, his home town, in his youth. We find him in Bridgeport, Connecticut, shoveling coal for a box factory. Then more road work and a nice Sharkey story.

One night when the watchman wasn't looking (our story goes), Jack crawled into an empty bear cage in the freight yards where Barnum and Bailey's circus was assembled. Came the dawn, and the day watchman was startled by ferocious snores from behind the front board with the image of a grizzly bear. To appreciate his alarm, you must understand that all the animals were supposedly on tour.

The watchman summoned a cop, and they decided to toss in a ham bone to distract the occupant. The bone struck Sharkey, who rolled over and made like a talking bear.

"They gave me a good licking," he related, "and sent me on my way." The way led to Gotham, where Jack hung around the Bowery pool room patronized by furtive pugilists. The manager hustled him out of doors so often that he withdrew his patronage, vowing vengeance at some later date.

Next scene: Jersey City, where Jack found work as a stevedore and studied Navy recruiting posters in his spare time.

"I was pretty big for eighteen," Sharkey observed, looking back on his tour of duty in the Navy. "About 160 pounds and growing fast. Funny, when I was a youngster in Binghamton, I used to run away from public school bullies. Then the Navy taught me that a fellow who can't take care of himself doesn't belong in hard-hitting company."

A fat little man named Johnny Buckley discovered Sharkey in the Kelly and Hayes Gym in Boston. Buckley was an undertaker who kept a small stable of preliminary boys as a kind of a hobby, and he knew a heavyweight prospect when he saw one. This big sailor off the USS Denver—hmmm. The kid looked like a Japanese doll with that wet black cowlick pasted over his brow. He was only clowning around, sparring with a shipmate, but Buckley could tell.

Buckley was waiting outside the gym when the two gobs piled out.

"Hello, boys! What ship you off of?"

"Who the hell wants to know?" Sharkey bawled.

Buckley was delighted.

"Now don't get sore, sailor," the undertaker remonstrated soothingly. "I'm just askin'."

"None of your blankety-blank business!" said Sharkey pleasantly. "How d'ya like that?" (Jimmy Cagney never did better!)

Buckley hooked a pair of fat thumbs in the pockets of his chequered vest and drew in a deep breath of raw January air. He hadn't felt so good in a long time.

The next morning he was down at the Navy Yard bright and early, perched atop his somber vehicle like a character from a Dickens novel. With long practiced patience he wooed the big boy with the pale Baltic eyes, and when Sharkey got his honorable discharge, the two were in business.

Sharkey always claimed he could lick an Irishman, and with the exception of only a few times, he fulfilled that boast. Celtic Boston was not amused when the twenty-two-year-old Sharkey knocked out Billy Muldoon in the first round of his professional debut in 1924. But Jack's "Irish complex" really dates from his frustrating feud with Jimmy Maloney of the Hub. Jack could lick every side of Maloney and frequently did. But every time he did, the Boston Irish would love their Jimmy all the more.

Jack wanted to be the hero of Beantown, ignoring the hard fact that Boston resents made-over Irishmen. So he turned his attention to the national scene and attracted lush raves when he outboxed Harry Wills, the perennial heavyweight challenger, at Brooklyn on October 12, 1926. Wills, who technically lost the fight on a foul in the 13th round, was gunning for Dempsey's title at the time, but for one reason or another, they never met. Some say Jack wanted no part of the black great. Others contend that Tex Rickard, mindful of the race riots set off by the Johnson-Jeffries match, did not wish to give rise to another incendiary situation.

Well, Dempsey lost to Tunney, and Wills bowed to Sharkey. "Dempsey picked the wrong man," the pundits said, and considering what happened to Sharkey in Yankee Stadium, July 21, 1927, they may have been right.

Dempsey regarded the Sharkey fight as a good tonic for his revenge meeting with Tunney. Sharkey, twenty-five, was the betting favorite; Dempsey, thirty-two, was the people's choice. Stories emanating from Dempsey's Saratoga camp suggested that Jack was soaking his left arm each night to keep it in shape. In the meantime, Sharkey was growing cockier by the minute.

On February 27, 1929, Sharkey won a 10-round decision from Young Stribling, in Miami. The boxing writers were all there. Among those in attendance were Nat Fleischer (front row, center, in tie, elbows on knees); Harry Grayson (third row, standing, second from left); Westbrook Pegler (dark jacket, to Grayson's left); Grantland Rice (center, wearing hat and bow tie); and Jack Dempsey (talking to Granny). Sharkey is the third man, left side of Dempsey, wearing cap, arms folded.

One day during a rubdown, Boston's Public Enemy No. 1 invited Grantland Rice to drop in.

"You know," Sharkey confided, "I could have had this fight with Tunney. Rickard offered it to me."

"Well, why didn't you take it?" Granny wanted to know. "It might have been a shortcut to the title for you."

"Tunney can wait," Sharkey said. "I know I can lick Dempsey, and when I beat him, it'll be a better buildup for the Tunney fight."

The fans at Yankee Stadium coughed up more than a million dollars to see if Sharkey could make good his boast.

You already know what happened. It is a memory Sharkey would like to forget. The devastating body punishment dished out by Dempsey that night ultimately took its toll.

A year after winning the crown from Schmeling, Sharkey put his title on the line against Primo Carnera. The Preem, a monster pawn in the hands of racketeers, had no business in the same ring with Sharkey on that June 29, 1933 night in New York. Even so, he scored a sixth-round knockout that was greeted with pinched noses by those who professed to know the inside story.

Jack Sharkey made his farewell appearance against Joe Louis in New York on August 18, 1936. He went out like a lamb in the third round.

12. Primo Carnera

THE most interesting if not the most important fight in 1931 took place at Ebbets Field, Brooklyn, on October 12th. It brought together towering (6 ft. 7 in.), hulking (275 pounds) Primo Carnera of Italy against Jack Sharkey of Boston. I say it was an interesting thing because nobody could tell in advance what was going to happen. The fact was anything could happen.

Poor old Primo had a very bad reputation on account of the numerous hippodromes in which he had participated, and Mr. Sharkey had by then just about established himself as the world's greatest in-and-outer.

Joe Williams, of the *New York World-Telegram,* candidly voiced his opinion a week before the bout.

"Put on the hot seat," he said, "I would have to admit I would not trust either one of the guys as far as I can throw the Empire State Building with my left hand. Which is another way of saying that in this fight you can make your own choice. I don't want any part of it."

Williams based his skepticism on the fact that Carnera was owned and operated by mobsters. It seemed he had been placed on earth for the sole purpose of being exploited by the most vicious of racketeers.

After touring around Europe in a phony buildup campaign, The Preem had been brought to America and introduced to the fight fans here by means of a cross-country tour, featuring quick knockouts. In one span of 34 bouts, he was credited with 30 "knockouts." Primo's opponents either came into the ring leaning or were more than normally sensitive to strong drafts, for Primo had only to swish his great glove through the air and–*crash!*–down they would fall. He fought 22 times between New York and Los Angeles, leaving a trail of flattened opponents and nose-holding experts behind him. In Chicago, one Elziar Rioux fell to the canvas for no particular reason after 47 seconds of the

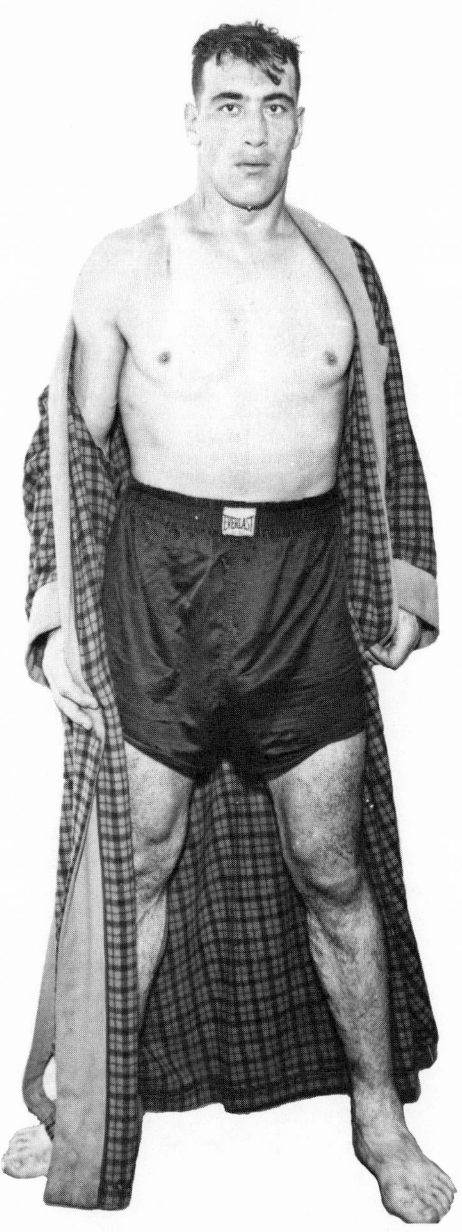

Six-feet-seven, 275-pound Primo Carnera of Italy was the biggest man ever to win the heavyweight championship.

first round. The Illinois Athletic Commission confiscated Rioux' end of the purse for play-acting unbecoming to a prize fighter.

In Oakland, a rugged individualist named Bombo Chevalier bombed the giant Italian with rights for a couple of rounds, splitting a gash above his eye and bruising his self-confidence. But the syndicate boys who owned Carnera were thorough. They had come prepared for just such a contingency. Between rounds one of Bombo's handlers rubbed rosin in Bombo's eyes. The blinded Bombo went out like a lamb in the sixth.

Another example? Well, Ace Clark, a rugged black, chose to ignore his corner's instructions and for five rounds committed violent mayhem on Primo. As Ace sat on his stool waiting for the bell, a cold, hard voice shouted up at him:

"Look down here, Ace."

Ace looked down. His mouth dropped open—for sitting at ringside was one of the mob's hoods, whetting a long, gleaming knife. P.S.: Carnera scored another KO in 30 seconds of the sixth.

In this manner, the line of victories grew longer.

Billy Duffy, a gutsy, low-bred character, listed himself as Carnera's manager by this time, and he signed for the match with Sharkey.

One afternoon, Joe Williams and Harry Grayson motored over to Primo's training camp to watch him work. The quarters were located across the Hudson from Manhattan and up in the hills of Jersey. It seemed to Williams very fitting that just before they turned into the road leading to Primo's place they passed an inn called "The Cuckoo's Nest."

Gus Wilson, distinguished as Georges Carpentier's old trainer, ran the camp. In every respect it was a very nice camp. Williams thought the ale was excellent. So did Grayson. In fact, it was with great difficulty that Jack Lawrence, the publicist, was able to tear them away from the grill to go out into the sun to watch the mammoth Carnera spar. They both tried to be critical. It seemed to them that Primo was using his left hand very well and that he was blocking punches much better than they had ever seen him do before.

"The man astonishes me!" Grayson said.

"I don't like the way he's shooting his right hand," Williams said. "It seems to me that he is merely throwing it and that there is no snap behind it."

Williams spotted George Engel in the crowd. George used to train Tunney. Williams said to Engel, "No man who throws a right hand like that can ever hope to be a fighter."

Joe could usually count on Engel for the right answer. But all he said was, "Will you have another ale?"

A few hours later Joe and Harry started back for New York to cover a bout between Loughran and Sekyra. Carnera asked to go along. He sat between Williams and Grayson. On the way over their car was stopped for speeding. "Pull over to the curb!" bellowed the motorcycle cop.

"Honest, officer, we were only going 30 miles an hour," Joe begged.

"Oh, yeah?" answered the cop. He looked inside the car. "Who is that big guy there in the middle?" Primo broke down and admitted he was Mrs. Carnera's first born in the flesh. "No kidding," grinned the cop.

"Well, follow me, I'll get you into New York in a jiffy," his very own words, too.

So they started out following the motorcycle. The cop opened wide his screeching siren, causing all other cars to move to one side and giving the middle-class occupants of the Williams-Grayson-Carnera car a feeling of great importance.

Everything was swell until they hit a fork turn in the road where traffic was not only active but populous. There was a head-on crash. At the moment Williams was talking to Primo about the time he had his nose broken. Neither of them saw the crash.

Primo was badly shaken up. Williams was knocked completely out, and had to be assisted to the nearest inn, where brandy was expertly administered. People crowded around. Where was he hit? An examination showed it was a scalp wound. A great sigh of relief followed. Apparently it was generally understood that a sports writer could not be hurt by hitting him on the head.

Then came the dawn. Primo and Joe were both sitting on an improvised couch in a gasoline station. Primo was moaning. "Ooooooooooo."

"Are you hurt?" asked Grayson, who had a faculty for asking the right thing at the right time. "Ooooooooooooo," answered Primo.

By this time Joe began to feel very bad himself, and he proceeded to tear off a few "Ooooooo's" just to see what effect they would have.

Primo was a very considerate fellow. He turned to Joe and said: "What we need is a bottle of pop." Well, as Joe always said there was nothing that would bring a fellow back to himself in a tough spot like a bottle of soda pop, so in no time they were heading into New York in a borrowed car with practically everybody agreeing that it was a narrow escape and that it might have been worse.

On the way over, Primo was himself again and talking to Williams and Grayson about the Sharkey fight.

"I am anxious to win this fight for two reasons," he said. "First, I want to convince myself that I am a real fighter. Second, I want to convince the American public that I am not a clown. I have seen Sharkey fight two fights, one against Schmeling and the other against Mickey Walker. I think he is a front runner. By that I mean he is a dangerous man for the first four or five rounds. I plan to rate myself accordingly. I am not going to try to do much against him in the early rounds, but after the fourth or fifth round I am going to try to knock him out. I may not succeed. I may be knocked out myself, but I am going to be in there swinging."

Substantially those were Primo's own words, as related to me by both Grayson and Williams some years later. Since he first arrived in the United States, he had improved his understanding and delivery of English quite remarkably. There was an instance in this connection at Primo's camp when Williams wanted to know how Primo would react to Sharkey's goat-getting tactics. He had put the question to Jack Lawrence. Joe assumed the remarks were too involved for Primo. The Primo was listening. "Don't ask him, ask me," he commanded. His answer was: "I pay attention to Sharkey's fists, nothing else."

Joe's own summation of Carnera was this: He came away from Primo liking him a lot. He was fully aware that he was a gorgeous hippodromer, that he had been involved in more broad travesties of the ring than any heavyweight in modern times, and that he was backed in America by the sinister Billy Duffy, whom Williams esteemed as a roistering midnight companion, and Owney Madden, whom Williams would not trust with last year's calendar—and yet Joe felt Primo could fight.

"Maybe not much," Joe wrote in his column the next afternoon, "but a little bit. And on top of that I have finally come around to the reluctant conclusion that it does not take a lot of fighting to beat Mr. Sharkey."

It was in this first fight with Sharkey that Primo got his first taste of canvas. Badly outclassed all the way, he went down from a sharp left hook in the fifth round and, as he was rising at the count of five, saw Sharkey rushing menacingly across the ring. Cringing visibly, Primo dropped back to his knees. The referee picked up the count and Primo, screwing up his courage, got to his feet at nine.

Primo managed to last the distance—all 15 rounds—and he clearly demonstrated, as he was to show countless times later, that while he lacked ability, he had not been short-changed when it came to courage. Sharkey disdained Primo's all but useless right and cut him to ribbons with left hooks and jabs. Yet Primo refused to quit. He stayed in there and absorbed a powerful beating.

At that, Carnera almost won on a disqualification in the wild fifth round when Sharkey, who had a history of losing his head at crucial moments, started to climb out of the ring under the misconception that Carnera had quit cold. Only quick thinking on the part of his handlers in blocking his exit saved the fight for him.

Billy Duffy was not discouraged. As far as he was concerned the Sharkey defeat was a detour but not a roadblock to the title. They would be back.

Carnera was taken to Europe to give the fans in America a chance to forget. He stayed away for a year. When he came back, Duffy masterminded another fast string of "KO's" for him. Although the metropolitan sports writers ridiculed these quick knockouts, Duffy decided that the time had come to move Primo into tougher competition. The best in the heavyweight division were Sharkey, Schmeling, Max Baer and Ernie Schaaf.

Duffy preferred Schaaf, a muscular ex-gob nicknamed the Blond Viking. Some experts considered handsome Ernie to be the best of the lot even though he had lost a close match to Max Baer earlier.

When the Carnera-Schaaf bout was announced, rumors began making the rounds that this was merely the first part of a "package deal." Schaaf, according to the grapevine, had agreed to lose to Carnera, thereby setting up a Sharkey-Carnera championship fight; then, if Carnera won, Schaaf would get his shot at the title.

True or false, both camps made the mistake of lending these rumors some credence by signing a contract for a Carnera-Sharkey bout on the eve of the Schaaf fight.

It was in this suspicious atmosphere, then, that Schaaf and Carnera battled each other on February 10, 1933, in New York. Almost from the opening bell a crowd of 20,000 skeptics booed the lame, colorless performance. Carnera won each of the first 12 rounds with his familiar shoving left as Schaaf, appearing dull and listless, failed to fight back. He never landed or even threw one good punch.

In the 13th, Schaaf staggered back from a light left lead. He clutched at the ropes with his right glove and slumped to a sitting position. At the count of five he toppled face downward to the canvas, while the fans booed bloody murder. They couldn't believe he was hurt.

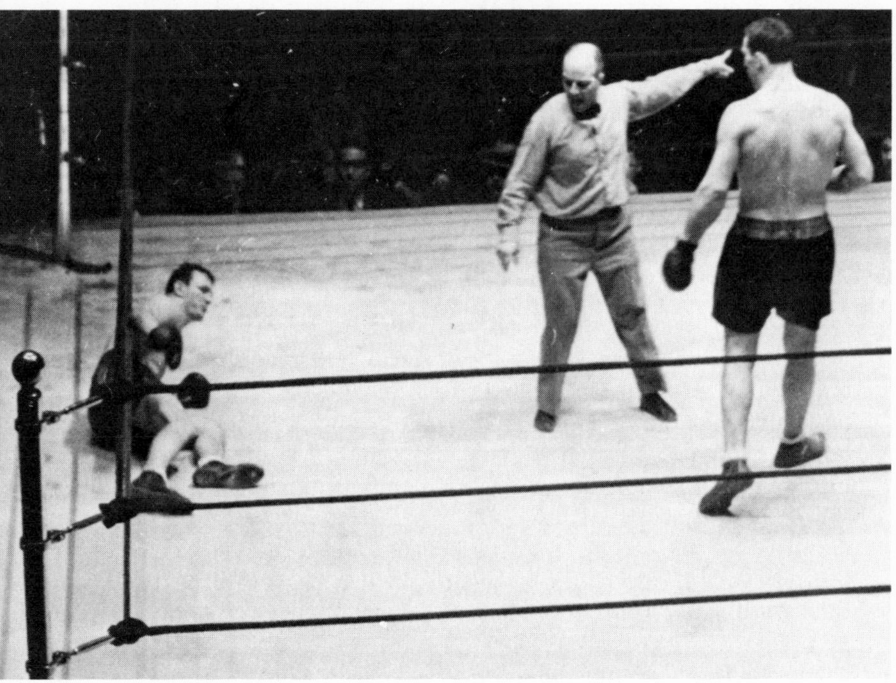

Carnera walks back to neutral corner after delivering a death blow to Ernie Schaaf in a New York ring, February 10, 1933. Schaaf died in the hospital five days later.

Amidst the hooting and cries of "Fake!" Schaaf's handlers worked feverishly to revive him. He was carried to his dressing room and 45 minutes later, still in a coma, was rushed to a hospital. There he lay in a state of semiconsciousness for nearly five days. At 4:10 A.M. on February 15th, a nurse walked over to his bedside and pulled a white sheet over his face. Ernie Schaaf was dead.

The autopsy showed the true cause of death to have been a blood clot left in the brain after the Baer fight. Further investigation revealed he had been bedded down with influenza one week before the fight. In simple language, Ernie Schaaf belonged in a hospital bed, not a prize ring, the night he met his death.

Carnera's owners quickly seized upon the tragedy and turned it into ballyhoo for the Sharkey match. They had no scruples. They pointed to Schaaf's death as proof of their young giant's "murderous" fists. His devastating strength, his ponderous blows and great bulk were simply too awesome for an ordinary mortal to cope with, they said.

The training-camp period leading up to the title match with Sharkey featured strange and shady doings. Some years later, Paul Gallico reminisced about the prefight atmosphere:

"Sharkey's reputation and the reputation of Fat John Buckley, his manager, were bad," wrote Gallico. "Both had been involved in some curious encounters. The reputation of the Carnera entourage by the time the second Sharkey fight came along was notorious, and the training camps of both gladiators were simply festering with mobsters and tough guys. Duffy, Madden, etc., were spread out all over Carnera's training quarters at Pompton Lakes. A traveling chapter of Detroit's famous Purple Gang hung out at Gus Wilson's for a while during Sharkey's rehearsals. Part of their business there was to muscle in on the concession of the fight pictures."

Rocky Marciano was only eight years old when Carnera won the title. Nineteen years later, after he himself was champion, he recalled how in the Italian section of Brockton, Massachusetts, they had big bonfires burning and they sang and shouted around them almost all night long in celebration of The Preem's victory over Sharkey. Rocky said he could still see those bonfires in the James Edgar playground right across the street from his house, and at the time he thought to himself: Gee, if he could win the title, he'd go back to Brockton and he'd throw a big party for the whole town and every kid would be invited and receive an expensive gift.

Right after Carnera defeated Sharkey he went to Brockton to referee at the old arena that was across Centre Street from the Brockton Hospital. Marciano's uncle, John Piccento, took him that night to see Primo, and on the way out the newly crowned heavyweight champion walked right by Uncle Piccento and Rocky and Rocky reached out and touched his arm.

When Rocky got home he told his father.

"I saw Carnera and I touched him," Rocky said. "I really did."

"How big is he?" his immigrant father, Perrino Marchegiano, asked.

"Bigger than this ceiling," Rocky said. "And you should see how big his hands and feet are!"

The giant Carnera towers over sports writers at training camp, describing the strategy he plans to use to win the heavyweight title from Sharkey, June 29, 1933.

Ominous things were shaping up indeed. Five days before the fight, Sharkey left his training camp and rushed back to Boston to check on the health of his children.

Still, Sharkey looked calm and confident as he climbed into the ring on that June 29th night of 1933. For five rounds he handled Carnera as he pleased. It was almost a carbon copy of their first fight. Toward the end of the sixth round, though, after a mild exchange against the ropes, Carnera swung one of his lunging right uppercuts. Sharkey went down and never moved a muscle as the referee counted to ten.

A strange hush fell over the audience. They sat in stunned silence, while Carnera danced happily around the ring. Manager Buckley, playing his role to the hilt, leaped into the ring and demanded that Primo's gloves be examined. His inference, of course, was that no mere mortal could cause such havoc with just skin, bone and leather.

Primo Carnera, for the record, was now champion of the universe.

Carnera defended his title only twice over the next dozen months. He won decisions in lackluster bouts with Paolino Uzcudun and Tommy Loughran. When the latter was asked by reporters if Primo hurt him, he replied: "Only once. When he stepped on my foot with one of those size-15 gunboats!"

The tip-off on what the experts thought of Carnera as champion was expressed by Petey Herman, the nifty little bantamweight champion of 1917 to 1920. Petey had since gone blind. He used to own a saloon on the edge of the French Quarter in New Orleans, where the fight mob congregated, and he would go through a patented routine in which he ran his hands over the body of a fighter and then tell him if he was of championship material or not. Sort of fortune telling by feel, you could say. Carnera dropped in one day on a visit to New Orleans and Petey gave him the touch treatment and then told him, "You're nothing but a big musclebound oaf!"

Max Baer stood in the wings, waiting to knock Carnera's crown off his head. The Carnera-Baer title bout was scheduled for June 14, 1934. Wrote Harry Grayson, in the *New York World-Telegram:*

"Seldom has there been a championship contest in which the principals have thought so little of each other's ability. Baer views Carnera as a set-up. Does Carnera boil over when told how Baer feels about it? He merely grins, and if pressed for an opinion sadly shakes his head, shrugs his mountainous shoulders and expresses regret for Max's temerity. 'We weel get reed of Baer and have eet over weeth,' he says. 'Mee feex Cuckoo.' Personally, Primo will be vastly more formidable than the good-natured big bloke who outfenced Loughran. He'll be ready for Baer."

Grayson's sidekick, Joe Williams, agreed with Harry.

"Primo is one of the few to outspear Loughran," Williams wrote. "Bowling over a clever one like Tommy is next to impossible once he starts concentrating on nothing more than remaining to the bitter end. Had Primo ironed out Tommy the majority would have said that he ought to be ashamed of himself for flattening a chap he outweighed 80 pounds. But when he outscored him, that was a frightful showing on his part. Nothing Carnera does is right. He starched Jack Sharkey, but somehow that didn't count, either.

"Baer was outpointed by Loughran. His closest friends didn't give him a round. He was outscored and outfinished by Paulino at Reno, where his pal, Jack Dempsey, gave the decision against him.

"Baer started building his reputation as a superman with the knockout of Tuffy Griffiths in Chicago on September 26, 1932. Griffiths, never without a china chin, was pretty well shot at the time. There followed the terrific engagement with poor Schaaf—the one in which the blond generally is supposed to have suffered the injury that led to his death following his meeting with Carnera. One judge gave Ernie a draw with Max as he lay on the floor at the final bell.

"Schmeling's training was widely criticized last summer. It was plain to close observers that the German's mind wasn't on his work. He hadn't boxed in a year and was dead in love. Steve Hamas' recent performance against Schmeling to some extent dimmed the lustre of Baer's achievement against him.

"In the coming contest, Baer finds himself more or less in the same position Schmeling was when they met. He, too, will have been inactive for a year, and surely has not led the quiet, restrained life of the well-mannered Teuton, not by a long stretch of imagination.

"But almost every one wants to see Baer stretch Carnera, and there is no question but that he has it in him to accomplish the feat. It would be a rare sight to see Primo fall again as he did in the first Sharkey scrap, but the real fun would come with Baer as champion.

"Can you imagine the handsome and cocky Californian wearing royal purple and living under the ancient legend that 'the king can do no wrong'? He'd have all the color and flamboyance of John L. Sullivan and something more besides. Did John L. drink a thousand beers? Then don't tell Baer or he'll try it."

Carnera vs. Baer for the heavyweight championship of the world was the maddest of all title fights. It couldn't very well have been anything else, considering the principals.

A week before the bout, reports from Asbury Park, where Baer had pitched his camp, were that Maxie was convulsing the crowds at his workouts and that he was devoting so much time to his comedy routine that he wasn't in shape. This caused the late Bill Brown, member of the New York State Athletic Commission and a stern, hard man, who had devoted his life to physical training, to visit the camp so that he might see for himself what was going on and determine whether or not Baer was fit.

The performance that Max and his manager, Ancil Hoffman, gave that day passed understanding. They had been warned of Brown's coming and of the purpose of his mission, yet Baer reached a new peak of hilarity in the ring, huffing and puffing meanwhile, and Hoffman's attitude toward Brown was one of studied indifference that bordered on insolence.

Brown's rage gathered like a darkening storm as he watched from a ringside seat and when the travesty was over and the grinning Baer had left the ring, the storm broke.

"Baer is a fat-headed bum," Brown said. "He is not in shape to fight Carnera or anyone else. He is not worthy of a chance to fight for the championship of the world and his attitude is an insult to the public. If I had the power to do so, I would call the fight off."

When this was repeated to Baer and Hoffman, the fighter laughed and the manager shrugged. The only one interested in Baer who was concerned was Jack Dempsey.

"Bill's right," Dempsey said, "and Baer is crazy. I've been trying to tell Max that something like this would happen but I might as well talk to a five-year-old boy. At that, I think the kid would understand what I was trying to tell him."

Bill Brown's attempt to bring about a cancellation of the fight failed. This, however, did not silence him. He repeated that Baer was a bum, denounced Hoffman for his obvious lack of control of the fighter and warned prospective customers that since the challenger was a clown, and out of shape at that, they could not expect to get full value for the money they laid on the line at the box office.

He was right in one respect, wrong in another. Baer was a clown and he wasn't in shape and the fight must have set the Marquis of Queensberry to spinning in his grave. But Baer won the fight and if the onlookers were bewildered at times by the spectacle unfolded before them, there was none who complained that he hadn't got his money's worth—part in excitement, part in laughs.

Carnera, a gentle giant, was strictly a book-taught fighter. He had learned by rote when to jab, when to hook, when to cross his right hand. He also had learned, by rote, how to throttle an opponent with his left hand while hitting him with his right, how to stick a thumb in his eye, how to give him the laces across his face and, considering the size of his feet—he wore size 15 shoes—how to stomp on his toes. In other words, he knew all the classic punches—and all the dirty tricks that had been invented by scalawags over a period of a hundred years or so.

Sometimes, however, he forgot. They told him, going into the ring with Baer, that the first time Max wound up to throw a right hand punch—to fall in. Never—and this was very important—they told him, never pull back. The first time Max wound up, which was approximately one minute after the opening bell, Primo pulled back. The punch hit him squarely on the chin and there he was, rolling on the floor.

Whatever happened after that... and plenty did... was purely incidental. Primo never completely recovered from that first punch. There was no rule in the book then that a fighter knocked down three times in a round automatically was through. Primo hit the deck 12 times. A couple of times, Max hit the deck with him, pulled off his feet by the power of his own punch. They roughed, they wrestled, they rolled on the rug. Baer needed no help from referee Arthur Donovan against Carnera's roughhouse tactics. He was rougher than Carnera.

In the 10th round, Carnera was knocked down three times. After the third knockdown, the referee got between the men, looking anxiously at Primo to see if he was fit to go on. Max jostled him, to get at the champion. From Max's corner, Hoffman and his seconds screamed curses at Donovan. Then the bell rang. Save for those at the ringside, the sound of the bell was drowned in the uproar all over the arena. Many thought Donovan had stopped the fight.

But now the fighters were coming out for the 11th round. Baer hit Carnera on the chin with a right hand and Carnera went down again. All the lessons he had learned had been blasted out of him long since, but punches could not rob him of courage. That was all he had left but it got him to his feet. Bleeding... dazed... his legs turned to rubber and not knowing quite where he was... he lurched into the ropes. That was when Donovan waved Baer to his corner and guided Carnera to his.

The fight was over. Baer was the new heavyweight champion of the world. But Bill Brown was correct about his condition. Baer, although winning all the way, had to stop several times to walk away from Carnera, hitch up his trunks for a stall and take a long, deep breath before he could return to the slaughter. Brown had the last word.

"He's still a bum," Bill said. "He won because he was in there with a bigger bum."

A strange case, Primo Carnera. He is remembered largely for two dubious distinctions: (1) He was the biggest man ever to win the world heavyweight boxing title, and (2) he was one of the prize ring's most tragic figures.

Carnera won no more than a handful of fights on his own merits in his entire career. Furthermore, his fights grossed more than $3,000,000, yet he was never known to have more than $500 to call his own after the racket boys who controlled him grabbed their share of his purses.

Primo was born on October 26, 1906. He weighed in at 22 pounds, the first son of a poor Italian stonecutter. By the time he was twelve, he was 6 ft. tall, weighed 220 pounds and was one of the landmarks of the tiny village of Sequals. He left home and for the next five years hoboed through northern Italy and southern France picking up what work he could find: laborer, bricklayer and, occasionally, stonecutter. At seventeen, now 6 ft. 6 in. tall and weighing 260, he signed on as a circus strong man and wrestler, billed as "The Terrible Giovanni, Champion of Spain." He was possibly the world's worst professional wrestler.

When the circus finally disbanded in Paris, in 1928, Carnera was picked off a park bench by a French pug named Paul Journee and brought to Leon See, an Oxford graduate, fight manager and promoter

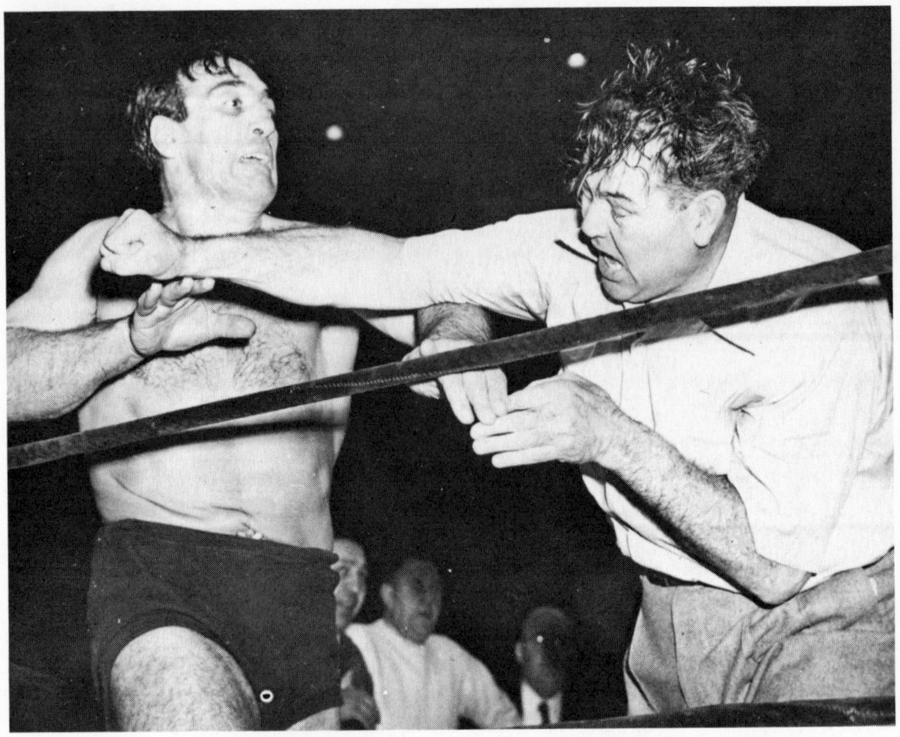

After mobsters had stolen all of his money, Carnera became a successful wrestler and finally earned some degree of financial security. Here he is being belted by referee Jack Dempsey, who felt Primo had been using unfair tactics on his grappling opponent, Don Eagle, in a 1950 match at the Boston Garden.

of anything that promised to bring him a franc or two. He trained the willing Italian in the manly art of self-defense for two weeks, then dumped him into a Paris ring with a tolerant heavyweight named Leon Sebilo. Sebilo conveniently collapsed in the second round and the pattern for Primo's subsequent ring career was established.

Before he arrived in America, mobsters already had cut in on his future.

In June, 1935, Primo was thrown into Yankee Stadium against the up-and-coming Joe Louis. The first punch the Detroit Bomber threw smashed Primo's mouth in. Bill Duffy, who had recently served time in prison for income tax evasion, was far from impressed. He sent Primo out for five more rounds and five more knockdowns before the referee stepped in and stopped one of the worst slaughters in ring history.

After the fight Primo sat unattended on his rubbing table. His face was still bloody, his forehead lumpy. His mouth was battered out of

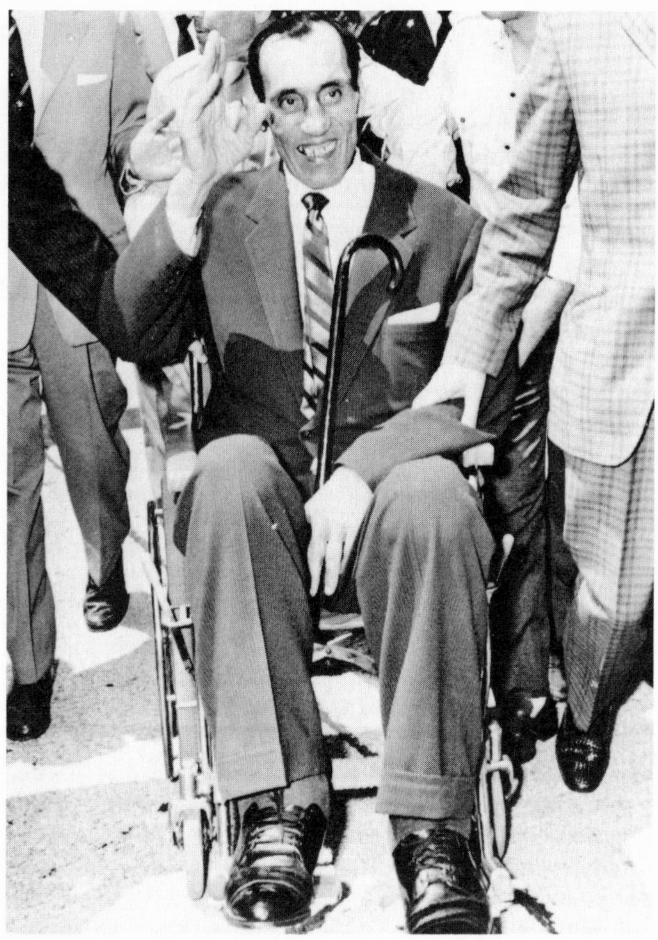

Carnera was only sixty when he died of sclerosis of the liver, on June 28, 1967. Here he waves goodbye to America as he boards a plane to return to his native Sequals, Italy.

shape. H. Allen Smith, the humorist who was then doing feature stuff for the *New York World-Telegram*, walked into the dressing room.

"Did he hit you hard?" he asked.

Primo stared at him through narrow slits for a long minute, then lowered his lop-sided head into his gloves.

"Jesus God, does he hit," he moaned.

"Do you want to fight him again?" Smith inquired.

"Oh Jesus God, no!"

Carnera was tossed back to the slaughter though. He fought on until a mediocre heavyweight named Leroy Haynes knocked him out twice within two weeks. After the second KO, Primo was dragged back to his corner, his left leg dragging uselessly.

The vultures abandoned him in the hospital. He was of no further use to them. They had picked the last ragged piece of flesh from his bones. Now that they could no longer feed off him they left him stranded. No prize fighter of note was ever treated with less decency, ever shorn more completely of dignity.

Primo Carnera died of sclerosis of the liver, on June 28, 1967. He was only sixty. But he didn't die broke as you'd suspect. After the Second World War, a Los Angeles wrestling promoter made a small fortune for Primo on the grunt-and-groan circuit–and for the first time in his life, Primo got to keep his share.

Before his death, in Sequals, Italy, Primo was philosophical about his unhappy life in the prize ring.

"Life has a way of evening things up," he said. "Where are those greedy vultures now? They were either killed by their own kind or put in jail. Some of them became little better than beggars and panhandlers. All that money. What good did it do any of them?"

13. Max Baer

YOU had to like Big Max. He introduced laughter to the prize ring at a time when there was nothing very funny about the heavies.

Max Baer was show business and wonderful copy.

Don't get me wrong. He could fight like crazy. Had he ever stopped clowning long enough, he could have become one of the greatest heavyweight champions of all time.

His huge enjoyment was infectious. Guys and dolls loved him. Handsome, carefree, incorrigible Max, who preferred a female "knockout" to a prize-fight knockout. Bill Saroyan, the author, should have been his press agent, though Maxie could make with the fanfare, the rolls and the flourishes.

"I'll kayo Ernie Schaaf in six rounds!" Max proclaimed, putting his foot through the drum. Then he hired a social secretary and did the night spots on 52nd Street in Manhattan.

This was New York's first look at the Golden Boy from California. The depression had all but ruined the fight game, and the heavyweights were a dull and dour lot.

The Garden was a haunted house. Max opened all the windows and let in the fresh air. That December night in 1930 he marched down the aisle like a conquering hero, bounded into the ring and took a shellacking from the veteran Schaaf.

But in defeat Max looked great, and his screwball performance endeared him to the crowd. In the third round, the Livermore Larruper missed by a mile with a haymaker and was practically reduced to hysterics by the *faux pas.* The next instant he was a scowling, seething killer—and still missed. And as he strolled to his corner between rounds, Max did not forget the ladies at ringside.

Max Baer was a creature of moods, and when the mood struck him, he was as brutal a heavyweight fighter as the prize ring has ever seen.

Baer had the last laugh on himself, and the fans gobbled it up. They stormed his dressing room after the fight and he regaled them with outlandish predictions and a madcap recap of what would have happened to Schaaf IF.

Max lived it up big in and out of the ring. His antics and showmanship kept boxing alive from 1930 until late 1934, when Louis came along. Grantland Rice called him "the New Deal for bored fight fans." His lusty sense of humor and irrepressible good spirits charmed the most cynical managers and even the gamblers who often dropped a double sawbuck because of his clowning.

Max Baer's hilarious antics and showmanship kept boxing alive from 1930 until late 1934. After one bout, a midget leaped into the ring and attacked him, and big Max pinned the little guy to the mat.

Who can forget the Magnificent Max, fighting for the world championship, suddenly pirouetting across the ring and wiping his feet in Carnera's resin box? Or Max toughening up for Schmeling by banging his leonine head against a lead pipe "to harden up my head for punches!"

The jester in Max would not be denied. Anything for a laugh, regardless of the risk. Baer worked overtime to build up the Baer legend.

Take that crazy afternoon when his manager, Ancil Hoffman, arrived at the camp ring to find Max flat on his back while a powerful trainer bounced a 14-pound medicine ball on his stomach. Pulling Max to his feet, the horrified Ancil turned to the scribes and remarked in his tired, quiet way, "Baer can do everything but *think.*"

"That's right," Max playfully agreed. "I got a million-dollar body and a ten-cent brain."

This popular, fun-loving fighter whiled away the smaller hours in night clubs surrounded by admiring frails and friends of every size, shape and description. Yet Max seldom took a drink and never smoked until he quit the ring.

A reporter offered Max a cigarette one night around 3 A.M. as he was "training" for the Carnera massacre.

"No siree!" said Max reprovingly as he squeezed the willing waist at his side. "You know I got to keep in shape for the fight."

It didn't require the James J. Braddock fiasco to demonstrate that Max was a sucker for a fast blonde. Women chased him, sued him, bobbysoxed him, threatened him. One enterprising babe tried to kidnap him. Whenever he appeared in the prize ring to do battle, the screams from the fair sex were fairly harrowing. And when he cast aside his robe, you couldn't tell the ladies from the women voters. Well over 6-feet tall, with magnificent wide shoulders tapering to a narrow waist, the 200-pound Baer was the best-looking hunk of man the heavyweight world had seen in quite a spell.

In 1938, when Max was training at Lakewood, New Jersey, for his second fight with Tommy Farr, the Welshman, the town's businessmen were alive to Baer's publicity value and sent their press agent over with a proposed stunt.

"Let's have Maxie rescue a girl from a runaway horse," said the p.a., entirely forgetting that Dempsey, Delaney, Sharkey, Tommy Loughran and Carnera had worn out that gag.

"Have Maxie rescue a girl from a runaway horse, eh?" snorted Walter St. Denis of Mike Jacobs' publicity staff. "Great! Wonderful!" And then after thinking about it for a moment, added, "But who's going to rescue the *girl* from Max?"

Dick McCann, who later wrote sports for the *New York News,* was Baer's press agent at the time. He recalled with delight that period of his career.

"Max was swell company," Dick said. "At the dinner table, he worried over whether everybody was getting enough; in card games, he would feign great distress over his bad luck; on long walks, he was an entertaining conversationalist. I spent one complete day alone with him in camp when his brother, Buddy, was taken up by manager Ancil Hoffman and trainer Izzy Klein to meet Gunnar Barland in the Garden a week before Maxie's tiff with Farr. Max was good for a laugh every hour...on the hour. After breakfast, he sat down and laboriously wrote three letters...one each to his month-old son (who grew up to star on the long-running television hit, *The Beverly Hillbillies),* wife and father. I had to spell every other word for him. After lunch, the cook came out and asked us if we wanted an apple. Max said yes but I said no. When the cook returned to the kitchen to get the apple, Max whispered: 'Hey, take yours and give it to me.' When the cook returned, Max said: 'He'll have one, too.' The cook went back for another. Maxie was proud for having put one over on her. On the way to the movies later, he mischievously munched on the second apple like a little boy who made off with a pie from the pantry window.

"That night, we sat and listened to his brother Buddy's bout with Barland. Maxie had been left at camp because he put up too much of a scene whenever Buddy fought. Max couldn't stand to see 'little' brother get hit. He kept shouting to the referee to stop the fight. But he was more restrained listening to the fight on radio. Still he suffered more through the bout than did Buddy. At first, he kept up a brave chatter as if he were trying to out-talk the announcer who was giving the blow-by-blow account of his brother's beating. But, as the fight went on and Buddy grew weaker, Maxie grew silent and sad. When the referee finally stepped in and stopped the bloodletting, Maxie snapped off the radio, grunted a hoarse goodnight and clomped to bed.

"The next morning, I found Max angrily reading the newspaper accounts of the fight, several of which claimed Buddy had quit. It was the only time I ever heard Maxie criticize a boxing story. 'I don't care what they say about me,' he said, 'but they shouldn't write those things about my brother.' "

Buddy Baer was a good heavyweight, but not in his older brother's class. Yet Buddy was good enough to earn two main events with Joe Louis. After the Brown Bomber knocked him out in the first round of their second match, in 1942, Buddy quit the ring.

"I'm glad I'm out," he told columnist Red Smith. "I never liked fighting much. I'm a Ferdinand, and that's no bull."

Years after Buddy stopped prize fighting, a man greeted him: "Hello, Buddy, where'd you get all the gray hair?"

"Did you ever fight Joe Louis twice?" Buddy asked. Then he added: "You've got plenty of gray there yourself."

"Yes," the man said. "I bet on you both times."

Like all comics, Max Baer had his serious side. While he was able to restore some measure of insanity to a baleful atmosphere, he knew the futilities of it all. The memories of Frankie Campbell, the fighter who had never recovered from a Baer smash to the chin, had become a part of him. Following this tragic accident, Max resolved never to fight again, and only the direst necessity forced him to return to the ring. The death of Campbell must explain in part Baer's spells of indifference throughout the rest of his career.

Maxie was a creature of moods, and when the mood struck him, he was as brutal a fighter as you would care to see. He could handle his dukes, and his right-hand punch was frightening to behold. In fact, he was right-hand daffy. Until he lost some of his confidence, Max had the courage and stamina of a bull. He came from behind in the Schmeling fight and ruined Herr Max. He battered down the tough Ernie Schaaf in his prime (1932) and lowered the boom on Kingfish Levinsky in the second round.

In that brief span between the Schmeling and the Braddock bouts, from June 8, 1933, to June 13, 1935, Baer merited the lofty title of "champion." He was willing to take on anyone. He believed himself to be invincible and was totally disdainful of what a rival might do to him.

Max Baer's preparation for a fistic career was fairly conventional. Born in Omaha, Nebraska, on February 11, 1909, he was the second of five children. His German-Jewish father, Jacob Baer, and Scotch-Irish mother, Nora Bales Baer, were both 6-feet tall and weighed well over 200 pounds.

The family moved to Livermore, California, when Max was fourteen years old. He quit the eighth grade and went to work on the ranch his father had rented. His parents hated to take him out of school, but there was a man-sized job to be done. Both he and his kid brother Buddy helped their father in a Livermore slaughterhouse.

"Our father was a champion, too," Buddy recalled, "at dressing a steer. That's opening the steer, removing the insides, splitting him, and turning back the hide. In a contest once dad dressed a steer and carved the American flag on the hide in 3 minutes and 36 seconds. So he was a champion, and he had two sons. One got to be the heavyweight champion, and the other fought for the title twice.

"Our family is full of coincidences like that. Dad wanted to be a fighter—he used to train with Tom Sharkey and Jim Jeffries—but his mother threw all his boxing equipment down the well, and that ended his career. I still have a wire that Thomas Beaudry, who was head of the Piggly-Wiggly stores, sent on June 11, 1914, the day I was born. It said: 'Congratulations on the new white hope.' Jack Johnson was champion then and they were looking for white hopes. So I grow up and another black fellow is champion and I fight him twice as a white hope."

Both Max and Buddy lugged huge sides of beef, and the gruelling slaughterhouse chores changed them from underweight striplings into marvelous physical specimens. At nineteen, for example, Max stood over 6 feet and weighed 190 pounds—all solid bone and muscle.

When Max was sixteen, Father Baer took him to Oakland to see his first professional fight. Max was not impressed. The only fighter he cared about was Jack Dempsey. When the Manassa Mauler lost the title to Tunney later that year, Max bawled.

At twenty, he persuaded his father to let him go to Oakland and become a fighter. There he took a job hauling huge iron castings in the Atlas

Diesel factory. Evenings he worked out at Jimmy Duffy's gym, where he attracted the attention of an old-time fighter named Ray Pelkey.

One night Pelkey invited Max to spar with him. He tossed a couple of light ones, and Max countered by whacking him to the mat. Pelkey leaped up, embraced the young novice and declared, "You're all right! I'm gonna make a champ out of you!"

When Max returned to the Diesel plant, his bellows of self-acclaim could be heard above the roar of the engines. I. Hamilton Lorimer, the son of the factory owner, took an interest in Baer. He arranged for a little pow-wow between his employee and an Indian named Chief Cariboo.

At the Oak Park Arena in Stockton, Max served notice to all and sundry that he was about the meanest critter on the Coast. He danced around like a maniac and yelled threats through the thin walls at the amazed Cariboo. Max drank five bottles of soda pop before entering the ring. He clouted the Chief lustily for a couple of rounds and then telegraphed a right-hand wallop that must have traveled two feet. The talented Cariboo went down, and Max collected 35 one-dollar bills. He thought he could retire.

In his second year as a pro, the ambitious Baer could rake in $10,000 a fight in California money. On the eve of the Campbell fight, he had scored over a dozen knockouts and lost only three bouts, two on decisions and one on a foul.

By this time Lorimer was at his wits' end trying to curb Baer's shenanigans and decided to let Ancil Hoffman do the managing. Hoffman promoted the Campbell-Baer fight because a victory for his big bad boy might lead to a ranking among top heavyweight contenders. Frankie, the brother of baseball's Dolph Camilli, was better than anyone Max had faced to date, and Hoffman had the Livermore Kid way up for this one.

In the second round a Campbell punch made Max slip to the canvas. Figuring he'd scored a knockdown, Frankie turned his back and headed for his corner. An enraged Baer leaped to his feet and went after Campbell, and as the young man wheeled to face him, Max let go with everything he had. The blow landed on Frankie's chin with a sickening thud.

Frankie defended himself for two more rounds but collapsed in the fifth. Six hours later he died in the hospital. That one punch had lacerated his brain.

The tragedy plunged Max into prolonged grief and remorse, and for a time one wondered whether he would ever be his old self again. On top of this he was flat broke. The house he had bought for his parents was only partially paid for, and his personal debts were staggering.

Hoffman and Lorimer finally convinced Max that he should not blame himself for Campbell's death and that a change of scene might revive him and the heavyweight division. They took him on a long trip that wound up in New York.

Max started working his way up the ladder again. He started slow.

He lost a 10-round decision to Ernie Schaaf, knocked out Tom Heeney in three, and then dropped another decision, this time to Tommy Loughran, one of the sweetest boxers of all time. Loughran had worked as Dempsey's main sparring partner for the first Tunney fight. He had held the light-heavyweight title of the world, outgrew the division in 1929, and moved on to the heavyweight class.

Tommy gave Max a boxing lesson he never forgot. Baer played chump for Loughran's jabs and lightning-like feints and the latter walked away with an easy decision.

Before the fight, the muddled Maxie had gone around New York selling pieces of himself to eager buyers. Everybody got a chunk of him, for sums ranging from $500 to $10,000. The fun-loving Baer quickly spent the dough on broads. So after losing to Loughran, he showed up the following day at Madison Square Garden to collect the purse for his end of the waltz.

"I walk into the room to get my pay," Max said later, "and there I see nothing but the awful lookin' faces of those guys who had bought pieces of me!"

The addlepated Maxie had sold exactly 113 percent of himself!

Baer had breakfast the next morning with Jack Dempsey, who had refereed the Loughran bout, and Max complained, "Tommy had me lookin' at left jabs all night... lefts, lefts, lefts... that's all I need."

"You could've stopped Loughran in the first round," Jack said.

"How?"

"Take off your coat," ordered Dempsey. Max shucked off his coat. "Now lead with a left, just as Loughran did."

Max led.

"YOW! You broke my arm," yelped Max, holding it painfully. Dempsey had dropped his huge right fist across Baer's left biceps with paralyzing force as Max led with his left. The left arm was useless for a half hour.

"But that's *illegal!*" said Baer.

"I know it," Dempsey said, "but the ref will usually only warn you the first time."

Though Dempsey never said so, Maxie was his favorite fighter. It was odd the affection the old Manassa Mauler had for the exasperating, unpredictable Baer. Max was not a fighter in the Dempsey tradition, in spite of the numerous and generous comparisons made of them after Baer won the championship. Maxie seldom exhibited any of the killer qualities that the fierce Dempsey brought to every fight. Some of the fiascos his protégé engaged in must have sickened the heart of the Dempsey of the mining-camp brawls, the street fights, the bloody battles of his turbulent ring days. Yet Jack clung tenaciously and loyally to Baer, coaching him, treating him like a son, scolding him, laughing at him, investing money in him, and protecting him.

Dempsey sometimes got into the training ring with Baer. He took part in the promotion of Max's 1933 fight with Schmeling, and as a stunt, Dempsey went over to Schmeling's camp and sparred a round with him. Then, the following Sunday, he showed up at Baer's training grounds to box a round with Maxie, his pride and joy. Dempsey was almost forty years old then and Max figured they would just clown a little for the benefit of the spectators. Jack came out of his corner bobbing and weaving like a maniac, scowling and snarling like he'd just been let out of a cage. As he closed in on Max, Baer said, "Hi, pal," and Jack nailed him on the button. The punch nearly tore the hair off Max's head. But, to Baer's credit, he shook the daffodils out of his eyes and let go with all the steam he had right into Dempsey's belly.

"OOF!" grunted Jack. he threw his arms around Maxie, grinned and said, "You dirty bastard! Whaddya tryin' to do, kill your *promoter?*"

Max hung on to him with all his strength and replied, "You dirty sonofabitch, you almost killed your *fighter!*"

Baer, in an infrequent reflective mood one time, admitted it was one of the toughest rounds of his career.

For years Dempsey tried to come up with a good new heavyweight who would adopt his style. Baer never quite came up to his standards. This was a great disappointment to him.

"I never succeeded in finding what I was after," Dempsey said. "I would have liked to. If I found a fella who had the ambition, he had some physical make-up that was wrong. I never found the right guy. But fighting, and my way of training, was too rough for the average fella. I'll tell you about a fella I brought up from South America. He wanted to be a fighter, and he was big enough to beat 20 guys, but when he got in the ring he wouldn't fight. He'd run away, and I couldn't stop him. So I just got myself a little stick and sharpened it, and every time he ran way I'd stick him with this little stick. Pretty soon he knew I'd do it to him, so he said, 'Why do you do that to me?' I said, 'I'm trying to make a fighter out of you. As big as you are, instead of running away, run into them.' He didn't like it. He didn't have any ambition to be a fighter. Did you ever see two chickens fight? Well, some of these fellas who think they're fighters, or have the ambition to fight–it's brutal to see two chickens fight. I don't advocate anything like it, but if a fella has ambitions to be a fighter, he should go and see two chickens fight. If you have the courage and the guts of a chicken, when you see them lying there almost dead, and they can't move and are still pecking at the other chicken, trying to get up, then you see a fighter."

Baer fought like one of those half-dead gamecocks the night he battled the toast of old Germany, Max Schmeling. It was the only bout Baer had in 1933, and he made it a good one. Schmeling was still burning over the Sharkey decision of the previous year. He knew that a win over Baer would give him the chance to win back the title. Schmeling trained hard, and Baer worked out a little for this one upon the insistence of his backers. He huffed and puffed in training camp, but the ringside odds in Yankee Stadium on the night of the fight were 3 to 1 on the German.

For seven rounds of mayhem Schmeling made those odds stand up. He scored heavily in the exchanges. His wicked left jab cut Baer's handsome face to shreds, and the Baer torso was wracked with pain. But Baer never stopped coming, and now and then he'd land a terrific right that would rock Schmeling to his foundation.

In the eighth round, Baer fought the way Dempsey always wanted him to fight. He hooked and backhanded Herr Max, cupped Schmeling's head with one hand while he massaged him with the other and in general behaved so atrociously that referee Arthur Donovan had to warn him to stop the alley tactics.

Schmeling boxed Baer's ears off through most of the ninth, but Baer cornered him and at the bell Schmeling was hanging on the ropes,

Baer fought only once in 1933, and this was it—Max Schmeling goes down in the 10th round. The German rose at the count of nine, only to have the referee stop the bout a minute later after severe punishment.

gasping. In the tenth round the referee stepped in. Schmeling looked like a drunk trying to learn how to skip rope.

Baer never fought another one like that.

By now, Primo Carnera held the heavyweight championship. With the sports pages expressing grave misgivings about the men behind him, the mobsters who owned Carnera desperately needed an opponent who was above suspicion. A match was arranged with Tommy Loughran, who had two undeniable virtues: his honesty was beyond reproach and his best days were beyond recall. Primo outweighed him by 105 pounds. The giant Italian won a decision in 15 rounds. The fight had drawn only 8,625 paid customers.

The Carnera crowd looked around for another opponent. They needed another payday. Prohibition had been repealed, leaving them in that awkward age between bootlegging and bookmaking. Their only liquid asset was poor old Carnera, and nobody wanted to see him fight.

The only real attraction around was Baer, who had just knocked out Schmeling and made a movie with Myrna Loy. Maxie, though, could think of dozens of things he'd rather do than fight, all of them involving wine, women and song.

When Maxie finally consented to take time out to fight for the championship, Carnera found himself—for the first time in his life—trapped in a ring with a fighter who could really hit and had not been handcuffed.

Baer was aware long in advance that he could beat Carnera, and how to do it. He found out about the champion in studio bouts, working in a motion picture out in Hollywood. During the filming Baer was only supposed to provide some spectacular movie opposition for the giant. But in those studio bouts Max discovered that The Preem could be hit by a long overhand right, his own most effective blow. Carnera had a fair boxing routine, and was not so slow for his size, but Baer found that the Italian was a sucker for a right swing brought up from the floor. What Baer learned in the Hollywood studio he applied in the Long Island ring, June 14, 1934. He cut Carnera down with sweeping, overhand rights. It was all over in 11 rounds. Baer was the new champion.

As champion of the world, Max was a disappointment. He held the crown only 364 days. He never engaged in one legitimate bout while he was on top. He fought a series of eight 4-round exhibitions against third-raters—and that was all. On the 365th day as champion, he finally put his title on the line against the "Cinderella Man," James J. Braddock. "I clowned away the champeenship in 15 rounds," Maxie later admitted.

Max married Mary Ellen Sullivan and announced he was through with prize fighting. But Mike Jacobs, the New York promoter, wasn't listening. He offered Max a $150,000 guarantee to fight the sensational rising young star, Joe Louis. Max said he would think it over. He had injured his right hand in the Braddock fight so he flew down to Johns Hopkins with Dempsey for X-rays and a rest. The doctor told him that an operation was necessary and it would take eight months for the hand to heal. Max typically decided to whip Louis so he could pay for the operation!

On September 24, 1935, Baer and Louis attracted a crowd of 88,150. It still stands as the largest Yankee Stadium fight audience in history. Joe jolted Maxie into semi-retirement in the fourth round. Max became a homebody.

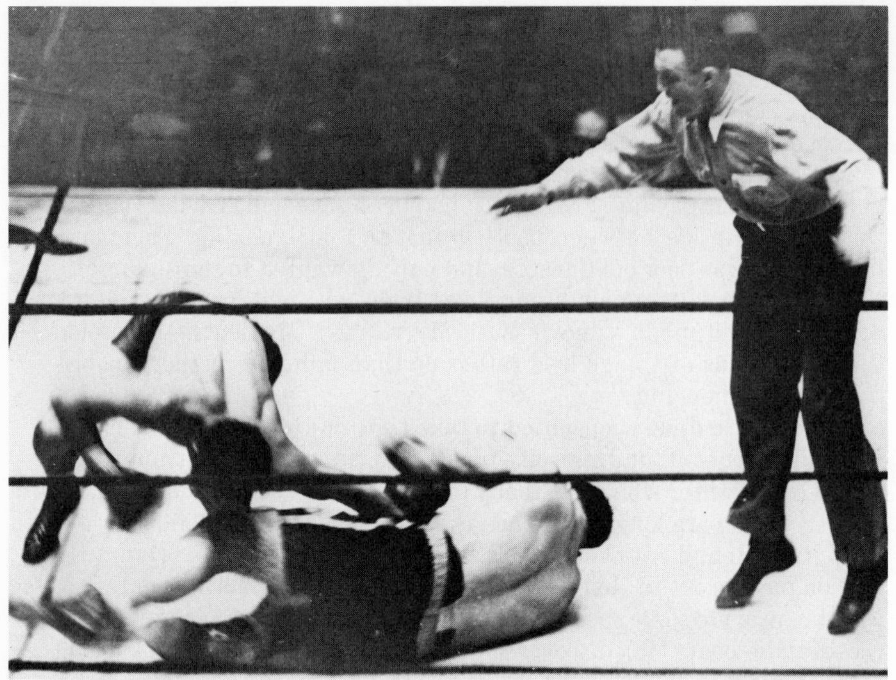

Grantland Rice called Max Baer "the New Deal for bored fight fans." Here he wrestles Primo Carnera to the canvas. He got up and knocked the giant Italian out in the 11th round to win the championship.

Then on June 1, 1939, at the age of thirty, boxing's greatest comedian slipped quietly into the Garden to do battle with fellow Californian Lou Nova. Too much "Nova-cane" put Maxie to sleep in the 11th.

This time he was really through, he declared, and on April 4, 1941, he actually retired after a second go at Nova and a grotesque outing with beer-soddened Two-Ton Tony Galento.

Max flunked the physical for World War II and browbeat the Army until they let him in. "How could they keep me out? Why, I started the whole damn thing, getting Hitler all riled up by beating Schmeling and then getting Mussolini against us by what I did to poor old Primo!"

As a staff sergeant, Maxie taught physical education with all the trimmings. A captain flew his private plane while a first lieutenant carried his bags. Or so Maxie said.

Only a few staunch friends stood by Baer in the twilight of his career. Ancil Hoffman was one, of course, and Jack Dempsey another.

But there was no need to feel sorry for Max Baer.

He had the time of his life, made scads of friends, and retired with all his marbles.

The brothers Baer are sworn into the Army Air Force in 1942. Max, center, said: "How could they keep me out of the service? Why, I started the whole damn war, getting Hitler all riled up by beating Schmeling and then getting Mussolini against us by what I did to poor old Primo!" Buddy Baer was a good enough heavyweight to earn two main events with Joe Louis.

14. James J. Braddock

THE night of June 22, 1937, at Comiskey Park in Chicago, on which Joe Louis knocked out Jim Braddock in the eighth round and so became the heavyweight champion of the world, Braddock hit the Brown Bomber on the chin with a right hand, following a stabbing left, and knocked him down.

Although the punch landed cleanly, it didn't seem to carry the force that most of Braddock's right-hand punches did and it was surprising to see Louis go down. The notion by many was that Joe must have been off balance, a notion heightened by the fact that he obviously wasn't hurt and immediately started to get up, although, in his corner, Jack Blackburn was bawling at him to take nine.

"Remember, Chappie," Blackburn had cautioned him, "you can't get up from a knockdown so fast the people didn't see you on the floor. The law gives you nine seconds to stay down. Take all nine, even if you ain't hurt."

Anyway, there was the sensational Joe Louis on the floor, but he got up and began to cut Braddock down, round after round. At the end of the sixth round Joe Gould, in Braddock's corner, said:

"I am going to stop it because you are getting hurt too bad."

"If you do," Braddock said, "I'll never speak to you again."

Gould, the manager, knew his fighter meant it and reluctantly sent him out for the seventh round. Jim got through the seventh somehow but in the eighth Louis hit him a fearful punch in the mouth and he pitched forward. He was completely knocked out, his face pressed against the canvas.

Years later, Frank Graham of the *New York Journal-American* was in Chicago talking to Tommy Thomas, who was the keeper of a tavern in town but who was the referee the night Louis knocked Braddock out.

Following a stabbing left, Braddock hit Joe Louis on the chin with a right hand and knocked him down in the first round of their title fight at Comiskey Park in Chicago, June 22, 1937. The Brown Bomber got back up and seven rounds later KO'd Braddock to become the new heavyweight champion.

"Tommy," Frank asked, "how close did Braddock come to knocking Louis out in the first round that night?"

Tommy shook his head. "As a matter of fact," he said, "Louis came closer to knocking Braddock out in the first round. You remember the left jab that Jim threw just before he let the right hand go? Well, that was more of a feint than a jab and Joe threw his right hand over it and, as Jim was throwing his right, Joe's punch hit him on the chin. When Joe went down, Jim almost fell over on top of him. 'Get back,' I said. 'Go to a neutral corner.' Jim was so dazed it was hard for him to make it, and when Joe got up I motioned them together again. Jim leaned on Joe to keep his own feet."

"Braddock was a game guy," Frank said.

"I never saw a gamer one," Tommy said.

"Did you know," Frank asked, "that Gould wanted to stop it at the end of the sixth round?"

"I did not," Tommy said, "but it's easy to believe. I knew Joe Gould only slightly, and that only later on, but he seemed to be a nice little man and, from what I hear, he and Jim were very good friends and he must have been suffering. As the referee, I had to remember that the champion of the world must be allowed to continue as long as he is on his feet and has a chance to win, no matter how bad he is being punished and so I could not stop it, but I could appreciate how Gould must have felt."

"How about the punch that ended the fight, Tommy?"

"It was, I think, the hardest I ever saw Louis, or anybody else, land," Tommy Thomas said. "When they got Braddock up and took him to his corner, I went over to look at him and I could see his teeth through the wide cut in his upper lip."

Seventeen years after losing the crown to Louis, Jim Braddock sat in the living room of his home in North Bergen, New Jersey, talking to Bill Heinz, the author.

"What do you remember about that fight?" Bill asked him.

Jim was sitting back in an easy chair. He had on a pair of tan slacks and a sports shirt, open at the neck. He made a cluster of the fingers of his right hand and put them to his forehead.

"I had bumps all over my head," he said. "My eyes, my ears, my lip, my nose was cut."

"How many stitches did you have?" Bill asked.

"Six in the lip," Jim said, "and 23 all over. The punch he finished me with was a right hand. It drove my tooth through the mouthpiece and the lip. I don't remember going down or hearing the count. I think the referee coulda counted a thousand over me."

Jim Braddock was always like that, honest, straightforward. In 85 fights he was stopped once on cuts, but Joe Louis was the only one who ever knocked him out. Why did he try to punch with Louis?

"I intended to box him," Jim said, "but in that first round I seen him get set to throw the right hand. I stepped back and naturally he come in, and I stepped in and let the right go. I didn't hit him on the chin, but he went down and I said to myself: 'If I hit him a good punch he'll stay down.' I went after him and spent a lot of energy, and after the fourth round he started layin' it into me."

Whitey Bimstein remembered the fifth round. Whitey and Ray Arcel worked Braddock's corner for the Baer and Louis fights with Joe Gould and with Doc Robb, who trained Jim.

Whitey said that Jim walked back to the corner and said, "What's the matter with the lights? They're getting' dim." Louis' punches had been taking their toll.

In the sixth round, Louis hammered a frightening left hook into Jim's stomach. Jim thought his stomach was in his mouth, and he said to Gould: "What did I run into tonight, a box car?"

At the end of the seventh round Gould wanted to stop it. But Jim wouldn't let him throw in the towel.

"If I'm gonna lose it," Jim told him, "I'll lose it on the deck."

He then walked out and carried the fight to Louis and Joe finished him in 1:10 of that next round. When the last right hand landed, Jim pitched forward on his face and, as the referee counted over him, he lay there in a growing pool of his own blood.

Few heavyweight champions have belonged to the people as did James J. Braddock. Here he looks over some photographic memories of days when he ruled the roost.

Mae Braddock, Jim's wife, said she would never forget what happened the day after the fight, when she and Jim left their hotel to return to Jersey.

"Usually everybody forgets a loser," she said, "but when we wanted to go to the railway station there was such a crowd in front of the hotel that the police had to take us out the back. To think that all those people came there to show Jim how much they thought of him—even in defeat. That was real nice."

Perhaps no big-league boxing writer of that era knew Braddock better than Bill Heinz. Bill wrote some stirring copy about the big, good-natured Irishman, and he said he suspects that Jim will never be properly placed among the heavyweight champions of the world.

"In no list that you will ever see will he be listed among the 10 greatest, but that is as it should be," Bill said, "He had a good left hand but he was not a great boxer and, although he could bang with that right hand, he was not a great puncher. He may, however, in the sense that others could see themselves in him and read their own struggles into his, have belonged to more people than any other champion who ever lived. His beginnings as a fighter were the beginnings of all fighters. What happened to him, though, happened to a whole country, and that is why I believe that no other fighter was ever as representative of his time."

Jim was the sixth of five boys and two girls. He was born in a brownstone tenement at 551 West 48th Street in what was known in New York as Hell's Kitchen. His father was a furniture mover, and later he worked as a guard for the New York Central and then as a pier watchman for the Holland-America line. His family moved across the river to West New York when Jim was nine months old. He quit school when he was fourteen and in the eighth grade, and got a job in a printing shop in New York. His brother Joe, who was four years older than Jim, had 19 fights as a pro, and he was the first one to teach and train Jim.

Jim was the amateur light-heavyweight champion of New Jersey in 1925 and '26.

He had his first pro fight in 1926 and lost a decision to a character who fought under the name of "The Astoria Butcher Boy." The Butcher outweighed him by 23 pounds.

Heinz recalled that Braddock was training in Joe Jeannette's Gym in Hoboken when Joe Gould walked in one day with his middleweight, Harry Galfund. Joe was trying to sell Galfund for $2,500, and he had hooked a couple of Jersey buyers into the gym to watch Galfund work out.

Gould spotted Braddock and he said, "I'll give you five bucks to go three rounds with my fighter."

"Sure," Jim said.

At the end of the three rounds the buyers cut the price in half. Joe walked over to Jim.

The future champ at the age of nine. The occasion was young Braddock's first communion.

"Here's fifteen bucks," he said.
"For what?" asked Jim.
"Who manages you?" Joe said.
"My brother Joe," Jim said.
"I'll meet the two of you here the day after tomorrow," Gould said.

"And that was the way it started for them," Bill Heinz recalled. "It developed into one of the great partnerships of boxing. Jim was 21 at the time and Joe Gould was 30. They looked like Mutt and Jeff and behaved like Damon and Pythias. Joe was a little guy out of Poughkeepsie, New York, the son of a rabbi. He was a dapper, smooth-faced talker and schemer, and served as a captain in the Army in World War II."

Whether Joe Gould was as colorful a fight manager as some writers said and whether he contributed substantially to Braddock's championship later isn't really important now and, except for barbering purposes, probably never was. If flamboyant dress, incendiary language, and brassy mannerisms add up to what passes for color in the prizefight racket then Gould had his full quota and any time a fighter gets to be champion it is reasonable to assume he got some help from his manager, in or outside the ring.

Sometimes a successful manager is a fellow who can throw his weight around politically. Billy Gibson, who had Benny Leonard and later Gene Tunney, belonged to that group. Gibson knew little about the actual mechanics of prize fighting. But he did know the right people. Tunney permitted Gibson to appear in his corner but took no instructions from him.

Sometimes the trainer is the most important member of a fighter's cabinet, as, for example, Jack Blackburn was to Joe Louis. There is no such thing as a natural-born fighter. A natural-born hitter, yes, but there is more to fighting than simply throwing punches. All Louis knew about the refinements of fighting he got from the razor-scarred Blackburn. This may have been the biggest break Louis got, being associated with the wise veteran from Philadelphia. None too bright himself, it is conceivable Louis might have been ruined in another's hands.

Ancil Hoffman was a sharp business agent, but he wasn't equipped to teach a fighter anything or plan ring strategy. Max Baer had the makings of a great heavyweight. But instead of expanding, his potentials diminished. Like so many young heavyweights, he was right-hand crazy. Hoffman was never able to sell Baer on the value of a two-handed arsenal.

"It always seemed to me that if Gould had been a good manager," Joe Williams said, "Braddock's career would have been less difficult and spotty. About the only thing that gives a touch of the unusual to Jim's ring story is that at one stage his personal fortunes fell so low he had to appeal to the state for support. Naturally when, months later, he beat Baer, the incident took on the rich flavor of sentimental drama. It just didn't seem to me that a good manager would let a fighter—who, as subsequent events were to prove, was good enough to win the world's heavyweight title—fade so completely into obscurity."

Williams was making reference to the Depression Years. In 1929, the roof fell in on Braddock as the great chasm opened on Wall Street. He lost to Leo Lomski, Tommy Loughran, Yale Okun and Maxie Rosenbloom. Jim had started out showing tremendous promise, but now he wasn't what he once seemed to be. Now the long lines formed in front of soup kitchens and the relief offices and Jim Braddock lost three out of five in 1930, two out of four in 1931, six out of eight in 1932. He was four and four on September 25, 1933, when he had a chance to pick up $300 against Abe Feldman at Memorial Field in Mount Vernon, New York. In the sixth round the referee threw them both out for not trying and held their purses. That had to be the end for Jim.

"Things were tough," Braddock recalled. "I figured all hope was gone. There were no jobs in sight, and now I had a broken hand and they were holding my $300. I went into the dressing room that night, and I cried."

Jim married Mae in 1930, and now there were two small sons, Jay and Howard. Each morning Jim would get up at 6:30 and have his breakfast and walk over to the Palisades and down those steep stairs at 69th Street to the docks for the shape-up. When he was lucky he would get in eight hours handling railroad ties, two guys to a tie, lifting them out of the ships from the South and up onto flat cars. Other times he worked on the coal docks, all night, at 60 cents an hour. Sometimes he would work both jobs. By now they were living in the basement of an old apartment house. The rent was $25 a month. Jim was earning $19 a week and, for eight months, they were on relief.

When there was no work, Jim sat on the bench outside Jimmy Johnston's office when Jimmy was the boxing promoter at Madison Square Garden. Inside, Joe Gould would be pleading with Jimmy to give Braddock a fight.

On June 14, 1934, Primo Carnera defended his title against Baer in the Long Island Bowl. One of Carnera's sparring partners was John (Corn) Griffin, a tough, young, right-hand puncher out of Fort Benning, Georgia. Corn had impressed sports writers with the way in which he belted Carnera around, and Johnston put him into the six-round semi-final bout of the Carnera-Baer card. Then he looked for an opponent.

"You have to give Braddock that spot," Gould kept saying to Johnston.

"Why?" Johnston said.

"Because he needs it," Joe said. "His wife and kids have to eat. Jim is desperate. Somebody's got to do something for him, and he doesn't want charity. He wants a fight."

"Can he stand up for six rounds?"

"Why not? He always has."

"All right," Johnston said, finally. "I'll give him $250 for six rounds with Griffin."

Johnston had a heck of a time getting the New York State Athletic Commission to approve the match, and if you wanted to bet Braddock you could get 6 to 1.

Joe Williams was at the Garden the day the Griffin-Braddock fight was made. "Charley Harvey was managing Corn and wanted to get him started in New York with a flourish," Joe said. "The best way to accomplish this was to get some washed-up name fighter and kick his brains out. Braddock, who had been out of action for some 10 months and was working as a longshoreman on the Jersey side, seemed to fit the bill perfectly. On two days notice he accepted the match, obviously without any training. This is what made me feel Gould had not put over a sleeper on Harvey as was later claimed. More likely, this was just a chance to split a small purse with a fighter he had given up on, and virtually forgotten. Like Baer, Braddock used to be right-hand crazy. But unlike the Magnificent Screwball, he developed a left, a very good left, too. Gould had nothing to do with that, either. 'I got it wrestling freight on the docks all those months I was not fighting,' Braddock once told me. An injured right hand forced him to use the bale hook with his left and somehow the arm action was close enough to punch-throwing to be of help. It was Braddock's left, if you'll recall, that enabled him later to outstab Baer for the championship."

Griffin and Braddock put on a hell of a fight. In the second round Griffin dropped Jim with a right hand, and Jim got up at the count of two and put Griffin down for nine.

In the third round Jim dropped Griffin with a right for a count of eight. When Griffin got up, Jim dropped him again with another right, and it ended with the referee holding Jim off and, with the other arm, trying to hold up Griffin.

As he and Joe Gould walked back to the dressing room, Jim said to Joe: "I did that on hash. Get me a couple of steaks and there's no telling what I'll do."

He got his steaks—and John Henry Lewis and Art Lasky. When he floored Lewis twice and licked him in the Garden they couldn't believe it. Jim took his end of his $750 purse and paid back, with the interest, the money he had received on relief. It came to $302.

Jim had everybody rooting for him now. Ray Arcel remembered that on the night Jim fought John Henry Lewis, he had Bob Olin fighting Maxie Rosenbloom for the light-heavyweight title in the main event. "And where was I?" Ray said. "I wasn't back in the dressing room with my fighter. I was out there in the arena hollering for Jim. You had to be for him. He was always the acme of human decency."

They were looking for someone to fight Baer for the title now. Art Lasky looked like the man. He had a knockout total of 30 in four years

June 13, 1935: Braddock walks out in the first round and takes charge of defending champion Max Baer. For 15 rounds he out-boxed Max to win the title at Long Island City.

as a pro. They put him in against Braddock, a 1 to 3 underdog. Jim won 11 of the 15 rounds. He picked up his check for $4,100.

Frank Graham told Jim that New York hadn't had a fight that stirred people like that one in a long while. Why, after the fight, Frank said, he met some hard-boiled guys who told him they were praying for Jim to win. Jim's priest over in his parish in Jersey said he was doing the same thing.

So, nine months after he got up off the floor against Corn Griffin, the New York State Athletic Commission named Jim the logical contender for Max Baer's title. Jim would get one good paynight, anyway.

Metropolitan sports scribes were skeptical.

"I am telling you," Paul Gallico wrote in the *New York Daily News*, "that Baer will knock Braddock out inside of three rounds, and the referee will have to look sharp because Jimmy is game and gets up, and if Baer hits him when he is groggy and can't get his hands up, Baer may injure him fatally."

Dave Walsh wasn't any more flattering. In his INS dispatch, he wrote: "It will be surprising to me if we don't all wind up in a police court."

At the weigh-in, before the fight, one of the newspapermen asked Braddock if he was worried.

"Naw," Jim said. "Let Max worry. He's got the title."

Jim was suffering from arthritis, though you would never know it.

Actually, the fight itself was not a great fight. Jim walked out in the first round and took charge. He just out-boxed Max. He made Max look so bad that at one point the crowd got to booing and hooting the champion. When referee Al Frazin raised Jim's hand at the end, though, the fans knew they had seen something special.

The sports writers had thought so little of Braddock's chances that when Francis Albertanti, who had been handling Jim's press, went around offering to give them copies of Jim's biographical history, they ignored him. When they didn't want them Francis said to hell with it and threw an armload of them under the ring. When Jim upset Baer all the writers scrambled under the ring looking for those press releases.

John Kieran wrote in his *New York Times* column that the story of Jim Braddock served as a great lesson for courageous plodders in any walk of life. He could have added that the saga of "Lucky Jim" had all the cliches of a Horatio Alger, Jr., novel:

From rags to riches.

Strive and succeed.

A man may be down but he's never out.

James J. Braddock—the "Cinderella Man"—made good copy. The country ate it up. The honeymoon was sweet while it lasted.

Braddock wore the heavyweight crown shakily for two years without defending it. And then came Louis. Jim received $320,000 as his end of the purse—plus a bonus. It has been written ever since that he also got 10 percent of Louis's earnings for 10 years. "Not many people knew it at the time," wrote Joe Williams, usually a reliable reporter, "but when Gould and Braddock signed to defend against Joe Louis they couldn't lose financially. Before signing, they forced the Louis crowd to cut them in on the Bomber's earnings if the title changed hands, a fore-

Jim Braddock was a popular champion. Here he is congratulated by J. Edgar Hoover, chief of the FBI.

gone conclusion. And since Louis went on to earn several millions they did much better than fair."

Williams was only partly correct. What Braddock and Gould got was 10 percent for 10 years of *Mike Jacobs'* profits from his promotions of heavyweight championship fights. That total came to $150,000.

Every morning after a Louis fight, Joe Gould went over to the Garden and collected from Jacobs.

"It got so, after a while," Gould said, "that Mike got very tired of me."

15. Joe Louis

THE second Louis-Schmeling grudge match, fought in a ball park, inspired one of the best leads I've ever read in a boxing story. It came out of the typewriter of Bob Considine, and began:

"The batteries at Yankee Stadium last night were—Louis pitching, Schmeling catching."

Joe Louis could do that to writers. He made terrific copy.

Aside from his obvious punching prowess, he was just as good copy outside the ring. No one in athletics did more to help his people advance with such speed. He was completely honest in a business that pampered and bred dishonesty. He was a beacon, a glowing example for black and white alike. Bundini Brown, Cassius Clay's self-described Svengali, recently told a New York television audience what the Joe Louis influence meant to him.

"Joe Louis," he said, "was a Martin Luther King with boxing gloves on. He gave us black people hope."

Louis was above most white men in their own game. He was a great champion. He defended his title 25 times, or more than all heavyweight champions of his era combined. He was a clean and fair sportsman.

For 17 years, 3 months, and 22 days Joe Louis fought for money. He collected millions. His ring record was the best of any heavyweight champion in history. At twenty-three, he became the youngest champion on record up to that time. He kayoed 5 world champions (a record) and held the title for 11 years, 8 months (another record). In one spree he not only won 61 of 62 heavyweight bouts (record), including 54 knockouts (record) but defended his crown those 25 times (record).

The story of Joe Louis Barrow's professional fist-fighting career began on the evening of a day that dawned July 4, 1934, and ended two hours before midnight of October 26, 1951. The latter was a long time on the way.

Joe Louis was above most white men in their own game. A great champion, he defended his title 25 times, more than all heavyweight champions of his era combined.

There is no better example than Joe Louis that the heavyweight title is still the shortest distance between poverty and big money.

"I can talk to you right out of my own life," Joe said. "I was born in a sharecropper's tumbledown shack on a dirt road in Alabama, on May

13, 1914. Later, I was a depression kid in the Detroit slums. Whenever I could, I earned a few cents after school working on an ice truck. I toted 75-pound chunks of ice three and four floors up.

"Nights I hung out at the corner with the Catherine Street boys. Most all they ever talked about was how much the big fighters took home in their purses. I had just started to take violin lessons, and one of the gang showed me that Kid Chocolate and Jack Dempsey made more money in one fight than a good fiddler could make in a couple of lifetimes."

The kids in Joe's neighborhood thought he was a mama's boy and a sissy because his mother made him practice the violin. Joe was too fond of his mother to mutiny until one day a pal named Thurston McKinney tipped him off about boxing.

"Joe," Thurston said, "it's more fun to box than play the violin. Come on down to the Boy's Club with me. The whole gang's down there, and I betcha could lick any of 'em."

"I never fought no one in my life," Joe said. "But maybe I could go just once."

The thing that clinched it for him, Joe said later, was when he discovered that amateur fighters received merchandise checks, usually $10, for their bouts. "I skipped the violin lessons and hid my fiddle in the locker at the Brewster Gym where I went to work out," Joe said. "When my mama found out, she never protested. All she said was that if boxing was something I really wanted to do, I could keep on with it. Incidentally, on my way home from my last violin lesson, some kid saw me carrying my violin case and called me a sissy. I hit him over the head with the violin and broke it in a thousand pieces."

Atler Ellis, the boxing instructor at Brewster Gym, took one look at Joe and promptly forgot all about his other pupils. Joe's natural ability stuck out like a sore thumb. Ellis taught him all the tricks he knew, including the stance that was to become Joe's trademark: chin sunk behind his left shoulder, right hand high at the ready and deadpan—always deadpan.

Ellis put Joe into some amateur bouts. His first opponent, Johnny Miler, was a seasoned light-heavyweight and a member of the 1932 Olympic team. "What he did to me!" Joe said. "I don't think I hit him solid once. He floored me seven times in two rounds—more than anybody ever did in my life again. Now the point is that if I could have gotten any kind of job I might have turned away from fighting right then and there. But I wanted more merchandise checks. My family needed them—there were seven of us kids. So I stuck with it and took all the punishment that a fighter's got to take."

Joe improved. He discovered he could dish it out as well as take it. John Roxborough, a wealthy lawyer and insurance man, heard about

Joe. One night he dropped by and watched Joe in an amateur bout. He liked what he saw, though he was not crazy about the fight racket as a character-building vehicle. He preferred basketball. But there was something special about this kid Louis. The lad was different. Mr. Roxborough sensed that right away. However, he decided not to rush the boy into professional boxing. Joe was only nineteen.

In 1934, Joe and his pal Dave Clark took a trip to Chicago to compete in the Golden Gloves tournament.

"What's that book, Dave?" Joe inquired as his buddy read beside him on the train.

"The Bible," Dave said. "I always read the Bible before I fight. Makes me feel better, Joe."

Joe hesitated before replying, "You might loan me that Bible when you're through."

Joe took to the Bible the way he took to boxing and it became a source of comfort and inspiration to him. Somehow boxing and the Bible seemed to complement each other.

Joe won the Golden Gloves title in '34, but it didn't pay for the coal and potatoes so he took a job in a Detroit auto plant.

"Those big automobile parts I had to tote around were awful heavy," Joe recalled in after years. "I only got twenty-five dollars a week. Thought maybe I could pick up some money fightin'. Thought it would be nice to make enough money to buy an automobile and a house for my Mom."

At first, Roxborough wasn't too anxious to handle Joe's fistic affairs. He distrusted money fighting and wasn't at all certain that Joe would make the grade as a pro.

"Why not wait a year, Joe? You're only twenty."

"I can fight all right, Mr. Roxborough," Joe doggedly insisted. "I'm tired of toting those auto parts."

"All right," the paternal politician decided. "You want me to handle your affairs? All right, Joe, but you'll have to do exactly as I say."

"That's all right with me, Mr. Roxborough," Joe answered with a grin.

As a wise man once said, professional fighting is four-fifths racket and one-fifth business. Backroom "influence" and front-office ballyhoo pave the way for most heavyweight contenders. A business man, Roxborough used business methods in directing Joe's affairs. He studied the youngster as though he were analyzing an insurance prospect. Then he and his partner, Julian Black, mapped out their campaign.

The partners were far-sighted and resourceful. Their first step was to hire Jack Blackburn to train and coach Joe. "Chappie" Blackburn had been a great black welterweight, yet smart men insisted that Louis couldn't get anywhere without a white manager.

"I've always done all right in business," Roxborough explained. "And I've done business with whites as well as Negroes. I find no prejudice. If we handle Joe well, I don't think the public will care who manages him."

Joe was already a big hit with the neighborhood, what with 43 knockouts, 7 decisions and only 4 losses to his amateur record. He fought his first professional bout on the Glorious Fourth, 1934. The whole East Side community jammed Beacon's Arena to watch the local boy flatten one Jack Kracken in a minute and a half of the first round. Joe earned fifty bucks for his brief exercise–the equivalent of two weeks' pay hauling auto parts.

Five months and ten opponents later he topped the bill at the world's largest indoor boxing arena, the Chicago Stadium. Lee Ramage was the sacrificial lamb, and $29,000 made the turnstiles spin.

Folks were saying that Joe had the best left hook since Dempsey. He stiffened Jack O'Dowd with an eight-incher. When Ramage came to, they asked him to describe the blow that felled him.

"I don't know," Ramage confessed. "I never saw it coming."

By the spring of '35 Joe was well on his way. The top promoters were after him, and the wary fighters were steering clear. He fought 5 times in 25 days, knocking out each opponent in short order. Then came June 25th and Carnera and Yankee Stadium.

"When Primo got up and faced me, he looked so tall I figured I'd almost need a stepladder to tag his chin," Joe recalled years later.

Joe spent most of the first round wondering what the heck. Just before the bell rang he thumped Carnera in the midsection to see if he was real. The big freak was so infuriated that in the second round he went after Joe with his long left. Louis immediately countered with left jabs and right crosses, and the battle was what you might call joined. By the fifth round Louis was calling his shots to the midsection. Shortly before the bell Joe realized that the Leaning Tower was beginning to wobble.

No need to pursue the details of this gruesome mis-match. Referee Arthur Donovan showed more humanity than the promoters when he halted the farce in the sixth round.

There was no stopping Joe now. Kingfish Levinsky was at his dangerous best when Joe met him in Chicago in mid-August. Fifty thousand customers turned out for this one, but it was all over in the first round.

Unretired Max Baer was next, and Joe celebrated the occasion by marrying Marva Trotter, a secretary, a few hours before the fight. When the bell sounded on September 24, 1935, Max was fully confident he could stop Louis in his tracks. But he lost his head and began trading with Joe in the very first round.

"You showed Mr. Baer who was the boss," Chappie told Joe before the bell for the second round. "Just keep working those lefts and rights on him, and it won't be long."

The Brown Bomber at twenty-two. He is pictured here with The Boston Tar Baby, Sam Langford, in 1936. Langford was one of the first great black prize fighters and once gave Jack Johnson a rough time.

It wasn't. In the fourth frame Max went by-by.

The first Louis-Schmeling fight on June 18, 1936, revealed Joe's basic weaknesses for all the world to see. Until that fatal evening his explosive power and hitting speed had been reminding oldtimers of Dempsey. But the clever Schmeling knew better. He had spent hours studying films of Louis and knew he could be had. And in the fight that followed, the husky Hun put Joe in a box and kept him there.

From the beginning, you could tell this was going to be a different Louis fight. Joe was completely baffled by a style he had never encountered before. Schmeling snuggled his chin in the hollow of his left shoulder, stuck out his left and kept his right hand cocked at the ready. His oblique stance puzzled Louis, who was unable to reach him with his right. He went into the old routine that had worked so well in previous fights. He tried to lure Schmeling closer with left jabs, purposely shortening the distance each time by letting the punch fall short of the mark. But Max wasn't buying. He knew that those retreating left jabs were bait for a murderous left hook. So he let himself be drawn in just close enough to unleash his own wicked right before Joe could hook him.

Schmeling's counter-measure worked to perfection for round after round until he finally scored a knockout in the 12th. In the fourth round his popping right sent Joe reeling to the canvas just before the bell. As the tocsin rang ending the fifth, Joe dropped his guard and the German floored him again with a sneak right that added brooding resentment to Joe's befuddlement.

Tactically speaking, Joe was in a rut. Through the next six rounds he was fog-bound and listless, an easy target for those punishing rights. He had no business even reporting for the 12th, but as he came out, he tried to score with a right to the midsection. His expression was dazed. Max saw it and—one-two... one-two. Joe was down and out.

It was the hardest defeat of Joe's career and a shocking revelation of his vulnerability. Time and again Schmeling had surprised him with

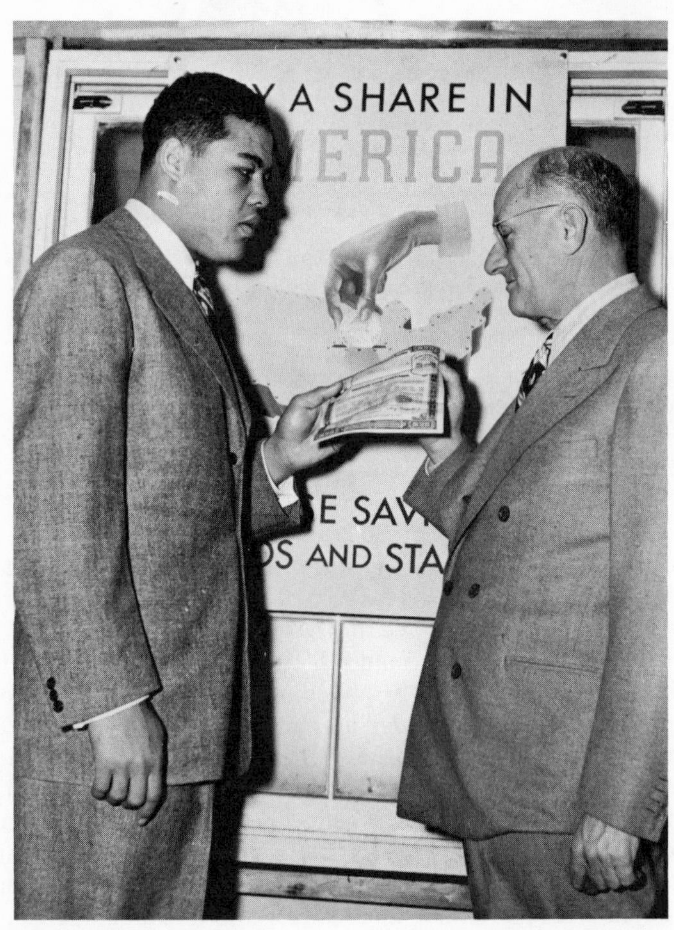

After winning the title from Jim Braddock, Louis quickly became promoter Mike Jacobs' meal ticket. Together they grossed millions. They are shown here shortly before Joe was inducted into the Army, January 14, 1943.

his booming right. But Louis was incapable of switching from a routine that had served him so well in previous bouts. Here then was the trouble–lack of imagination.

Between fights Louis could be trained to follow most any pattern of combat, and between rounds Chappie Blackburn could correct a basic fault or advise a certain change. But at the first punch Joe would repeat the same old mistakes. He couldn't think a problem through during a fight, and there wasn't enough time between rounds to correct his errors.

Before Louis could settle his score with Schmeling, he met Jim Braddock for the title. Of course, the "Cinderella Man" figured Joe was a sucker for a right and promptly knocked him down with one. But that was all for James J., who held on stubbornly until the eighth when he was forced to drop his guard from sheer exhaustion.

In a wild first round, Buddy Baer clubs Louis out of the ring, but Joe climbed back in and knocked out Buddy only 2 minutes and 56 seconds after the fight started. Held at Madison Square Garden, January 9, 1942, Louis donated his share of the purse to the Naval Relief Fund.

Louis had now become promoter Mike Jacobs' meal ticket, and his immediate plans called for a promotion in New York with London's Tommy Farr. Complications developed. Farr's handlers began to look with greater favor on a match with Schmeling in Europe. Jacobs summoned Nat Fleischer, the influential boxing publisher. "You are close to Farr's handlers," Mike told him. "If you can get 'em to take Louis I'll give you 10 percent of my profits."

Nat swung his weight around. Farr signed to meet Louis in New York. "As for Jacobs' agreement with me," Nat said, "he forgot all about it after Farr signed. He didn't even reimburse me for transatlantic phone calls and cables I made in consummating the deal. But that was Mike for you. While he never went back on his word with fighters and managers, I learned in private matters with him that he was far from the honorable gentleman the press so often made him out to be."

The Louis-Farr program attracted 32,000 to Yankee Stadium and a $320,000 gate. This was Louis' first defense of the championship. Surprisingly, Farr was still on his feet at the end of the 15th round. Louis' explanation: "The man fight me sideways all night. That ain't no way

June 22, 1938: Louis avenges his earlier defeat by Max Schmeling—2 years, 2 minutes, and 4 seconds later. The German fought two foes at Yankee Stadium that night: Joe Louis and hate.

to fight." The truth is Farr was tough, rough, utterly unawed and actually thought he won.

Between February 23, 1938, and January 9, 1942, Louis put his title on the line an amazing 20 times. He gave extra meaning to the expression, "a fighting champion."

After the Farr match, he kayoed Nathan Mann in three, and Harry Thomas in five. That brought him up to the night he had been waiting two years and three days for: the rematch with Max Schmeling.

"With one exception, money was the only reason I ever fought," Joe said one time. "The exception was the return bout with Schmeling. The writers would come from his camp and tell me all the things he was saying about his Nazi super-race. He was still gloating over his first knockout of me. When I got in the ring with him that second time I was in there for a lot more than money. He came out fast and he tried me with that right hand that had beat me all over the ring in our first fight. But not this time. I had trained very hard. I slipped the right and then I cut loose. I brought his guard down with a good left and I let go with one of the hardest right hands I ever threw. I'd been carrying that punch for Mr. Super-race for two years. I tore into him on the ropes and put him down three times until finally he couldn't raise himself any more."

"I'm glad I don't have to play catch with that baby," Jack Dempsey remarked as he viewed Schmeling's prostrate form. "Louis is such a good boxer and such a paralyzing hitter that all you have to do is make one wrong lead, one mistake and—boom!—it's all over."

Black America went wild that night. Great was the rejoicing on Detroit's East Side, along Lennox and Beale and Basin and in cotton-picking Chambers County, Alabama, where Joe was born in a crude board shack. Joy in the clean, savage kill. Pride in the fine young man who had brought honor and glory to his people.

While the Joe Louis legend was fully vindicated, the champion received $350,000 for one of the briefest heavyweight fights on record. All of Joe's fistic assets were brought to bear in this quick encounter, the most dramatic of his career.

Picture a head like Baby Dumpling with the mumps, an expression drained of all emotion but the most intense preoccupation, eyes watching and waiting with unnerving candor.

"It's the eyes," a sparring partner once said. "They're blank and staring, always watching you. That blank look—that's what gets you down."

Once Joe laced up his gloves, he was merciless. He hired the best sparring partners available, all black men, and whaled the stuffin' out of them. While training, he was entirely ruthless.

To learn more about Lou Nova's "cosmic punches," NEA Sports Editor Harry Grayson joined the husky Californian in his roadwork at Pompton Lakes, New Jersey. Louis later finished off Nova in six rounds in their September 29, 1941, bout at the Polo Grounds.

And now take another look at those sloping, loose-muscled shoulders, the short-coupled torso and powerful legs of the prime Louis. Though slower afoot than Dempsey, his soft shuffle was a ritual war dance. Joe had wonderful rhythm, grace and poise, and he was a superb boxer. What's more, he revived the lost art of feinting with head, shoulders, elbow, hips, even eyebrows. Finally, he could play the waiting game like no other heavyweight in modern history. If his intense concentration on an opponent left him open to assault, there were few who cared to dismantle a human bomb capable of blasting them out of the ring.

Louis ducked no one. He was a busy champion. Schmeling, John Henry Lewis, Tony Galento, Bob Pastor, Arturo Godoy, Johnny Paychek, Abe Simon, Billy Conn, Lou Nova—they all stepped up and tried to knock the crown off Joe's head. The script generally followed the same plot. Find a challenger, build him up, put him in against the Brown Bomber—and then carry him out, feet-first.

The "Bum-of-the-Month Club" came in many different sizes, shapes and philosophies. Each man was sure he was destiny's choice to end the Louis string. The sports writers went along for the ride. Harry Grayson went one step further. He went over to Pompton Lakes, New Jersey, and made the mistake of accepting Lou Nova's invitation to accompany him on his last stretch of roadwork before he fought Louis. Then Harry wrote this lead story for NEA Service:

Lou Nova is making sure that his tremendous body is in perfect condition because he expects to climb off the canvas to win the world heavyweight title from Joe Louis at the Polo Grounds, Sept. 19.

The very intelligent and determined challenger respects the dynamite in the Louis fists and fully realizes that traveling 15 rounds without getting tagged is not one of his pugilistic virtues.

That is why he spent five weeks in the Maine woods before pitching camp here. He did 12 or 15 miles of road work every other day. He chopped wood. He rowed and paddled a canoe. He made one four-day trip with a 50-pound knapsack on his back. Every time he feels like letting down, he just says to himself: "Think of Joe." And he goes back to work again.

It's quite all right with Nova that Louis, with enough fighting under his belt, did his early training for this fight sparring with his estranged wife in court, playing golf and softball and showing horses.

Nova hopes to beat Louis to the draw, and believes the fight will be decided in the first four rounds. "If I'm still there at the end of four, I'll knock Louis out or win going away, and I have a hunch I'll be there," Nova says, confidently.

Nova insists that his new cosmic punches are in no sense a gag. Pictures of him illustrating his dynamic body balance look like those of the stances of old English fighters. "The funny part of it is," Lou maintains, "John L. Sullivan and those old English fighters were right. They were in the proper position to punch the hardest."

Nova got his cosmic theory from Prof. Walston Crocker Brown, who has an exhibit at the Rockefeller Museum of Science and Industry in New York. "I don't understand it any too well myself," Lou says. "But what harm can it do if it makes me believe I can hit harder?"

Don't worry. Lou Nova won't waste any time thinking about applying the cosmic system when he crawls in there with Joe Louis. He'll take the shortest distance between two points—and fast.

While Harry was over at Nova's camp, Grantland Rice was spending some time at the Louis quarters.

"I'm going up to Lou's place tomorrow, Joe," he said. "Do you have any message for him?"

"Just tell Nova I'm changin' my style for this fight," Joe said. "In my last two fights I fought flat-footed. Tell Nova for this one I aim to be on the balls of my feet. I'm comin' to him."

Nova wasn't happy with the news.

"That's not the way I wanted it," he told Granny.

Nevertheless, Joe did come to Nova in that fight as Nova's "cosmic stance" was shattered in the sixth round.

Three months before knocking out Nova, Louis had come close to being toppled from his throne. In a fight that surprised everybody, Billy Conn, the light-heavyweight from Pittsburgh, came within an eyelash of upsetting the odds with a brand of battle few had dared expect, Louis least of all. The doughty Conn, 25 pounds lighter than the champion, frail in comparison and with none of Joe's heavyweight fighting experience, held him even in action and on rounds through 12

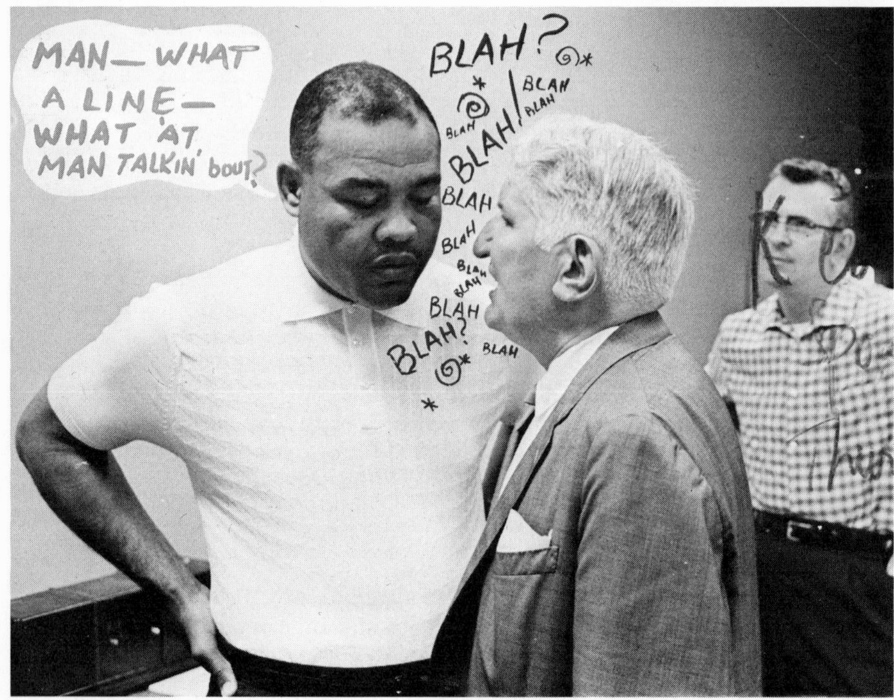

Our NEA artist's conception of Harry Grayson—a man of a few million words—interviewing Joe Louis.

rounds while 54,487 wildly excited fight fans, who shelled out $450,000 in the Polo Grounds, yelled themselves hoarse as they envisioned one of the major upsets of the century.

Louis mixes it with Billy Conn, one of his most warlike opponents who was winning on points until Joe KO'd him in the 13th round in New York, on June 18, 1941.

Billy the Kid came within 6 minutes and 2 seconds of stealing the title. He was ahead on points. Then the fight ended as it had been predicted it would end. Billy left himself open for one dangerous blow. A desperate, harried Louis, fighting with fury, whipped home through the opening with a right to the jaw. The blow landed high, but it packed plenty of power. Billy tottered backward. His knees buckled. The Brown Bomber was the Alabama Assassin once more. He leaped in savagely, his fists pumping like pistons. Billy crumpled under the barrage. A final right to the jaw sent him careening to the floor. At 2 minutes and 58 seconds of the 13th round, Referee Eddie Joseph counted him out.

James P. Dawson, of the *New York Times,* called the bout "one of the greatest heavyweight battles of recent years." In his coverage of the event the next morning, he wrote: "The struggle was waged in an atmosphere reminiscent of older and better times in boxing. The great crowd saw Conn fight a battle that was true to his style, of necessity, but better than usual, though it proved inadequate. And the crowd saw Louis fight as a champion should, a champion who refused to become discouraged though he was buffeted about outlandishly at times.

"Louis weighed 199½ and Conn 174. Louis was the favorite at 1 to 4 to win and the price on him to score a knockout was 5 to 11.

"Unmistakably Louis has slipped. Even making allowances for style—the contrast in styles was inescapable—the champion is not the champion of old. He was not sure of himself last night, a fact which might be explained by the circumstance which found him in the ring with a veritable wraith for speed. But the speed that Louis once boasted himself is gone, the accuracy behind his punch is diminishing. He is becoming heavy-footed and heavy-armed, weaknesses which were reflected as he floundered at times in his quest of the target that was Conn.

"One thing remains undiminished with Louis and that cannot be denied. He still is an annihilating puncher. His right hand claims a victim when it lands. His left hook jars a foe to the heels and props him for the finishing potion that is in the right hand."

Joe Louis did everything that was expected of a great champion and more. And he was as good a soldier while serving Uncle Sam in World War II. He entered the Army as a private and was discharged after the war a sergeant. During this time in uniform he toured the North African and European theatres as well as hospitals and billets throughout the United States. All told, he performed in 96 exhibition bouts before 2,000,000 GIs. His Legion of Merit citation refers to him as "a model soldier and an inspiration to all soldiers."

There was talk of a commission for Joe, but he firmly declined the offer.

"If I were an officer," he said, "the boys wouldn't feel at ease with me. Now they slap me on the back, shoot questions at me and call me Joe."

When Sgt. Louis left the army with a fistful of citations and $1.10 railroad fare, he was credited with one of the prize epigrams to come out of the war. Upon hearing that some joker had questioned the black serviceman's lot during World War II, Joe said, "There's nothing wrong with America that Hitler can fix."

Louis' tremendous popularity with blacks everywhere was exemplified by their total acceptance of his stumping for Wendell Willkie, the Republican Presidential candidate, in 1940. Because they were proud of Joe, they were proud of whatever he did. Joe handled himself on the campaign platform with dignity, wit and poise. When they gave him the raspberry in Philadelphia, he stepped back from the rostrum and announced in his unassuming way, "Listen, you fellas, I don't really care whether Mr. Willkie or Mr. Roosevelt gets elected. It don't concern my business. Neither one'll get in the ring with me."

Joe had a refreshing sense of humor. When interviewed on the radio before the fight with Max Baer, he was queried concerning a rumor that Baer would storm out of his corner firing as many low blows as possible to bring down Louis' guard.

"Oh, he ain't gonna do that," Joe calmly observed.

"Why not?"

" 'Cause he ain't crazy," replied Joe casually.

On June 19, 1946, one of the richest gates in boxing history stormed Yankee Stadium to watch a rematch of Louis-Conn. It was the first major boxing event since the war, and 45,266 paid $1,925,564 to be there. Only the second Dempsey-Tunney fight topped the gate receipts. This time, Louis had better control of Pittsburgh Billy. He knocked him out in the eighth round.

Louis began to slow down now. He wasn't defending his title nearly so much. He kayoed Tami Mauriello in a wild first round three months after disposing of Conn, and then only defended his title once in 1947 (a 15-round split decision over Jersey Joe Walcott) and once in 1948 (11-round KO of Walcott this time). For the next eight months he limited his fighting solely to exhibition tours. On March 1, 1949, he announced his retirement.

While Louis spent the next 14 months out on the exhibition trail picking up loose change to pay his back taxes, Ezzard Charles won a 15-round decision over Walcott in Chicago to claim the NBA version of Louis' vacated crown.

Needing money, Louis agreed to come out of retirement and try to win his championship back. Seeing him in training again for a title bout was like mislaying 15 years. As time is measured for fighters, 15 years isn't a great deal short of always. Thirteen years before, when

Louis fought Braddock for the championship, Ezzard Charles was just a kid of sixteen, reading about fighters in the comic strips. And there Joe was now, fighting for the title again. Red Smith, then with the old *New York Herald-Tribune*, asked him if it didn't seem like a long time ago.

"It don't seem long," Joe said. "It seems more like I never been away. I never felt I was fully retired."

"When you look back over 15 years," Red said, "what do you remember? What fights? What fun?"

"I don't know," Joe said. "Not fights so much. Training camp, I guess. Things that happened."

He broke into a sudden broad smile.

"Training for the second Schmeling fight," he said, "and hot? Oooo, it was hot! I'm doing six miles on the road, and Blackburn is telling me, 'Chappie, 'at's nothing. You can do it easy.' One day Blackburn and me and a couple others, four of us, get in the car and take a ride all the way out to the end of the road, six miles. We're walking around out there cooling off, and one of my sparring partners—Mickey MacAvoy, I think—is out there rowing a boat around in the crick. They all start th'owing rocks at him and I jump in the car and drive home and make 'em all walk. I stay just two, three blocks ahead of 'em so they can see the car, and I make 'em walk six miles. That Blackburn, he died."

Joe laughed, slapping a thigh, and Red said, "Go back a dozen or 15 years and think of the Louis of that time coming up to the Baer and Braddock and Schmeling fights. How would that Louis rate Ezzard Charles?"

"I don't think Charles can fight like Baer," Joe said.

"Another John Henry Lewis, maybe?" Red asked.

"I think John Henry was a better boxer," Joe said. He groped back through the years of his own fights, seeking a comparison for Charles. "I'd say about like Bob Pastor. Just about like Pastor. Tommy Farr? Charles could beat him, a tough fight. Godoy too, but he wouldn't beat Godoy easy."

"And yet," Red said, "you say Charles is the best man around today?"

"Sure, who else?" Joe said. "Ain't his fault there's nobody better around for him to beat."

Since the Charles match was first signed, Joe made no secret of his conviction that he could whip Charles.

"I don't mean that in the cockiest sort of way," Joe explained, "but I think I can win."

The years were rolling the odds up against him, however. By his own admission, Joe was only 75 percent of what he was for the second Schmeling fight. He had lost his reflexes. Though he was physically fit for Charles, no amount of training could restore the reflexes of his youth. In the first Walcott fight he missed plenty of openings, but Louis discounted those errors, saying he had overtrained. "I was sluggish-like, couldn't get going," he said. "That was condition, not reflexes."

When Joe lost a 15-round decision to Charles, a good many honest tears were shed by people who had admired him so much they had hoped never to see him beaten like that. It was a sentiment not shared by all, however, for Joe had been a professional prize fighter in all his adult years, and if they keep on fighting, all fighters get licked sooner or later. What happened to Joe happened to all heavyweight champions before him except Gene Tunney. It has happened to all champions after him, unless they retire first. It doesn't hurt a fighter much to lose.

Louis fought Charles for money. There was nothing wrong with that. Fighting was his business, and he was entitled to go on doing business as long as it offered him a chance of profit. One could not help feeling, however, that Joe must have felt the need of money very keenly to go on making public exhibition of his physical and artistic decline. When he read the reviews of his comeback bout with Charles, he must have gulped hard a couple of times to swallow his pride before going up to collect his pay. Still, he did get the pay, and that was something.

An item in the paper quoted Joe as explaining that his chief reason for coming back was a desire to prove to himself that he could, at thirty-six, regain "some measure" of the ability which made him the best in the world for 12 years. He couldn't really believe that was possible. He must have known that every time he climbed into the ring he would be a little older than the time before, a little slower, a little wearier.

Louis refused to admit to himself that he was washed up. He had looked bad against Charles. He was not even a pale carbon copy of the old Joe Louis. He was just an old Joe Louis. He had floundered and missed punch after punch. Several times his deadly left had Charles set up for a knockout. The Louis of old would have finished him. The old Louis could not. He had slowed down perceptibly.

It was odd that Joe's celebrated punch appeared to have deserted him. According to the most profound thinkers in sport, the big wallop is the very last thing to depart from any athlete. Jack Dempsey and all the other killing punchers could hit with their usual authority to the very end. Babe Ruth hit three home runs just a day or so before he quit baseball for good.

But against Charles, the Bomber would connect with his left and never follow through with the right. It was almost as if his right hand never knew what his left hand was doing. He couldn't put together two consecutive punches. Once again he demonstrated that his aging reflexes were shot, gone beyond recapture.

Arthur Daley summed it up for the whole boxing world when he wrote: "Sad as it is to have to admit it, Louis is through..... The road ahead has to be strictly downhill."

At least twice Louis formally called it quits. But each time he recanted. He first retired when he surrendered his title. Back he came, though, to fight Charles. Then he quit once more in his dressing room after his defeat. He said he had abandoned all thought of ever trying again for the title.

The second retirement didn't stick for long. Two months after losing to Charles he got into the ring against Cesar Brion and won in 10 rounds. In 1951, he beat Freddie Beshore (KO, 4), Omelio Agramonte (Decision, 10), Andy Walker (KO, 10), Omelio Agramonte (Decision again, 10), Lee Savold (KO, 6), Cesar Brion (Decision, 10) and Jimmy Bivins (Decision, 10). Louis was now reduced to fighting for money, and for money alone. There was nothing those matches could gain for him, except money. There was nothing those matches could prove, beyond the fact that the name of Louis still had some magic at the box office, that he remained a figure of such magnitude that the public would pay money to see him model short pants and mittens in a style show.

Even Joe could read the handwriting on the ring posts. The public money tree was drying up. Only 8,866 non-owners of television sets had paid to see him in action against Cesar Brion of the Argentine. Joe said he wanted one more good payday and then would retire for good. You couldn't ask for a more candid confession than that.

The end came two hours before midnight of October 26, 1951, at Madison Square Garden. A rugged young heavyweight from Brockton, Massachusetts, launched the punch in the eighth round that was a long time coming. Rocky Marciano knocked the old man out. The Joe Louis Story was ended. That was all except—

Well, except that this time Joe Louis was lying down in his dressing room, his right ear pillowed on a folded towel, his left hand in a bucket of ice on the floor. A handler massaged his left ear with ice. Memory retained scores of pictures of Joe in his dressing-room, always sitting up, relaxed, answering questions in his slow, thoughtful way. This time only, he was face-down on his stomach on a rubbing table.

His words were muffled. The sports journalists had to kneel on the floor in a tight little semicircle and bring their heads close to his lips to hear him.

"The best man won," he said. "He's a good puncher... I won't know until Monday whether this has been my last fight."

Did Marciano punch harder than Schmeling did 15 years ago, on the only other night when Louis was stopped?

"This kid," Louis said, "knocked me out with what? Two punches. Schmeling knocked me out with—musta been a hundred punches. But I was twenty-two years old. You can take more then than later on."

Ray Arcel was standing nearby, listening to the questions. One of the writers turned to him and asked, "How did you feel tonight?" For years and years Ray trained opponents for Joe and tried to help them whip him, and in a decade and a half he dug tons of inert meat out of the resin.

"I feel very bad," Ray said, looking down at Louis.

Even Marciano showed feelings for Joe. "I hated to do it," he said. "He's such a decent guy and did so much for boxing. I feel lousy about knocking him out."

Rocky's words were repeated to Louis.

"Tell Rocky not to feel bad," he said. "He's a fighter. He was only doing his job. I was trying to knock him out."

An old man's dream ended. A young man's vision of the future opened wide. "Young men have visions," Red Smith wrote, "and old men have dreams. But the place for old men to dream is beside the fire."

Joe Louis discovered you can't fool a punch on the jaw. He finally got the message. He retired for good after the Marciano defeat.

16. Ezzard Charles

THE trouble with Ezzard Charles was that he became heavyweight champion of the world too soon.

He stepped into the throne room with such ease after Joe Louis retired the first time that not too many people took notice of his ability. They didn't notice him when he beat Louis, who was trying to come back in 1950. They only felt sorry for Old Joe. And they didn't notice him when he beat Jersey Joe Walcott twice. But everyone took heed when Walcott won the title away from Ezzard.

It just was never right for Charles even when he was the heavyweight champion. There was no big talk in him and he was not conceited. The fame was tainted because he was the guy who beat Joe Louis; a lot of people resented that. The money was good but it didn't come in the way he had anticipated it.

Ezzard told Jimmy Cannon one time that if he could have begun all over again, he would have tried to alter his attitude.

"I'd change my personality as a fighter," he said. "When I was young, I patterned myself after Louis. Sometimes, times change and all. It didn't work out for me. Trying to pattern myself after his stone face. I'd try to tell the truth about certain things instead of keeping them inside. I should have been more braggadocio. But then I wouldn't have an idol."

He stared at the palms of his hands. It was clear that it was very important to him. Weren't all the kids that way? But how many of them had to fight Louis? There could only be one Louis.

"That's about all I regret," he said. "Guys asked me about a fight, I'd say I don't know. I knew but I didn't say why. Why not? It was a fixation then. Then it got to be an obsession. Like in school, the teachers always talked about Louis. If you were an athlete, he was the type of

It took Ezzard Charles 10 years to get to the heavyweight championship, but, once there, he was the best fist-fighter of his particular time.

guy you were supposed to pattern yourself after. So I took that shy stuff on account of all that. I didn't tell anyone any lies. But I held the truth in."

Ezzard Charles was a serious young man who held a cracked shaving mirror up to life. His droll pronouncements on Life, Mom and the Pursuit of Ezzard Charles endeared him to the scribes while his devastating *non sequiturs* made more sense than most fight managers.

Red Smith collected Ezzardians. Red recalled that during the course of some table talk with the Sage of Cincinnati, reporters asked Charles to account for his rise to fistic prominence. "Well," he said in his offhand way, "it took Stephen Foster a long time too." This was in reference to the fact it had taken him 10 years to get to the championship. You'll recall it took Jim Jeffries only 10 fights to get there.

"Snooks," as they called him, was perhaps too conservative to be regarded as a great champion, yet in the words of Red Smith: "Some day, maybe," he wrote in 1951, "the public is going to abandon comparisons with Joe Louis and accept Ezzard for what he is, the best fist-fighter of his particular time."

Red made that observation the day after Ezzard's eighth successful defense of the title, in which he completely outclassed Joey Maxim, the light-heavyweight champion, in Chicago. Charles won 14 of the 15 rounds by any rational scoring, as distinguished from the referee's count of 7 to 4 with 4 rounds even.

It was generally agreed that it was Ezzard's best performance since he succeeded to Louis's title. He went in against a man recognized as a spoiler, a cutie, a superior defensive boxer, and he punched the whey out of him. Ezzard fought three minutes per round, hit from all angles at all times, and chewed up Maxim with the ruminative deliberation of a cow working over last night's supper.

His left hand was especially admirable, except in Maxim's view, as he jabbed and hooked Maxim's profile out of shape. In the ninth round, Ezzard took five rights on the chin and scarcely blinked. This was the round that most scorers awarded to Maxim, although it could be argued that Charles had accumulated enough points before this flurry to earn a shade in the heat, too.

For about two hours after he quit the ring, Maxim lay in his dressing room, snuffling through an oxygen mask. Then a doctor took him to his hotel and put him to sleep. He was all right, the doctor said, except for complete exhaustion. Meanwhile, Charles dressed for a fairly plush reception in another hotel suite.

"Do you think it was your best fight?" Charles was asked.

"A man can't see hisself," he replied, "but I felt good. This time I could get up—" he demonstrated, moving about on his toes—"where in other fights I was just kinda dragging." He came down on his heels and shuffled heavily.

In advance the fight had looked like one in which Maxim had nothing to lose. He might have won the heavyweight championship. Even if

Charles had knocked him out, he would have awakened the next morning as light-heavyweight champion, same as before. But afterwards it wasn't quite the same. Charles was asked whether he thought Maxim could beat Bob Satterfield, who was theoretically booked for a light-heavyweight title bout.

"I don't know who he can beat after tonight," Ezzard said thoughtfully. "He took a pretty good going-over."

Charles said that night he was willing to fight once a month, barring injuries. He had already signed for a Pittsburgh match on July 18, 1951, with the eternal opponent, Jersey Joe Walcott, who had lost two 15-round decisions to him in the past two years.

Charles was managed by Tommy Tannas and Jake Mintz. Tommy handled the finances, Mintz the talking.

"There has been so many champions wouldn't fight this guy or wouldn't fight that guy," Jake told reporters. "We are going to be the fightingest champion in history and we are already ahead of Joe Louis's record on time. What's the use of kidding ourself? We got the greatest thing they is around, and Izzud's a very smart kid, too. It only takes him a few rounds to figure an opponent out and then he walks in and takes care of him. Izzud is a very thinkable guy."

Charles had a striking facial resemblance to Joe Louis.

"His resembling is very close to Louis," Mr. Mintz agreed.

Louis and Charles fought only once, when Joe came out of retirement and tried to win his title back. This gave the writers an opportunity to compare the two.

On the afternoon of the fight (September 27, 1950), Frank Graham went on record in his *New York Journal-American* column with this commentary:

> The notion here is that Ezzard Charles will beat Joe Jouis in the Yankee Stadium tonight and thereby make very clear his title as heavyweight champion of the world. It is possible that Charles will win by a knockout... or that the final bell will be rung as Louis still is trying to catch up with Charles, still trying to land the punch on which he is depending, since he can depend on nothing else. But, by a knockout or on a decision, Charles will win.
>
> This is a logical conclusion. Louis was a great fighter but if, when he was at his peak, he had no more than he has now, he could not have achieved greatness, you cannot say he is a great fighter now. Charles, seven years younger than Louis, is not a great fighter, either, and, it may be, he never will be one. But, bar a stunning punch, he has everything that Louis carried—and more. He is faster than Louis ever was, he is a better boxer than Louis ever was and he is equipped, as Louis never was, to make his opponent fight *his* way.
>
> There is no fighter in the ring today more resourceful under punishment than Charles. Ezzard has an aversion to being hit in the face or the belly. That is not a way of saying he isn't game. It merely means that he would rather hit than be hit, and that, when he is hit, he knows what to do. He goes away.

The notion here is that Ezzard Charles is the best fighter in the world today. Maybe you do not believe it. Maybe you will not believe it even if Charles beats Louis tonight. But I think he is, and so I must believe that he will win.

So what happened? Listen to Grantland Rice's followup story the next afternoon in his syndicated column:

They don't come back is still across the gates of Never-Never Land. Joe Louis found that out when Ezzard Charles proved that youth and speed and skill still have the call over age and power. Louis, slow of foot, slow of hand with his reflexes burdened by 36 years, found his nimble challenger far too good.

I gave Charles 13 rounds and Louis two. Louis took the worst beating he had ever known since the first Max Schmeling fight, for in this last battle he was completely outclassed in every department. Charles astonished spectators by walking into the dreaded Louis punch in the first round. Charles not only led the assault but he began by throwing right-hand punches known as the sucker punch, which Louis couldn't duck.

Round after round, Louis took a terrific physical beating. Outweighed by over 33 pounds, the slender Charles, at 182, ripped into Joe and almost tore him apart. It was evident from the first round that Charles had no intention of running away.

As the first bell sounded Charles tore into Louis and nailed him with a hard right-hand punch. In that round Charles landed at least four right-hand leads. They came in fast and hard.

Louis was having trouble all the way. He was dead game, marching forward, throwing wild punches that seldom landed. It was not until the 10th round that Louis finally cornered Charles and had him in trouble. The crowd, strictly for Louis, came to its feet when Joe landed with a right and a left, but he couldn't put him away.

Both men were willing to fight every second, but Charles had all the weapons. He kept piling into Louis with lefts and rights, driving for both head and body, as the slow-moving Louis found himself unable to offer any defense.

There is no questioning the fact that Charles belongs at the top. His battle with Louis was his all-time masterpiece. You can say for Charles that a real champion has arrived at last.

After his victory over the hero of his boyhood, the fight mob filled Ezzard's dressing room. He had not wanted to fight Joe, obviously for sentimental reasons, but finally now he did and won. "How do you feel tonight?" Ezzard was asked.

"Uh," Charles said, hesitating. "Good fight."

"You didn't feel sorry for him, Ezzard?"

"No," he said, with a kind of apologetic smile that explained this was just a prize fight in which one man beat an opponent.

It would have been easy to say, and it was said, that it wouldn't have been like that with the Joe Louis of 10 years before. It wasn't a surpassingly bright thought, though, because it wasn't 10 years earlier. The Joe

Louis of September 27, 1950, couldn't whip Ezzard Charles, and that was the only Joe Louis there was in the Yankee Stadium that night.

For the past two years, Charles had improved with every fight. The Fancy's growing respect for him was evidenced by the fact that nobody any longer suggested that there might be a heavyweight around who could outfight him. When the work bell rang he would stalk out there and whack his opponent soundly, punching sharply and incessantly with both hands. He didn't look mean; just confident and competent, a skilled workman at his job. The most anybody suggested was that this opponent or that one might have a style that could confuse and rattle him; they talked of guys who might louse him up, not guys who might whip him.

Charles didn't rattle easily, though. When he was preparing for his January 12, 1951, showdown with tough Lee Oma, whose style of guerrilla warfare could bother him, he just shrugged. "I've never seen Oma," he said. To him Oma was, as all other fighters had come to be, just another opponent, another job of work. So he knocked Oma out in the 10th round.

Ezzard Charles was born at Lawrenceville, Georgia, on July 7, 1921, and grew up in Cincinnati. At first he showed no particular enthusiasm for prize fighting, even though he did win 42 amateur bouts in a row. Since he was sixteen years old—or, as they say in the business, since he was a baby—he learned how to fight. Haunting a gymnasium in Cincinnati where fighters trained. Coming up through the amateurs. Moving into the professional ranks at eighteen. Fighting anybody who would fight him. Having an appreciation not only of his skills but of his faults. Working to polish his skills and overcome his faults. Winning 64 of his first 68 pro fights.

The critics accused him of being a cautious fighter, which he was. But back him into a corner and he no longer was cautious. He was desperate. In spite of his knockout record—43 in his first 73 starts—they said he couldn't hit. But he could. He could, believe me.

In his 69th fight, he decisioned Jersey Joe Walcott in 15 rounds to earn the heavyweight title. That was in Chicago, on June 22, 1949. One writer described the fight as "drearily pacific."

At first, Ezzard didn't seem to catch on with the public. Exactly how little he stirred emotions was evidenced in an anecdote that happened at Jack Dempsey's Broadway restaurant in New York a couple of days before Charles fought Walcott out in Chicago for the vacant title. Some of the guys were sitting with Dempsey at lunch, talking about the heavyweight championship and how it sets a man apart, gives him something that nobody ever can take away. There were crowds outside Dempsey's, too, knots of strollers stopped to stare through the window at the table where the old champ sat signing autographs.

Charles connects with right on chin of Jersey Joe Walcott and beat him twice, but then in their third meeting Walcott turned on the champion and flattened him in the seventh round to win the title in Pittsburgh, July 18, 1951.

This was 23 years after Dempsey lost the crown to Tunney.

A stranger stopped by that dining table and saluted Jack, telling him he'd seen him win the title from Jess Willard in Toledo. Jack was giving him the "Hiya, Pal" routine when the man said earnestly:

"Jack, I hope you knock the brains out of that guy tomorrow night."

He walked away and Dempsey stared after him.

"He thinks I'm still champion," Jack said softly.

No one would be ever saying that to Ezzard Charles. No matter. Ezzard went about his duties with the methodical patience of a mechanic going to work, lunch pail under arm. He punched his timecard, toiled diligently at his job, and returned home to wife and kiddies. It was all in a day's work.

The record played on. He defended his shiny new crown twice within two months in 1949; thrice in five months in 1950; and twice between January 12 and March 7, 1951. Those he left for dead along the roadside included Gus Lesnevich (KO, 7), Pat Valentino (KO, 8), Freddy Beshore (KO, 14), Louis, Nick Barone (KO, 11), Oma, and decisions over Maxim and Walcott. Each successful title defense nudged him a trifle closer to popular recognition as the excellent champion that he was.

And then on July 18, a strange thing happened to Charles on the way to the arena in Pittsburgh. Jersey Joe Walcott, loser to Ezzard in two previous bouts, turned on the champion and flattened him in the seventh round. Evidently Charles had gone to the well of wisdom once too often.

Old Pappy Guy Walcott had his number now. They fought again a year later in Philadelphia, and this time Jersey Joe came out ahead on points in 15 rounds. So all right, Walcott had somehow discovered the Fountain of Youth, but what happened next to Charles was inexcusable. Eight weeks later Charles boxed a large young man of limited talent named Rex Layne. They went ten rounds in Ogden, Utah, where the referee was the sole judge. Layne won the decision, two rounds to one. "The other seven rounds?" said the referee. "That was fighting? Phooie, give 'em to the doorman." The referee-judge was a man named Jack Dempsey!

Ezzard managed to stop this backward slide, and he won 11 of his next 13 bouts. By now, Rocky Marciano, the Brockton Blockbuster, ruled the heavyweights and signed to defend his title against Charles. The match was billed for New York, on June 17, 1954. Ezzard told reporters he was happy he was getting a chance to try to be the first heavyweight to regain the title.

Jimmy Cannon asked him how he felt about fighting a guy who could turn a fight around with a single punch. Charles was a calm man and his manner was mild and matter-of-fact. He said, "I'm glad to get a chance at Rocky. I know more about boxing than he does. I punch pretty good. I'm not the slowest fellow in the world. You can take out any guy with one shot if you catch him and hit him. Marciano punches good, sure. But he has to have a man in position."

The complaint against Charles was that he was too cautious. Jimmy Cannon talked to him about his last Walcott fight in Philadelphia when he allowed Jersey Joe to bull him.

"That was my trouble in Philadelphia," Ezzard conceded. "I don't want to do it again and blow this chance against Rocky."

There was a time when Charles depended on agility and punched with amazing accuracy. In recent fights he had been reckless. It would be a dangerous style against a brawler such as Marciano.

"You can't swap punches with anyone who has position," Charles said. "Things will unravel as the fight progresses. I don't know what I'll do. I'll be in good condition and I'll have an idea of what it's all about and see what happens as the fight progresses. Rocky is a good fighter. He punches hard and is always busy but he can be handled. Even in a gym you're conscious of what he has. I mean the one punch. You're always conscious that one good punch can lay you out, no matter who you're fighting. The puncher must nail you and nail you right. Marciano will have to be sharp to nail me. He has to land right. Just because he punches doesn't mean he can take you out. Punching alone isn't enough. You hit him. He'll go if you hit him right. But he has to be real sharp because he's the puncher."

It was pointed out to Charles that Marciano would be in condition because no one worked harder.

"He'll be strong and he'll be in shape," Charles agreed. "I don't know about the sharpness, though. He might be rusty. He hasn't had a fight since Roland LaStarza. I've been fighting all the time. He might be rusty. And if he isn't sharp...what good is being a puncher if you're not sharp?"

Charles came up to the Marciano bout with a sound mental attitude. He was ready for 15 rounds of championship fighting.

In all of sports there is no other day that holds quite the same carnival quality of excitement as the day of a heavyweight title fight. Everybody was excited, that is, except Charles. He spent his spare hours in the deep and peaceful slumber that usually overtook grown men *after* they started trading punches with Marciano, not before. For days, he really packed in that shut-eye. Perhaps he was "slept out," as the saying goes, when he arrived in Yankee Stadium that Thursday night. That would explain why he could not be induced to doze under the most powerful anesthetic Marciano was able to supply. However you wanted to analyze cause and effect, this was a great championship fight. And it was no disparagement of Rocky to point out that it was Charles who made it so.

Early in the first round, Rocky fetched Ezzard a right-handed wallop on the side of the gizzard. Analyzing this punch in more peaceful surroundings later, Charles declared: "That punch was one of Marciano's best, and I said to myself, 'If that's all he's got, I can stay with him for 15 rounds and maybe knock him out.' I did stay the 15 rounds, and I almost knocked him out in the middle of the fight."

When Ezzard was expected to retreat and cover, he fought boldly, moving in at first with right swings to the body and a left hook to the head, later countering with good right crosses. Where it had been felt he would seek safety in sticking and running, he made virtually no use of the sharp left jab he used to employ.

It had been believed that Marciano's strength would prove too great for any opponent who sought to tie him up inside, yet Charles seemed stronger than Rocky at the start, and the champion could do little at close quarters in the first few rounds.

Knocking out 40 opponents in 45 fights, Marciano had convinced virtually everybody that the man didn't live who could trade blows with him and stand through 15 rounds. Charles traded with him. Ezzard's countenance was his receipt for the transaction. His features slowly changed, until the man who came out of the challenger's corner for the 15th round bore scarcely a recognizable resemblance to the one who had walked out for the first.

Yet when the final bell rang, Charles walked back unassisted, an unconquered loser.

If it was Ezzard's best fight, then for that very reason it was also Rocky's best. Charles was the best man Marciano ever fought. He had better scientific equipment, at least as much courage, and a greater capacity to endure punishment. Consequently, Rocky had to make his best fight to win. Doing so, he exhibited again the two qualities for which he had been chiefly distinguished in the past—his incredible indifference to pain and the numbing force of his punch. Rocky never let up, even when his vision was impaired by blood from a cut above his left eye.

Dazed and weary, Ezzard Charles is caught in dramatic pose as he takes count of 10 in the eighth round as he tried to win back the title from Rocky Marciano at Yankee Stadium, September 17, 1954. Three months earlier, he lost a 15-round decision to the champion.

There were times when Charles, sitting in his corner, looked as though he wanted to cry with discouragement and pain. He always came back for more, though, riding with most of Marciano's best blows, countering gamely and accurately. Perhaps Red Smith summed it up best of all the post-fight newspaper stories with this tagline: "It is difficult to believe there is another heavyweight extant who could give the champion so good a battle."

The first fight Ezzard Charles fought for money was on March 15, 1940. His last fight was on September 1, 1959, against Alvin Green. He was beaten on points in 10 rounds. He had become a punching bag. He was all but forgotten.

Only a short time before the Green bout, Milton Gross, the late New York sports columnist, saw Charles. "He still had his good looks," Gross said. "His mind was sharp. He smiled easily and sincerely. The gold in his teeth shone."

Gross had said to him, "Why are you going on, Ez? You're going to get hurt."

"Do you know any other way I can make $25,000 a year?" Charles asked.

"It's your life," Gross said.

"It's the only life I know," Ezzard said. "I've got a wife, three kids and a mortgage. Tell me a better way to take care of them."

Several years later there was a story in the paper of how Charles no longer could take care of his family. He was jobless, broke, the mortgage which could and should have been paid off long ago was about to be foreclosed. The telephone in his home at 303 Forest Avenue in Cincinnati had been disconnected. The garage was empty. His car had long since been sold.

Milt Gross' immediate reaction was outrage. He asked, "What happened to Charles' money? In 13 title fights alone his purses came to $769,499. He earned more than a million dollars during his pro career. He owned an apartment house in New York City and several businesses in Cincinnati, but all of them are gone."

Questions were put to Tom Tannas, who had co-managed Charles with the late Jake Mintz. "For the time I had him," Tom recalled, "his purses were about $600,000, closer to $700,000. He got his money clean. I took care of his expenses. All I took out was tax money so he wouldn't get in a bind. When I took him over he owed $18,000 in taxes. I cleaned that up. He didn't have tax trouble after that that I know of."

"So what happened to his money?" Tannas was asked.

"I don't know," Tom said. "Lots of people imposed on him and when he didn't have it anymore they backed away from him. He went in with some fellows in Cincinnati, a night club deal, a delicatessen deal, some other things. None of them panned out. He said they were going to sell

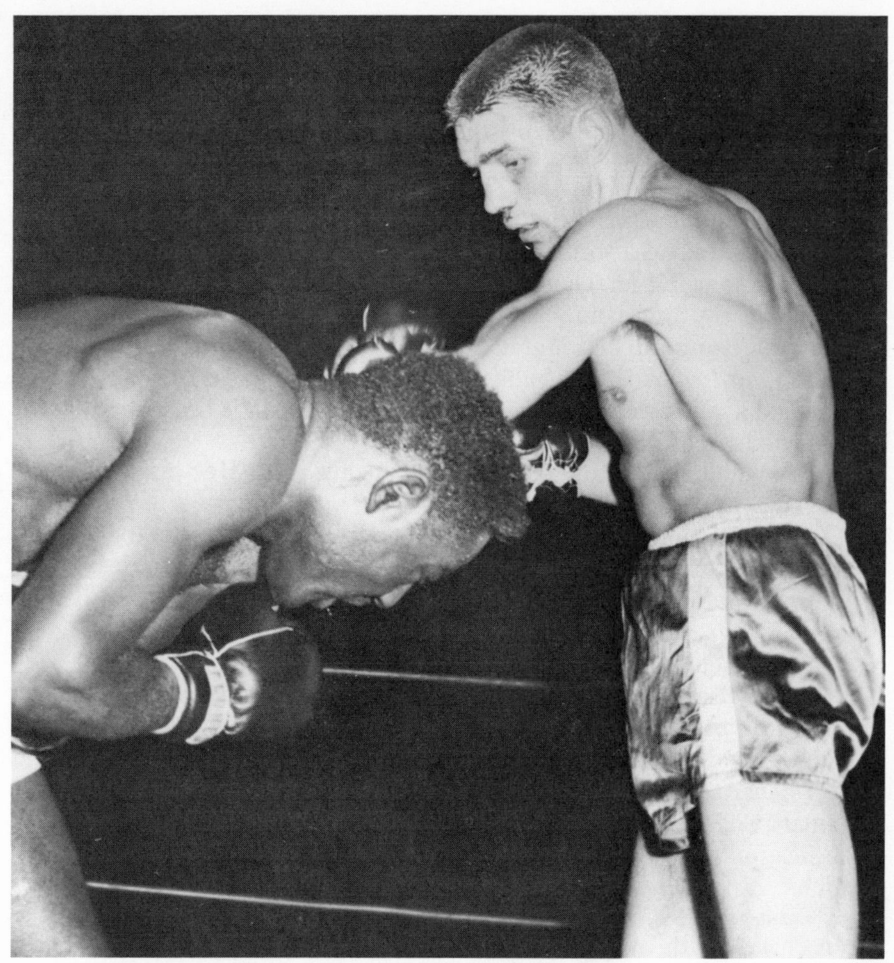

Eighteen years after starting his professional career, Charles was still drawing big crowds. He is shown here losing a 10-round decision to Irish Pat McMurtry in Lincoln Bowl at Tacoma, Washington, on July 13, 1956. McMurtry, an ex-Marine, was the fifth-ranked heavyweight in the world at the time and a red-hot attraction in fight-crazy Tacoma. The bout drew nearly 11,000 and grossed some $55,000. The referee was Davey Ward.

his house, but he was still trying to live like he was making big money. He had to taper off, but he wouldn't. I hate to see something like this happen to him. He was such a nice guy. He was, above all else, intelligent. He was a bright fellow. That was part of the trouble. You couldn't tell him how to take care of his money. He thought he knew how to take care of it himself. I guess that's the story. He really didn't."

The shame of it all was not that Charles was just another fighter who found the product of his pain squandered faster than his passing years. That has happened to so many fighters over the years. The irony was that Charles never cared for prize fighting. Few fighters like the tedium of waiting for the actual combat, but many of them enjoy the fight itself. Charles was not one of them. He enjoyed music. He was a jazz buff and loved playing the bull fiddle. He prided himself on his vocabulary. He had a sort of secret joy that he could never enjoy making another man bleed. There was almost an esthetic quality about him, unlike Rocky Marciano.

After losing the first Marciano bout, Ezzard's face was a caricature of itself. His lower lip was badly cut on the inside and swollen so that it seemed a quartered apple was hidden beneath it. His head literally was punched out of shape.

"I made friends tonight," he said in his pain. He was glorious in defeat.

At thirty-eight, Charles tried a comeback. Tannas wouldn't handle him. Tom advised him against fighting again. Later, Charles was in New York to try to hook on as a wrestler. He called Milt Gross. "I can't get hurt wrestling," he said, "and I can make some money."

"You shouldn't," Milt told him.

Milt Gross didn't know then that the shame of it couldn't go deeper than the pain of the ring or the hurt of an ex-heavyweight champion who wound up being nothing.

I never saw the name Ezzard Charles mentioned in the papers again until 1972. There was a tiny item from one of the wire services out of Chicago:

> Ezzard Charles, 51, heavyweight champion from 1949 to 1951, is seriously ill in Chicago with lateral sclerosis of the spine. He became ill about five years ago and his health has steadily deteriorated since.
>
> Believed to be virtually penniless, he is now paralyzed from the waist down and barely able to talk. He lives with his wife in an apartment on Chicago's South Side.

Leo Durocher was right.

Too many nice guys finish last.

17. Joe Walcott

JERSEY JOE WALCOTT was a black man's version of the James J. Braddock bust-and-boom, rags-to-riches theme.

He was the "Cinderella Man" all over again—in *color*.

Everything—bad and good—that had happened to Lucky Jim on the way to the heavyweight championship of the world, happened to the Great Black Father of Camden, New Jersey.

Consider these striking similarities in their respective sagas:

Both lived in Jersey. Both were clean, moral men, with a devout belief in God. Both were forced on welfare during the Depression Years. Both turned to boxing to support their families. Both grew discouraged and quit the prize ring before coming back to strike gold. Both were well past their primes when they finally wore the championship belt.

Jersey Joe's checkered career experienced more stops and starts than a bus driver. He officially "retired" from boxing no fewer than *six* times on his way to the title. By his own calculations, he labored for 21 years in the fist-fighting salt mines before he got there. That's a whale of a lot of gut-persistence.

Though only 9 years separated them in age, Walcott won the title 16 years after Braddock held it. Some say that Jersey Joe actually was 41, and not 37, when he knocked Ezzard Charles out to become champion; in that case he would be only 5 years Braddock's junior. There is no birth certificate.

Jersey Joe, in any event, was the oldest champion in history. He was living on borrowed time when he came back in January of 1945 after having quit the ring for the sixth time and being on the sideline for 3½ years.

When he dropped the 30-year-old Charles flat on his face in Pittsburgh, Walcott did more for the middle-aged than Ezio Pinza, Satchel Paige and

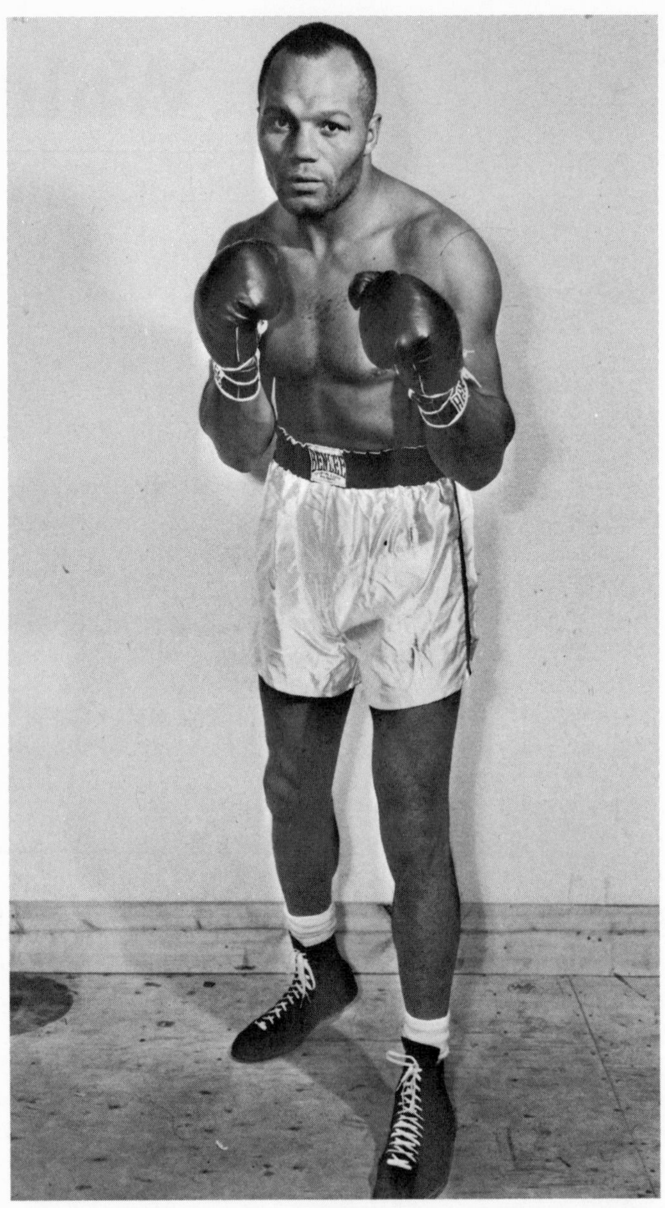

Jersey Joe Walcott was the oldest champion in history. Some say he was 41, and not 37, when he KO'd Ezzard Charles to win the title.

Geritol®. His story was the old heartbreak of boxing. In some ways, his edition of a Cinderella story was even more amazing than Braddock's. He had hit rock bottom so hard and long he almost dropped clear through.

The darkest moment was one day in 1936—coincidentally, six months after Braddock won the championship from Max Baer.

"I broke my arm," Jersey Joe recalled. "I couldn't work because of it. There was only $9.50 in weekly relief money to feed my wife and six small kids. I couldn't have gone any farther down, even if I pulled the stopper."

So 16 years later, Walcott wasn't just talking when he spoke these words into the microphone from the Forbes Field ring in Pittsburgh after putting the slug on Charles in the seventh round:

"I want to thank God for helping me win. I've always said that if God's on your side, you're bound to win sooner or later. I want to be a worthy champion, and try to help the youth of this country. I want to visit every church and Sunday school where they want me. I want to tell the young folks what it means to have God on your side."

This was not idle chatter. Jersey Joe Walcott, whose real name was Arnold Cream, was a very religious man.

The metropolitan press quickly dubbed him "The Praying Puncher." I think my old boss, the late Harry Grayson, was the first nationally syndicated sports columnist to use the expression. I remember Harry got right over to Camden and talked to county officials the day after Jersey Joe was crowned champion, and they told him how much time Walcott spent helping combat juvenile delinquency, speaking to groups of youngsters in schools, at playgrounds and meeting places. Prayer to the deeply religious champion meant sitting down and talking things over with God.

Walcott told Grayson what he felt deep inside an hour before a highly important meeting with Jimmy Bivins in Cleveland, on February 25, 1946. The fight was important to Walcott because he was coming back to the ring after a long layoff.

"Bivins' dressing room was next to mine," Walcott said. "All the time before the fight, he had a record player going with loud jump numbers, and he was singing and jumping. The minutes before the fight, and here was this guy jigging around with jive."

Walcott had clean habits. He didn't smoke. His favorite and strongest drink was the milk shakes he and his brother-in-law and pal, Joe Homes, got at a certain spot on Jersey's Black Horse Pike. His wildest playboy motivations were movies, blues records and a card game peculiar to Camden, known as "sixty-one" or "outhouse rummy."

Jersey Joe Walcott began his prize ring career at sixteen as a middleweight. Jack Blackburn had him under his wing for a brief spell, before being lured away to develop the up-and-coming Joe Louis.

Jersey Joe, stricken with typhoid, was ill a full year. He married, and family financial worries left no time for training. He went into fights with no more preparation than a hair comb. He went as far as he could before keeling over from sheer exhaustion.

In June, 1941, Walcott hung up his gloves for what he believed was for good. There were five little Walcotts by this time, and he couldn't feed them on the peanuts he got for being beaten up in the ring. But along came James J. Johnston, one of the superior managers of the day, and Jimmy convinced him that he could work in a defense plant by day and still fight at night. Jersey Joe's boxing license had run out during his retirement, and he applied for a new one. John Hall, the New Jersey Boxing Commissioner, had seen Walcott fight several times when Jersey Joe obviously was not in the pink of condition. He insisted that Walcott undergo a complete physical examination.

There was so much red tape connected with getting Walcott back into the ring that Johnston lost interest, and Jersey Joe's only appearances from June 27, 1941, to January 11, 1945, were two inconsequential bouts in tiny Batesville, New Jersey.

Walcott applied for a post on the Pennsauken Township police force. He landed a job in the Camden shipyards. Some weeks the pay was as high as $90. Contrast that with the check for $49,782.28 he received when he won the heavyweight championship from Charles.

Jersey Joe's victory over Ezzard in his fifth title attempt after 21 years of fighting is preposterous, but no stranger than the story of Felix Bocchicchio picking him up from the jaws of poverty and disillusionment. If ever a man had faith in a human being, Bocchicchio stuck with the New Jersey-born son of a West Indian black.

Felix Bocchicchio knew nothing about boxing when he drifted from the Pennsylvania coal country to Camden, New Jersey, where he became a bit of a racket guy and boss. Felix met Vic Marsillo, a matchmaker and manager, and started promoting fights at the Camden Armory.

Business wasn't doing too well at the gate just before Christmas of 1944, when Marsillo mentioned an old heavyweight who had retired for the sixth time 3½ years before. The fighter, Marsillo said, had named himself after the old and great welterweight champ of 1901 to 1904, the West Indian Joe Walcott. The modern edition of the old champion knew his way around, and Marsillo figured he might draw a few quid as a local attraction.

Bocchicchio looked Walcott up and proposed one more whirl, with his career properly financed this time.

Jersey Joe hesitated.

"Mr. Felix," he admitted honestly, "my family is getting along for the first time. I don't know if I want to take another chance on boxing."

"I'll give you enough every week so that you won't have to worry about them," Bocchicchio promised.

That was the Walcotts' first real Christmas.

With the wrinkles out of his belly, his mind finally relieved of family and financial problems, Jersey Joe showed what he might have done had the opportunity come several years before. Even then, there were none

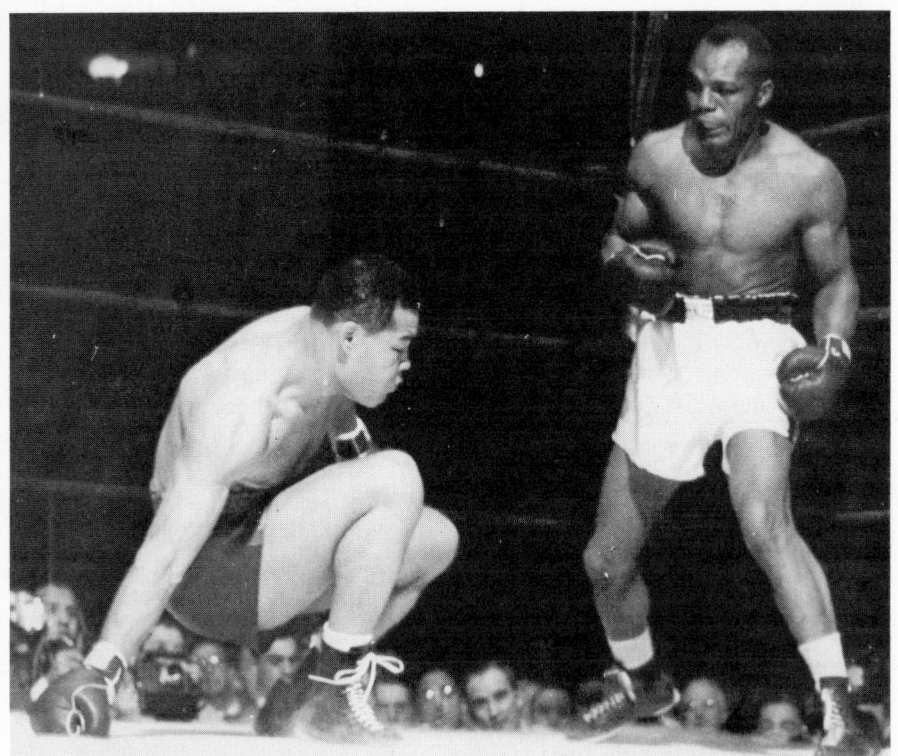

Walcott shocks the New York crowd by flooring Joe Louis in the first round—and again in the fourth—in a 15-round bout, December 5, 1947. Though referee Ruby Goldstein voted for Jersey Joe, the judges gave the decision to Louis.

of the money matches he had tried unsuccessfully to get for 15 years. So Felix Bocchicchio, the gambler, rolled the dice and set sail for potential heavyweight championship challengers whom Joe Louis had either politely refused to fight, or just plain cold-shouldered. One was Curtis Sheppard, the Hatchet Man. The venerable Jersey Joe put a lily in his hand in the 10th round in Baltimore. He also out-fenced cutie Lee Oma.

Early in 1946, Louis predicted that Jimmy Bivins would be the next champion. The Brown Bomber gave the chill to a $100,000 offer to fight him in Cleveland. Walcott floored Bivins and handed him a wicked lacing.

Mushky Jackson dispelled the legend that Walcott knocked Louis down at Lakewood, New Jersey, in early June of 1936, when Louis was preparing for his first and disastrous duel with Max Schmeling. Jackson hustled sparring partners for Louis, and Jersey Joe was one of them.

"Louis half-slipped, that was all," Jackson said. "Walcott refused to go another round for $25, so I chased him out of the camp."

Walcott went along with the legend because it was good ballyhoo. It was good for the box office.

Though he had come back to twice repulse Joey Maxim, Jersey Joe was still so lightly regarded that his first match with Louis, on December 5, 1947, was billed at first as a 10-round, no-decision exhibition. It finally was put on over the 15-round championship distance and to a decision—only because a heavyweight title-holder brings his crown along every time he's in the ring with six-ounce gloves on his dukes.

A Buffalo firm tried to rent the soles of Walcott's shoes as advertising space when Louis made his toes turn up.

Walcott shocked the crowd when he floored Louis in the first round and again in the fourth. He punched the champion's ears off. At the end of 15 rounds, referee Ruby Goldstein voted for Walcott, but the judges gave it to Louis, causing considerable wonder as to which fight they were watching.

Walcott won the championship that night in New York just as surely as Louis knocked him deader than yesterday's newspaper in the 11th round, six months later, at Yankee Stadium. Jersey Joe blamed part of the problem in the second fight on Frank Fullam, who was the referee this time.

"Fullam kept hollering at me and riding me constantly," Walcott said afterward.

"Did he affect the outcome?" Jersey Joe was asked.

"He certainly didn't help me," Walcott said.

Jersey Joe had no license whatsoever to be getting a third title shot at Charles in the early summer of 1951, but having fought himself out of challengers, including Louis, Charles decided to give Walcott another whack. In the meantime, Jersey Joe had lost puzzlingly to Rex Layne in New York. It was enough to cancel the match, but, no, Ezzard kept his part of the bargain. He was as much a son of Pittsburgh as of Cincinnati, and he wanted to show off his title in the Steel City. Originally the opponent was to have been Joey Maxim, but Ez fought Joey in Chicago. So nobody was left for Pittsburgh—nobody but Walcott.

Beyond all doubt, Walcott came up with one of the great performances of his career when he flattened Charles in the seventh round. He shrewdly switched over from his better-publicized right cross and turned sharpshooter with his left hook. His tactics called for a wearing down of the body, then changing to the head.

In the third round, Jersey Joe pinpointed Ez's right cheekbone, directly under the eye, with a ripping hook. He followed with a right to the head. Ezzard's legs bowed and Walcott pressed on for the kill. The bell stopped him but he never thereafter lost command of the situation.

In the seventh, with the round yet very young, Walcott got off a left hook to the jaw. Charles turned rag doll as he flopped backward to the floor. Before the count reached 10 he wobbled to his feet but fell down again. After only 55 seconds of the seventh round, the referee raised Walcott's big right arm in victory and cried:

"The new champeen of the world...Jersey Joe Walcott!"

"If I'd known where the punch was coming from," Charles bluntly explained later, "I wouldn't have gotten hit."

"I felt like a sixteen-year-old out there tonight," the new champion told reporters. "I could do it again to him tomorrow."

But Jersey Joe didn't do it again tomorrow. He kept Charles waiting in the wings for nearly a year before he gave him a return match, but when they finally fought for the fifth time Walcott accentuated the positive and won on points in 15 rounds.

Walcott and Rocky Marciano did much to put the fight business back on its feet in Philadelphia, on September 23, 1952. The bout provoked tremendous speculation. The smart money was on youth, Marciano. Oldtimer Billy Roche, still hail and hearty at eighty-four, liked the odds. He was going with Old Pappy Guy Walcott.

"I'll have to see Rocky in the flesh to believe he is as good as they say," Roche said before the fight. "Walcott will knock Marciano out within six rounds."

"Marciano most certainly is no 2 to 1 bet," asserted Lew Burston, the veteran manager.

"Walcott is either going to make a monkey out of Marciano, or be killed," said Al Mayer, the same Al Mayer who handled Luis Angel Firpo and Paulino Uzcudun.

Senior Citizen Roche pointed out to me that Walcott was one of the comparative handful of fighters around in '52 who thoroughly knew prize fighting. Billy dated back to the days of the Three Jacks, too: John L. Sullivan, the original Dempsey and McAuliffe. He managed the roughest and toughest fighters he ever saw—Mysterious Billy Smith and Elbows McFadden. He had a hand in the early development of Gene Tunney. He refereed 15 world championship fights. When Harry Grayson brought him to New York from San Francisco to write a special boxing series, comparing the oldtimers with the more modern gladiators, I was assigned to be his ghost writer.

"Walcott may be thirty-eight," Billy told me at the time, "but he's been active, and is still an extremely dangerous man until he falls apart. Lee Savold, another old geezer, only recently made Marciano look terrible by moving away, blocking and tying him up in the clinches. A jagged cut above Savold's eye gave Rocky an out after six rounds. Now, if Savold could render Marciano's attack almost totally ineffective, what do you suppose the more mobile and skillful and hard-hitting Walcott will do? The Marciano I saw in the Savold bout had two left feet and was nearly always off balance. Tunney tells me that Marciano's overhand style of punching would leave him vulnerable to Dempsey's inside hooks to the body and head. Well, you take my word for it that Walcott, while perhaps not quite as devastating in the overall, is a more polished hooker than Dempsey was. I want to see Rocky react when hit solidly and is hurt. I also want more of a line on how he performs when tired. Sure, Marciano is young and strong and can knock Walcott out with a punch, but Jersey Joe has been in the ring with young and strong fellows before, and didn't he floor Joe Louis three times and drop Ezzard Charles flat on his face as though shot dead by a left hook? Charles, remember, had youth riding for him, too."

Lew Tendler, who twice fought the matchless Benny Leonard in bouts which attracted record lightweight crowds and gates, lined up on the side of Jersey Joe. "Walcott steps around like a lightweight," he said. "Forget about age here. Walcott is no ordinary athlete. He is like Satchel Paige—once in a lifetime. I agree with all those who feel he won the first fight with Louis. The second time he was far ahead on points when he got careless, and Louis nailed him. Louis had to hit him close to 20 shots to put him down. Does Marciano hit harder than Louis?"

The Old Guard—Roche, Burston, Al Mayer and Tendler—were a long time finding one of their own they could cheer for, and they were sticking together.

It was a grand fight, possibly the best for the heavyweight championship since Dempsey's famous "long count" match with Tunney a quarter of a century before. It was a wonderful fight in its own right, close and bruising and bloody and exciting, but especially good because Walcott's performance was so unexpected by the public. Billy Roche and Company looked very good indeed in their prefight appraisal of Jersey Joe.

Highly aware of the fact that Marciano was an unschooled slugger, Walcott proceeded to give the Brockton Blockbuster a lesson he never forgot. Rocky at one time had aspired to be a baseball catcher, and he most certainly was in nine of the 13 rounds with Walcott. He never caught a niftier pitcher.

Nothing in Walcott's reign as champion became him so well as the night he lost his title to Marciano in Philadelphia. Maybe that's wearing a threadbare line to tatters. It's true, though. Here was a pacific old gentleman who was justly recognized as a prince of prudence, an antique tiger who had lost to assorted mediocrities, who had never beaten any fighter of lasting distinction, who had shown himself possessed of many small skills and great contempt for the calendar's spite, but had never exhibited a consuming urge for combat. Yet on that September 23rd night of 1952 he stood his ground against a young, rough, resolute bruiser and fought such a battle as nobody believed he could make, and he was winning when the sands ran out. He came suddenly to the end of the string, got nailed, and went out as a champion should, on his shield.

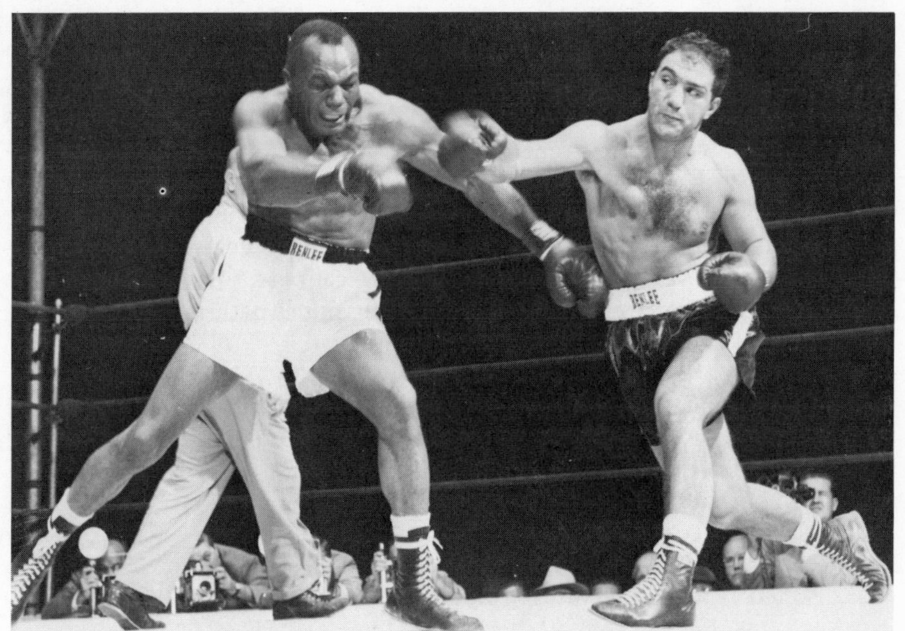

Jersey Joe and Rocky Marciano did much to put the fight business back on its feet in Philadelphia, on September 23, 1952. Walcott was winning until Marciano caught up with him in the 13th round and knocked him out.

A majority of ringside experts had Walcott ahead until he was stiffened. The fight actually was so soft for Walcott, as he predicted it would be, that he took liberties. Which was why he was nailed by a right-hand punch to the jaw while propped against the ropes after 33 seconds of the 13th round.

Practically everybody after the fight said age finally caught up with Jersey Joe. That was because it figured to, but Walcott returned to his corner as straight as a soldier at the end of the 12th after chopping Rocky to ribbons. The fact was that the law of averages caught up with the old man after a magnificent stand. Anybody who threw as many punches as Marciano did that night *had* to land one now and then. And, as someone remarked, "when Rocky hits 'em, they stay hit!"

All Walcott had to do was keep his feet. But when it was time for him to do what he could do best, sidestep and retreat, he obviously decided to change tactics and press the battle by out-punching the much younger challenger. Perhaps he figured Rocky had shot his bolt, that it was time to wrap up the title and get back home with the wife and all those kids. That figured, too, but it was a fatal error.

Passing briefly in review, the fight went like this: Walcott outclassed Marciano at the start; the younger man won the middle rounds; then the old guy came on again and took charge, and it looked as though he was going to get away free when Rocky caught him. On the official scores, Marciano couldn't have won after the 12th round except by a knockout. Off the action in the first round, it didn't look as though he could win with hand grenades. Walcott used his weapons superbly. He couldn't miss with his left hook. He was magnificent, feinting, punching, showing up Rocky as a gawky novice. As he slugged Rocky to the floor, it seemed impossible that Rocky could last five rounds. But Rocky had what everybody thought he had–courage, great recuperative power, and the strength to throw a killing punch after punishment that would have finished most fighters.

The calendar finally caught up with the odd old gentleman from Jersey, eight months later. Marciano, making his first defense of the title he won from Walcott in Philadelphia, only had to throw one respectable punch at Joe before a crowd of 13,266 at Chicago Stadium. It was a right uppercut to the head, and it knocked Walcott to the floor. There old Joe sat like a darkly brooding Buddha, dazed, while 10 seconds drained away. He seemingly made no effort whatever to get up.

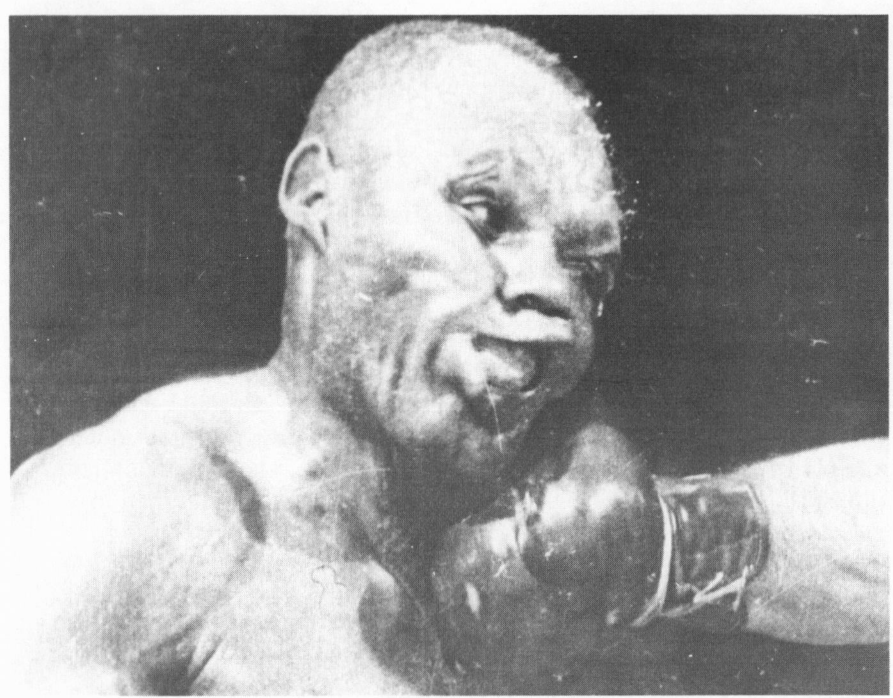

Camera catches the knockout blow that earned Marciano the heavyweight championship. For 12½ rounds, Walcott was never greater.

That's all there was. There was a hint of disgust in the words of Red Smith's column the next morning: "Last Autumn's wildly wonderful battle, one of the finest, closest, and most exciting of all heavyweight title fights, was replayed as one of the most sordid of all time. Walcott was guaranteed a quarter of a million dollars for this night's work. If its finish guarantees his departure from boxing, the price was not too great. After 23 recorded years as a professional fist fighter, the former champion went out in a total disgrace that no excuses can relieve. If he

After retiring from the ring, Walcott was elected Sheriff of Camden County in New Jersey. He is shown here just after being sworn in, in 1971.

was truly knocked out by the only real punch of the bout, then he didn't belong in the ring. If he was not knocked senseless and did hear the count of the referee, Frank Sikora, then it was a disgrace, because it was evident through the last several seconds that he was not going to get up, or even try. If he did not hear the count, then he was befuddled by Marciano's blow or else his hearing is no better than might be expected at his age..."

Harry Grayson called this second Marciano-Walcott match a "dangerous as well as a stupid one." Harry wrote: "Being whacked by Marciano isn't precisely healthy for anybody, especially a shopworn bloke of 39 going on 49. Everybody but Walcott and members of his party predicted that the much younger, stronger and harder-hitting Marciano would knock him out quicker in the rematch, and then seemed surprised when The Rock did it so quickly. All those years and Marciano's big right hand simply caught up with the antiquated geezer. Scarcely anyone at the fight saw the right thrown, but in reviewing the punch in the three-dimension pictures it comes across as a smashing half uppercut, half swipe that landed on Walcott's face. It further stresses the amazing quickness of the Marciano right. The punch didn't travel more than 18 inches. That's the kind of stuff that made all outstanding punchers.

"The one ironical note of the proceedings was Marciano moving over to Walcott's corner in the post-fight turmoil. Putting a hand on Walcott's shoulder, he said, 'Are you okay, Joe?' Walcott nodded. And Rocky said, 'Nice fight, Joe.' Sez who?"

It was too bad that Jersey Joe Walcott had to bow out under such disgracing circumstances. A lot of folk have never forgiven him for choosing the Chicago Stadium ring to put on his sit-down strike.

Shortly thereafter, he announced his retirement.

Rocky Marciano had taught him one of the axioms of the prize ring: You can't out-smart a sock on the chin.

18. Rocky Marciano

IT was a typical day at Stillman's Gym, on the West Side of Manhattan's 8th Avenue between 54th and 55th Streets. The place was crowded with fighters and managers and trainers, for this was nearly a quarter of a century ago, before the doors of the famous old boxing gym were closed forever.

Prominent at Stillman's was Charley Goldman, who had more than 400 fights as a bantamweight. He stood 5 ft. 1 in. and had two broken hands and a broken nose. He had trained four world champions.

"How are you making out with that fighter from Massachusetts?" he was asked on this day at Stillman's.

"He's just a beginner," Charley said. "I had him up here one Sunday because the CYO gym was closed, but I keep him down there because he looks so crude that, around here, somebody might laugh.

"He scares me, though," Charley reflected, thinking about it. "I mean, he does so many things wrong, but I'm scared to change him much because, trying to give him something else, I might take away what he's got."

Charley Goldman never took away from what the fighter had. Carefully he molded him into the only undefeated heavyweight champion in history; for the fighter was, of course, Rocky Marciano.

"The first time I saw Rocky was when he came into the CYO gym on 17th Street," Charley recalled. "He came in with Allie Colombo, who had written me a letter with a Brockton postmark on it back in June of 1948. The letter told about the fight prospects of his friend, Rocco Marchegiano, and it said the two of them would like Al Weill to manage and me to train this fighter. I answered the letter and now here they were. They both were broke and had come down to New York in a fruit truck that day. I certainly hope the cabbages on the truck didn't

Rocky Marciano might have been the crudest heavyweight ever to get a crack at the world title, let alone win it, but no one ever beat him.

look as bad as they did. Both of them looked like they had come to sweep the place up.

"Well, I immediately put the big lumbering boy to work on the heavy bag, and then sent him into the ring with a kid by the name of Wade Chancey. Rocky was so awkward when I had him punch the bag and when he was in the ring with Chancey, I couldn't stop myself from laughing. Once he was backed against the ropes and he put both his hands up over his head and just leaned back while the other fellow hit him a mile a minute. I stopped it and asked Rocky what he was doing, and he told me, 'The guys who taught me to fight always said that when a guy got me against the ropes I should put my hands over my head and let him hit me in the belly until he got tired and then I should clout him on top of the head and knock him out.' I had to take a walk down to the other end of the gym when I heard that, but when I told them to fight again, Rocky hit this other fellow with a right hand which nearly put a hole in the guy's head and I knew that something could be done with this boy."

Rocky remembered that first meeting with the little man who was to become one of his best friends.

"I was a little timid I guess when I came into the gym," he said. "You know, I had always read about these big-time trainers and where they worked. When I first saw Charley I couldn't get any words out. Allie (Colombo) did the talking and then Charley looked at me. He had a white sweater on and was smiling a little. 'So you're a fighter,' he said to me. I told him I was, and then he just sighed a little and said, 'If you're a fighter let's see you fight. Go in and put your duds on and come back out here and we will see how much of a fighter you are.' Gee, he's only a little guy and all that but something tells you when you talk to him that he knows all the answers, and I was a little afraid of him..."

Well, that was how it started. Little Charley Goldman went to work on big Rocky, although the Brockton boy was twenty-three and too old by boxing standards to start out as a four-round prelim boy. But Charley poured it on. Rocky obeyed him. He was the teacher. Al Weill had told Rocky: "I'll manage you, but you got to remember this. With me, I'm the boss. I do the managing and all you do is the fightin'. You don't ask me who you're fightin' or where you're fightin' or how much you're gettin'. When you go to the gym you do what Charley tells you, and after the fight you get your share."

Charley took one fault at a time, corrected it, worked on it and then forced Rocky to do the right thing in the ring. And the first fault that was corrected was Rocky's manner of handling himself on the ropes.

"I did that for his own protection," Charley said. "Even if the boy never became a fighter I had to tell him that. If he ever got into a street fight and a guy backed him into a wall, I think Rocky would have been killed. I did that to save his life."

Charley agreed that Rocky was unquestionably the crudest heavyweight ever to get a crack at the crown, let alone win it. He was the first heavyweight champion who had to be schooled. Just how raw he was is told in this anecdote by Dan Walton, who was Sports Editor of the *Tacoma* (Washington) *News Tribune* for many years.

"This happened back in 1947," Dan remembered. "Harold Bird, the local businessman who was a great booster of boxers in our area, had been talked into taking over a good-looking young giant named Big Bill Little. Big Bill had dreams of becoming the heavyweight champion. Bird was tutoring his *protégé* in Homer Amundsen's gym in Tacoma one day when in walked a stocky G.I. from Fort Lewis who says he's a fighter and is willing to work out with Big Bill. When he gets his tights on and with those short arms, hairy chest and waddling style, he makes Harold think of a bear. Anyway, Big Bill stood 6-5 and weighed 225. He was pretty fast for a big guy and was in excellent condition. The soldier looked to be about 5-9 and weighed around 180. He was hog fat.

"Well, they worked a couple of rounds and Big Bill didn't even work up a dewy sweat. The G.I. from Fort Lewis didn't back up though, and he took some good cuts at his towering opponent, but with his stubby arms he didn't come even close to tagging the big guy.

"After the workout, Bird handed the soldier $8 and he was happy. Bird told him to come back the next day, but for some reason or other he never showed up—and that was the very last that Harold Bird saw of Rocky Marciano until after he won the heavyweight championship and returned to Tacoma to referee a bout."

It was an intriguing story, so I asked Rocky about it later. He was stretched out on a rubbing table at his Grossinger's camp, and at the mention of the name of Big Bill Little his eyes brightened and he raised his head.

"Yes, that's all true," he said, after the tale was repeated to him. "I was in the Army out near Tacoma and one day a notice came to the camp that sparring partners were wanted at this Tacoma gym and anybody could apply. I was flat broke, so the next day I went in there, and they put me in against this giant who must have been seven-feet tall. I don't think I even came close to hitting him. They asked me how much I wanted, so I mentioned two dollars a round would be okay, so they gave me four dollars. I really was rich then. When I was out in Tacoma the last time I asked Harold Bird whatever happened to Big Bill, and told him I thought he had a champion. Bird admitted he thought he had one too, and told me about his sad awakening. One night Big Bill got hit on the lug and it was curtains, and although he was big enough and game enough his chin just wasn't made to take punches. Bird made him quit fighting."

At the outset, Al Weill wasn't putting any money into Rocky; fight managers don't put money into question marks. So Rocky would hitch-hike from Brockton to New York as much as possible and work under Charley. Then Rocky got his first real professional chance.

On July 12, 1948, he was put in the ring with one Harry Balzerian at the Providence Auditorium. He knocked Balzerian out in the first

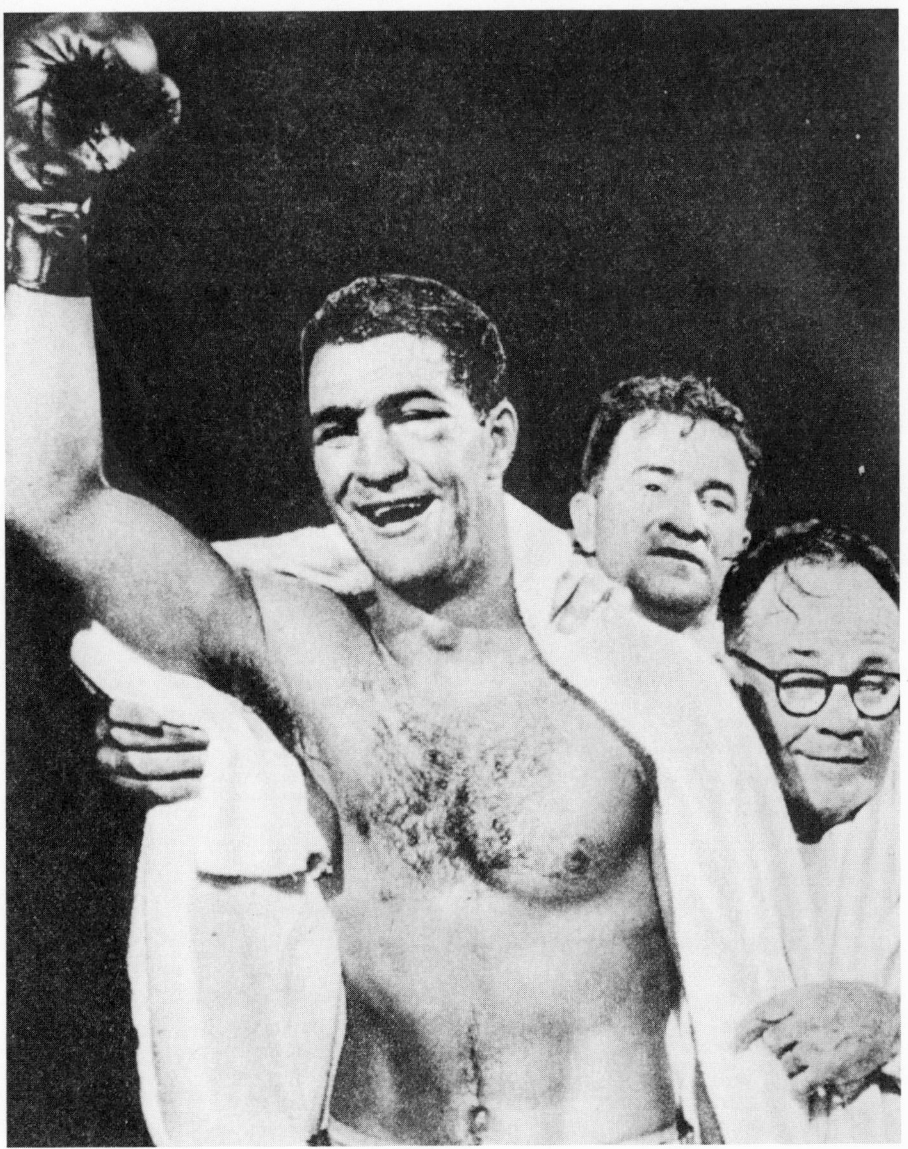

The winner and new champion, Rocky Marciano! Little Charlie Goldman, right, deserved much credit for the Brockton Blockbuster's success.

round. He followed up with a few others—quick wins—and soon Goldman was taking the three-hour train ride to Providence to work in Rocky's corner. The diamond in the rough was beginning to smooth out and Weill was beginning to make the front-office moves calculated to ease Rocky's path to the title.

Charlie couldn't make Rocky champion but he could show him the way to become one and in those sessions at the CYO gym he showed Rocky plenty. "But I never showed him that Suszie-Q of his," Charley said. The Suzie-Q was Rocky's murderous right-hand punch, one of the most devastating weapons in ring history. "Anything I did, I always told Rocky to disregard it completely if he thought it was bothering the way he threw his Suzie-Q. That was one thing he had...that and a steel chin. Jack Dempsey has always said that there are two things a successful fighter must have: The big punch and the ability to take a big punch. Any real champion must have both—and Rocky had 'em. As long as he had those I had a chance to lead him along. If he didn't have those things, nothing could have been done."

Charley always had the Suzie-Q in mind as he turned Rocky into a crouching fighter and started working on his left hand, teaching him to hook it, snap it straight out in a jab or use it to shove an opponent's right out of the way so that Suzie-Q could ride in, unmolested.

As heavyweight champions go, Rocky was not big. He was only 5 ft. 10 in. and weighed 187. Shortly after he won the title, Al Weill and Rocky received a letter from the White House saying that President Eisenhower didn't get to see many sports events and so he was having a sports luncheon to meet some of the famous stars. They wanted Rocky to come.

Joe DiMaggio, Ty Cobb, Cy Young, Clark Griffith, Ben Hogan, Gene Sarazen, Florence Chadwick and about 40 others were there, and to begin with they were all formed in a semicircle in the White House when President Eisenhower walked in.

The President moved down the line of celebrities, shaking hands with each one. When he came to Rocky, he stepped back and looked at him and smiled. "So you're the heavyweight champion of the world," he said.

"Yes, sir," Rocky said.

"Somehow," he said, "I thought you'd be bigger."

"No, sir," Rocky said.

After the luncheon the President and his guests posed on the White House steps, and one of the photographers who was a real fight fan took a picture of General Eisenhower looking at Rocky's right fist.

There's a bit of the small boy in all men, and, later, Rocky said to his mother: "Can you imagine me, Rocco Marchegiano, a shoe worker's son and a Pfc in the Army, posing with a five-star general who became the President of the United States?"

No man reached the championship with more physical handicaps than Rocky. He was stocky of build and his arms were so stumpy that he had the shortest reach of any champion, 68 inches. For purposes of contrast the reaches of other champions were these: Jack Dempsey and

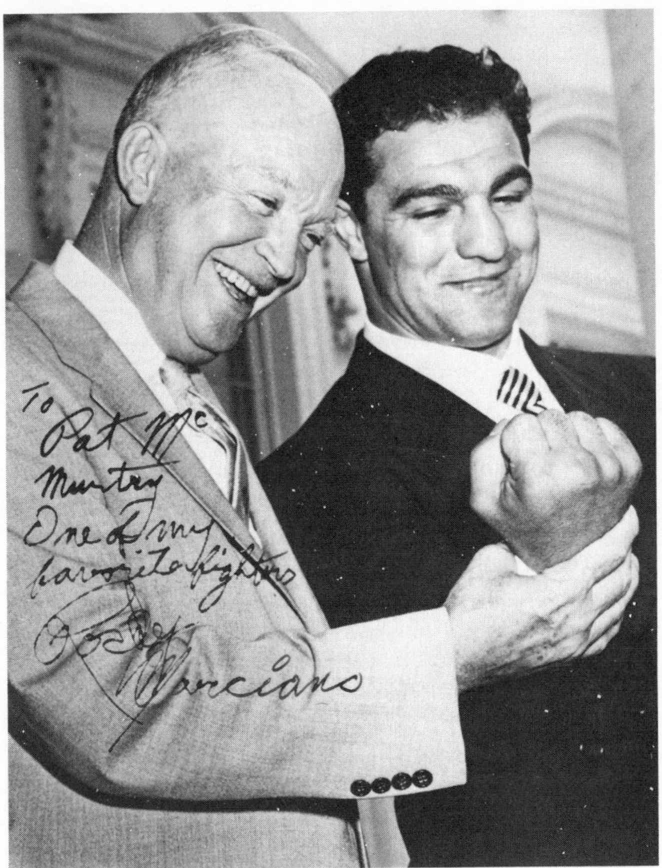

Rocky shows President Eisenhower the fist that knocked out 43 opponents. Somehow, General Ike told him, he thought Rocky would be bigger. The photo was taken at a White House dinner for sports stars. Rocky later autographed the picture and sent it to Pat McMurtry out in Tacoma, where Rocky once worked as Big Bill Little's sparring mate for $2 a round.

Gene Tunney, 77 inches; Joe Louis, 76; Primo Carnera, 85⅕; Cassius Clay, 82; and George Foreman, 78½.

The short reach eliminated the jab from Rocky's arsenal. By getting inside, of necessity he became the Brockton Blockbuster, hurting foes with every punch and butchering superior boxers. To counteract his short arms, Goldman sent Rocky into a pressing crouch. There, with his right leg serving as an anchor and his first advances being made on the left, he became a constant aggressor. To get his best punches in, he had to get inside an opponent's longer reach. Naturally, if Rocky were to be backed into the ropes, it would not be his kind of fight. And it would not be Charley's kind of fight for his guy. So if Rocky even got near the ropes during workouts, he heard Charley yell at him.

Charley insisted that Rocky stay close to his opponent, and then if his man started running away, as many did, Rocky could leap after him with those wide battering hooks. You did not run away from Rocky under the pattern Charley taught him. You could stay and swing, as Walcott did—but you seldom went as many as 13 rounds with him.

Marciano's rise to fistic fame began with a deadly flourish when he nearly killed Carmine Vingo in Madison Square Garden in December of 1949. On the way up Weill got him opponents who, with only one exception (and he got timid after Rocky hit him a good punch) gave Marciano a good fight for as long as it went.

"You see," Goldman used to tell Rocky, "you're learnin' while you're earnin'."

After that came a close decision over Roland LaStarza and a thrilling knockout of Rex Layne. The Layne fight convinced Rocky he was going to be a champion, but it was the LaStarza fight which settled the matter in Goldman's mind.

"I didn't think he could win that one," Charley said. "But when I saw him outboxing LaStarza and winning the fight, I said to myself on the way back to the dressing room, 'This boy is going to do it.' "

Marciano recalled some years later that when he was training for LaStarza, Jersey Joe Walcott dropped in to see him work. After the photographers had finished posing the two of them, Joe and Rocky got to chatting, with nobody listening. This was after they had fought for the title.

"Joe," Rocky said, "how's the motel going out there in Jersey?"

"Fine," Joe said. "Very good."

"I hope you make a lot of money with it," Rocky said.

"Rock," he said, "I want to say this. I liked that title. I didn't want to lose it to anybody, but if I had to lose it, I'm glad I lost it to you. You're a good fighter and you're gonna be a great champ."

"I appreciate that, Joe," Rocky said. "And I think you're a great guy."

That was a warm scene, decent, and very human.

"And why not?" Rocky asked. "Walcott fought his greatest fight against me, and I fought my greatest against him. That was something that people will talk about for the rest of their lives, and Joe and I can be proud of it. I never wanted to lick a man more, because I had to get his title. I can remember the night that Walcott and Louis fought for the first time and Walcott had Louis down twice but didn't get the decision. I had had only one pro fight 10 months before, and I was working for the Brockton Gas Company and I was sitting on the bed at home listening to the fight. It never occurred to me that I would be the

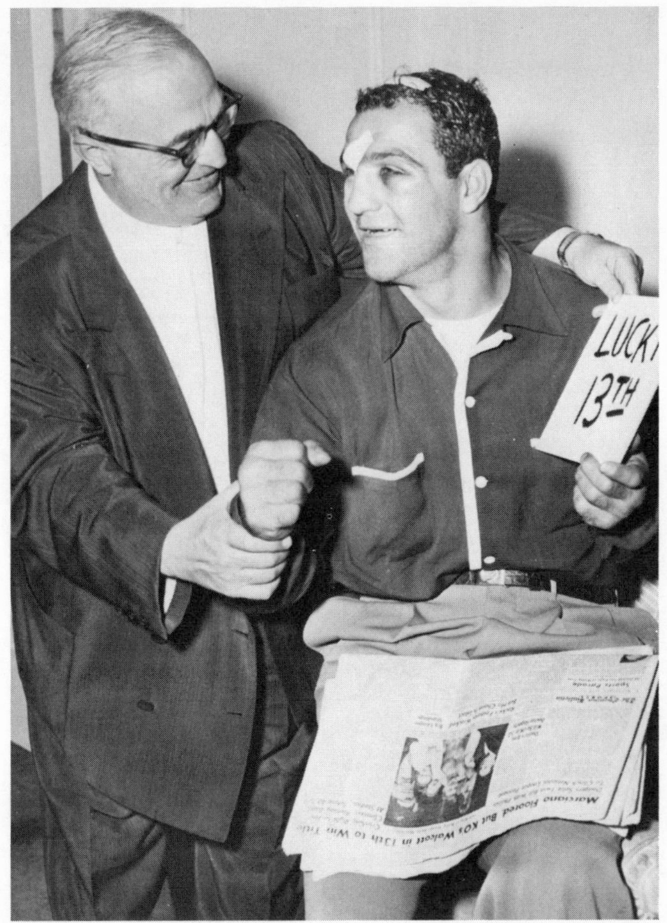

Rocky and Al Weill, his manager, hold "Lucky 13th" card designating the round in which Marciano knocked out Jersey Joe Walcott to win title. But it was no easy victory, as shown by Rocky's puffed eyes.

guy to knock out Louis and retire him and then knock out Walcott and take the heavyweight championship of the world."

The Joe Louis fight was Charley Goldman's crowning triumph. "Keep pressing him, don't give him time to take it easy," he kept insisting at the end of each round. "He's an old fellow and if you make him work all the time, he'll get tired and then you will have a good chance to get him out of there."

Louis, tiring rapidly from the pressing pace Rocky put on him, went down for good in the eighth.

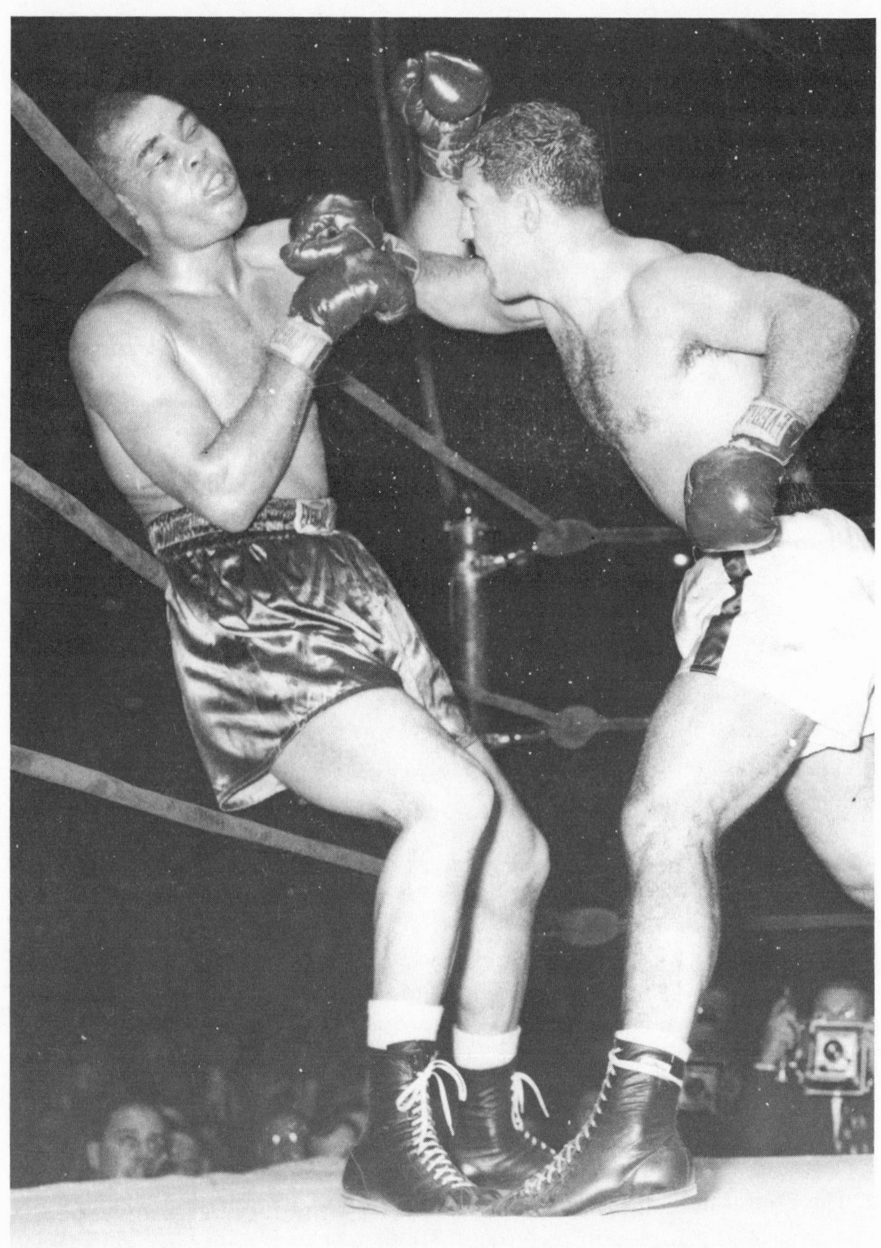

On his way to the world championship, Marciano KO'd Joe Louis in the eighth round. The fading Brown Bomber was no match for the younger man. With the exception of Gene Tunney, no heavyweight came close to matching the dedication and self-discipline of Marciano.

There are those who will tell you that Marciano won the first Walcott fight in spite of his corner directions—and they are right. For Charley Goldman wasn't allowed a free hand in the corner that night. Weill was the guy who was giving the directions and most of the time Charley couldn't even get near Rocky, much less talk to him, because Weill was in the way between the rounds. Charley had helped Rocky through 41 fights without defeat, but now Weill was taking over, in person.

There were people in the $40 ringside seats that night who didn't like the idea that Charley could not talk to the fighter and give advice on how to get to Walcott, who was winning the fight easily. Those people had a lot of money bet on the fight and a lot of them were mob guys and mob guys don't like to lose the bets of $80,000 and $100,000 they make. Along about the ninth round they were muttering about Weill's tactics. If Rocky hadn't landed that punch in the 13th round they would have blamed the loss on Weill and they were not the best guys in the world to have mad at you.

"Now Weill is said to be the best manager in the boxing business," Jimmy Breslin told me after the fight. Jimmy, who has since become a celebrity in his own right with his books and TV appearances, was writing sports with me for NEA at the time. "But Weill," Jimmy continued, "is not a trainer as Goldman is and the suspicion persists that if

Murray Olderman, left, and Harry Grayson get the lowdown for NEA from Rocky at his Grossinger's training camp.

Charley had been able to speak his mind and have his man go for the midsection, then maybe the fight wouldn't have continued so long."

With the possible exception of Gene Tunney, no heavyweight could come close to matching the dedication and self-discipline of Marciano. When he trained at Grossinger's, he lived the life of a monk at an old farmhouse on the edge of the hilltop airport, miles away from the glitter and glamour of the complex below.

"The last month before a fight I don't even write a letter," Rocky explained once. He was not complaining. He was only stating the way it was with him and his life. "The last 10 days I see no mail and get no telephone calls and meet no new acquaintances. The week before the fight I'm not allowed to shake hands or go for a ride in a car. Nobody can get into the kitchen, and no new foods are introduced."

Arthur Daley told exactly how deep this subordination of self was. He saw it first-hand one time when he dined as a guest of Marciano's at the champion's hilltop hideout. Rocky was training for a title defense and had not seen his wife and baby daughter for two months. While Arthur and Rocky were eating, Rocky's wife phoned from Brockton and Rocky came back from the call, a troubled look in his dark brown eyes.

"Gee," he told Arthur yearningly, "I sure miss my family. But I have a job to do and the only way to do it is the right way. That's the price I have to pay and I have no regrets."

Marciano stuck by his self-imposed training rules. Even the conversation was watched around him. In camp, Allie Colombo was his constant companion and tried to take his mind off the grimness of the life, but they talked very little about fighting. The name of Rock's next opponent was never mentioned. And newspapers were taboo because, as Goldman explained it to Rocky, "somebody might write one idea that might stick in your mind. Besides," Charley said, "think what fun it will be to read the clippings after the fight and see who was right and who was wrong."

For two or three months, then, every minute of Rock's life was planned for one purpose. He didn't even think about what he would be doing the day after the fight, because that was going to be like an adventure, and exciting. Everything on Rocky's part and on the part of the hired hands was directed toward one goal—to lick the other man. Rocky saw him in front of him when he was punching the bag. When he ran on the road he had him in mind, and always he worked on certain moves that he hoped would lick him.

Marciano recalled how it was when he was training for the return match with Walcott.

"Willie Wilson, one of my sparring partners, had Walcott's moves down very good," Rocky said, "He'd feint me and pull away or, after I'd hit him a punch, he'd pull down and try to tie me up. The big problem was to figure out what I was going to hit him with for a second punch, and one night Colombo and I were talking about it, walking for about 45 minutes after dinner, and then we talked it over with Goldman and Weill. We decided to try right-hand uppercuts after a left hook, and I practiced it a lot on the big bag and then against Wilson. As it happened, the fight went less than a round, but the 3-D movies showed why very well. I hit him with a hook, but as he ducked to take it high on the head he moved right into the power of that uppercut, because, with an uppercut, the power is right after you start it. When he went down I moved to a neutral corner, and when the count got to eight I said to myself: 'You know, this fella ain't going to get up.' "

In many respects, Rocky Marciano reminded boxing fans of Dempsey. He had a knockout punch in either hand. He took a punch beautifully. He had courage, a fighting heart. He feared no man, and would not have feared Dempsey. "I don't want to sound like a braggart," he told me one time, "but I don't think anybody in the world can lick me. I've never been defeated as a pro, and I hope I will still be undefeated by the time I retire. Once in a while when I'm building up to a fight, the thought does occur to me that supposin' this guy does lick me? What then? What'll happen to all my grand plans? But that's as far as it goes. I never believe it can happen, really. It's just a passing thought, and it passes quickly."

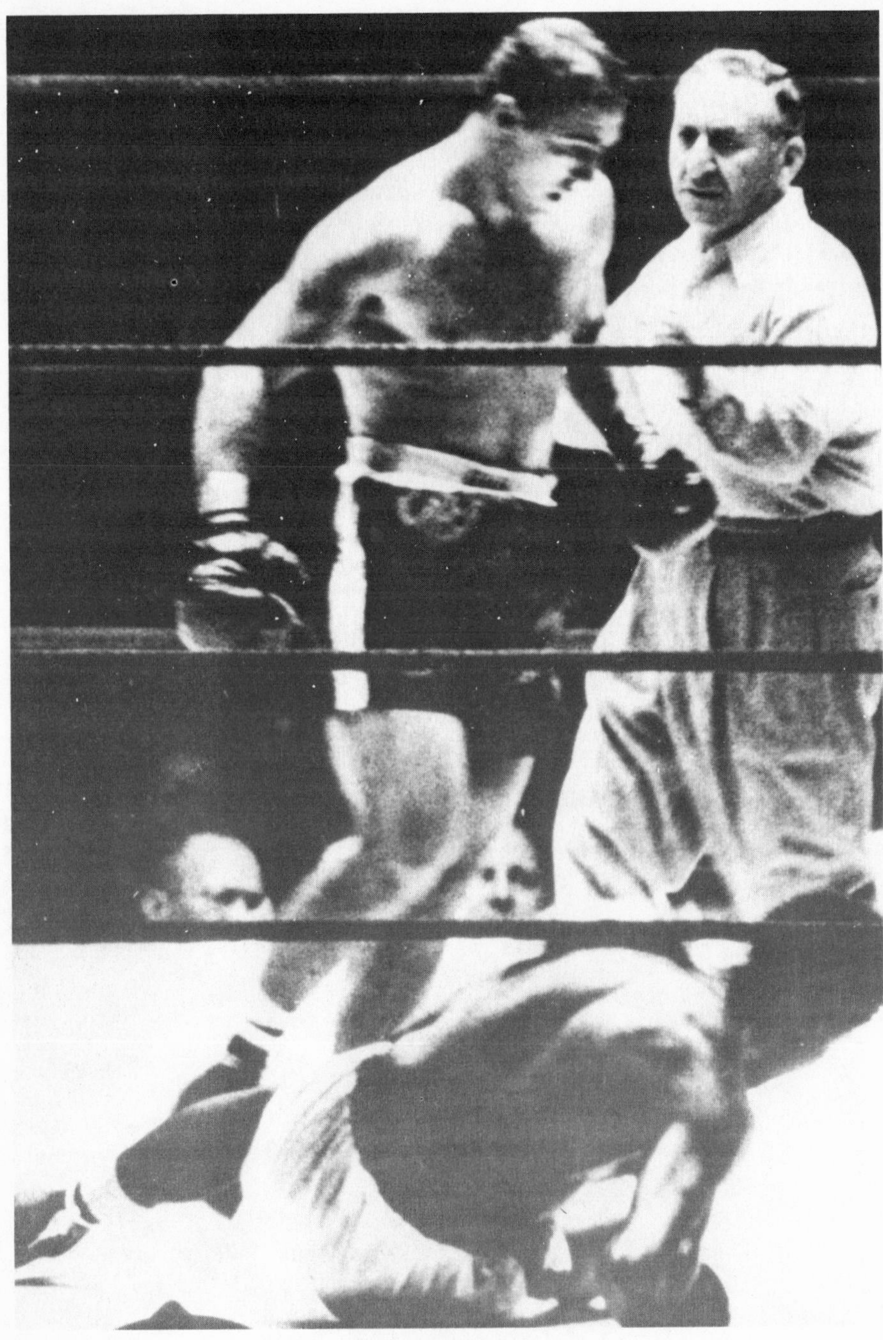

September 17, 1954: In their second fight in three months, Marciano stays undefeated and untied by belting out Ezzard Charles in the eighth round at Yankee Stadium.

Marciano knew only one way to fight: Slam in, throw punches, take them. No less an authority than Tunney believed a Dempsey-Marciano fight would have been a cheek-to-jowl brawl that would have had the crowd in a frenzy. His guess was that it would have provided the wildest first round since Firpo clubbed Dempsey out of the ring at the Polo Grounds.

In Los Angeles one night, Grantland Rice was having dinner with Joe Benjamin, the former star lightweight, and Abe Roth, one of the country's top referees. They talked about the relative power to be found in the punches thrown by Marciano and Dempsey. Some intruder made the point that when Rocky nailed you, down you went for an unplanned snooze. Against this, Granny said, Dempsey registered eight or nine knockdowns in the first round of the Willard fight, about the same against Firpo. "But both kept getting up," a Marciano man said. "They would've stayed down if Rocky had hit 'em."

Joe Benjamin then spoke up.

"I'll tell you the difference," Joe said, and he was backed up by Roth. "Marciano goes all-out on his punches. He gives about everything he has to give. Dempsey always threw a *controlled* punch. His left hooks were short. He wanted to be sure he knew where each punch would land and he wanted to be sure he was still in position to block if the other guy was throwing a punch."

"Not so many know it," Roth said. "But in addition to being a stunning or jolting puncher, Dempsey also was a first-class boxer. You'd never find him throwing a punch that took him off balance. For this reason he kept his punches much shorter than Marciano or other sluggers. Louis was another who kept his punches under control. Once Marciano lands with that all-out wallop, he can murder you. The thing that made Dempsey so dangerous was his spirit, even above his speed and his power. He thought only in terms of attack, never in terms of defense except in the case of the controlled wallop."

When Marciano was at his peak, I asked Al Weill to explain him. "Rocky has something you don't see unless you're around him all the time," the manager said. "After a while, you know it's there, and so do the guys who get in there with him. Nature gave Rocky everything he needs as a champion. He has unusual strength and stamina, a terrific punch and plenty of guts. No one ever trained harder or took better care of himself. Put all that together and you can see why it doesn't really matter who he fights. When he was going to fight Joe Louis, a fellow he worshipped and in a fight he knew would make or break him, he went to sleep in the dressing room. We had to wake him up 10 minutes before it was time to go into the ring. It has been written that Rocky hasn't fought anybody worthwhile. That has been said of every heavyweight champion. No one called Louis and Walcott tired old men until Rocky knocked them out and put them in that class. Roland

LaStarza was far from being an old man, and he was supposed to be the clever boxer, the one who wouldn't get banged up. So what happened? LaStarza was full of bruises after the fight in which Rocky didn't take a long breath and didn't have a scratch on him. Believe me, Rocky has something you don't see until you're on the receiving line. He has improved with every start."

The Beau Ideal of the fight mob was what the late Francis Albertanti used to describe as "a gutter fighter." It wasn't a nice-sounding term and wasn't meant to be one. But it graphically characterized the pugilist as to type. In the generic sense Albertanti meant a fighter who learned his trade in the gutters, every battle being a battle for survival. Jungle tactics always proved the most effective. The gutter fighter swarmed all over the other fellow, spurred by his inborn lust for combat, and swung away furiously until the other fellow dropped.

Rocky Graziano was a gutter fighter. So was Jack Dempsey, although Jack substituted hobo camps for gutters. Mickey Walker was one. Stanley Ketchel was one. The list is a long one. Some of them learned

Marciano was an all-around athlete. In high school, he starred in both football and baseball. The Chicago Cubs had him in their organization as a catcher. Here he wore the baseball uniform of the Chicago police in a 1956 benefit contest in the Windy City.

boxing skill but the most important factors by far were the killer instinct and the big wallop.

In the strictest definition of the term, Marciano didn't qualify entirely as a gutter fighter. He avoided brawls in his youth except when they were forced upon him. I remember a story John Piccento, an uncle of Rocky's, told Harry Grayson and me soon after Rocky won the title. We had gone up to Brockton to write a four-part background series on the new champion and his Uncle Piccento told about the time when some neighborhood kids had jumped on his nephew. Rocky was only seven then and he came home crying. Uncle John told the lad to take nothing from anybody, and hung up a speed and a heavy punching bag in the backyard. Allie Colombo, who was four years older and lived next door, took over immediately.

A year later, when Rocky was eight, thirteen-year-old Jimmy DiStaci was the neighborhood bully in Brockton's Ward Two. So, when "Manager" Colombo thought his tiger cub was ready, he matched Rocky and Jimmy in his backyard. The boys went 10 rounds with gloves on their hands, and those who saw it talked about that fight for long afterward.

Marciano, as mild and soft-spoken out of the ring as he was rough and hard in it, did not have gloves laced on his square fists again until he fought Big Bill Little in Homer Amundsen's gym in Tacoma.

He was twenty-eight years old when he won the championship. On the night he roared from behind to knock out Joe Walcott, he stirred the boxing world as it hadn't been stirred in years. Marciano was colorful. Marciano was exciting. Marciano could hit. Marciano was a champion who breathed new life into prize fighting.

He might not have qualified precisely as a gutter fighter.

But he sure fought like one.

Rocky defended his title six times. All ended in KO's except his first bout with Ezzard Charles. On September 21, 1955, he finished off Archie Moore in the ninth round—and seven months later announced his retirement.

Before his last fight, it became evident that he was beginning to regard the price he was paying to be champion as unnecessarily high. He still did as he was told but he had begun to rebel against the harsh restrictions of Al Weill, who had dictated his life. There were instances when the manager publicly degraded Rocky as if he found pleasure in it. I wondered aloud one time why he allowed Weill to humiliate him so.

"I wanted to be champion," Rocky said. "I wanted what I got now. How was I ever going to get out of Brockton if I didn't do it prize fighting? I'd be working in a shoe factory like my father. So I took it and kept quiet because I wanted to be on top and stay there."

It was his father, Rocky said, who influenced him the most when he was debating whether or not to retire.

"He was around the training camp and bugging me before the Archie Moore fight," Marciano said. "He used to have such a good time around the camp but this time he was different. He was pestering me. I

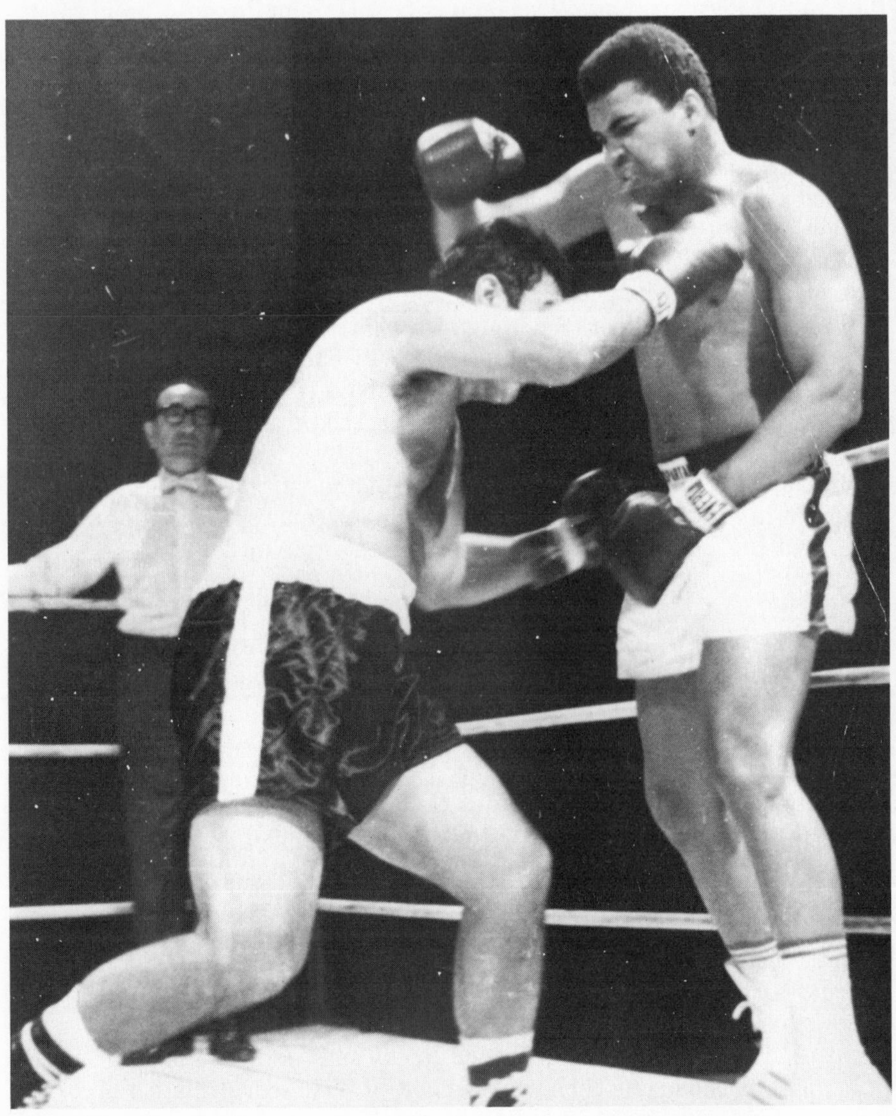

A much heavier Rocky Marciano lands a right to the jaw of Cassius (Muhammad Ali) Clay in their secret August, 1969, "championship computerized" match for the benefit of closed-circuit television cameras. With a computer dictating the action and outcome, Marciano was declared the "winner." The exhibition was staged just three weeks before Rocky's death.

said to him what's the matter. He said you want me to live 10-15 more years, Rocky? I said what's the matter with you, Pop, you're bugging me. He says my son, I watch you sacrifice and I watch you train. Then I watch you fight. I can't stand it anymore, Rocky. If you want me to live a few more years, don't fight no more. I saw the change in Pop. I saw what it was doing to him. I knew it was time to hang up the gloves."

Rocky Marciano was probably the only athlete in any sport who was ever offered a million-dollar guarantee and turned it down. Jim Norris, the millionaire promoter, told Rocky after he retired that he would write him a check for a million dollars if he would agree to come back and fight Floyd Patterson.

"No kind of money can make me fight again," Marciano told him. "It's not a question of money. Fight for what? How much money does a guy need? I got what I need. I never went in for grandeur. No amount of money can tempt me."

It couldn't, either. A group from Kentucky offered him a $1,250,000 guarantee to fight one more time, but Rocky stuck to his guns.

On September 1, 1969, the morning papers brought the sad and shocking news of Rocky's tragic death. He and two companions were

Rocky Marciano's last flight. The former heavyweight champion was killed in this private plane wreckage near Newton, Iowa, on August 31, 1969.

on their way to Des Moines, Iowa, to visit friends when the private single-engined plane in which they were travelling crashed near Newton Airport, about 30 miles east of Des Moines. The crash took place about 10 P.M. the night before in a wooded area two miles east of the airport as they were coming in for a landing.

Among the many who grieved at his loss as memories flooded back in almost tumultuous confusion was Arthur Daley, one of his closest friends among the press.

"The Rock was a man of gentleness, kindness, compassion and affability," wrote the distinguished *New York Times* sports columnist. "He brought dignity to the championship he held with such modest graciousness."

Let that serve as his epitaph.

19. Floyd Patterson

FLOYD PATTERSON was a man of contradictions. Here was a prize fighter who brought immense natural skill and devout dedication to his craft. He was the youngest heavyweight champion of all time. He stands in boxing history as the only one ever to regain the championship. He must go down in the record book as one who belonged to the ring as few men have. And yet–

The strange thing about Floyd Patterson is that he wasn't cut out to be a fighter. There has never been another heavyweight champion quite like him. He devoted more than 20 years of his life to prize fighting, held the title twice, barely missed winning the WBA piece of it for a third time when he lost by the slimmest of margins to Jimmy Ellis in Stockholm in 1968–and yet somehow he has never seemed a part of the violent business which left him wealthy.

Slugging another man with your fists and being slugged in turn should brutalize a man, yet that part of Patterson which might be termed his soul inexplicably remained detached from it all. He bled and he suffered and compassionately picked up opponents he knocked down.

He was the enigma of the essentially nonviolent person who found the only identity he ever knew in a business of violence and what comes back now is not Patterson's distress at having been beaten by Ellis but his sincere regret at having broken Jimmy's nose.

"I'm sorry to hear that," Floyd said in his dressing room afterward when told he had shattered Ellis' beak with a second-round punch.

"Sorry?" he was asked. "What were you in there for?"

"Not to break a man's nose," he said.

Can you imagine an answer like that ever coming from Jack Dempsey or Joe Louis?

Floyd Patterson, the youngest heavyweight champion (twenty-one) of all time, stands in boxing history as the only one ever to regain the big title.

The day of the second Ingemar Johansson-Patterson fight they weighed in at noon at the Commodore Hotel in Manhattan. The big room was crowded with boxing people. Johnny Attell, who promoted fights around New York for many years, was there and he ran into Billy Conn.

"Who do you like tonight, Bill?" Johnny said to him.

"Me?" Conn said. "I like the Swede for his punch."

"I don't know," Johnny said, shrugging. "Patterson's got the equipment to beat him if he fights him properly."

One of the nicest men ever to hold the world's heavyweight championship, Floyd Patterson receives thanks from President Richard M. Nixon at the White House for his work with youth groups.

"You hear the remark Patterson is supposed to have made?" Conn asked.

"What?" Johnny said.

"Patterson is supposed to have said that when he gets a guy in trouble he lays off the eye and hits him in the belly," Conn said. "I don't believe he said it. Somebody put words in his mouth. You know he'd pour salt in a cut if he could."

"No he wouldn't," Johnny said.

"Are you kidding?" Conn said.

"No," Johnny said. "Floyd's really that way."

"Then he's got no business being a fighter," Conn said.

Left hooks and the only anger he ever carried into a ring won back the heavyweight championship for Patterson. The anger was born of a resentment, not of Johansson but of the many who Floyd felt deserted him after he lost to Ingemar the first time they fought. And yet—

When Patterson left the Polo Grounds on that June 20, 1960 night, the promoters had a car and chauffeur waiting for him. He sat in the back seat alone, and he felt good as the limousine travelled through Harlem. No fight in New York had caused so much excitement since Louis knocked out Billy Conn.

Then Floyd thought about Johansson. He thought how Ingemar would have to drive through Harlem, too, and that he would have to go through the pain Floyd went through after their first fight. Floyd thought that he would be even more ashamed than he, Floyd, was, because Ingemar knocked him out the first time. Then Floyd felt sorry for him.

Later, when Patterson made this confession to Bill Heinz, Bill asked him if he thought he could call up the same kind of anger and viciousness the third time he fought Johansson.

"Why should I?" Floyd said. "In all my other fights, I was never vicious, and I won the majority of them."

"But you had to be vicious against Johansson this time," Bill said. "You had to turn a boxing contest into a kind of street fight to destroy his classic style. When you did that, he came apart. This was your greatest fight, because for the first time you showed emotion. A fight is nothing without emotion."

"I just hope," Floyd said, "that I'll never be as vicious again."

The inherent decency of Patterson was illuminated many times. In January, 1953, for example, he fought Chester Mieszala in Chicago. The week before the fight, the two were training in the Midtown Gym, but Patterson refused to watch Mieszala.

His manager, Cus D'Amato, couldn't understand it.

"I'd be taking unfair advantage of him," explained Floyd. "I learn a lot watching another fighter, and he wouldn't have a chance."

During the fight, Floyd knocked Mieszala's mouthpiece out, and Mieszala stopped and bent over to recover it. He was having trouble picking it up with his glove, so Floyd stooped down to help him. When the mouthpiece was back in place, they touched gloves. Floyd finally finished Mieszala in the fifth round.

He once had Tommy Harrison out on his feet in the first round. He dropped his hands and waited for the referee to stop it. In another fight, Floyd opened a cut over Roy Harris' left eye, then began banging punches to the body. Was he sorry for Harris?

"It wasn't necessary for me to ruin him," Floyd said. "And besides, I don't like to see blood. It's different when I bleed, that doesn't bother me because I can't see it."

I thought of Rocky Marciano.

He didn't feel compassion for certain opponents, you say? Wrong. He once confessed of his reactions to the two most important fights of his unbeaten career. The first was with an aging Joe Louis, no longer the champion. The other was with Jersey Joe Walcott for the title.

"When Louis went down," said Rocky, "I was glad that he wasn't getting up. But then I remembered what a wonderful career he had had and I felt terribly sad instead of elated."

Marciano sandbagged Walcott with the perfect punch in the 13th round and won the championship. As Old Pappy Guy was being counted out, Rocky looked down on him and had strange thoughts.

"'He must feel awful,' I said to myself," declared Rocky with an embarrassed grin. "There I was, the new heavyweight champion of the world and I was behaving like a soft-hearted slob. What's the matter with me anyway?"

Nothing ever was the matter with him. And nothing ever was the matter with Floyd Patterson, either. Both fighters had plenty of handicaps to overcome to reach the championship. They were winners in the ring and out of it, too.

In 1952, Floyd won an Olympic Gold Medal at Helsinki. Pete Mello coached the United States boxing team that year. He had been in box-

Patterson won the middleweight Gold Medal at the 1952 Olympic Games in Helsinki. Members of the United States boxing team were, left to right, Nat Brooks, flyweight; Charles Adkins, light-welterweight; Patterson; Norval Lee, light-heavyweight; and Eddie Sanders, heavyweight.

ing for more than 40 years, and in all that time he said he never met a nicer person connected with the prize ring than Floyd Patterson.

"For example," Pete recalled, "we're over in Helsinki and we have to line up for chow. I noticed that Floyd would gather himself three or four steaks, so I watched to find out what he was doing. It turned out that some of those Finns didn't have too much to eat, so Floyd was making up packages of food for them."

It was sometimes written of Patterson that he "is a kind of a stranger." After more than 20 years he was still a stranger to a multitude of people. They simply couldn't understand how a man who was something of a mystic could find such gratification in a business where sensitivity is so heavy a liability.

After Sonny Liston bludgeoned him in the first round to win the title in Chicago, September 25, 1962, Floyd was so embarrassed he hid behind a false beard and mustache to escape the stares of the public.

When Sonny Liston bludgeoned him in the first round to win the title in Chicago, September 25, 1962, Floyd drove off into the night from the Midwest to New York and hid behind a false beard and mustache because the shame was more than the physical pain. On November 22, 1965, when Muhammad Ali tortured him and taunted him through 12 tormenting rounds, Patterson's body was hurt but his pride was intact because he had not been counted out. When he became the only man ever to win the heavyweight championship a second time, that should have been his finest hour. But he considered it his most debasing.

"I was filled with so much hate," he said. "I wouldn't ever want to reach that low again."

Floyd's evaluation of himself always was important to him. The shame of his two first-round knockouts by Sonny Liston haunted him.

"In my whole career," he said, "I could never think of any fights where I didn't give the fans their money's worth, except in the Liston fights. I fought those fights stubbornly. If I had it to do over, I'd fight my fight. Cassius Clay made Liston fight his fight. Clay always makes

his opponent fight his fight. But to me, giving the people a good show, a good fight, is more important than winning. When you're a fighter, you're an entertainer. People pay big money to see you. I'd rather fight a good fight and have people stand and applaud and lose, than fight a bad fight and have people boo and win. After the Ellis fight, some people told me that they had bet on Ellis, but that they had refused to take their money because they thought I had won."

When Patterson stepped from a plane at LaGuardia Airport, in New York, boxing gloves looped around his neck, Cus D'Amato was there to meet the 1952 Olympic Games middleweight champion. This was before Floyd had had his first professional fight, and, pointing to the gloves, Cus made a long-range prediction.

"By the time you hang up those gloves you'll be a heavyweight," Cus said. "You'll also be the youngest heavyweight champion in history. And by the time you retire they will call you one of the greatest fighters in history."

"Fine," Floyd said. "When do I start?"

"Right now," his new manager said.

D'Amato put the Olympic champion in against Eddie Godbold on September 12, 1952–only weeks after his return from Helsinki–and Patterson belted him out in four rounds. D'Amato signed him up for four more fights, and Floyd belted them out, too. Five professional fights, five knockouts. You would have thought this would've had Cus turning cartwheels, but he wasn't.

"Why so glum?" I asked D'Amato one day at the gym.

"He lacks the killer instinct," Cus said. "He's too tame, too nice to his opponents. I've been trying all the psychology I can think of to anger his blood up, but he just doesn't have that zest for viciousness. I have a big job on my hands."

Like Marciano, here was a boy who had to take boxing lessons in the gym. Floyd had a lot of faults to correct. D'Amato noticed that he punched with both feet off the floor. He crossed his right foot behind his left when he stepped to the left. He was easily hit. He didn't follow up an advantage; he, instead, stayed back with his hands up. And, oh, if he would only be a little meaner.

But Cus D'Amato stayed with Patterson. He did an admirable job in bringing the boy along. An even better job than Al Weill did with Marciano. Cus first saw to it that Floyd mastered the fundamentals, then exposed him by degrees to experienced competition. He built up his confidence along with his skills until finally he felt Floyd was ready to campaign among the big-timers. He won his first 13 professional bouts, 8 by knockouts.

The first time Patterson was down in a professional fight was in his 15th bout. Jacques Royer-Crecy dropped him to one knee with a right

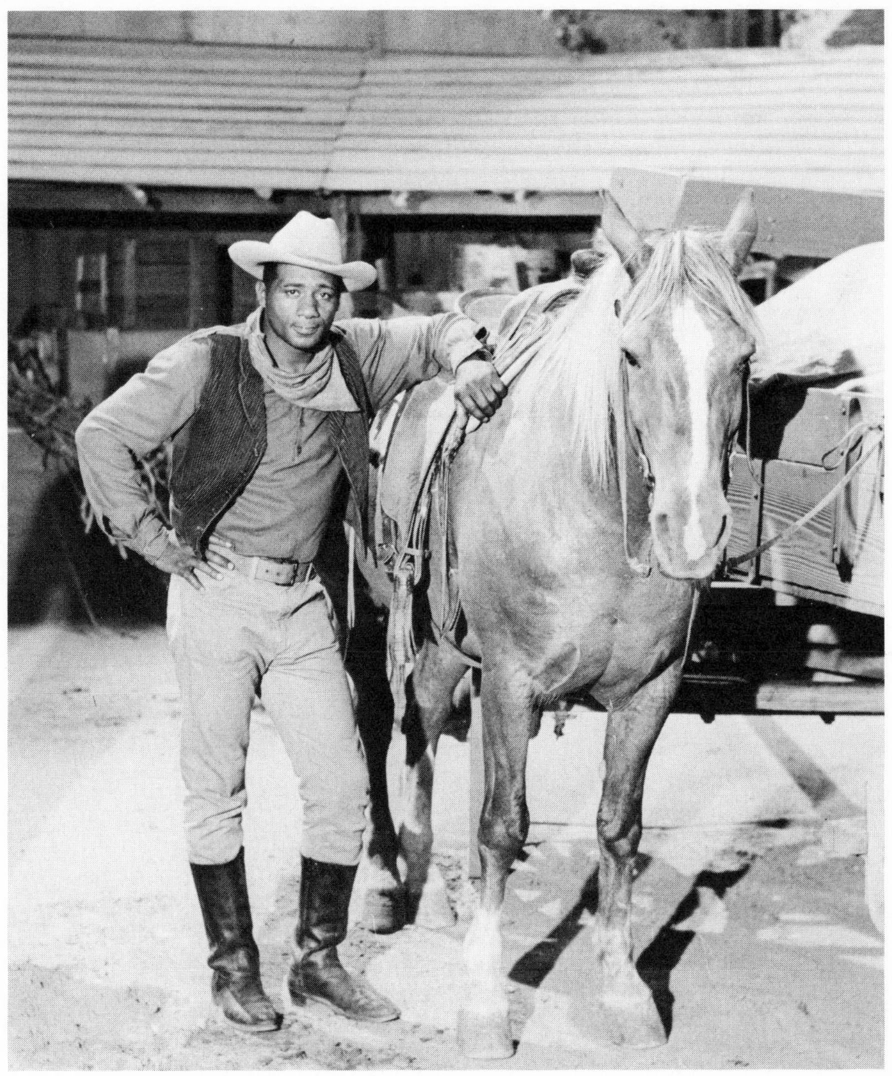

Millionaire Patterson raises horses on his own farm and has had roles in westerns on TV and in movies. He has also handled himself extremely well as a boxing commentator on radio-TV from Madison Square Garden.

hand in the first round at the St. Nicholas Arena in New York. Floyd came up before the count, but in the dressing room later, fight writers asked him about it.

"He slipped," Cus D'Amato said.

"No," Patterson said. "He knocked me down. I know he hit me because I don't remember going down. Otherwise I'd remember."

Floyd's first loss as a professional was to Joey Maxim. Until that time, he had been tangling only with kids like himself or veterans whose progress had been arrested before they had learned anything and, one and all, they were comparatively easy victims. Then, in an eight-round bout at the Eastern Parkway Arena in Brooklyn, Maxim just managed to move him around enough to grab the decision. Eleven of the twelve boxing writers at ringside thought Patterson had won and they told him so in the dressing room.

"Don't you think you beat him?" one of the reporters asked.

"The officials could see it better than I could," Patterson replied. "I was too busy fighting."

That was Floyd's only defeat on his way to the championship.

The loss rankled D'Amato. It shouldn't have. If Floyd had to lose, at least he lost in a good cause. Joe Louis lost only once on his journey to the title. That was to Max Schmeling and it was, undoubtedly, an important one in his life. Schmeling taught him, after his incredible streak of early success against boxers, punchers and brawlers. By the same token, Maxim taught Floyd plenty. He taught him that somewhere, somehow, he could lose, too.

On April 27, 1956, Marciano retired. Seven months later, only a month and four days after his twenty-first birthday, Patterson kayoed ancient Archie Moore, the light-heavyweight champion, in five rounds to become the youngest man in history to win the heavyweight crown. Cus D'Amato, the prophet, could now take bows as a resident genius.

In the first year and a half as champion, Patterson kept pretty much out of circulation, due largely to his manager's running feud with James D. Norris and the International Boxing Club. It was impossible for outsiders to fully understand what the argument was all about, but the fact remains that Patterson defended his title against only Hurricane Jackson and Pete Rademacher.

The critics had a field day at the expense of D'Amato and his champion. Sample, Joe Williams, writing in the *New York World-Telegram:*

"If Floyd Patterson isn't the worst managed heavyweight champion in history he'll have to do until someone can produce a more enigmatically bizarre character than Cus the Christian.

"By comparative standards, Patterson has little money and even less prestige, a minor tragedy as these things go, because the young man is a good fighter, in time, could be a great one. In recent weeks four prospective challengers he could have made money with, handled rather easily and, in the process, sold himself as an exciting, valid champion have been expunged from the lists.

"All of a sudden the heavyweight division has been shot to pieces. The men Patterson could have fought, but wasn't permitted to because they were socially unacceptable to his manager, have eliminated themselves. First, Machen and Folley, then Valdes and DeJohn. Who else is there?

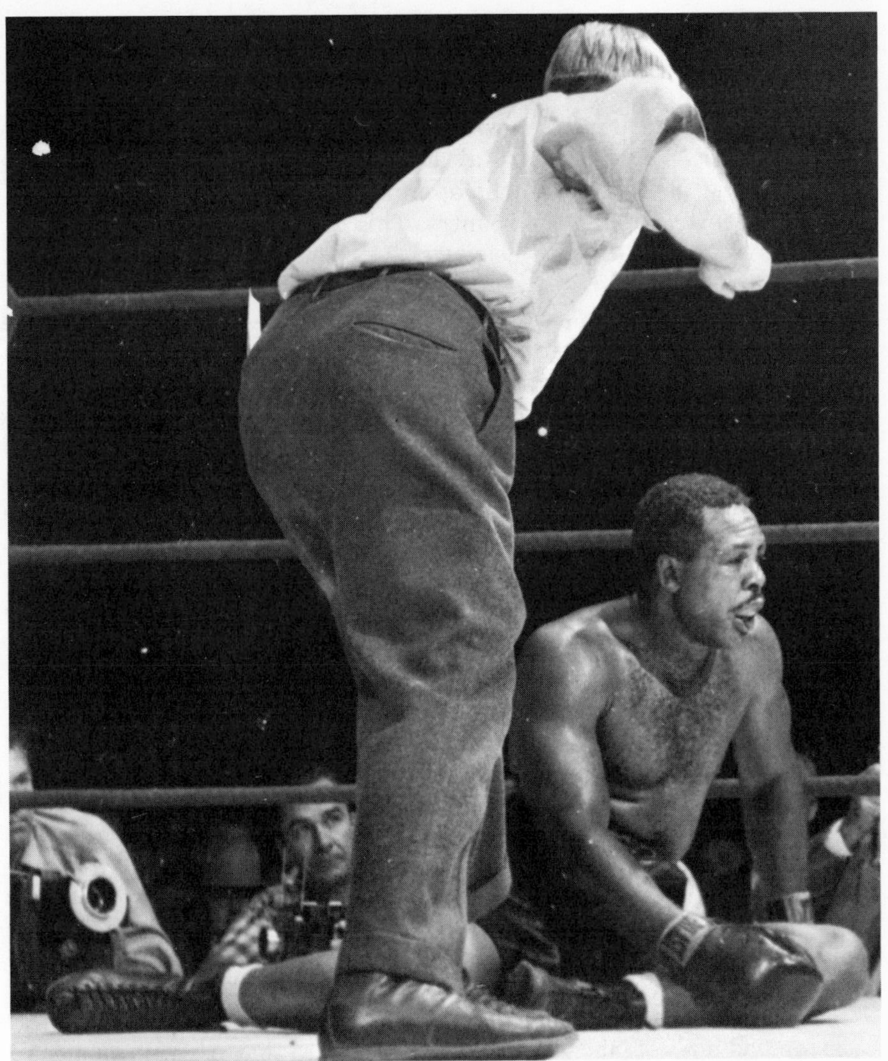

When Rocky Marciano retired undefeated, Patterson fought Archie Moore for the vacant heavyweight championship. The bout ended with referee Frank Sikora here counting out Archie in 2:27 of the fifth round in Chicago. Thus on November 30, 1956, Floyd, at twenty-one, became the youngest heavyweight champion in history.

"Another penalty Patterson has paid for is his minor rating as TV merchandise. It's minor because he hasn't fought anybody of consequence since belting out ancient Archie Moore to win the title vacated by Rocky Marciano. He hasn't been given the opportunity to build himself up as a TV attraction.

"On home screens for free a sponsor would go for the tab, but who would pay to see him on theater TV against a Roy Harris, a Valdes, or, heaven forbid, another big bag workout against amateur Pete Rademacher? And theater TV is where the big money is now. A month ago 17,976 paid $351,955 to see Ray Robinson and Carmen Basilio in the flesh, while 364,876 others paid approximately $1.5 million to see them on theater TV around the country. This course is closed to Patterson. There is no market for a heavyweight champion who has been managed into obscurity.

"A fight manager who unblushingly admits to scruples is rare enough. One who clings to them at financial sacrifice is rarer still. In this case, however, the sacrifice is not borne alone. In addition to money, Patterson's loss in prestige is incalculable."

Harry Grayson, in his nationally syndicated NEA column, took the same hard line as Williams:

"In the strange boxing world of James D. Norris, Constantine D'Amato finds himself with the heavyweight champion and nowhere to go. Floyd Patterson, who could do so much toward putting boxing back on its pins, sweats it out in training at Greenwood Lake, N.Y., with no plans to date for a summer defense of the title. It's inconceivable that the manager of such an attractive heavyweight titleholder as Patterson cannot obtain employment for his fighters from the far-flung International Boxing Club, under the auspices of which Floyd scaled the heights. But Cus D'Amato insists that this is the case.

" 'I have paid for my opposition of Jim Norris by lack of work for my fighters,' he said. In Patterson, D'Amato obviously has what Norris needs, so he was asked to give just one good reason why Norris should give him the silent treatment. 'I must consider Norris a vindictive man,' the manager said. 'Perhaps he was embarrassed because I made him come to me and out-smarted him when Patterson boxed Hurricane Jackson last June (1956). Now, I'll give you a story that has never been printed. A year ago, when the Jackson match was made, Rocky Marciano had not yet officially retired, and I heard that Al Weill was quarreling with Norris. Without talking to Weill, I learned that the quarrel was authentic, so I said right out loud in a public place: 'If the IBC doesn't stop fooling around, Patterson will box Marciano for another promoter.' I knew what I said would get back to Norris, and to Weill's credit, he kept his mouth shut. The thought of such a tremendous match as Marciano and Patterson going elsewhere beat Norris completely. It wasn't long before a friend of mine asked me to meet Norris in midtown, assuring me that he would talk on a reasonable basis. We can wait. Jim Norris isn't going to put himself out of business.' "

Grayson wrote that on March 29, 1957. Norris did not talk to D'Amato on a reasonable basis. And Marciano did not sign to fight Patterson. In fact, when Marciano was in Kentucky on some business, he

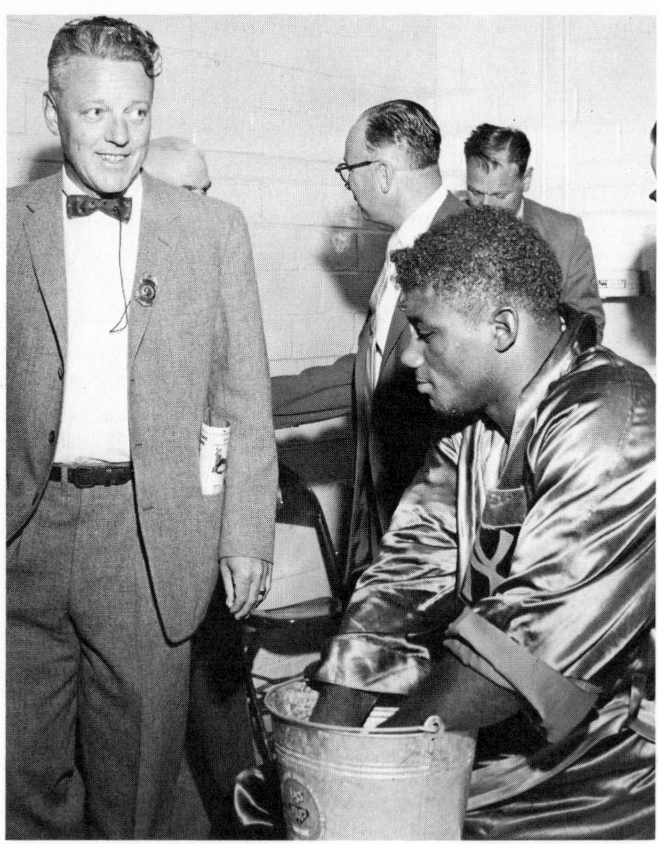

Dr. Charles P. Larson, eminent Tacoma pathologist and President of the World Boxing Association, watches Patterson soak his hands in brine before his August 22, 1957, title bout in Seattle against Olympic Games champion Pete Rademacher. (Photo by Ken Ollar)

visited the office of Happy Chandler, former Commissioner of Baseball. Chandler had heard of the million-dollar offer that Norris had made to Rocky to fight Patterson.

"Rocky," Chandler told him, "don't you fight."

"Don't worry, I won't fight again," Rocky said.

Patterson, to keep busy, took his show on the road in 1957. He fought a series of inconsequential four-round exhibitions in places like Kansas City, Minneapolis, Joplin, Wichita, and Ft. Smith. Then, twice within 3½ weeks, he put his title on the line.

The first was against Hurricane Jackson, who had nothing to offer but courage, endurance and a completely screwball style. Patterson put him out of his misery in the 10th round. He pounded Hurricane into reeling, staggering helplessness. It was a hard and cruel and dirty job he had to do and one that he didn't relish, but Floyd brought it off. I covered the bloodbath for NEA and as I left the Polo Grounds, I thought to myself, "Patterson had the killer instinct tonight."

On August 22, 1957, only weeks later, Seattle was the scene of about as bizarre a title match as you could imagine: Patterson vs. Pete Rademacher. Here was a case of the heavyweight division coming down to a challenger for the championship who never had had a professional fight. Rademacher's sole credentials were that he won a Gold Medal in the heavyweight division at the 1956 Olympic Games, and at Washington State University he had been a rough, tough football lineman. Pete, to his credit, knew how to promote himself. He was a super-salesman, and he had sold himself to a group of Georgia sportsmen who called themselves Youth Unlimited, Inc. The group guaranteed Patterson $250,000 to fight Pete. At the urging of Seattle promoter Jack Hurley, D'Amato accepted.

Patterson brought immense natural skill and devout dedication to his craft. To keep in shape, he works out here with a medicine ball.

If Pete Rademacher had ever been proposed to Al Weill as a challenger for Marciano when Rocky was king, he would have dismissed it with a shrug. He would have sniffed the air and said, "There ain't gonna be no Rademacher match. The people won't stand for it so why should I take a match where they're gonna start laughin' at us. I ain't got the kind of a fighter you should laugh at."

The build-up was on. Harry Grayson and I flew out to Seattle to cover the bout for NEA and the *New York World-Telegram and Sun.* D'Amato, talking as fast as his lightning-fisted champion, tried to make the upcoming fight interesting. He denied that he held Rademacher lightly.

"Anyone who weighs 210 and can punch can be dangerous," he told us. "Rademacher won the Olympic title and you have to be good to do that. When my boy won the middleweight title in the 1952 Games, I thought he could beat Bobo Olson even then."

Patterson, meanwhile, trained hard. He sparkled. We mentioned his improvement to D'Amato.

"He's been a good fighter for years," Cus said. "The so-called experts and critics just didn't recognize it. Floyd's been criticized for those leaps he makes. But those are 'spot' punches. He never uses them except when he knows the opening is there. He's not going to get counter-punched when he jumps in."

A total of 16,961 paid a gross gate of $243,060 to watch a professional champion fight an amateur champion. Youth Unlimited, Inc., had to pitch in another $125,073 to make up the guarantee.

In the opening round, Rademacher forced the fight. It looked as if Patterson were sizing him up. At least he did not open up with a volley of punches as he did in the first round of his last fight with Hurricane Jackson.

The big moment of the Seattle encounter came in the second round when Rademacher floored Patterson. It was no fluke. Rademacher actually and legitimately dumped the champion. The punch was a good, fairly straight right-hand that landed on the cheekbone and a bit toward Patterson's left ear. There was nothing phony or faked about the knockdown.

Referee Tommy Loughran did not usher Rademacher to the farthest neutral corner, as the rules specify, but he did pick up the count and appeared to toll off three. Patterson did not appear hurt, taking about the normal time to get up and protecting himself against Rademacher's right-hand shots for the remainder of the round.

At one spot in the third round, the fighters got in an awkward position and Patterson actually was holding Rademacher up with one hand around the latter's body. Floyd later explained this, saying, "If I'd let him drop or given him a push, it would have looked like I was fighting dirty." In that same round, Patterson dropped Rademacher with a sneaky right-hand lead to the chin for the first of seven trips to the floor for Pete. Floyd was in total charge after that, although Pete continued to wing right hands. But his strength was fading and his punches lacked explosive prowess.

Rademacher hit the deck four times in the fifth round, and some of the fans seemed to think Loughran should have stopped it then and there, but the referee let the fighters carry on. Pete was floored twice in the next round–both times from right hands–and on his second knockdown, he didn't get back up.

The bout was pitiful in its anti-climax. Patterson went about the grim business of cutting down an amateur. At times it appeared that he had no particular heart for the job. Once more, his compassion showed. The trouble with Rademacher was that he did not have the equipment. At twenty-eight years, he was too old to start a professional career. He was too slow of foot. He had little defense. He went down too easily from seemingly light blows to the head. Jimmy Cannon later asked Pete why he went down so easily, and Pete said, "I don't know. I tried after the fourth round and ran into a lot of hell. I never blacked out. I lost control of my knees. Soon as I hit the deck I was all right. He never hurt me. I was going a little too strong in the first couple of rounds and ran out of gas."

Red Smith was at ringside, too. He came up with the best line of the night.

"Patterson," he wrote, "looked like a man who wanted to carry an opponent and didn't know how."

Floyd Patterson paid a big price for his manager's prolonged feud with the IBC. D'Amato's one-man crusade brought this blast from Jack Dempsey:

"D'Amato's break with the IBC may be commendable, but the sad part of it is that the manager is hurting Patterson more than Jim Norris. Gene Tunney was right when he said it was a shame to see Patterson win the championship at 21. As Gene points out, Patterson as champion couldn't possibly fight often enough to learn. No one then could imagine D'Amato keeping Patterson as idle as he has been. Any good fighter will tell you that a fighter learns to fight well only by fighting."

Dempsey said he admired Floyd's loyalty to his manager, but the old Manassa Mauler could not imagine a champion with any sense and pride allowing a manager to foul him up like that.

"I would not have stood for it," Dempsey said. "Neither would have Tunney, Joe Louis or Rocky Marciano."

Patterson could have collected $200,000 each for fighting ex-Marine Pat McMurtry out in Tacoma, Washington, a red-hot fight city since the days of middleweight champion Freddie Steele; Eddie Machen in

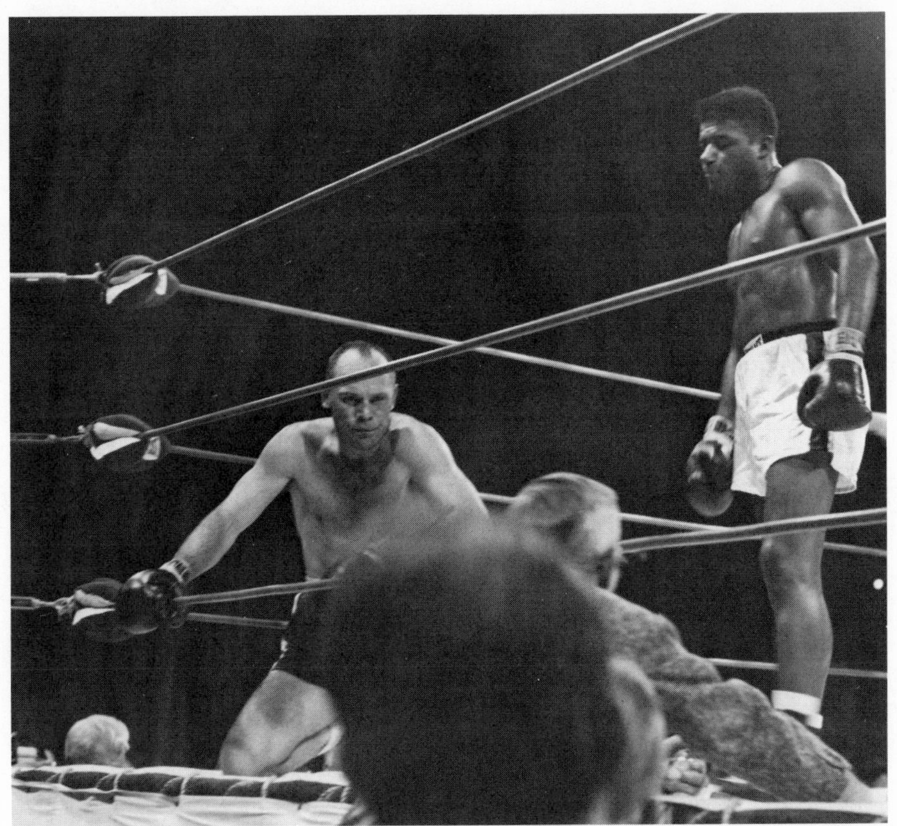

Seattle's Sick's Stadium was the scene of about as bizarre a title match as any in history. It marked Pete Rademacher's first *professional fight. Yet in the second round Pete floored Patterson for a count of three. Then the fireworks exploded—on Rademacher's chin. Pete is shown here getting up after the first of seven knockdowns. Referee Tommy Loughran finally stopped the one-sided match in the sixth round. (Photo by Ken Ollar)*

San Francisco; Zora Folley in Phoenix; and Mike DeJohn in Syracuse. Instead of taking the matches, D'Amato permitted these acceptable challengers to slide by.

"D'Amato got off on the wrong track fighting the monopoly," Dempsey said. "Patterson should have knocked off all those guys at championship prices and made himself the No. 1 figure in boxing. Then D'Amato could have written his own ticket."

When D'Amato refused to do business with the IBC, he set up his own private fights for Patterson. He hired fighters, from middleweights to heavyweights, to box Floyd. The idea was to give the champion work and to let him fight under regulation conditions. These were real fights, too, 22 of them in all, every one a *secret* bout. Patterson fought one guy in secret on three successive days. He knocked him out in the first round each time, except on the first occasion, when it took him a round and a half. *Three knockouts in three days!*

In the winter of 1958, Patterson travelled to England and gave British fight fans, long used to home-bred horizontal heavyweights, a sample of his talents in three-round exhibitions with his sparring mate, Dusty Rhodes. At London's Empress Hall, his speed and finesse inspired one journalist to write:

"The heavyweights of these shores could flatter but never flatten Floyd Patterson."

Nor could Roy Harris (KO, 12) or Brian London (KO, 11) with the title on the line.

That brought Patterson up to his first match with Ingemar Johansson, of Sweden, June 26, 1959. Associated Press correspondent Murray Rose wrapped up the details for the wire service in this manner:

> Ingemar Johansson's "mystery" right hand turned out to be an atomic weapon—an explosive force that propelled him to the world's heavyweight championship. The "thunder and lightning" that the undefeated Swede had promised was unleashed in a pulsating third round that saw defending champion Floyd Patterson felled seven times and stripped of his crown in rain-soaked Yankee Stadium last night.
>
> It was a right-hand bomb that burst against the jaw of the 5-1 favored American seconds after the start of the third round. The power-packed right smashed Patterson to the floor on his back and left him bereft of his senses.
>
> Calmly and coldly, as if he were sighting a rifle, the handsome, blue-eyed Viking dropped his bleeding and reeling foe to the canvas until referee Ruby Goldstein ended the slaughter with a wave of his hands.
>
> It went into the record books as a technical knockout. But this was pure destruction. It was a massacre. The mighty right hand made the 26-year-old, 196-pounder the first Swede ever to win a world boxing championship.
>
> The astonishing upset—witnessed by some 30,000 at the ball park and thousands more in theaters coast to coast—must rank with such shockers as Max Schmeling's kayo of Joe Louis in 1936, Jim Braddock's triumph over Max Baer in 1935, and Jersey Joe Walcott's annihilation of Ezzard Charles in 1951.
>
> The great triumph earned Johansson a purse of about $248,000. Patterson will collect approximately $560,000.

After Johansson knocked him out, Patterson went into seclusion for a month. When he came out of it, he set up a training camp in an abandoned roadhouse in Newtown, Connecticut, and trained for nine straight months.

"Do you resent Johansson?" he was asked one day.

"No," Floyd replied. "I was inclined to at first, but then I realized that all he did to me was what I tried to do to him, and there was no reason to resent him."

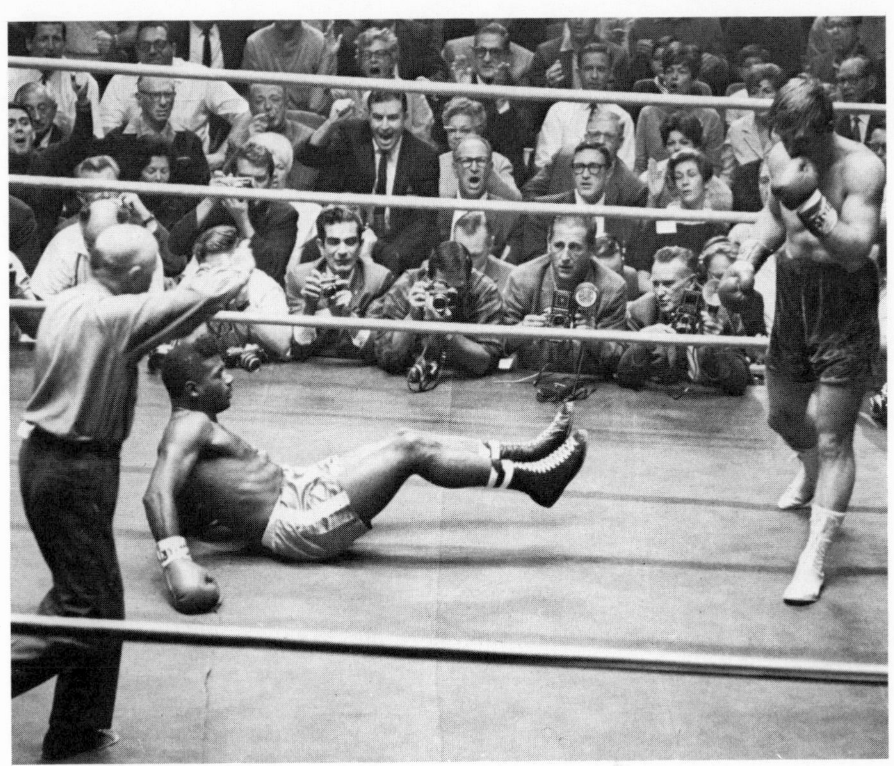

When Cassius Clay had his title taken away from him, an elimination tournament was organized and Jerry Quarry, of Los Angeles, bounced thirty-two-year-old Patterson out of the championship picture by winning a split decision. The hard-punching Quarry floored Floyd in the second round. The bout was held in Los Angeles on October 31, 1967.

"At any time when you were down in that fight, did you recognize anyone at ringside?"

"Yes," he said. "I recognized John Wayne. I think it must have been the third knockdown, because there I was on the floor, looking right at John Wayne and John Wayne was looking right at me. I've never met him, but he's my favorite movie actor. I think I've seen him in every picture he's made. At first I couldn't figure out how I could be seeing him there at ringside. I found out later he was plugging a movie during the broadcast of the fight, but all I knew then was that I'd seen John Wayne in person, and when I got back up I was still thinking of that and I was embarrassed that John Wayne had seen me down on the floor."

Cus D'Amato was not discouraged.

"Patterson," he told reporters after the defeat, "will be the first heavyweight champion in history to regain the title."

Three-hundred and fifty-nine days later—and Cus would look very good, indeed.

20. Ingemar Johansson

INGEMAR JOHANSSON was the first European to hold the heavyweight championship since the days of the freakish Primo Carnera—and only the fifth such champion born outside the United States since John L. Sullivan established the modern title, in 1882.

Ingo Johansson's sensational knockout of Floyd Patterson marked the end of an era in prize fighting; an era of American domination, an era of glory, but also an era of shame, in which boxing had rotted to a dirty business in the hands of monopolists and hoodlums working in cahoots.

The Sockin' Swede—6 ft. ½ in. and 196 pounds—did not prove to be as great a fighter as some of his illustrious predecessors, but he did have some very definite qualities going for him:

The quiet elegance of James J. Corbett.

The animal magnetism of Jack Dempsey.

The studious determination of Gene Tunney.

The simple sincerity of Joe Louis.

Johansson, blond, smiling and soft-spoken, was gifted with a special greatness, a compound of brawn and personality. He was master of a style that few professionals were able to solve, master of a punch that knocked out 14 of his first 22 opponents. In those days when so many contenders were half-baked, he fought Floyd Patterson coolly and shrewdly with the poise of a genuine professional, nullifying the defending champion's speed of hand with his own speed of foot, staving him off with a relentless barrier jab, saving his big right hand for just the right moment. When that moment came the right hand exploded just as he had said it would, a straight punch precisely designed to penetrate Patterson's peek-a-boo defense as no hook could do.

In less than nine minutes of fighting the main issue was settled by that single punch—a punch that had been derided as a publicity man's hoax.

Sweden's Ingemar Johansson was the first European since Italy's Primo Carnera to hold the heavyweight championship of the world. He stood 6 ft. ½ in. and weighed 196 pounds.

Those who knew Johansson best said his left hook was almost as good as his straight right, that he adapted to any opponent's style, moving in on counterpunchers as he wisely stayed away from Patterson's attempts to start those swift combinations. His was a cool head in a hot fight.

With Johansson's stunning victory the person of the world heavyweight champion suddenly became important again. Patterson, a natural recluse, had been willingly all but obscured from public view by his manager. The new champion, a natural extrovert, came much more sharply into public view and proved to be the very prototype of the clean, intelligent and independent athlete whom neither promoter, manager nor hoodlum could shove around. Europe idolized him and he was known in America for more than his good right hand. In television appearances his natural personality rivaled the practiced charm of Dinah Shore, with whom he once sang a respectably melodious duet. In a TV version of Ernest Hemingway's "The Killers," he won a solid hand of critical applause. He even made a movie.

Johansson's introduction to prize-fighting in the United States would have disillusioned a lesser man. He was told brusquely that he would not get his chance until he signed what he was later to describe as a "slave contract." Under it a man he had never heard of would collect 10 percent of his earnings (reduced from an original demand for 33⅓ percent) and tell him where and when and whom he could fight. Shortly before winning the championship from Patterson, he personally made this dark deal public. The New York State Boxing Commission then denounced the scheme and Ingemar was free, free to fight Patterson on honest, sporting terms.

Then, after the fight, it developed that one of the promotion's hidden backers, introduced to the sport by Promoter Bill Rosensohn, had been a gangster named Tony (Fat) Salerno. The disclosure led to suspension of licenses right and left and to a perjury indictment for Salerno's lawyer, Vincent J. Velella, charged with being a front man for the gangster. Before this happened, however, Johansson found himself adroitly maneuvered, quite as if by accident, into the company of James D. Norris and Truman Gibson of the dissolved and dissolute old International Boxing Club. The idea was to tie Johansson at least indirectly to the organization most responsible for the decadence of prize fighting. Ingemar forthrightly said he would have none of it.

"I will not have anything to do with gangsters," he declared publicly. "I will not fight for the IBC."

A highly professional man when a dollar was involved, Johansson was also dedicated to boxing as a sport and resented the cheap chicaneries of fast-buck hustlers. His true feeling for prize fighting was as amateur as his love of fishing, sports cars, light planes and hacker's golf, none of which ever made him a krona. He was deeply distressed by the state of prize fighting in the United States in 1959. His big punch came at a time when boxing in America had only two places left to go—up or out. He came to greatness in the year that boxing fell to a new low state.

Johansson's sensational third-round knockout of Floyd Patterson, on June 26, 1959, in New York marked the end of America's domination of the world heavyweight division.

Boxing now had the man—Ingemar Johansson—who had struck the blow for good against evil.

Unlike baseball, the "world" championship of which is determined entirely within the United States, boxing is a genuinely international sport, but for many years the heavyweight division was understandably dominated by the United States through the magnificence of its Sullivans, Dempseys, Tunneys and Louises.

Ironically, the drive that accounted for this domination decelerated more and more in the years of economic acceleration. Boxing came to greatness in America, and great American boxers were developed, because the sport offered opportunities of truly bonanza proportions to recently arrived ethnic groups and to the recently freed black. It was, Horatio Alger notwithstanding, at one time the only escape hatch from grinding poverty for boys of the lowest economic order and the lowest education level. At first, Irish and Germans were most prominent, later Jews and Italians, most recently blacks and a few Puerto Ricans. But today's prosperity and the concurrently sorry economics of prize fighting combined to militate against the development of American fighters in the Fifties and Sixties. Most American fighters could not earn a living by fighting alone. Free TV network shows ruined the small clubs where American boxers once learned the trade and made a good livelihood while learning.

By 1960, America no longer was the center of boxing. Of the 88 world champions and ranked contenders in all eight weight divisions, 55.6 percent were from outside the United States, an unprecedented proportion. In 1940, this percentage was 37.5. America had all but abandoned the two lightest divisions–the bantam and flyweight–which once were so exciting. Not a single American was ranked in either division. Even the television promoters made no effort to revive interest in the little men.

Nor was the United States doing so well in its historic specialty, the heavyweight division. On June 26, 1959, we had lost the championship to Sweden. Even before that, our top-rankers of the day–Eddie Machen, Zora Folley and Willie Pastrano–had been defeated in Europe by fighters who were little regarded on this side of the Atlantic.

Prize fighting in the United States was groggy, certainly, but it was not necessarily knocked out. Ingemar Johansson had come along in the nick of time to furnish the badly needed transfusion.

"When Johansson flattened Patterson so savagely," wrote Harry Grayson, "he gave the heavyweights their biggest boost since Dempsey established the million-dollar gate."

This was the same Harry Grayson who only a month before had questioned the Swede's credentials. Harry had bumped into James A. Farley, the best boxing commissioner New York ever had, at the Waldorf-Astoria, and Big Jim asked him, "Can Johansson fight?"

"How does anybody in this country know?" Harry told him.

Farley had ruled boxing during its golden days–from 1924 to 1933–with the great William Muldoon.

"Jim," Harry asked, "were you still chairman of the boxing commission today, would you approve a Patterson-Johansson match?"

"I am inclined to believe I would make Johansson fight someone else in this country first," the former Postmaster General said. "I would make him prove himself. I am positive that Bill Muldoon would have done this. He would not have permitted the public to be fed an untested package. But the present commission is so eager to get Patterson active that it was willing to OK the bout without first having seen the Swede."

"What do you know about him?" Grayson asked.

"Only that he's been as delicately guided as Patterson," Farley said. "The first thing I must question is his number of fights. He's fought only 21 times in six solid years as a professional. That's a rather skimpy schedule for a youngster being put through the mill. What line do you have on him, Harry?"

"He's the same Johansson who was disqualified for refusing to fight in the finals of the 1952 Olympic Games. Since then he has been fed a rare assortment of bums from Europe and the British West Indies, with practically all of the action confined to his native Sweden."

The first recognizable name in Johansson's record was Hein Ten Hoff, the towering German who was a veteran in 1955. Joe Bygraves lasted 10 rounds with him in 1956. The same Jamaican had quit to Wayne Bethea after five rounds at St. Nicholas Arena in New York.

Johansson won the European championship by knocking out Franco Cavicchi in Bologna, on September 30, 1956, after which there was some question about the Italian's moxie in the ring. Henry Cooper, the Englishman, was demolished in five rounds in 1957, but Archie McBride, an extremely ordinary American, forced Johansson to go 10 rounds. The following year, Joe Erskine had enough after 13 and Heinz Neuhaus, a German showing wear and tear, went out in four.

That brought us to what appeared to be a smashing victory over Eddie Machen, who was knocked down three times and out in 2 minutes and 16 seconds in Gothenburg, on September 14, 1958. It later developed that Machen was suffering from a pulled muscle in his left shoulder which restricted his jabbing and hooking. Those acquainted with the facts claimed this accounted for Eddie's miserable 12-round draw with Zora Folley.

Machen worked out in a warm sun in the afternoon, while Johansson had worked at night. "It was an outdoor fight and the night was cold," Machen told his friends. "It has always taken me some time to warm up. They told me Johansson would run and he did the first time I went after him. But the second time he took a half-step back and caught me cold with a right-hand punch to the chin. All his weight was behind it. That's all there was to the fight, although he hit me a lot of punches after the first one."

On that sole recommendation, Johansson got his opportunity to fight Patterson for the championship.

"Let's hope he can fight," Grayson said, before the bout, "at least good enough to give us some line on Floyd Patterson."

Now that the Patterson-Johansson match was set, Floyd came out of his shell and talked candidly to the press about himself, his hopes and dreams. He said he hoped to put his title on the line four times a year—providing he beat Ingemar, of course. "What I want," he said, "is to get into the ring and meet whoever the No. 1 challenger is. After I beat whoever is the top man, move the next man up and I'll meet him. What I've been doing—these long layoffs—hasn't done me any good. I haven't been the kind of champion I should be and I'm not now. I've lost that competitive edge I once had and the only way I'll get it back is to be fighting."

Floyd made it clear that he had no disagreement with his manager Cus D'Amato over the way he had been handled, but at the same time he didn't try to hide his discontent that except for defenses against Hurricane Jackson, Pete Rademacher and Roy Harris he had been a champion on ice who hadn't reached the peak he should have achieved after two years as a titleholder.

"Of course," Floyd said, "I do what Cus says. I've no complaint with what the championship has meant in money to me so far, but there are other things besides money."

D'Amato had defended his handling of Patterson with the explanation that the champion was in the 90 percent bracket down at the tax department.

"The year I had the two fights–Jackson and Rademacher–I was in the 91 percent bracket," Floyd said. "If I have four fights a year I won't be in any higher bracket and I'll still be making some money. At the same time I'll be getting the kind of experience and work that you don't get no matter how long, consistently and hard you train in the gym. I am aware that I am not fighting up to my form. Against Harris last August, I just couldn't get myself together. I'd bob and weave and that boy would be open for all kinds of punches and instead of punching I'd pull back. It was the first time in all the time of my fighting that I was disgusted with myself in a fight. I knew I could beat him and that I'd take him sometime, but I actually was discouraged. Even when I threw a punch I didn't do it naturally and instinctively. I had to think before letting the punch go and that's no way at all to fight. The last time I was at a peak I considered right for me was against Archie Moore when I won the title. I wasn't satisfied with myself against Jackson, but against Moore I made every move that had to be made. I've seen the movies over and over again and I can't find a place where I did something then that I'd want to change now. After the fight I wrote a letter to Archie. I told him that maybe the result would have been different if I'd fought him when he was younger. I figured the beating he took from Marciano helped me whip him."

From what the oldtimers saw of Johansson in training at Grossinger's convinced them that for him to beat Patterson, he would have to knock out the champion quickly or be slowly and methodically chopped up and stopped in no more than nine rounds.

Ingemar did not look good in practice.

"Frankly," Harry Grayson said, "Johansson has looked so bad that most boxing men actually wonder whether he will turn out to be a real test for Patterson. His pawing left has looked as ineffectual as a Geneva conference. The right hand with which he is supposed to slay dragons is as invisible as Patterson between engagements. He hasn't the slightest idea of what infighting is. His hands and feet are slow and he is an easy target. The best his sparring mates can say about him is that he is strong. Ingemar looks good physically to the naked eye, but then, so does Errol Flynn—and Errol couldn't fight his way out of a roomful of gorgeous blondes. Those who have seen him in European rings say he is just a shade better than Brian London—and you'll recall what Patterson did to him (KO, 11)."

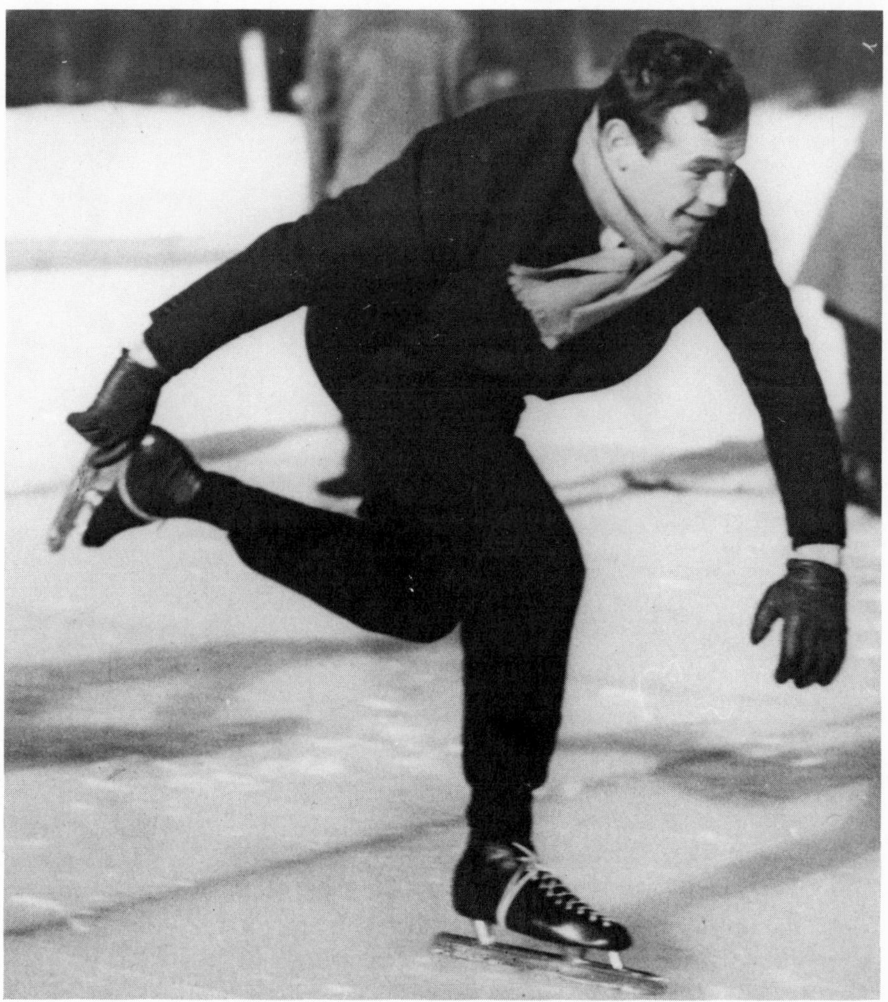

Ingemar Johansson, blond, smiling and soft-spoken, was gifted with versatility in athletics. Here he sprints across the finish line to win 1,000-meter speed-skating event at Malarhojden, and he puts his foot into soccer ball playing for Goteborg against Malmo, Sweden.

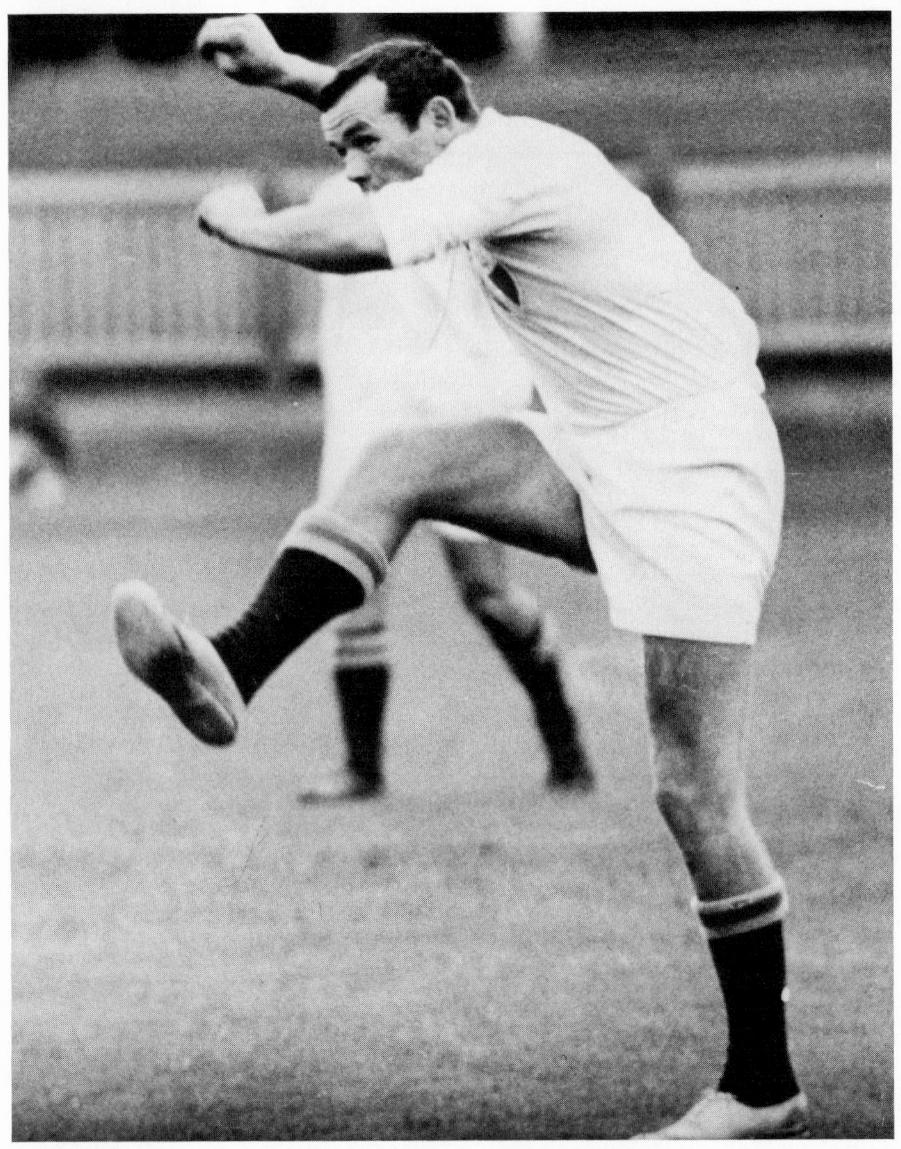

Martin Kane, of *Sports Illustrated*, felt the picture painted by the veteran Grayson was too pessimistic. He believed that Johansson had a reasonable chance to win.

"The chance depends almost entirely on the challenger's right hand," Kane said. "Everyone Patterson has fought in recent years has hit him with a solid right-hand punch. Pete Rademacher, the amateur, even knocked him down. Conceivably, a really powerful right-hand puncher could knock Patterson out."

Johansson knew all this—and he had the biggest right hand of them all.

From any sensible standpoint, the fight was a natural. Whether it went long or short there would be suspense in every round. No one had yet hit Patterson hard enough to test him truly. No one the champion had fought since Moore had been able to punch as hard as Johansson.

The quality of the challenger is what makes an attractive fight when a championship is at stake, and challenger Johansson had attractive fighting and personal qualities. He was a young man of great social charm, and at the same time he was pleasantly aware that the title he sought was worth a million dollars to him.

Despite what Grayson thought of Johansson's training program, the Swede did, in fact, train with the body-punishing dedication of a Rocky Marciano. Where Patterson ran three to five miles, Johansson ran six. Where Patterson boxed four rounds, Johansson boxed six or seven. And where Patterson satisfied himself with a few rounds of bag-punching and rope-skipping, Johansson added his own extraordinary Swedish calisthenics and at least two rounds of punching on a strange contraption, a Swedish girls' *slungboll,* which is normally hurled in girlish imitation of the hammer throw. Suspended from a bang board by its 18-inch strap handle, it was much harder to hit consistently than the ordinary speed bag, which moves with a swift but definite rhythm. The *slungboll* moved with the approximate speed and unpredictability of an opponent's bobbing, weaving head. Johansson's reflexes were thus being trained, in other words, to catch Patterson's head going east with a Johansson punch going west. The very first of the three Machen knockdowns proved the value of this device, invented by Trainer Blomberg and perfected by Johansson.

There was, of course, a sensible reason for the difference in the training methods of Patterson and Johansson. The champion weighed only 182 pounds for his fight with Brian London the previous May 1st. In training for Johnsson he had dropped at times to as little as 179, just four pounds above the light-heavyweight class. And, as his trainer, Dan Florio, said, "What Patterson puts into one round of boxing or bag-punching is worth three rounds by another fighter." Patterson aimed to come to the weigh-in scales at 182. Johansson, on the other hand, was a natural 196-pounder.

On fight night, the odds were 3 to 1 in favor of Patterson. These seemed excessive to the late Wilbur Clark, proprietor of Las Vegas' Desert Inn, and to make his point he wagered $10,000 on Johansson after paying several visits to Ingemar's training camp.

It took just nine minutes for Johansson to make Harry Grayson and the skeptics eat their prefight words. Grayson was more than happy to. The handsome Swede was just the young man who could quickly restore to the heavyweight championship of the world the prestige and dignity which it so richly deserved. Grayson told his national audience:

"It remains to be seen whether Johansson is a good all-around performer, but he can punch—at least hard enough to wreck Patterson, whose chin always has been suspect. Johansson once more proved how simple prize fighting really is for a young man with a wallop. You don't need all the preliminary folderol. All you have to do is hit the other guy at the right time with the right punch, the earlier the better."

The real story of Ingemar Johansson—the son of a City of Goteborg maintenance foreman—began with Edwin Ahlqvist. The Goteborg publisher and promoter first saw Ingo as a fourteen-year-old at Lorensberg's Circus in Goteborg. He said he actually first heard of the boy when Ingo was thirteen, but he waited a year before tracking him down.

"It had always been my ambition to develop a heavyweight champion," Ahlqvist said, "but I had been terribly disappointed with four other hopefuls and had given up the dream as a bad job. Then I saw Ingemar. He was only fourteen but weighed 180 and had the awkwardness of a growing boy. They had him matched with a husky 195-pounder from the shipyards. The big fellow started after the kid as though he would eat him alive, but Ingemar dropped that right on his chin and the referee counted out the shipyard worker. When the big fellow came to, he asked who in the hell threw in the towel. Like Floyd Patterson 12 years later, he didn't know what hit him. Ingemar was born with that short right hand."

Johansson, as an amateur, won 60 out of 71 bouts. In 1951, he competed for a European team against an American Golden Gloves team in Chicago and knocked out Ernie Fann in the second round. Then something happened to him. He was thrown out of the ring for "not trying" against big Ed Sanders of the United States at the Olympics in Helsinki after he had fought his way to the finals. Only by knocking out Patterson was he able to wipe that stain from his career. It had taken him seven long years to live down his countrymen's derision. There had been no room in him for rancor at the scorn of his proud people, because he was too filled with quiet determination to win the biggest title of them all, heavyweight champion of the world.

The press met with Patterson two days after he lost his title. Cus D'Amato was with him. When the reporters asked Floyd if he believed he could beat Johansson in a return match, D'Amato insisted on answering: "I think Patterson will be the first heavyweight champion to regain the title."

Patterson, still shoved into the background, answered one question much to the discomfiture of his manager. Someone asked him whether he had ever been hit so hard before, and Floyd said, with a wistful grin, "Evidently not."

It marked the first time professionally that Patterson had ever been kayoed. He had won his last 22 straight fights and 16 of his last 17 by knockouts.

Thus Ingo became the fourth heavyweight ever to win the crown without a defeat on his pro record. John L. Sullivan, Jim Jeffries and Rocky Marciano were the three others. Jeffries, however, had two draws to mar his record.

The second edition of the Johansson-Patterson championship series took place a year later in the Polo Grounds. Ingo went into the ring that night confident he had Floyd's number. Listen:

"Nothing has changed," he said. "My best punch is still my straight right hand. Straight, and so quick you cannot see it! It is always good to use the short right when Patterson is coming on. He comes right to it."

"But Patterson does not come straight on into a punch," I corrected him. "He bobs, weaves and feints."

"Still, at some point, he must drop his peekaboo guard," Johansson said, "and that's when I nail him."

In training, Johansson concentrated on his jab almost to the exclusion of his right hand. Clearly, he planned to use the left to pile up points while waiting a chance to throw his big right, the right that floored Patterson *seven* times in the third and final round of their first fight. "So he will come out with his two hands up on his face again," Johansson said, "and I will jab and jab and jab straight and hard and this will do something, this will annoy him and he will do something with his hands."

The champion gave two versions of his left-right combination. His favorite had the two fists arriving almost simultaneously, the left a fraction of a second ahead of a fairly short right. In the other version the jab was used with almost a pawing motion to confuse the opponent in the instant before a powerful, much longer right was launched with plenty of shoulder behind it to give the punch full authority.

"When Patterson misses," Ingo said, "I do not know what hand I'll use. The main thing is to go on him then. By going on him I mean moving in close, probably after throwing a punch. To solve his peekaboo defense I will probably go to the uppercut, but I don't know. I must really be careful. If I miss, my hand is up here and he will voom to the body."

Some people got the impression that Johansson did not train seriously for his first and only defense of the title. But those closest to him—among them the very skilled Whitey Bimstein, who shared training responsibilities with Nils Blomberg, Johansson's Swedish trainer—were half inclined to think quite the opposite—that Ingo trained too hard, although Whitey expressed loyal admiration for the champion's persistence and dedication.

"He trains like the oldtimers," Whitey said one afternoon while Ingo was exhausting spectators with his customary long routine in the gym. "The oldtimers loved their work and so does this fellow. I can remember Johnny Dundee boxing 20 rounds at Stillman's Gym because he felt he was learning something every round. Who does that anymore?"

Still, Whitey had wished Ingo would slow down on hot days. "But if it is a hot night at the Polo Grounds?" Ingo asked. He had been studying the torrid climate that frequently strikes New York in late June and he wanted to be ready for it.

The fight itself had the crowd of between 40,000 and 45,000 in a frenzy. In the second round, the champion came out of his corner and nailed Patterson high on the head. Had he been able to follow up his best punch of the night it might have been lights out for Floyd then and there. Patterson was stunned but he was able to retreat and Ingo didn't get in the followup right. It was the only round Ingo won.

Patterson fought differently this time. He upset Ingo's own piercing weapon—the left jab. Floyd lanced repeatedly and effectively with the jab. He opened a cut under Ingo's left eye in the first round. He raised a lump under the same eye in the next round. In the fifth round he sent Johansson to the ropes. The first leaping left hook thudded against Ingo's jaw and dropped him. Ingo got up on one knee and took the count of nine. Patterson tore after him fiercely, battering him with both hands. For a few moments, Johansson escaped. Then came the crushing final left hook and Ingo hit the canvas. Referee Artie Mercante could have counted 500 over him. It was several minutes before Ingo was propped up on a stool in the ring and several more minutes before he was able to leave for his dressing room.

For the second time in his life, Floyd Patterson was heavyweight champion of the world—the first former heavyweight champion to regain the title. He had shown the world emphatically that he had a lightning left hook to match Johansson's thunderbolt right.

"I think it was the hardest blow I ever hit anyone," said the twenty-five-year-old New Yorker afterward. "For the first time I feel I'm a real champion. I think the public finally will accept me. At least, I hope so. I told Ingemar he positively will get a third shot. I'd like it soon. In 90 days, if possible. I'm going to be a real champion."

Johansson was downcast. A third straight fight with Patterson?

"I want time to think it over," he said.

It didn't take him long to make up his mind. The decision was to go ahead with Bout No. 3. The title rematch drew heavy bidding. Los Angeles, Chicago, Philadelphia and Dallas all tried to get it. Miami Beach finally won.

Deacon Jack Hurley had picked Johansson to beat Patterson in their first fight and then tabbed Floyd to win the second bout, but now when

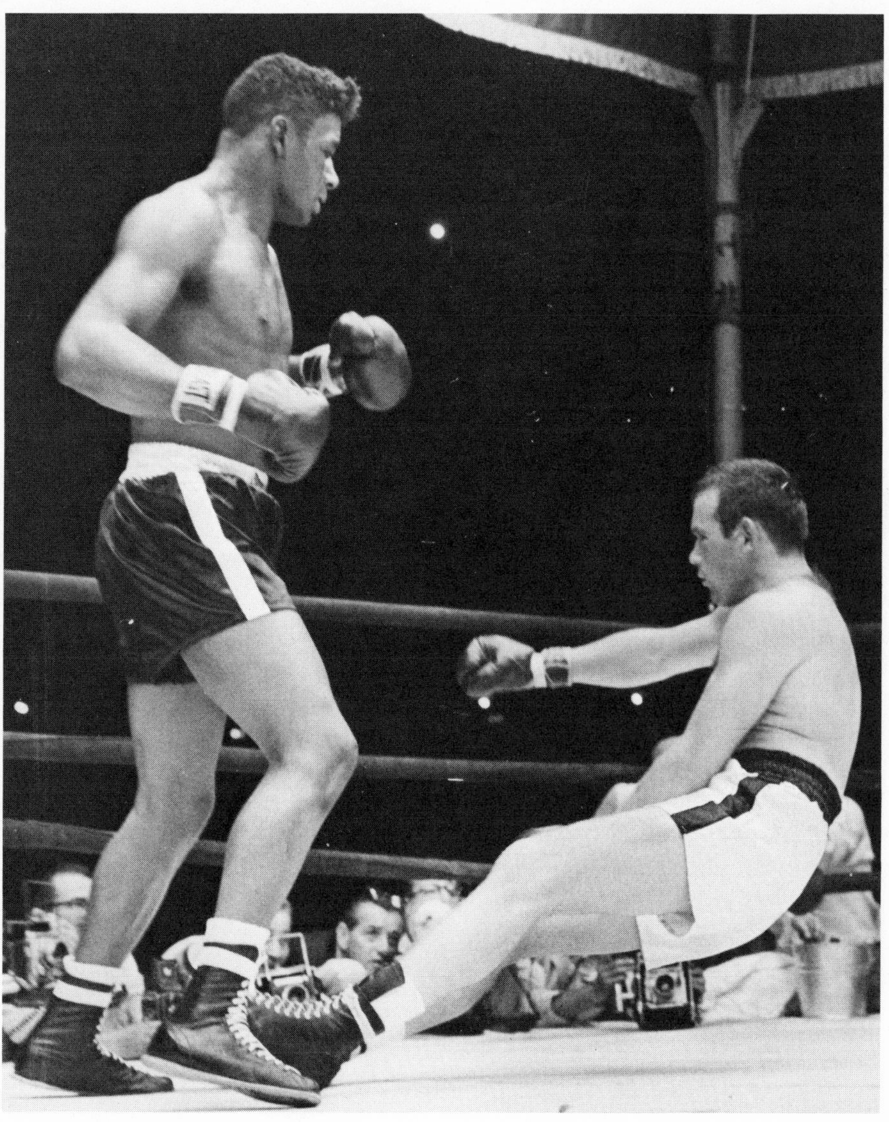

Fast camera work caught Johansson in mid-flight as Patterson KO'd the Swede in the fifth round to become first man ever to regain the heavyweight title. The bout was held in New York on June 20, 1960.

I asked him to predict the probable winner the third time around, he backed off. "I'm not going to pick anyone this time," he said. "I'm terribly in doubt. Even after Patterson knocked Ingo out this last time, I don't know. The Swede hit Patterson on top of the head and hurt him.

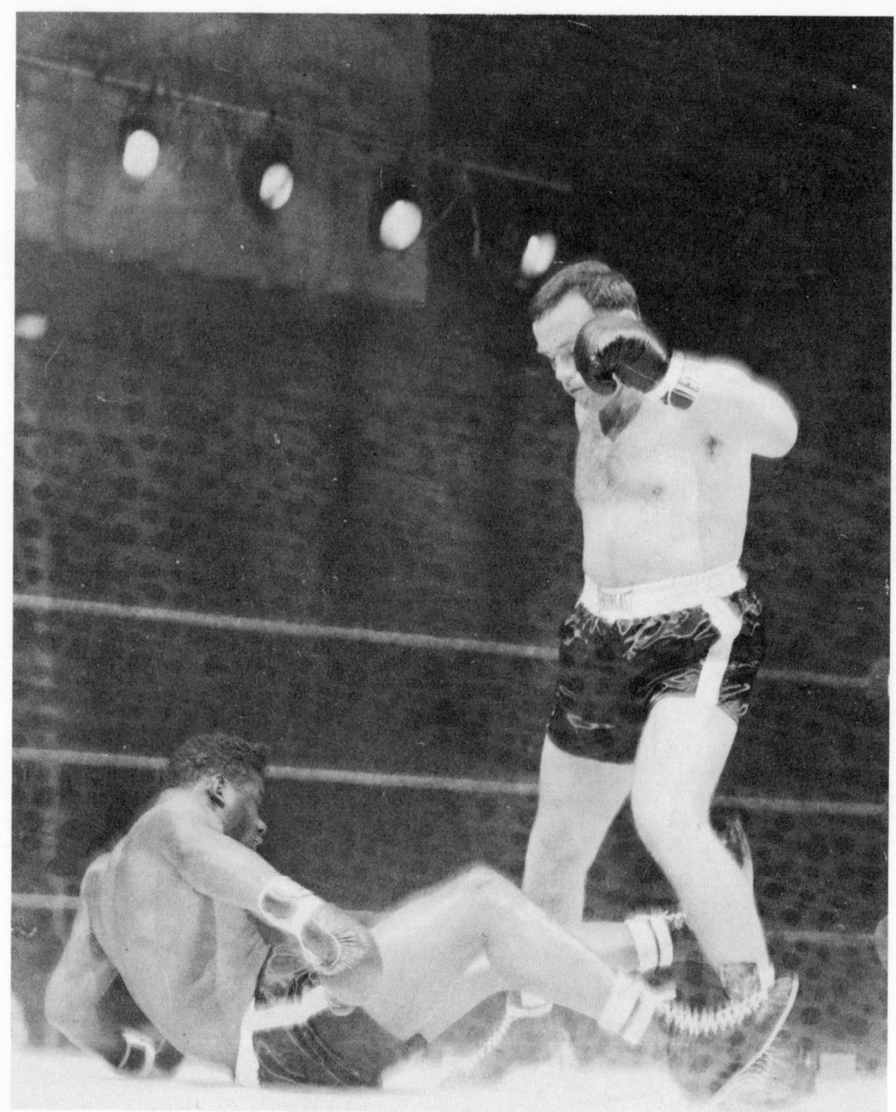

In their "rubber" match in Miami, March 13, 1961, Johansson and Patterson fought a barnburner. Ingemar was the first to light the fuse by flooring Floyd twice in the opening round, then being knocked out himself in the sixth round.

The third could go like the first. You've got to remember Ingo could lose 14 rounds and still knock out Patterson with one punch. He's that dangerous. Ingo is the best one-punch knocker-out among the champions since Dempsey. Tunney, Charles, Walcott, the rest of those guys

couldn't take you out with one punch. Ingo can. Maybe you don't realize it but Johansson has a better record as a pro than Patterson. He has lost only one fight as a pro—that to Floyd. Patterson has lost two—one to Joey Maxim and the other to Johansson."

The Patterson-Johansson series made history. It marked the first time that the same two men fought in three consecutive championship bouts (1959, '60 and '61).

In the final chapter, Patterson sent Ingo Johansson back to his heavy contracting business and fishing boat in Sweden with a sixth-round knockout.

Thus ended the longest playing dramatic TV performance since Abie's Irish Rose.

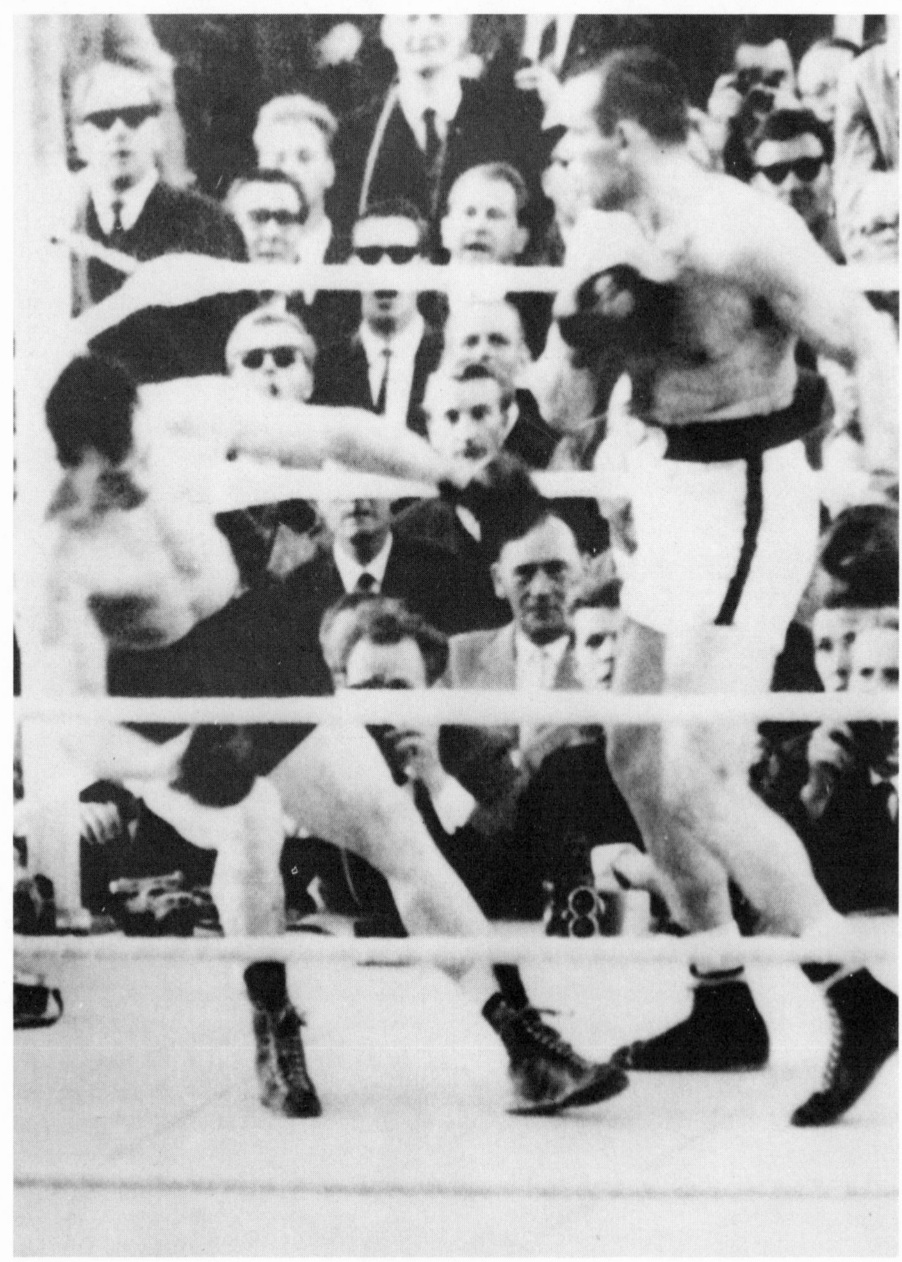

Johansson connects with his famous "hammer-of-Thor" right-hand punch to put Dick Richardson of Wales asleep in the eighth round and regain the European heavyweight championship at Goteborg, Sweden, on June 17, 1962. Ingemar fought only once more—a 12-round decision over Brian London—and then retired in 1963 to enter private business.

21. Charles (Sonny) Liston

SONNY LISTON was tricked most of the thirty-eight years of his life. Except for the night of September 25, 1962, when he knocked Floyd Patterson out in the first round to become heavyweight champion of the world, not very much ever turned out as he expected. He was born with a mischievous deviltry in his eyes and he died under mysterious circumstances with his face turned to the wall, the bitterness beyond acceptance. He wanted everything, got very little. Sonny Liston, born into a family of 25 children, was a study in despair.

His biggest fault lay in the fact that he grew up thinking that criminals were great people. Even when he had wealth and could afford to change his ways, he seemed to prefer hanging around with the bottom of the social scale–a rowdy collection of foul-mouthed pugs, small-time managers, ten-cent politicians, tarts, boobs, bookmakers, dope peddlers, hoodlums, mobmen, gangsters. They were in general hard-eyed, cold-faced men with fearsome reputations–the palace guard, war ministry and state department of the invisible gangster empire.

Not that he was having any official traffic with such revolting characters during the 17 months he was heavyweight champion. It was just that their tough, virile, explosive and animalistic personalities drew him to them out of sheer similar backgrounds. They talked his language. It was the only real language he knew.

Liston obviously did not feel comfortable in a refined and erudite atmosphere. He felt almost repelled by the social graces.

The boys he hung around with were not the types you could ignore without entailing considerable risk.

Recently, I talked to Dr. Charles P. Larson about Liston. Dr. Larson has served with distinction as President of both the NBA and WBA. He was also President of the College of American Pathologists and for

Sonny Liston stood 6 ft. 1 in. and weighed 213 at his peak. There was just too much dynamite in both hands for most fighters to handle him.

years has been recognized as one of America's leading crime experts. Dr. Larson has helped police solve many crimes. It was thus only logical that I would talk to him about Sonny Liston.

Dr. Larson did not pull his punches.

"Sonny was a true illiterate," Dr. Larson said. "He was a poor, dumb man. When he was champion, we had a hell of a time giving him a decent image. He was always in trouble. He drank too much, he hung around with criminals, punks. We assigned detectives to tail him just to keep him in line."

"Dumb?" I asked. "Do you mean Sonny couldn't read or write?"

"Barely," Dr. Larson said. "We finally sent him to Denver to Father Edward P. Murphy, S.J. The Catholic priest taught him to read and write some."

"Are you saying, Doctor, that Sonny was mentally deficient?"

"Not by any means," Dr. Larson said. "When he had the opportunity to learn—to read and write—he proved he could do it. But those things were unimportant to him."

"How well did you know him?"

"Better than the other champions," Dr. Larson said. "I had many conversations with Sonny, both officially and informally. In our private chats I found him to be a hard man to draw out. He was introvertish. When he decided to open up, he made quite a bit of sense. He reasoned out his thoughts pretty well."

"Do you feel, Dr. Larson, that Sonny wanted to be a good person?"

"That's very hard to judge," Dr. Larson said. "His entire background, from his childhood to the years he spent in the penitentiary, was in association with criminals. Hoodlums of the worst sort. Through his childhood and early adult life, those associations made such an impression on him that he actually developed an adulation for the low-life criminal element. He especially idolized those who beat the law. To Sonny Liston, those who made a lot of tainted money and got away with it were heroes."

"His judgment of right and wrong was all distorted," I said.

"Yes," Dr. Larson said. "But I did not blame him for this attitude, because most of his life he dealt with people in business who gave him the short end of the stick. I think it finally dawned on him that he seldom got a fair deal from anybody; the reason being, of course, was that those who managed him and had a piece of him were crooks themselves."

"It is significant that the record books do not list Sonny's manager," I said. "Who was his manager? I could never find out."

"We never did find out who really owned his contract or who got his money," Dr. Larson said.

"When you were President of the WBA," I said, "what action did you take to correct those matters? What steps were enacted to chase the criminal element out of prize fighting?"

"We adopted several rules which made it impractical for the underworld to continue profitably in boxing," Dr. Larson said. "One such rule prohibited championship return matches. Until then, it was almost a foregone conclusion that any champion losing his title would automatically get a rematch with the winner before the new champion fought anyone else."

I said, "That put a stop to those title series, such as when Patterson and Johansson fought three times in a row."

"Right," Dr. Larson said. "It was not fair to the other worthy challengers. Liston, for example."

"For years," I said, "boxing was plagued by gangsters owning pieces of some fighters. How did you combat this?"

"We instituted a rule whereby it was illegal for any known underworld character to own a piece of a fighter," Dr. Larson said. "If it

Dr. Charles P. Larson, shown here holding his presidential plaques from both the NBA and WBA, knew Liston well. The renowned pathologist says that the late ex-champion's biggest fault in life was that he grew up thinking criminals were great people. (Photo by Ken Ollar)

could be proven that a champion had such ties, then he'd lose his crown and was forbidden to fight for the championship. Rules were also adopted making it mandatory to produce a complete financial disclosure of any prize fighter's ownership. We went even further when we wrote into our laws that the commissioners of boxing in any state could not have a financial interest in any boxer; nor could a commissioner accept any type of fee for his services at any prize fight. This includes refereeing a bout on the part of a boxing commissioner, judging a fight, or taking money or gifts for his presence at a bout."

"Doctor," I concluded, "did you personally ever bump into any of the mob element while you were President of the WBA?"

"Once," he said, "and I will never forget it. One day, in Chicago, this hoodlum walked up to me at one of our boxing conventions and offered me $50,000 under the table if I'd help Liston get a license to fight in a certain state. I told him in no uncertain terms where he could go! Later, at our WBA meeting in this hotel conference room, one of our officials saw this same guy's pocket bulging. He walked up to him and purposely brushed past him to feel the pocket. Inside, was a miniature tape recorder. The hood had been taping his bribe offer to frame me later. That's when I decided to clean up boxing."

Sonny Liston was a man with two records–one inside the ring and the other inside prison walls. He was arrested 19 times and served two prison terms. To his credit, he never attempted to dodge his past. "I have been in the limelight two ways," he once said. "Good and bad. Ever since I was born I've been fighting to stay alive. I had nothing when I was a kid growing up on this little cotton farm outside of Little Rock, Arkansas. All I had was a lot of brothers and sisters (24), a helpless mother, and a father who never cared about any of us. We grew up with few clothes, no shoes, little to eat. My dad worked me hard and whipped me hard. If he missed a day, I felt like saying: 'How come you ain't whipped me today?' I have often wondered where all these people who work with kids were when I was growing up. My first serious trouble came when I got mixed up with a bad crowd. One night we wanted to do something exciting. We stuck up a restaurant and I wound up in jail. I served my first prison term in 1952, at the Missouri State Penitentiary. I was back in again in 1957. I didn't mind prison. It was the first time in my life I got three square meals a day."

The first person to show a sincere interest in Liston was Reverend Alois Stevens, who was the athletic director at Missouri State Penitentiary. He saw Sonny's antagonistic contempt toward the world and, naturally enough, channeled these energies into boxing. Liston's fists were big, he was big and there always was that cold, menacing look in his eyes.

Liston often tried to explain his bad-guy countenance.

"I try to look tough because I'm trying to get the scare on the other guy," he said. "The way some of those suckers fight I guess they are scared. But a boxing match is like a cowboy movie. There's got to be good guys and there's got to be bad guys. That's what the fans pay for–to see the bad guys get beat. So I'm a bad guy. But I change things. I don't get beat."

At a weigh-in for one of his early bouts, his opponent said to him: "Sonny, you can talk to me. I'm your friend. Why do you scowl so much at me?"

"You'll find out tonight," Sonny said.

The poor guy went out like a light 118 seconds after the opening gong rang.

Liston began his professional career in 1953 with a one-round knockout of Don Smith in St. Louis. After that there was a long string of KO's as he climbed the ladder toward the heavyweight championship. There was just too much dynamite in both hands for most fighters to handle him. Until Cassius (Muhammad Ali) Clay stopped him in 1964, Sonny's only defeat in 36 fights was on points to Marty Marshall the second year after he started fighting.

By 1960, Liston's march to the title was slowed up somewhat by the Patterson-Johansson "ping-pong" game. For two years he didn't stand a chance to get a crack at the crown even though he demolished Zora Folley, No. 2 in the heavyweight rankings, in Denver. The three-round KO of Folley stamped him as the most formidable challenger around. It also left him without any opponents and employment. No one wanted to fight the heavy-fisted bully boy. Eddie Machen, for example, ducked a $25,000 guarantee rather than expose his classic profile to Liston's terrifying punches.

Liston did not complain at the runaround.

"I'm only 26," he said. "I'm in a position to wait as long as Patterson and Johansson want me to. But I'll be ready for the winner."

Liston was generally accepted by boxing people as the finest heavyweight in the world in 1960. All they had to do was point to his record. He had beaten every fighter who dared risk his neck, and usually for short money. The major portion of his purses went as a bribe to get an opponent into the ring with him. He knocked out Billy Hunter in two, Wayne Bethea in one, Mike DeJohn in six, Cleveland Williams and Nino Valdes in three, Willi Besmanoff in seven, Howard King in eight, Williams again in two, and Roy Harris with a casual left hook in less than two minutes.

Hunter was a ranking heavyweight who went nine with Machen, against whom Johansson ran out of a return match. Liston tackled Williams when the Houston knocker-outer was being given the brush by everybody else. Patterson turned down a flat guarantee of $300,000 to box Valdes at Madison Square Garden in 1959. Harris surrendered after 11 rounds with Patterson because of facial cuts.

It used to be that a defeated champion or challenger had to qualify for a return match. Even the great Jack Dempsey did it between his two fights with Tunney. The rules called for a champion to defend his title within six months, but this was now being disregarded in the case of the heavyweight champion, due to the heavy tax. The overlapping contract, closed-circuit television and taxes were taking all the fun out of prize fighting.

So a good, aggressive left-hooker like Sonny Liston was kept cooling his heels in the hallway while Patterson and Johansson settled their differences.

I began digging into the Liston case as far back as the spring of 1958. I discovered even then that he undoubtedly would have been challenging Patterson for the championship had his earlier manager, Tom Tannas, belonged to Cus D'Amato's union. In 1955, Tannas took time out from trying to talk Ezzard Charles out of fighting and sent a letter to the late Nat Fleischer, publisher of *Ring Magazine.*

"I have a heavyweight prospect who might have it all," Tannas wrote. "His name is Sonny Liston. I'm having trouble getting him fights and maybe a plug would help. Don't worry about him standing up."

When Liston finished Julio Mederos in six minutes flat on TV, May 14, 1958, three years after Tannas wrote Fleischer the letter, Nat was duly impressed and went digging into his files for the Tannas note. It was the only available background information on Liston; that's how little he was yet known after serving another hitch in prison in 1957.

The information supplied by Tannas, who was no longer managing Sonny, revealed that Liston was twenty-six years old and came from Pine Bluff, Arkansas. He was now fighting out of Philadelphia. "Liston can fight like hell," Tannas said, "and those in boxing know it. That is one of the principal reasons he can't get fights. He's too good. No one wants any part of him these days."

Joseph (Pep) Barone of Allentown, Pennsylvania, was listed by this time as Sonny's manager, but I was told to contact Frank (Blinky) Palermo at his offices in the Shubert Building in Philadelphia when I phoned to say I wanted to write a piece on Liston. This explained Liston's sudden ability to get all the fights he could handle. Palermo held a strong hand in the fight racket. He was a paid-up member in good standing of the right union!

Liston's classic moves quickly caught the eye of schooled boxing men. I learned that the big fellow had once been a sparring partner for Ezzard Charles, and the former champion could box like blazes. Sonny picked up numerous pointers from the old master. Now he was in the hands of Jimmy Wilson, a veteran and a smart trainer, who had brought out Ike Williams, the former lightweight champion.

Liston was a stand-up fighter with long arms and marvelous legs. When he knocked out Mederos, he hurt Julio with a vicious left jab that was remindful of Gene Tunney's. Liston packed a right-hand wallop and could take a punch. Even Cus D'Amato was sold on him—and Cus had made a habit of disparaging young fighters who were threats to his tiger's championship.

"Liston is a good fighter," Cus conceded. "A good fighter. He was too good for a Mederos. Why didn't they stick him in with somebody better?"

Like a Floyd Patterson, maybe?

It was inevitable that Patterson and Liston would meet finally. The bout was held on September 25, 1962, in Chicago. It took Liston just 126 seconds to finish his night's work. In the third fastest finish in heavyweight boxing history, 2:06 of the first round, he crumpled Patterson to

In winning the heavyweight championship, Liston made short work of Floyd Patterson with first-round KO in Chicago, on September 25, 1962. Ten months later Sonny duplicated his victory over Floyd with another one-round knockout in Las Vegas.

the canvas with two ponderous left hooks. Almost before a disappointing Comiskey Park paid crowd of 18,894 and a whopping closed-circuit TV audience had time to dig into their popcorn, the fight had ended in stunning fashion.

Patterson's share of the gate was $250,250; Liston got $69,515. Both fighters also cut in on the closed-TV revenue. This brought Floyd's total to $1,165,253, while Liston's rose to $282,015.

After the bout, Liston held a press conference. His words sounded like they had been written for him by a Hollywood press agent. The idea was to give him a brand-new image. Just like that. Win the title and change your personality. Influence the public and win new friends. Good ol' Sonny.

NEA Sports Editor Harry Grayson studies Liston's huge right hand. It measured 15½ inches (2½ inches larger than Cassius Clay's).

The press conference went something like this:

"I have reached my goal as heavyweight champion," Sonny said. "When you reach your goal you have to be proud and dignified. You represent something and you have a responsibility to live up to it. There was a time I was convinced I would never get out of the jungle I once lived in. In those days I didn't care what I did and had little regard for the feelings of others because I thought everybody was against me. I realize now that a man can't be successful or happy with that attitude. As champion I can do something good for somebody else. As champion I have the opportunity to do things that would not be possible otherwise. I want to prove to people who have proved they trust me that I appreciate their concern. Regardless of the people who don't like me, I intend to be a decent, respectable champion. I intend to model myself after Joe Louis, who I think was the greatest champion of all and my idol. He did everything I want to do. I intend to follow the example he set and would like to go down in history as a great champion too."

Liston and Patterson presented the second chapter of their serial, "The Perils of Patterson," at Las vegas, on July 22, 1963. After Sonny so rudely interrupted their first meeting by knocking out Floyd in 2:06 of the first round in Chicago, there seemed no overwhelming demand by the public for a rematch. Floyd's feelings were hurt probably worse than his chin and he insisted on the chance to regain the crown jewels. He just happened to have a return-bout clause in the fine print of the original contract.

Since the Chicago fiasco, promoters managed to build up some curiosity for the second bout. The seating capacity at Las Vegas was limited but the closed-circuit television and other ancillary revenues brought the receipts to more than a million dollars.

The ballyhoo for the return match was directed at building up Patterson. The principals did not cooperate with their press agents, however. Liston insisted in his interviews that he would flatten Floyd in a hurry. Patterson seemed timid in rebuttal.

Liston was a 4 to 1 favorite.

Most fight prophets went along with the odds. They picked Liston to kayo Patterson in four rounds at the most. Sonny was so convincing in their first match that it seemed Patterson was not physically or psychologically able to beat the Big Bear. "Patterson is not big, strong and tough enough," wrote one writer. "He hasn't the fighting equipment to do it. He can't match Liston in punching or catching a wallop. He can't outbox and keep away from Liston for 15 rounds. Sonny will catch up with him along the way. And that will be that."

And it was.

It was The Chicago Story all over again. A fast first-round KO relegated the thirty-year-old Patterson to boxing's scrapheap. He didn't even give the champion time enough to work up a sweat.

Patterson never lived down those two defeats to Liston. After the second one, he hid behind a false beard and mustache for a month because the shame was more than the pain. He even talked about retirement. Then he said he would only fight again if he could get another shot at the title.

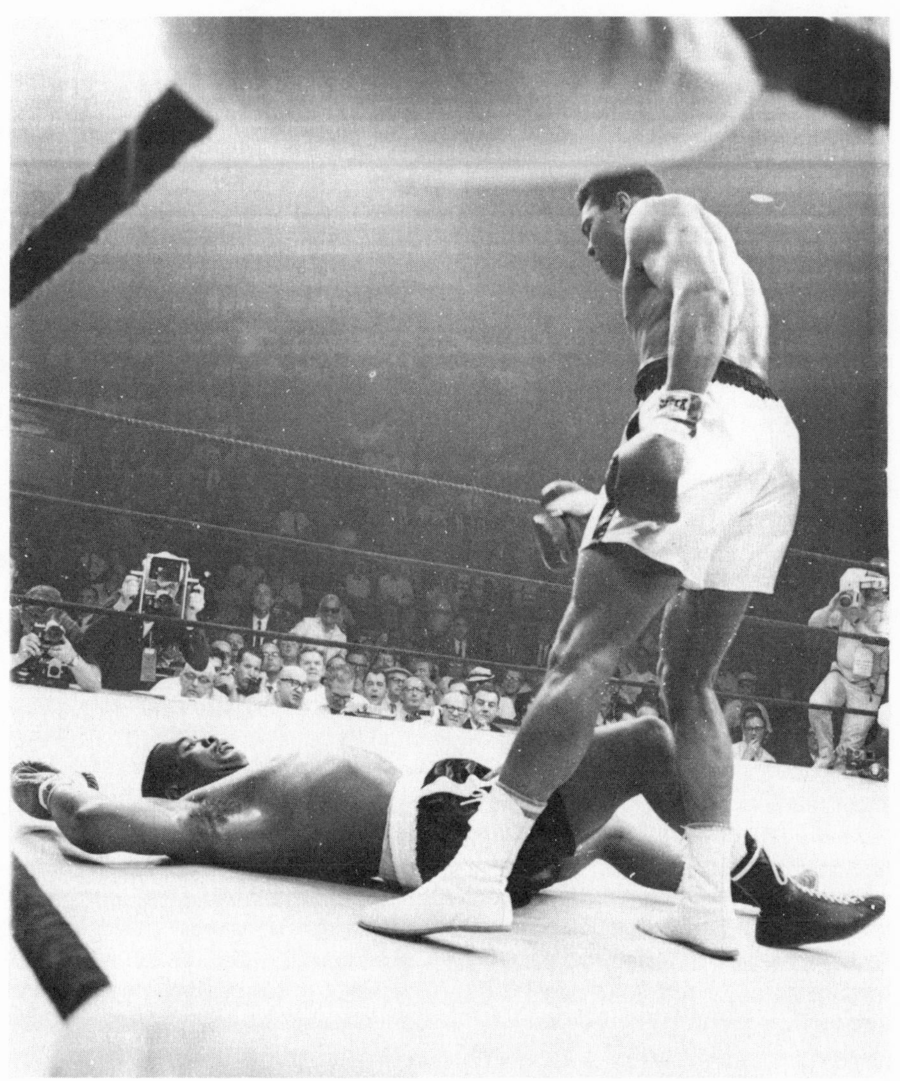

Liston and Clay fought twice. In the first meeting, Sonny failed to come out for the seventh round and lost his title to Clay in Miami Beach, on February 25, 1964. The second bout, at Lewiston, Maine, on May 25, 1965, ended with Liston flat on his back 1:58 after the first round started.

"The first person I want to fight is Liston," he said, after his wounds healed. "I've been beaten a number of times physically, but never mentally. God knows how many times I've fought Liston in my sleep, how many times and in how many different styles."

When Dick Young, the *New York News'* flame-throwing columnist, heard that, he offered this advice to the ex-champion: "Floyd Patterson is a good guy, and if he wants to pursue his profession of boxing, why not? But the thing I don't dig is his particular motivation. He says he wants to even the score with Sonny Liston, who twice knocked him out in one round. Kids around the block say, 'I'll get even with you,' not professionals. Besides, how do you get even with a guy who has knocked you out twice in one round short of knocking him out twice in one round? And I question Patterson can do that before Sonny is 60, which still is a couple of years from now."

So Sonny Liston turned to new worlds to conquer.

And waiting in the wings for him—Cassius Clay.

22. Cassius Marcellus Clay (Muhammad Ali)

YOU could laugh at him or you could hate him, but there's no getting away from the fact that at his peak (1964 to 1968) Cassius Clay—or Muhammad Ali—deserved to be ranked among the best heavyweights of all time.

Certainly he must be remembered as one of the most controversial and complex men the prize ring has ever known.

His life style is filled with contradictions.

He criticized Floyd Patterson for buying a house in a white neighborhood instead of living among his own black people, then bought his own estate in a well-to-do white community.

He attacked the fight racket as a degrading business staged largely for the entertainment of "whitey" but was prepared to fight seven-foot basketball star Wilt Chamberlain in a freak title bout.

He loved the limelight, was a noisy showoff—and yet without publicity of any sort has been known to slip away to children's hospital wards to give comfort to little amputees.

He scorns ostentation, preaches against materialism, but fills his garage with a Rolls Royce, a new Cadillac, a new Lincoln, a new camper and a model of an antique Oldsmobile.

He is devoted to a religious movement that looks on the white race as devils—and yet he has more genuine white friends than almost any black fighter around.

He can shout in one breath, "I want that championship again," and in another, "My life isn't wrapped up in fist-fighting anymore, I use it only as a platform to reach my people."

Cassius Marcellus Clay—it's still his legal name, it has never been changed in any court—always has had a genius for creating excitement. It is to be doubted, however, that even the dynamic Mr. C. will ever be

Cassius Marcellus Clay—or Muhammad Ali—will go down in history as one of the most controversial and complex men in boxing, but he saved the business at a time when it was at its lowest. At his peak, he had a genius for creating excitement.

able to top the uproar he created just before he fought Sonny Liston for the championship in Miami Beach in 1964.

Not many people gave him much of a chance against the Big Bear. Sonny had demolished Floyd Patterson twice and was generally regarded as a superman. Some columnists even said that the fight should be cancelled, warning that Liston might do permanent damage to poor little Cassius. None of this had any effect on Clay. He was the same fighter in the gym he had always been, and he was as confident of beating Liston as he had been of beating any of the fighters he had met during the three years he had been fighting professionally.

He took the psychological play away from Liston. In training for the bout he began to destroy the superman image that Liston had used to psych most of his opponents. Liston had a thing going for him. He always tried to look bigger and meaner than life. He would climb into the ring wearing a hood and a robe with a couple of towels under the shoulders, so that he looked even bigger than he was. In training he'd go through the medicine ball routine, letting Willie Reddish pound him in the stomach with it, and if you didn't know better you had to believe he really was superhuman. Any fighter in good condition can take a medicine ball in the belly.

Aside from the antics Clay went through to bug Liston, he created additional excitement by proclaiming for the first time he was a Muslim. Cassius had decided that henceforth he would be called Muhammad Ali. Angelo Dundee, his trainer, suggested he keep Cassius Clay as a ring name and use Muhammad Ali in private life.

Dundee said, "You've built up a big reputation as Cassius Clay. It is foolish to change now."

"But Elijah Muhammad has given me the name of Muhammad Ali," Cassius said, "and I am going to use it."

The question was settled.

Cassius had managed to get everyone on edge by the time of the weigh-in. He had heckled Liston at the airport in Miami and at his training quarters. He had turned Bill McDonald, the promoter, gray, and he had made most of the writers forget the image of Liston as the unbeatable monster. The scene at the weigh-in was his own idea. It was a put-on, but everyone thought he was serious. He yelled and screamed and tried to get at Liston. When the boxing commission doctor took his pulse rate and blood pressure both were way up. The doctor threatened to call off the fight. Cassius then settled down and passed the examination.

Later, Cassius said to Dundee, "Did I have Liston shook up? Did you see his face? I shook him up, didn't I?"

"You shook him up," Dundee said, "and a lot of other people, too."

Liston didn't really present that much of a problem. Cassius was confident from the time the bout was signed that he could beat him.

At the opening bell, Cassius danced out and moved around and made Liston miss. For three rounds he kept up that blazing pace. Liston didn't reach him at all. Cassius would feint a punch and then not throw it. Liston would react and Cassius would give him a target to shoot at and he'd shoot and miss. Liston had to plant himself to punch, and in those first few rounds he was throwing his left hand so hard that his fist turned when he missed. When you miss a punch that swift you wear yourself out, and that's what happened to Liston. He discovered he couldn't hit Cassius, and that made him angry and tired him even more.

Liston also found out that Cassius could hit him and dance away. Liston grew more desperate by the minute. Cassius hit him with punches that broke him up. He turned his hand just as it landed, and it punished Liston. It was breaking Liston up. Liston was made to order for Cassius, and he showed it in Miami Beach.

The only real problem was in the fourth round, when some of the coagulant they put on Liston's cut eye rubbed off on Clay's forehead and then into his eyes from the sweat coming down. Clay returned to the corner and said that his eyes were burning. At the end of the one-minute rest period, Dundee told him to stay away from Liston. "Keep moving!" he shouted after him. "Run!" Liston wasn't able to follow up his advantage.

By the end of the sixth round Liston knew he was whipped. His shoulder might have been hurt, as he claimed it was, but it wouldn't have made any difference if it had been healthy. He knew he was in the ring with a superior fighter. At the beginning of the seventh round Liston remained affixed to his stool, and the world had a new heavyweight champion.

"I'm going to be a clean champion," Cassius Clay said after the fight. "I am going to be a sparkling champion."

And he was. No smoking. No drinking. No messing around.

Clay went off to tour Africa. He signed to fight Liston again, in Boston, but when he came back from Africa he had to undergo a hernia operation and by the time he got over the surgery and started working again the fight had been moved to Lewiston, Maine.

It was decided that the thing Clay had to do in the second fight was remind Liston what had happened to him in the first bout.

Angelo Dundee told Clay in training: "The thing that sticks in Sonny's craw is that he still thinks he can lick you. You gotta take that confidence away from him early. You got to bring back memories of Miami Beach."

The plan was for Cassius to get off fast and then coast and make Liston fight his fight. Physically, he was in perfect shape. He had no ill effects from the hernia operation, and he trained real well.

As usual, the scene before the fight was pretty hectic. On TV, Clay was asked to predict what round he expected to knock out Liston in. Usually Clay was loud and boastful in front of a television camera, but on this day he spoke softly and calmly. He shook his head slowly. "No predictions," he said quietly. "Not for this fight."

The TV host closed off the program and Clay turned to a man next to him and said, almost inaudibly: "If I said I will knock out Liston in one minute and 49 seconds of the first round, it would hurt the gate. So" –he winked–"I better not say it."

Six days later Liston went down in the first round in the ring at Lewiston. The time of the knockout was announced, incorrectly, as one minute even, but the next day someone held a stopwatch on the fight film. Liston was seen hitting the canvas at 1:48 and did not rise from his slumber until 2:05. Had there been no mixup when referee Jersey Joe Walcott failed to pick up the count from the knockdown timekeeper, Liston presumably would have been counted out at 1:58–only 9 seconds away from Clay's off-the-record estimate.

Maybe it was just as well that Cassius didn't advertise his prediction. Skeptics would have claimed that Clay knew something, and that would have provoked loud shouts of "Fake... Fake... Fake!"

Nothing is beyond suspicion in boxing, but there was absolutely no evidence to support a claim of fakery. There certainly was no motive, either. The defeat not only disgraced Liston, it also destroyed his career. Never again would he get another crack at the championship. Suspicion of Clay's victory stemmed from two factors: one, that Clay's right-hand punch was not a powerful blow and, two, that Liston seemed content to stay on the canvas. Only Liston knew how hard he was hit–and he claimed it was substantial.

Floyd Patterson didn't like Clay's big-mouth act and openly admitted he hated the Black Muslims, but in Lewiston he was sitting in the third row and he saw the punch.

"Liston got hit real hard," Floyd said. "Liston was chasing Clay. They were right above me and Liston was leaning toward him about to throw a left jab. Suddenly Clay threw a short right hand that I thought hit Liston on the chin. Liston was rocked. And when he started to get up, he was bewildered. I could see it in his eyes. It was a good punch. It was the best right hand I've seen since Joe Louis."

Joe Louis, himself, did not accept Patterson's appraisal of Clay.

"Clay is lucky there are no good fighters around now," Louis said after the fight. "I'd rate him with Johnny Paychek, Abe Simon and Buddy Baer–a lot of guys would have beaten him if he was around when I was. There hasn't been a real good heavyweight around since Marciano."

"People underestimate Clay," Patterson pointed out. "He talks so much about himself that people figure he can't possibly be that good. Believe me, he's a terrific fighter."

Billy Conn was undecided.

"He's big," Billy said. "But Clay pulls away from punches. That's what an amateur does. I think he can fight, but how can you tell yet? I know this, though: he's a giant."

Not many people realized at first how big Clay was. He is 6 ft. 3 in., much taller than any of the most famous heavyweight champions.

Dempsey was 6 ft. 1 in., Louis 6 ft. ½ in.–the same height as Liston. Gene Tunney was 6 ft. ½ in., Rocky Marciano 5 ft. 10 in., Patterson an even 6 ft. Clay towers over all of them. And, in his prime, he was a perfectly proportioned 210 pounds. Louis was heavier, usually around 215, and since Clay came back from his exile he has been fighting at around 220. But Dempsey and Tunney each were around 190, Marciano around 185. Patterson usually came in at around 190.

Most surprising, however, was Clay's remarkable speed. Patterson always was considered a fast-moving fighter, but Clay was faster than any heavyweight champion in history. After Cassius disposed of Liston the second time, Patterson said, "Clay is really fast. You can tell that from the way he carries his hands. Low like that. You've *got* to be fast if you carry your hands down there. If you're not, you're going to get popped."

Cassius called the blow which put Liston away his "phantom" punch. "I'm fast," he said. "They've timed my punches, and they say I can punch faster than you blink your eye. If you blinked at the Liston knockout, you missed the punch."

Cassius chuckled.

"This guy came all the way from Los Angeles and paid $150 for a seat," he said. "He stopped to get a Coke and a hot dog. Before he could sit down, the fight was over, and he said, 'Liston sat down before I did.' "

Cassius was the first to admit that his reputation as a loudmouth was only an act of showmanship to build up the gates for his fights.

"Talk got me the title fight with Liston," he said. "It dates back to my first real hard fight. I was fighting a guy named Duke Sabedong in Las Vegas in 1961. He was about 6-7 tall, unorthodox and awkward, and he made me look bad. It took me a while to figure him out, but I won a decision and learned a lot. I also learned something else at that fight. While in Vegas I was on a radio sports program with Gorgeous George, the wrestler. When the host asked me a question, I just said the usual things, but when he got to Gorgeous George the air suddenly came alive. Gorgeous George told him how he was going to tear up his opponent and they shouldn't even allow the match because he was so much better. He boasted how he was going to kill the poor bum the next night, and I got a big kick out of it. I wanted to go see Gorgeous George wrestle, and when I went the joint was jammed with people. That impressed me. After that I started talking, and the fans started thinking, 'This bag o' wind needs a good whuppin'.' This loudmouthin' made the promoters think they could get rich. I was talky, different–and I ran to the bank laughing."

Clay's last bout in 1965 was against Patterson. His championship was on the line. This fight ended one phase of Clay's career and marked the beginning of another. There had been some complaints by columnists here and there about Cassius being a Muslim, but it wasn't a big thing to him. But because Patterson made it a factor and because that aroused Clay, from the Patterson fight on you read as much about Clay's religious beliefs as you did about his ability to fight. After knocking Patterson out in the 12th round, he never changed much. He became more aware of being a Muslim and the effect that had on other people, because other people made him aware of it. But in his personal relationship with close friends he didn't change. He was just as relaxed as ever and just as fond of practical jokes.

The world around him was changing, however. The pressures were bigger and the problems were bigger. His draft status and his beliefs and his stubborn refusal to compromise with anyone or anything cost him. The worst of it started when the press quoted him as saying, "The Viet Cong ain't done anything to me and I ain't mad at them." His remarks caused an uproar. The Illinois Athletic Commission refused to approve his scheduled fight with Ernie Terrell in Chicago unless he went there and apologized for his unpatriotic statements. Clay flew from Miami to Chicago and met with the commissioners. Whatever chance there might have been to hold the fight in Chicago blew up when one of the members heckled Cassius. Clay walked out of the meeting.

After that, the fight bounced around all over the country, and Clay wound up fighting George Chuvalo in Toronto instead of Terrell in Chicago. He didn't have much opportunity to train properly for the Chuvalo fight, because he was traveling constantly, going to draft-board hearings and the like.

Cassius brought out the best in Chuvalo but there never was any question about who won the fight. At the end of 15 rounds it was Clay on points.

Anti-Clay feeling in the United States had been gaining momentum by this time. Although he never talked much about it, this mass feeling disturbed Cassius. It worked on him. The lightheartedness and gayety were gone. Luckily for him, as his popularity fell off in America it grew in Europe. The public statements that made him the villain whenever he fought in the United States actually made him a hero to the fight fans overseas. So he travelled to Europe and twice fought in London. He knocked out Henry Cooper in 6 and Brian London in 3, and then flew over to Frankfurt, Germany, and kayoed Karl Mildenberger, a southpaw, in 12.

Clay always had trouble with left-handers, and Mildenberger was no exception. The champion was exceedingly unimpressive. The German just didn't have the physical equipment to linger for 12 rounds against a man of Clay's obvious talent; yet he lasted far longer than he had any right to last. About the only damage Mildenberger did was to let a little air out of the "I-am-the-greatest" balloon that Cassius had taken so much effort to inflate. It was impossible to conceive of a Jack Dempsey, a Joe Louis or a Rocky Marciano letting the likes of a Mildenberger survive as long as 12 rounds. Clay had the German on the hook with knockdowns in the 5th, 8th and 10th rounds, but let him wriggle free each time. He seemed so lacking in the killer instinct that Joe Louis commented on it from ringside. This is a serious flaw in any fighter's armament, especially a heavyweight. The longer he exposes himself unnecessarily the greater is the risk that the other man can disable him with a butt, a cut, a lucky punch or whatnot. It is a risk no heavyweight should take.

"As long as the other guy is on his feet," Dempsey used to say, "he can hit me. So I try to knock him off his feet as fast as possible."

It seemed that Clay fooled around with Mildenberger and wasted time. He eventually got the job done, of course, but it definitely was not one of his better exhibitions.

Perhaps Cassius had some valid excuses. The year 1966 had been a long campaign for him. Since March he had fought Chuvalo, Cooper, London and now Mildenberger with little rest in between. He didn't look smart against the latter and missed punches far more often than normally. Staleness had caught up with him.

Next on his schedule was a November 14th championship fight with Cleveland Williams in Houston. Cassius routinely finished him off in 2½ rounds.

Clay fought only twice in 1967. He decisioned Terrell in Houston and scored a 6-round KO over Zora Folley in New York. Then the roof caved in. His draft board suddenly clouded up his future. For the next 3½ years it would remain undecided while the courts pondered over his unwillingness to go into the service. He was willing to go to jail for his beliefs.

This pause in the action enables us to go back now and review the Cassius Clay history...

Once upon a time, Cassius had been a model teenager, bearing a grand old name, striving for championships and Cadillacs and the adulation of beautiful young "foxes." Drawn into boxing at the age of twelve by a friendly Louisville cop, Cassius swept up through the ranks: the Golden Gloves, the AAU, and on to the 1960 Olympic Games. Here Angelo Dundee, his trainer, picks up the story:

"The first time I ever talked to Cassius was in 1957 in Louisville," Dundee recalled. "I was in town with Willie Pastrano, who was fighting John Holman there, and we were in Willie's room watching television. The telephone rang and this kid was on the other end. He said he knew all about me and my fighters from watching us on TV. He said, 'My name is Cassius Marcellus Clay, the Golden Gloves champion of the city of Louisville.' He went on and gave me a long list of all the things he had won, and he wound up by saying he was going to win the 1960 Olympics and he wanted to come up to the room and talk to me and Willie. I covered the mouthpiece and turned to Willie and said, 'Some kind of nut

Cassius Clay, age twelve.

is on the phone telling me how great he is and he wants to come up. Okay?' Willie said he was tired of TV, so send the nut up.

"So in a few minutes he came up. He was a long, rangy kid. He weighed maybe 184, 185 then but I could tell right away by the way he

Cassius Clay, light-heavyweight Olympic Games champion in 1960.

was built he was going to get bigger and wind up as a good-sized heavyweight. He was really hungry for information. He asked Willie how many miles he ran a day, when he ate, if he was nervous before a fight, when he went to bed, what he did the day of a fight and what he did when the fight was over, whether he drank or smoked–things like that. They hit it off right away.

"One afternoon, Willie and Clay sparred for a round in the gym. When we got there Clay had already been punching the heavy bag for an hour getting ready. They got into the ring and went this one round, and Clay did everything right and Willie did everything wrong. I said to Willie that he looked terrible. I asked him, 'What's the matter with you?' And he said, 'This cat is good, Angie,' Then Clay came over and told Willie that he was a shoo-in to beat the guy he was going to fight. Clay had already boxed the other guy, so he said he ought to know. It made Willie feel better, but I found out later that Clay had told the other guy the same thing. He was always that way. He liked to con you even when he was young.

"In those days Cassius walked everywhere, bounding along with a carefree air and saying hello to everybody. He liked to kid a lot, but he was always a gentleman. He never missed a fight if he could help it. I don't think he ever saw a fighter he didn't think he could whip.

"One night, he went to Indianapolis to watch Floyd Patterson fight Brian London. He came back to Louisville and told me that he told Patterson he was going to take the heavyweight title away from him.

"Then he went to Rome and won the Olympic championship, just like he said he would, and when he came back a lot of big-time managers were after him. I never made a move toward him. That wasn't my style. I never approached amateurs. So this group of Louisville businessmen took him over after the Olympics and the first thing they did was to send him out to San Diego to work with Archie Moore. They felt Archie would be good for Cassius, take some of the cockiness out of him. But it didn't work. Soon Cassius was back in the gym in Louisville. When I asked him what happened, he said, 'I ain't gonna sweep floors and wash dishes for nobody.'

"The Louisville group was looking around for a trainer by then and I got the job after they came down to my gym in Miami Beach and asked me how I would handle Cassius. I guess they liked my answers. I told them he would have to be brought along gradually, no main events.

"Cassius arrived in Miami Beach in November of 1960 and immediately he wanted to box everybody in the gym. He loved boxing. It was not unusual for him to go 150 rounds before a fight.

"At first the group split 50-50 with him. They paid all expenses. Later that shifted to 60 for him and 40 for them. At the beginning the group paid him $400 a month. With this he supported his mother and father and brother Rudy. Now and then he would run short and he'd say, 'Angie, give me some walking-around money, man. I ain't holding.' I'd give him a couple of bucks and tell him not to ask for any more. He'd always pay me back after the next prize fight.

"Cassius had that dedication required to be champion. Lots of times, I remember, he'd leave his room and run to the gym wearing blue jeans and a shirt and heavy shoes. He'd run about six miles and get to the gym all sweaty and take a shower and then work for a couple of hours in the ring. He never got tired. He was truly dedicated. He was willing to give up all pleasures and devote his life to really hard physical work and training. And he was willing to accept all the pain that goes with the life.

"Most of today's up-and-coming young heavyweights think they can be another Muhammad Ali. But don't you believe it. I don't think we'll ever see another one like him. He was the one and only."

Under the stewardship of the syndicate of white Louisville businessmen, Cassius Clay began his professional fist-fighting career on October 29, 1960, with a six-round decision over Tunney Hunsaker in Louisville. That was a month before Angelo Dundee got him. "Clay's backers asked me to come up to Louisville for that one," Dundee said, "but I didn't want to step on anyone's shoes. I think Fred Stoner, a local man, handled him in that fight, and I thought that it would be bad for me to move in on him so soon. The first fight Cassius had with me in his corner was with Herb Siler in Miami Beach on December 27, 1960, and he knocked Siler out in the fourth. Siler was just an opponent. I wasn't looking for anyone real tough at that time. I wanted to build up his confidence so that he would always know he was going to win when he climbed into the ring."

In the next three years Cassius won 19 fights, defeated several contenders, and took dead aim on his dream, the heavyweight title. But small experiences had already eroded the dream, and the title no longer seemed the sole objective in life for Cassius Clay. He had worked hard at his trade for the reasons young blacks often cite: "It's all I could really do. There wasn't nothing to do in the streets." Yet those reasons were being challenged for the first time by growing numbers of militants, who demanded to know why whites could enjoy the entire range of career choices while blacks were expected to cheerfully and gratefully choose sports over the streets. In public, the young Clay was alternately a promising athlete or an entertaining, if overtalkative, clown. Away from the ring, in a simple, visceral way, he was one of the first black athletes to question his role in society.

Cassius recalled one particular jolt to his psyche, when he strode into a Louisville restaurant wearing his Olympic medal around his neck, only to be denied service because of his color. Many other incidents troubled him in less dramatic ways, until the day in 1961 when he met a young Muslim minister, Samuel X. Saxon, who was hawking the newspaper *Muhammad Speaks* in Miami. Quietly, Cassius began attending meetings; once he even visited the Chicago home of the sect's leader, Elijah Muhammad.

Boxing fans knew nothing of the meetings or the obscure religious group; but many were already recoiling from Clay, the incredibly cocky kid who was daring to challenge and ridicule the fearsome world champion, Sonny Liston.

"Aint't I pretty?" shrieked Clay as their 1964 showdown approached. "Ain't that big old bear Liston ugly?" Drew (Bundini) Brown, Clay's confidant and adviser throughout his career, coined the phrase that was to become a ringing slogan: "He'll float like a butterfly, sting like a bee." Clay, a 7 to 1 underdog, fulfilled the prediction exquisitely. He told the world: "I am King."

The effect was electric. Instead of welcoming a colorful new personality, most boxing fans and writers rushed to condemn the loudmouthed new champ. Many hoped Liston would regain the title in the rematch. Liston was a strange hero. But he was also something of a sporting archetype—the strapping black gladiator who provided entertainment and kept his mouth shut. Clay, lithe and unprecedentedly fast, was the physical antithesis of the traditional "black stud," and many whites could never feel comfortable with him as champion.

If anything, Cassius was a throwback to Jack Johnson, the laughing, outspoken black who thumbed his nose at the ring establishment, whipped white fighters and slept with white women. Shortly after win-

Cassius Clay, heavyweight champion of the world.

ning the title, Clay seemed to complete the parallel: instead of enraging whites by taking their women, he did it by announcing his membership in the anti-white Black Muslims. Later that year, Elijah Muhammad conferred the name Muhammad Ali upon the champion; but it would be years before most of the press and public would accept the name or anything it stood for.

Ironically, Clay's popularity declined as precipitously as his skills were increasing. His most serious troubles began far from the ring, at his Louisville draft board. In 1963 he had flunked a pre-induction mental exam and been classified 1-Y. Then he was shocked when in February of 1966, without a re-examination, he was reclassified 1-A. "How could they do this to the champion?" he asked. "The taxes from my fights alone pay salaries for 200,000 soldiers a year." Angry at the American draft system, he then bristled, "I ain't got no quarrel with those Viet Congs." That was when miffed veterans' groups and politicians across the nation moved in swiftly to take the case into their own hands and drive Clay into obscurity.

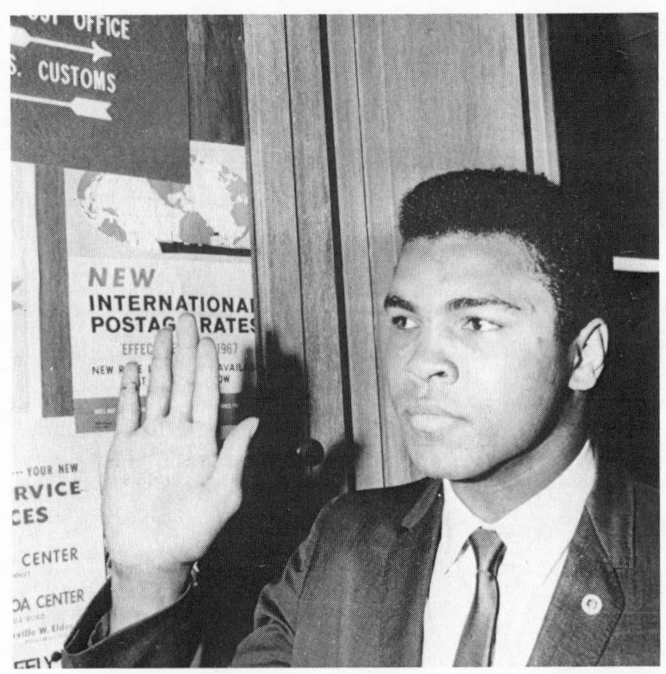

Cassius Clay waves to fans as he arrives at the Army Induction Center in Houston, where he voluntarily forced his exile from boxing by refusing induction, April 28, 1967. Shortly thereafter he was stripped of his title.

Cassius took his title out of the United States and put it on the line in Canada and Europe against Chuvalo, Cooper, London, and Mildenberger. At home, meanwhile, his lawyers grappled with the draft system, seeking his exemption first on grounds of hardship, then as a conscientious objector, and finally as a Muslim minister. At one point, after a 1966 Louisville hearing, a former judge and specially appointed court officer, Laurence Grauman, recommended that Cassius be granted CO status. The Justice Department disagreed, insisting that Clay's objections were "primarily political and radical." The battle dragged on until, a month after his ninth successful defense against Zora Folley in New York, he formally refused induction into military service on April 28, 1967. Two months later—after boxing commissions had already acted to strip away his title—he was found guilty and sentenced to five years in prison and a $10,000 fine. Thus began the round of appeals by his lawyers that cost him hundreds of thousands of dollars in legal fees—and 3½ years at the peak of his career. They were years that can never be recovered.

For 3½ years Clay was deemed a nonperson by the various boxing commissions. To grub out a living for his wife and children, he dog-

After three years in exile, Clay formally filed for a license to fight in the state of Washington. The power behind the move was Tacoma sportsman Morley Brotman.

gedly took what was given—lectures, a Broadway musical, everything except his real livelihood—and then in the summer of 1970, he signed an application for a license to box in Seattle. He signed it as "Cassius Clay." I was part of a Tacoma-Seattle group, headed by popular businessman Morley Brotman, ready to sponsor Clay's return to the prize ring. That signed application of Clay's caused lots of commotion. When the Associated Press heard about it they called Cassius for the story. Cassius called Bob Arum, the attorney who represented him in so many of his fights before the boxing commissions around the United States decided he was too hot to handle.

"What do I tell the AP?" Clay asked.

"Tell them you have no comment," said Arum.

Instead of saying "no comment," Clay told the AP he knew nothing about the reports that he had filed an application to fight in Seattle.

Clay had two postures, a private and a public one. Both were revealed when a TV crew had him on camera. He was asked where he stood on an application to fight Joe Frazier or Jerry Quarry out in the state of Washington.

With the camera on, Clay solemnly swore it was not his doing. Nobody, he said, had the authority to make the application.

"It was great when I was a boxer," he said, "but I'm not a boxer any more. I'm retired. I'm a lecturer."

Then the little red lights on the TV camera clicked off and the interview was over and Clay turned on.

"Just get me that license out in Seattle and bring on Frazier," he cried. "Smokey Joe? Man, I'll put out his fire."

Why the duality?

"He's been embarrassed going around the country begging for anything," Bob Arum explained. "The Government has reduced him to that level. He no longer wants the stigma of rejection. The last three years have ripped him apart psychologically. Now all he's doing is hoping. He's been disappointed so much in the past. He's afraid to do more than that."

Some of the Eastern sports writers voiced skepticism when rumors reached them that Clay had actually filed an application to make his comeback out in the far Puget Sound country. But it was true. Here is the proof—a copy of Clay's actual signed application for a boxer's license in the state of Washington, dated June 8, 1970:

The drama was building up now. Attorneys at both ends of the country were handling mountains of legal papers swiftly. Tacoma attorney Neil Hoff represented the Washington group, while Bob Arum handled the paper work for Cassius.

Meanwhile, Morley Brotman, the power behind the proposed promotion, kept in touch with Clay directly. In a letter dated June 9, 1970, the day after Clay's signed application arrived, Morley wrote:

Dear Cassius:

We could write a book about what has taken place the past six months regarding trying to put the pieces together to get you licensed to fight in the State of Washington. It looks great right now—even though we still have strong opposition from the Chairman of the Commission.

Some of the people we have in our camp include:

1. Fifteen coaches and athletic directors of High School and Colleges. Everyone prominent in their field.

2. Three editors of union newspapers.

RING RECORD

(This Must Be Complete and Accurate. If No Ring Record, Say So)

Date	Place	Opponent	Result
3/22/67	New York, N.Y.	Zora Folley	KO 7
2/6/67	Houston, Texas	Ernie Terrell	W 15
11/14/66	Houston, Texas	Cleveland Williams	KO 3
9/10/66	Frankfurt, Germany	Karl Mildenberger	KO 12
8/6/66	London, England	Brian London	KO 3
5/21/66	London, England	Henry Cooper	KO 6
3/29/66	Toronto, Canada	George Chuvalo	W 15
11/22/65	Las Vegas, Nev.	Floyd Patterson	KO 12
3/25/65	Lewiston, Me	Sonny Liston	KO 1
2/25/64	Miami Beach, Fla.	Sonny Liston	KO 7
6/18/63	London, England	Henry Cooper	KO 5
3/13/63	New York, N.Y.	Doug Jones	W 10
2/24/63	Pitts. Pa.	Charlie Powell	KO 3
11/15/62	Los Angeles, Cali.	Archie Moore	KO 4
7/20/62	Los Angeles, Cal.	A. Lavorante	KO 5

NOTICE TO BOXERS

Conditions Qualifying for a Boxing License

No one should present himself or apply for a boxing license who has any physical deformity, or any disease of the vital organs, whether acute, subacute or chronic, e. g.:

Bodily deformities such as—
1. Curvature of the spine.
2. Missing fingers.
3. Recent fractures, etc.

Condition of—

Right eye Good

Left eye Good

Diseases such as—
1. Valvular heart disease.
2. High blood pressure from any cause.
3. Bright's disease.
4. Recent recoveries from acute illnesses such as pneumonia, typhoid, etc.
5. Venereal diseases.
6. Skin diseases.

Any other disease or condition, such as deaf and dumb or partially deaf, which in the estimation of the examining physician would be detrimental to the boxer, the arena, or boxing in general.

Are you free from the above physical defects or diseases? Yes

If not, describe in detail your present physical condition

Sworn to before me this 8th day of June 1970

Michael Heitner
Notary Public

MICHAEL HEITNER
Notary Public, State of New York
No. 24-1744795
Qualified in Kings County
Commission Expires March 30, 1971

Cassius X Clay Jr
(Applicant's signature)

Muhammad Ali
(Applicant's ring name)

(LEFT AND RIGHT THUMB PRINTS)

Approved:

Date , 19

STATE ATHLETIC COMMISSION
OF WASHINGTON

Chairman

Executive Secretary

Commissioner

The Commission *must* be notified promptly of any change in manager or terms of contract with manager. Failure to so notify the Commission may result in the suspension or revocation of this license.

All applications must be typewritten.

Fee, $3.00, to be remitted by certified or cashier's check, postal or money order.

DO NOT SEND CURRENCY.

If a minor, parent or guardian's consent, legally acknowledged, must be attached to your application.

A manager is not necessary, but if one is selected he must be licensed by this Commission and a copy of contract between boxer and manager filed with this office.

Have signatures legally acknowledged.

Two photographs required, PASSPORT SIZE, full face, without hat. Any other size will not be accepted. Photos are for identification purposes.

State Athletic Commission of Washington

210 E. Union
OLYMPIA, WASHINGTON

DANIEL J. EVANS, GOVERNOR

COMMISSIONERS

W. B. REESE, CHAIRMAN
515 10TH, OTHELLO 99344

HARRY J. LYNCH
117 NO. TACOMA AVE., TACOMA 98403

James L. Rendek
660 West Ewing
Seattle Washington 98119

O. Receipt K.

No. ....

Received ....

Cash ..... M. O. ..... Check ....

Considered ....

Photos ....

License No. ....

APPLICATION FOR BOXER'S LICENSE

FEE, $3.00

(Give real name in full)

TO THE STATE ATHLETIC COMMISSION OF WASHINGTON,

The undersigned, enclosing the fee of three dollars ($3.00) as required by law, hereby makes application for a license to act as a boxer.

Date June 8, 1970

Name CASSIUS M. CLAY Phone 215-TR-9-1112
(Give real name in full)

City Philadelphia Zip .... Street 1835 North 72nd Street

Present occupation V.Pres.-Champburger Corp. ~~Lecturer~~ Previous occupation Boxer-Heavyweight Champion of World

Business address 1175 N.E. 125th Street, Miami, Florida

Ring weight 210 Height 6' ft. 3" in. Age 28

Place of birth Louisville, Kentucky Date of birth Jan. 17, 1942

Married Yes Single .... Citizen of United States of America

REFERENCES (Give five)	ADDRESS
Robert Arum	477 Madison Avenue, New York, N.Y.
Michael Malitz	345 Park Ave., New York, N.Y.
Fred Hofheinz	99Indian Trials, Houston, Texas
Howard Cossell	c/O ABC, 1330 Ave.of Americas, New York, N.Y.
Chauncey Eskridge	123 W.Madison Street, Chicago, Ill

Name of Manager None

Address of Manager ....

Is Manager authorized to contract for your appearance or services? ....

Is Manager licensed with Athletic Commission? .... Manager's license number ....

Was applicant ever disqualified anywhere in any contest for any cause? No

Was applicant ever penalized or disciplined by any state or boxing commission? Yes

If "yes" to either of the foregoing questions, state where, and complete circumstances

See Insert A, attached

Have you ever been convicted of a felony or misdemeanor? Yes

If so, when and where? (Give full particulars) June 21/67, U.S. District Ct.Houston Texas, for violation of Selective Services Act. Conviction on appeal before U.S. Circ. Ct. for Fifth Circuit

Has applicant any financial interest in any club, corporation, association or organization promoting boxing in this state or any other place? No

Or, has any promoter, club, association, corporation or organization any financial interest in your earnings as a boxer? No

3. Dr. Charles P. Larson, past president of NBA and WBA, and past Chairman of Washington State Boxing Commission.

4. Wayne Sheirbon, National Commander of the Disabled American Veterans in 1969.

5. The Lt. Governor of our State, plus many more County and City officials.

A meeting with the three-man Commission is being set up immediately, at which time, if you get two out of three votes, you will be granted a license to fight here. Harry Lynch, the Chairman and who opposes the license, told one of our people that he was sure we had two votes and if the two voted the license, he would not stir up a stink. He has also assured us the Governor will not interfere.

Kindest regards,
Morley Brotman.

Brotman's optimism quickly dissolved into dark gloom. He could not pin Chairman Lynch down to a definite date for the hearing. Angry words went back and forth. Brotman accused the Chairman of stalling. Lynch said he was not stalling. He claimed he must follow protocol; that he was waiting for a date when all three members of the Commission were free at the same time.

A week passed. Another week. Bob Arum, back in New York, grew restless. On June 22nd, he sent Neil Hoff the following wire:

CONFIRMED YOUR AUTHORIZATION TO FILE CLAY BOXING APPLICATION. OTHER STATES HAVE INDICATED THAT CLAY MAY BE GRANTED LICENSE THERE FORTHWITH. UNLESS WE HAVE A SPEEDY DETERMINATION NO LATER THAN FRIDAY JUNE 26 FROM WASHINGTON STATE WE MAY ACCEPT FIGHT ELSEWHERE. BUT YOU HAVE ASSURANCE FROM CLAY OF DESIRE TO FIGHT IN SEATTLE IF LICENSE IS GRANTED.—BOB ARUM, ESQ.

With pressure from the news media building daily, Chairman Lynch finally set Friday, June 26th, for the hearing. The meeting was scheduled for 10 o'clock that morning at the ancient Winthrop Hotel in Tacoma. All the regional press was there, the TV news cameras—and hundreds of people, who crowded the conference room to overflowing. The question of Clay's application for a license to fight in the state had become front-page news. Hal Conrad, vice-president of Sports Action, Inc., flew out from New York to personnally represent the Bob Arum group and testify at the hearing.

The first member of our Tacoma-Seattle group to testify in behalf of Clay was Dr. Charles P. Larson. Since Clay's trouble involved the military, attorney Neil Hoff pointed out to the Commision members that Dr. Larson was also a retired Army colonel. He told the Commission:

"Clay's case is an outstanding exception to what we have always considered to be justice in the United States of America. During my term as president of the WBA, we had many breaches of conduct far more serious than what Cassius has done. Sonny Liston, for example, the

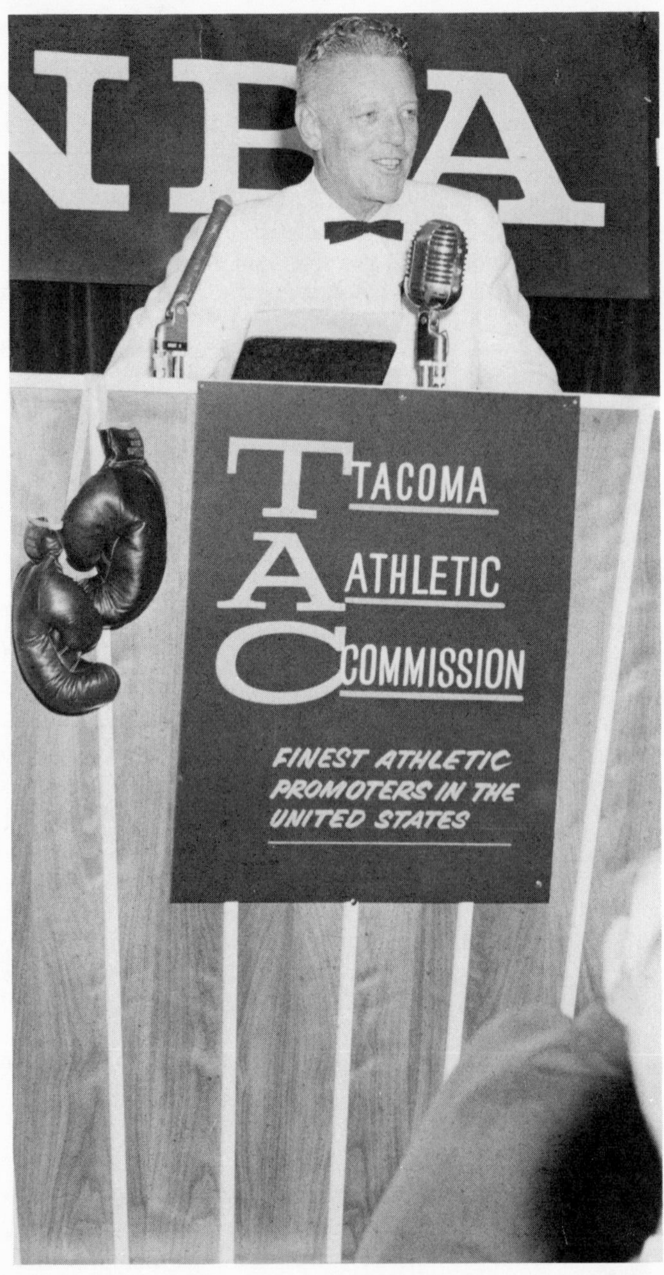

One of those feeling Clay should be granted a license to fight again was Dr. Charles P. Larson (shown here addressing a World Boxing Association convention in Tacoma, Washington, where the organization was born). (Photo by Lyle M. Lathrop)

man that Clay beat for the title. I'm worried, too, about the country's status in the boxing world. Boxing champions are symbols of manhood and superiority over other countries. At one time, all 11 champs were from the U.S. Today, there are only four. And, in 10 years, there may be none. On recent tours I have taken in behalf of the WBA, I have found lots of sympathy for Clay and his problems. I think he should be allowed to fight again–and I think his next fight should be right here in the State of Washington."

I chose a similar platform. Only recently I had completed a 32-week lecture tour across the United States. The itinerary had covered some 400 cities and towns and drawn more than 600,000 listeners. I had found very little anti-Clay feeling.

"It is not easy to estimate present public reaction," I told the commissioners. "The national climate has changed since Cassius Clay refused to take that one step forward three years ago. Then he was condemned as a draft dodger and his claims to conscientious objection were hooted. He was a man beneath contempt. But since he first delivered his empty vaporings against the war in Vietnam, Senator Fulbright and other officials in high places have campaigned against the war in angrier and more persistent fashion. Even the Supreme Court has broadened the base of conscientious objectors. Religion is not the only guideline anymore. A man's conscience is enough. Furthermore, it appears that the Army never really wanted any part of anyone as controversial as Cassius. I still don't know why his draft board finally tapped him. I think it's time to let him get back to the business of being a prize fighter again. Keep in mind that the Supreme Court has yet to hand down its verdict on his case."

Then it was Morley Brotman's turn to speak. He produced some interesting figures. They were taken from a private poll he had conducted. Morley had mailed out 8,000 postcards to a list of World War II, Korean, and Viet Nam veterans. To his question, "Do you believe Cassius Clay should be licensed to fight again," he received more than 2,000 replies. There were 1,057 YES votes, 783 NO scores, and 204 NO OPINIONS.

Brotman told the Commissioners: "We have worked on this proposed Clay-Frazier match for seven months, and during all that time I have had only one phone call against it."

The Commission–comprised of Chairman Lynch, seventy-six, of Tacoma; W. B. "Red" Reese, seventy, former head football and basketball coach at Eastern Washington State College; and the younger Jim Rondeau, fifty-two, who had refereed four world championship fights in his career and was later elected President of the North American Boxing Federation–denied the license for Clay by a vote of 2 to 1. Rondeau was the only one who voted for approval.

"I think they made a mistake," Dr. Larson said in a TV news interview immediately following the hearing. "There isn't any doubt in my mind that the fight is going to be held somewhere. The State of Washington should have had it."

I asked Colonel Red Reese (retired) to explain his vote.

"I actually decided about a day ago to vote no," he told me. "Nothing you people said today changed my mind. Most of the pro athletes in the U.S. lose two of their most lucrative years of their careers by going into the service. None of the other 49 states has approved a license, and I don't know why we should be sticking our necks out. I've received a lot of phone calls, some of them vicious, from parents of young men stationed in Viet Nam. Those calls were split down the middle on the question of Clay. But in all good conscience I could not vote for him."

The Cassius Clay affair was ended. He would not fight Joe Frazier in Washington state. Morley Brotman immediately asked for Chairman Lynch's and Colonel Reese's scalps. He wanted them either to resign or be fired, but Governor Dan Evans shot such notions down by publicly stating at a news conference, "I have a great deal of confidence in the members of the Commission. I have absolutely no desire, no plans to seek any changes whatsoever."

Earl Luebker, a transplanted Oklahoman who has been writing sports for the *Tacoma News Tribune* since he left the Army after World War II, caught the consensus of public opinion with the following words in his daily column:

"Lynch, Reese and Rondeau each voted his honest conviction on Clay's application. It was one of those situations, however, that whatever they did would be wrong. If the license would have been granted, howls would have been raised. And it's obvious that the denial has managed to stir up something of a ruckus. Clay has long been a center of controversy. He managed to keep things boiling even before he refused induction into the armed forces. It has reached such a point that emotion, rather than reason, is the dominant factor whenever Clay is discussed. His opponents, and there are many of them, point out that American citizenship requires certain obligations. They argue that Cassius failed to live up to these by refusing induction. Lynch and Reese certainly aren't alone in their feeling that a Clay-Frazier fight would not be the greatest thing that ever happened to this state. They voted the way they thought was right, and lots of the friendly natives agree with them."

Officially, Tacoma sportsman Morley Brotman's efforts to land the proposed fight were dead. Morley, however, had one more ace up his sleeve. The idea came from Dick Francisco, a veteran Seattle boxing man. Dick had been a Marine fighter pilot in World War II. He had a strong background in aircraft and suggested to Brotman that he contact Boeing about the possibility of leasing one of their giant 747 jumbo jets and stage the Clay-Frazier bout 17,000 feet in the air.

"No license would be required," Dick told him. "It would be like the old days when boxing was still illegal in many states and they were forced to run from the cops and fought on barges. As long as the fight isn't staged *on* U.S. soil they can't stop it."

Dick Francisco checked with Boeing engineers and military flight surgeons, who deemed it feasible to hold the first athletic event in history aboard a Boeing jumbo jet. Stan Farber, boxing writer for the *Tacoma News Tribune,* did some investigating, too, and learned from several space medicine specialists that fighting while flying at 17,000 feet would be the same as fighting at sea level. The Clay camp began to show some genuine interest.

Brotman drove to the big Boeing plant in Seattle and was told that the company had one 747 jumbo jet trainer available without seats. It would rent for $8,000 an hour. Two-hundred and fifty special seats would be installed at $1,000 per boxing customer. The 747 was large enough to hold a standardized ring.

The fight, according to Brotman's plan, would be beamed via closed-circuit television, and if any problem developed with the transmission, the super jet would land immediately at the conclusion of the bout and the film would be rushed to videotape cameras to complete the national and international telecast.

"You'll recall," Stan Farber pointed out, "that it was Dick Francisco who earlier had tried to launch Clay's comeback by offering to stage a match between him and Billy Schellhas on the Tualalip Indian Reservation in western Washington near Marysville. Since it was federal property, Dick argued that no state boxing license was required for Cassius. It might have worked, too, except that the winter weather and outdoor arena facilities killed the plan."

If the setback out in the Pacific Northwest dampened Clay's hopes, they hadn't even been noticed by a brash and brilliant New York lawyer named Robert Kassel. At thirty, Kassel was board chairman of a sports conglomerate called Tennis Unlimited, Inc., as well as a promotional concern called Sports Action, Inc.

"I didn't care what had happened to others who'd tried to get Ali back in the ring again," said Kassel. "Bob Kassel hadn't even made an attempt yet."

Sports Action, Inc., was an outgrowth of Main Bout, Inc., the partially Muslim-owned firm that had promoted Clay's last seven fights. After Clay's conviction, Muslim manager Herbert Muhammad had bowed out and the remaining owners, led by Bob Arum, had run an elimination tournament to find a successor. Then Kassel, in turn, bought out Arum, hoping that Sports Action would be the vehicle for Clay's return.

In August, a month after Brotman apparently threw in the towel, Kassel called his father-in-law, Atlanta businessman Harry Pett, and inquired about staging Clay's comeback there.

"If anyone can do it," said Pett, "It's Leroy Johnson."

Johnson, elected in 1962 as Georgia's first black state senator since Reconstruction, was probably the most powerful black politician in the South. He delivered the votes that elected Sam Massell as Atlanta mayor; he even wielded enough votes to intimidate Lester Maddox. In short order, Massell okayed a Clay appearance, and Maddox tacitly agreed to limit his opposition to some belated criticism rather than any real obstruction. Johnson formed an ad hoc promotion organization called House of Sports, Inc., and prepared to welcome Kassel and Clay to Georgia.

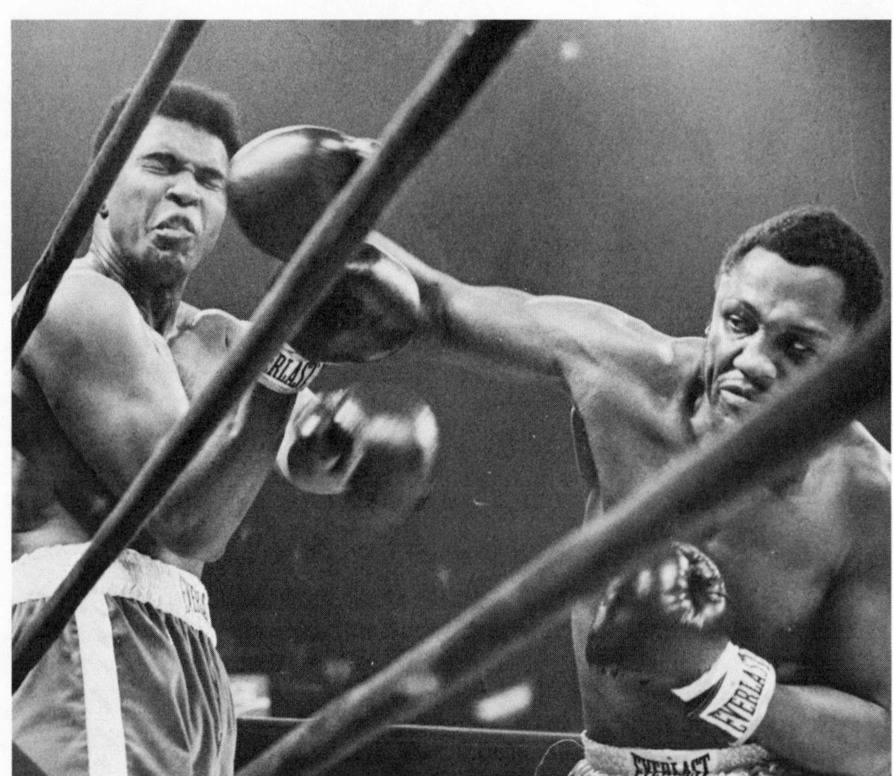

Defending Champion Joe Frazier had too much firepower for Cassius and retained his crown in a title bout in New York, on March 8, 1971.

Kassel and Johnson staged one Clay exhibition, tried briefly and futilely to get Frazier for an immediate match, then settled for Jerry Quarry. The bout was scheduled for October 26th, in Atlanta.

Seven days before the bout, a press conference was held in Atlanta. Clay and Quarry were there. So was Joe Louis. The old Brown Bomber was on hand to help publicize the fight. Brotman and those of us who had been instrumental in trying to lure the match to the Pacific Northwest arranged with the telephone company for the conference to be piped into Brotman's office back in Tacoma. I took notes. This is the way it went:

QUARRY: I'm going to win the fight. We'll find out Monday night which of us is faster.

NEWSMAN: Jerry, do you consider this a championship fight?

QUARRY: Yes. In my book, Ali is still the champion.

JOE LOUIS: I don't think it's going to be easy for Cassius to come back. He's going to have a tough time. I laid off 4½ years, the World War II years, and had a tough time against Conn. But I'll pick Clay in this one because he hasn't lost a fight yet. Yet the long layoff is bound to hurt his legs and coordination. He'll get hit by punches that previously he would've ducked. He should have a few more fights before he challenges Joe Frazier for the title.

NEWSMAN: Joe, if you were fighting Ali next Monday night, how would you fight him?

LOUIS: There's only one way to fight Clay, and that's the way Frazier would fight him—keep him on the ropes and on top of him. If Clay's legs hold up and he can move as he did three years ago, he'll win. I don't think he'd stack up against Frazier right now, though. He needs a few more warm-up fights—and I think Quarry will serve as a stern test.

NEWSMAN: Ali, do you have any predictions for Monday's bout?

(Cassius spoke in a low, soft voice. It was uncustomary to find him so subdued.)

NEWSMAN: For the first time in your life, Clay, no one can hear you!

CLAY (raising his voice): I said I have no predictions for this fight. All my predicting days are over. I weigh 209 now, but I'll come in at 205 at fight time. But I don't think about losing. I don't know what it is to lose. My next fight? I don't know. I have to get past this one first. But I'll fight whoever the public wants me to fight.

NEWSMAN: Ali, you're three years older than when you last fought. How would you describe yourself physically?

CLAY: I'm stronger, faster, wiser. I'm training harder...more seasoned...more mature. Yes, I'm a *better* fighter than I was 3½ years ago before my retirement. I've been running about two days a week for the last three years, which is good enough to keep my legs in shape for today's heavyweights. I'm just twenty-eight now. I don't drink, I don't smoke. I sleep well, eat well, stay in shape. I've changed my boxing style a bit. I've been taking some tricks from Johnny Bratton, Kid Gavilan, Sugar Ray Robinson and Jersey Joe Walcott. I've been putting it all together.

NEWSMAN: Ali, Jerry said he considers Monday's fight a championship fight. How do you rate it?

CLAY: I agree with him. Yes, I consider this a title fight. Whichever of us wins it should be considered the world's champion. I *know* I'm still the champion.

NEWSMAN: (John) Condon, do you anticipate any demonstrations by hard hats at next week's fight?

JOHN CONDON (New York Knicks' public address announcer who was handling the publicity for the Clay-Quarry bout): We expect no commotion whatsoever. At the New York Knicks basketball game the other night I did a commercial on the fight and it provoked no derision at all—nothing but cheers.

NEWSMAN: Ali, do you agree with Joe Louis' estimate of your chances?

CLAY: It's hard for Joe to estimate my condition. He can't predict on me. I'm much faster than Joe ever was and it's hard for him to imagine how fast I really am. I've prepared myself mentally and physically for this fight. I'm prepared not only to beat Quarry but all those oldtime experts who are predictin' I'm over the hill. Listen, all this talkin' doesn't help you when the bell rings, so I'm not sayin' much this time.

It was like old times once more. Cassius Clay was back and suddenly his 43 months of enforced exile from the prize ring seemed part of a remote past. Suddenly, it no longer mattered where he would fight; now all that mattered was the fact the one-time heavyweight champion had returned.

At last, Cassius was ready for his first fight since that fateful day in April of 1967, when he stood at a draft center in Houston and refused to step forward to accept induction into the armed service.

Physically, the ex-champ appeared lean and taut, just as fast and stronger than he had been in his last ring appearance in March, 1967. But the years of exile and controversy had plainly changed him. Now he was a fuller, more mature man. Now his face, which once was alight with mischief, was rather somber, the planes wider and beginning to grow heavier with age. Now he was a far more meaningful symbol to his followers.

"It is God's will for Ali to come back and be champion," Bundini Brown said. "He was born to be the King. His mission is to do the impossible."

"I'm no black leader," Cassius said. "Other people may want to hold me up as a symbol, because my case says a lot about America. But right now I just feel like a fighter. I've been locked out of my profession for three years and now I'm back. That's the important thing."

In the old days, Clay was always on stage. In his hotel room before the first Liston fight he was never still. He was on his feet, dancing, watching himself in the mirror, talking about what he would do to Liston, appreciating the appreciation of his audience, even if the audience was only one person.

But now, 43 months later, he lay quietly in his room in Atlanta going over a thick sheaf of cards upon which he had made notes for a lecture he was preparing. That morning, lying in bed, he had said, "I don't have to go through the act anymore. Used to be, before the Liston fights, all I thought about was fight, fight, fight, be the greatest, be the loudest, be the champion. Now it's like I go to work, put in eight hours a day, do my job. I got other things on my mind, heavy things."

In public, he wore the mask of the old Cassius. But in the privacy of his room, he'd drop the laughing posture and his face would be solemn and thoughtful. He had just rejected the offer of sponsorship for a professorship of poetry at Oxford, extended by Nicholas Stern and Duncan McLeod, dons of St. Catherine's College. "My main concern is to further the cause of black people in the United States," he explained.

Clay could still be the showman when the spirit moved him, though, and whatever his political impact may have been, his drawing power had clearly been enhanced by his absence from the ring. Some 550,000 people crammed into more than 200 theaters and arenas across the United States to view his return on closed-circuit television.

Cassius sounded like the old Cassius as he thought about it.

"People are coming from Pakistan and China," he said. "From Philadelphia, from Detroit, from Watts. Satellites are flying around the sky just to take this fight to Africa and Asia and Russia. Millions and millions of people, watching and waiting—just to see me jump around a ring."

He paused. Then the voice rose again, and the words poured out.

"I'd better win," he said, "because as much hell as I catch when I'm winning, I hate to think of what would happen if I lost."

Cassius was a heavy favorite to defeat Quarry at Atlanta's old Municipal Auditorium, crammed to the rafters with 5,100 people, but it was the manner in which he won it which showed that indeed he once more was a major force in boxing. From the opening bell of the scheduled 15-rounder until the fight was stopped at the end of the third round with blood gushing from Quarry's split left eyebrow, Cassius was in complete command. Using his 5½ in. reach advantage and showing he had not lost his punching speed, he peppered Quarry with stinging left jabs and jolted him with left hooks and rights. It was a straight right in the third round that ripped Quarry's eyebrow, a wound that required 15 stitches.

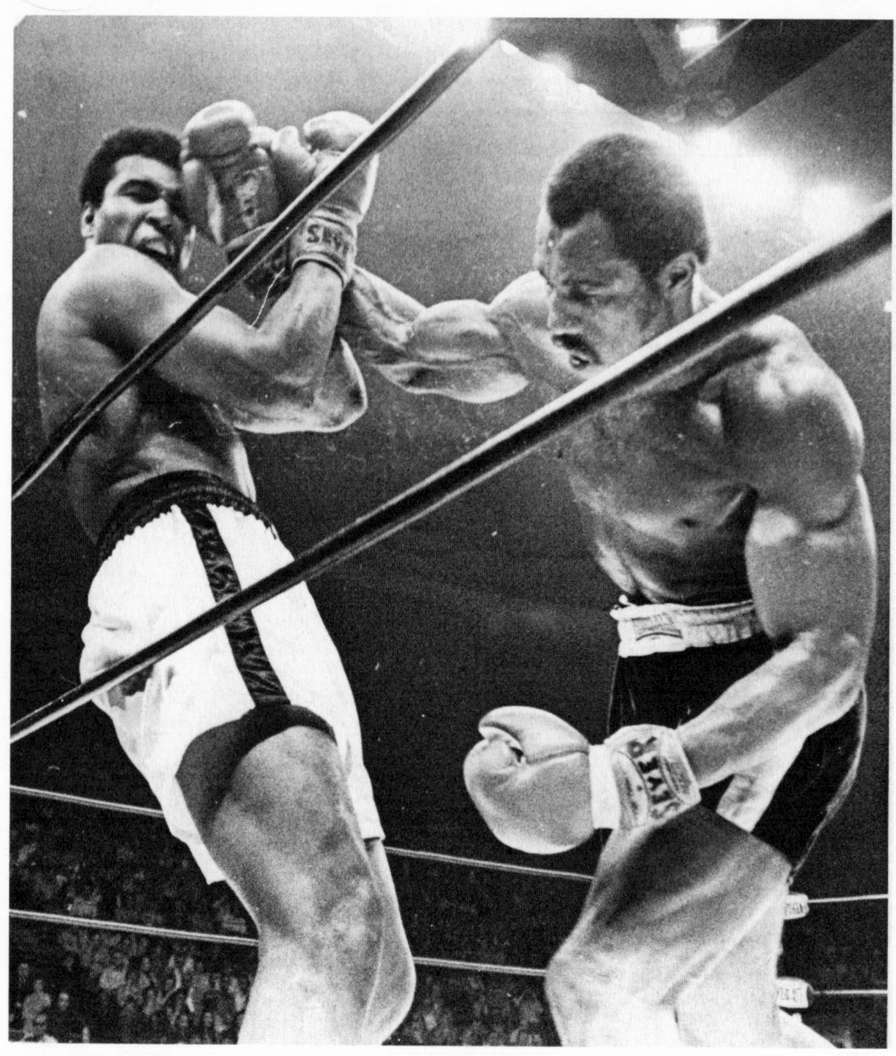

Cassius didn't have much to say after San Diego's Ken Norton broke his jaw and won the decision on March 31, 1973. Clay blamed the stunning upset on his failure to train properly.

Climbing out of the ring and down the ringsteps, Cassius spotted sportscaster Howard Cosell at the TV mike and said, "Do you still think I'm all washed up?" Clay later said the Jerry Quarry fight was as good a fight as he ever fought in his entire career.

Clay's victory not only opened the way for him to get a crack at regaining the championship, which he claimed he never lost in the ring, it opened the way for one of the most lucrative fights in history.

In his absence, Joe Frazier had been made champion after a fifth-round KO of Jimmy Ellis, Clay's old sparring partner, in a 1970 elimination match.

"I'm still the champ," Clay said after beating Quarry. "They say Frazier is the technical champ, but technical stuff doesn't mean much in the country any more. People are rebelling, fighting, demanding what's right. No old man on a boxing commission can tell them Frazier's the champ now. But I'm ready to get on with fighting him. I'm goin' home now to listen for the phone calls from all those fight promoters."

Cassius Marcellus Clay–or Muhammad Ali–was indeed back.

23. Joe Frazier

PROFESSIONAL boxing, lacking the continuity that other major sports gain from their regular schedules, is always in danger of being counted 8...9...10...and out by various experts. When some champions were controlled by mobsters, when Floyd Patterson ducked most of the competent contenders for his crown, and when Muhammad Ali Cassius Clay ("Macc") shocked the Establishment and was told to take his eight-ounce gloves and go home, many observers professed to lose all hope for the business.

The fact is, however, that boxing always has drawn its life's blood from heavyweights with the big punch, and at the time "Macc" was getting the heave-ho there was a dandy candidate able and willing to step up and take Old Big Mouth's place.

He was Joe Frazier, who like his predecessor was a former Olympic Games gold medalist, and an undefeated professional. Though "Macc" had been stripped of his title in what some people thought was shoddy fashion, there was nothing tainted about the way Frazier, then twenty-six, ascended into the vacated championship. On his way to the title he met and soundly thrashed every available contender. He settled all questions with a five-round KO of Jimmy Ellis on February 16, 1970, in New York.

Joe Frazier was the right champion at the right time.

He was remarkably free of the sport's traditional underworld influence; his management went by the name of Cloverlay, Inc., a Philadelphia syndicate of some 200 investors that gave him an immaculate corporate image and was rewarded with substantial profits and a lot of fun.

Because they fought and were built much alike, Frazier often has been compared to the late Rocky Marciano. The Brockton Blockbuster scored 19 knockouts and 2 decision victories in his first 21 pro fights. That was a

Joe Frazier was the first man ever to win both the Olympic Games and the professional heavyweight championship.

.905 knockout percentage. He finished with 43 kayoes in 49 bouts for a .878 knockout percentage, tops among all heavyweight champions.

Frazier, an inch taller and 15 to 20 pounds heavier than Rocky, equaled the latter's early pace with 19 KO's and 2 decisions. Rocky was twenty-four years old by the book, but actually closer to twenty-six when he started fighting for money. Frazier turned pro when he was

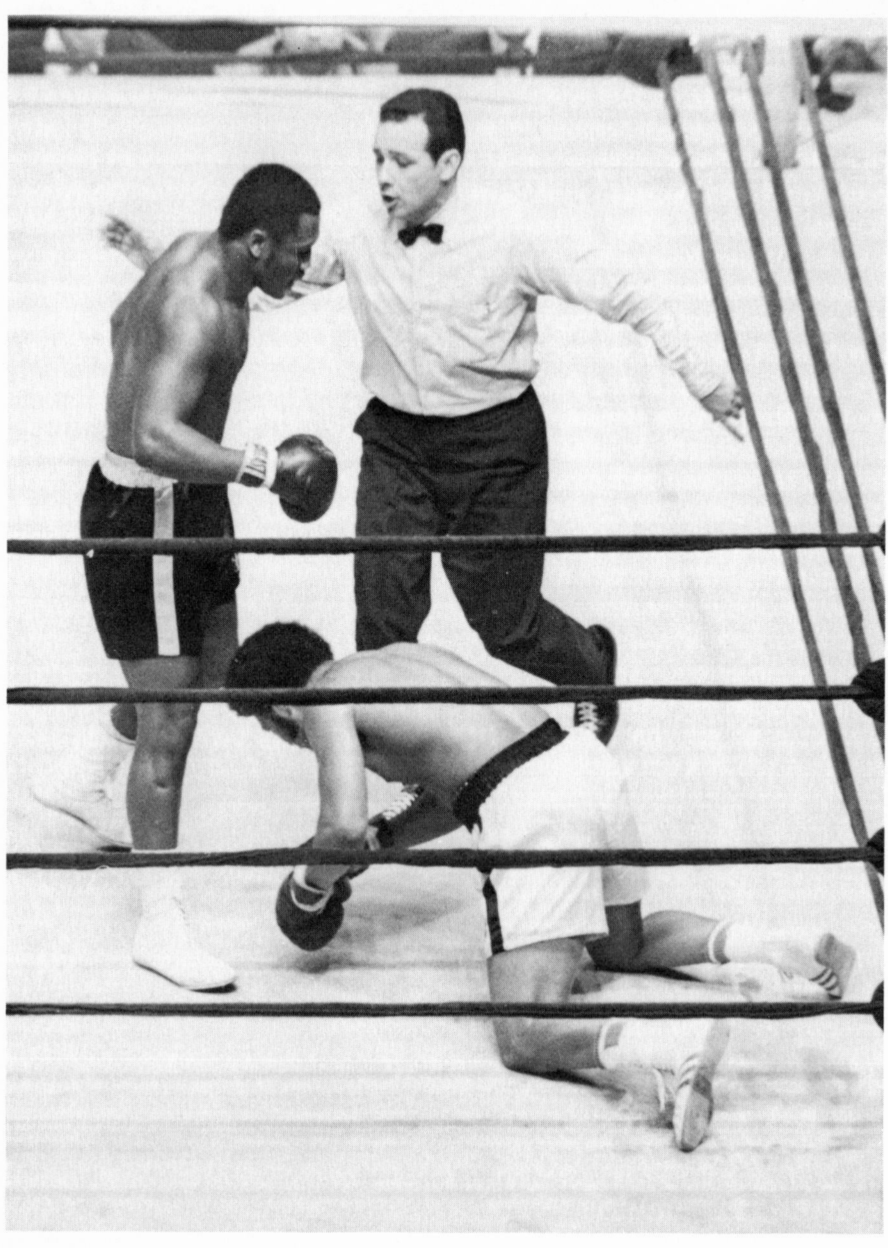

On his way to the world's title, Frazier met and soundly thrashed every available contender. He settled all questions with a five-round KO of Jimmy Ellis on February 16, 1970, at Madison Square Garden. Ellis goes down here for the second time in the fourth round and failed to answer the bell for the fifth round.

twenty-two, after winning the 1964 Olympic heavyweight title, and was twenty-four by the time he had his first 21 bouts.

Marciano had 25 fights before he fought his first name fighter, Roland LaStarza, and won a close decision. At the same age, Frazier had already beaten Oscar Bonavena, Eddie Machen, Doug Jones, George Chuvalo, Buster Mathis and Manuel Ramos. Machen and Jones were over the hill, and while the others were not very highly regarded they were among the best of what was around at the time. Chuvalo, the durable Canadian champion, had never been knocked out before and that included a 15-rounder with Cassius Clay. Frazier pounded Chuvalo's face into a lopsided mess and stopped him in four rounds. Mathis was unbeaten and had never been floored until Frazier draped him over the ropes and knocked him out in the 11th round.

Ramos had won 15 straight and had never been floored or stopped in 28 fights until the strong, muscular Frazier dropped him twice and forced him to surrender under heavy gunning in two rounds.

Like Marciano, Frazier came to fight. His pet expression on the way to the title was, "I'm comin' out smokin'."

The resemblance to Marciano was striking in many more ways, too. Frazier was dedicated in his training just as Rocky was. Marciano trained as he fought and his gym fights were wars. The same was true of Frazier. Rocky was willing to take a punch to land one of his own. He used to batter an opponent's arms to force him to drop his guard. He broke blood vessels in LaStarza's arms. Marciano smashed away at the body to soften up an opponent and to open up the head defenses. "When the body dies, the head rolls," was the way oldtimers described it.

Frazier used this same jungle technique, but with one difference. Rocky was vulnerable to cuts, and Joe was not. His tank-like body was wrapped in a tough skin. He was still a few fights short of the championship when Teddy Brenner, matchmaker for Madison Square Garden, said, "Frazier throws more punches and throws them faster than Marciano. He's a helluva fighter now and he has tremendous potential. When he's in there, you're guaranteed a good fight. He comes to fight."

When Muhammad Ali Cassius Clay was telling the world how he was going to destroy Joe Frazier on March 8, 1971, for the world championship, Jerry Quarry, who had been stopped by them both, spoke up loud enough to be heard and said bushwash.

"Until I fought Clay," he said, "I thought he would beat Frazier. But I did not realize he could not hit. Clay's a big, strong guy, but he can't break an egg. I was quite shocked. Clay hit me flush on the chin with a right. I said to him, 'If that's all you can hit, you can't hurt a flea.' He doesn't have much sting in his jab, either. Either you have a punch or you don't. Clay has had to compensate by improving his mobility. But Frazier is something else again. He's more aggressive. He's quick—surprisingly quick. He's there all the time. He makes most guys panic.

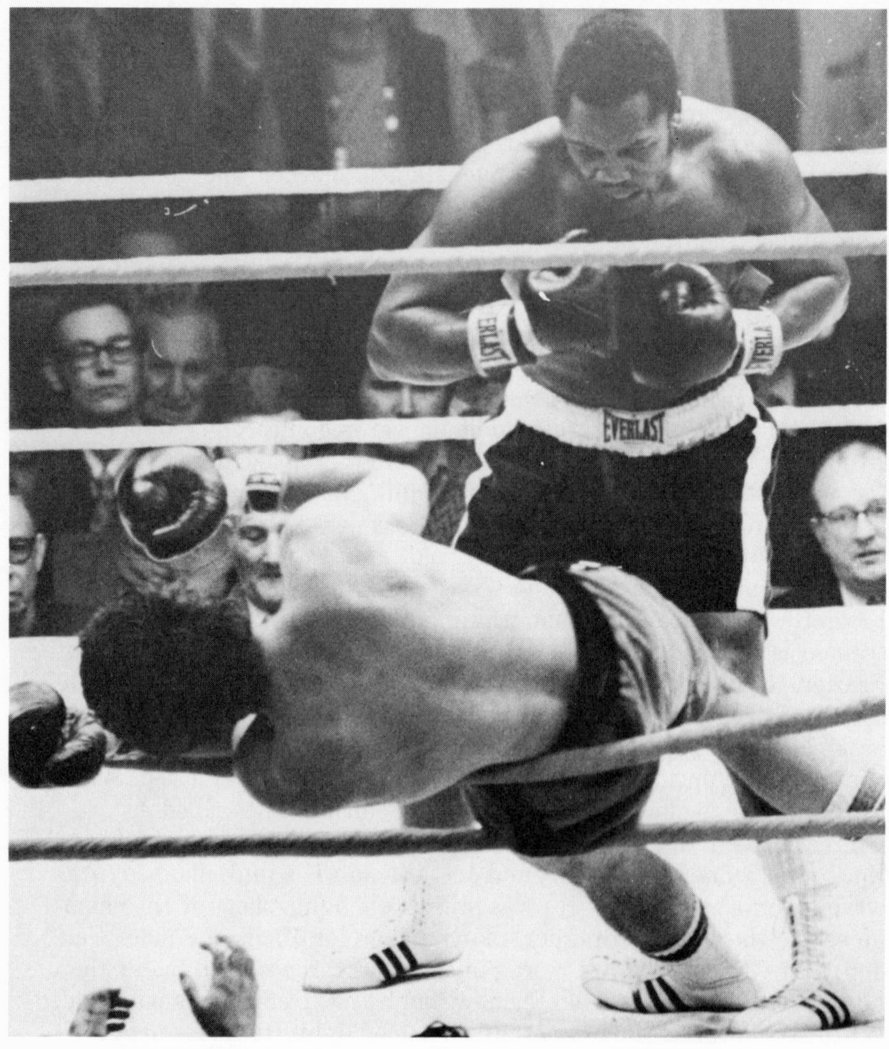

Frazier took only 3½ rounds to dispose of challenger Terry Daniels in the January 15, 1971, championship bout in New Orleans.

Clay can't keep him off and he'll panic. It's the mental pressure that gets you against Frazier. It isn't so much that he hurts you, it's just that he's always right there, boring in."

The road traveled by Frazier to his multi-million-dollar showdown match with Clay had been long and dusty. It had started on January 12, 1944, at Beaufort, South Carolina. He never finished the ninth grade; a teenage dropout who drove a tractor on his father's poverty-pocket farm.

When he was seventeen, he went north to Philadelphia where he was just another 230-pound guy named Joe when he was spotted by trainer Yank Durham in a local gym trying to melt all that fat off his frame. There were 12 kids in his family and he had a job slaughtering cattle in a Kosher slaughterhouse. "In those days," Frazier recalled, "my legs were so round I couldn't get my pants on. That's what I was doing in the gym, trying to slim down."

Under Durham, Joe trimmed down to a muscular 205 pounds and won the Olympic championship—the first man ever to win both the amateur and professional heavyweight title. He won the Olympic Gold Medal with a fractured thumb, but never told anybody about the injury until the officials had hung the Gold Medal around his neck.

When he was training for the Clay bout, Frazier made a point to clear up some matters about himself.

"People say Clay's got a cause and I don't," he said. "But what's the cause? What's it mean to be a black champion? What's it ever meant? What's it mean for Jack Johnson to be champ? Or Joe Louis? Do it help the black folks? Do it? I don't need a cause to fight because I fight for my family, for myself, for my pride. But I ain't no Uncle Tom and I ain't no black white hope. Know what I mean? I do what little I can. They're tryin' to build a chemical factory in the town I was raised. In Beaufort, South Carolina. People starvin' down there, and this plant give maybe 4,000 or 5,000 jobs. But the whites don't want it. They say pollution, man. Pollution wouldn't be able to stay, man, not in the South, because there's too much space. I'm gonna talk with one of the factory people who want to build it, and maybe we can get it goin'. But look, man, I'm a fighter, that's all. I simply go out there to do a job. Man get hit on the button, he gotta go. Cause? Hell, my cause is *me!*"

With the bout expected to gross an astounding $18 million to $20 million in closed-circuit television revenue, both Clay and Frazier were understandably anxious to meet in the prize ring. By this time, each had flatly claimed the championship for himself, but rather than stall things by bickering about who was the "real" champ, they agreed to an even split of the record purse. They were guaranteed a fantastic $2,500,000 apiece! And who said boxing was dead?

The story behind the historic match was almost as fascinating as the fight itself. Bob Considine, the Hearst columnist and former sports writer, broke the details first. He told how a relatively young theatrical agent named Jerry Perenchio put the package together.

"Jerry Perenchio had never even met a fighter in his life before he mitted those two bruisers and signed them for $2,500,000 each," wrote Considine. "His previous experience as an entrepreneur covered such activities as booking college dances at UCLA, small-time acts and bands for Air Force posts in World War II, and as one of the faceless flesh-peddlers in Music Corporation of America until the Justice Department busted it."

Perenchio pushed out on his own, Considine said, and with his charisma and know-how built his own agency which was grossing $30 million a year handling such clients as Glen Campbell, Andy Williams, Henry Mancini and Jane Fonda. But Perenchio was as remote from boxing as Pluto from Mars when he received a phone call from his friend Frank Fried, owner of Chicago's Aragon Ballroom. Perenchio was in London at the time, hustling his stable of theatrical stars.

Fried had some news. He told Jerry he had been talking to Herbert Muhammad, the Black Muslim who was Ali's manager of record. Ali, he said, wanted to fight Frazier.

"Can you put the package together?" Fried wanted to know.

"Sure," Perenchio said.

Jerry flew back to the States and learned that there would be much competition for the rights to the fight. One combine had already offered a bid of $1 million. So, all on his own, Perenchio decided he would up the ante to $5 million, plus $1.5 million or 50 percent of the profits for a rematch.

He met in Philadelphia with the fighters and their lawyers. He put up $250,000 of his own money in the hope of firming the proposition but nobody was impressed. Nobody knew Perenchio. They wanted him to produce a site, the Houston Astrodome or Madison Square Garden; then they'd talk turkey. The Astrodome was out. It, too, was bidding high for the match and thus was a foe. Frustrated after the four-hour Philadelphia meeting, Perenchio was leaving when Frazier's manager, Yank Durham, took him aside and suggested he make a pitch at the Garden. Jerry sped to New York by car–it was Christmas Eve–and found Alvin Cooper, the Garden's Executive Vice President, still at work. They came to an understanding in ten minutes: the Garden would put up $500,000 against a percentage; Perenchio must raise the remaining $4.5 million. "I can get the money in a day or two," Perenchio promised.

Perenchio flew back to Los Angeles for a late dinner with his wife and six kids at 11 o'clock on Christmas Eve. The next day he called a man he hardly knew, Jack Kent Cooke, the owner of the Los Angeles basketball Lakers and part-owner of the Washington football Redskins. Cooke said, sure, he'd put up the $4.5 million if the fight was held in his Los Angeles Forum. He also wanted 60 percent of the profits, 10 points more than Perenchio wanted to give away.

Perenchio prevailed. He talked Cooke out of holding the battle at the Forum–neither Clay nor Frazier was licensed in California–and, after the deal looked as if it might fall through completely, Cooke voluntarily took 50 percent, not 60. What nearly collapsed it was the Garden's insistence that Cooke's word was not enough; it wanted an "irrevocable certified check" for the $4.5 million.

Jack Kent Cooke was furious. "How dare they!" he stormed when Perenchio gave him the news. "Why, I'm worth a lot more than Madison Square Garden!" He finally calmed down and gave them the front money. The whole historic deal was wrapped up in just two weeks.

For the benefit of the press, Clay dug up his old act and went back into action. He predicted that Smokin' Joe Frazier would be easier for him to handle than Quarry. No one took this statement seriously, but they printed it anyway. They had come prepared for many tongue-in-cheek put-ons and put-downs in the coming weeks. In reverting to his old style, Clay offered the public one of his breezy poems:

Now, this might shock and amaze ya'
  But Ali will destroy Joe Frazier,
Muhammad's got such endurance,
  Frazier's gonna need some insurance...

Overnight, Clay's return had made the whole fight scene more exciting again. It was a sequential thing. An exciting boxer on the scene made all fights seem more important. Thus, for all the premature death notices, prize fighting suddenly found itself the most money-making, headline-grabbing sport again.

Cassius had not lost the touch. In a private talk with Charles Maher, of the *Los Angeles Times,* he was asked if it wouldn't have been wiser to fight several softer opponents first before meeting Frazier.

"After all," Maher told him, "you've had a long layoff. I'd think you'd want to get in a lot of rounds before taking on Frazier."

"You don't understand," Clay said. "Joe Frazier will be *easier* than Quarry or Bonavena. I'll just hold his head like this and I'll tell him, 'Come on, champ.' I'll just play with him. He'll be trying all those short hooks and not reaching me and I'll be moving and saying, 'Come on, champ. You can do better than that.' "

"Do you know Frazier?" Clay was asked.

"Oh, yeah," Cassius said. "We met at my house a few months ago. We drove to New York together. I spent four or five hours with him."

"What kind of guy is he?"

"Nice fellow. Good fellow."

"What did you talk about?"

"About who can whip who."

"That's all you talked about for four or five hours?"

"Yeah, mostly."

Clay then confessed to sports columnist Maher that he not only composed his own prefight oratory but often wrote material for his opponents as well.

"I tell 'em what to say," he admitted. "I tell 'em, 'I'll say this and you say that.' I told Liston things to say. I told Patterson, told Chuvalo, told Ernie Terrell, told Quarry."

"Did Quarry follow your instructions?"

"Yes."

"And the idea was to build up interest in the fights?"

"Yes," Cassius said. "And it works, too."

It was hard to write about the much quieter, less colorful Joe Frazier when Cassius Clay was around. Clay was the Pied Piper of Pugilism, a put-on artist, a man of many facets, and he was good copy. You never knew what he would talk about. One interview it would be how he was going to "whup Joe Frazier," and in the next his voice would suddenly become bitterly cold when the conversation turned to the subject of white people.

"If you were willing to hold your hand out just a little farther," Clay was told, "you'd probably find there are a lot of white people who would like to grab it."

"I'm still a Black Muslim with Elijah Muhammad and more so than ever," Cassius said. "And I ain't anxious to grab no hands. Black hands come first. Then if we've got some more room left, I'll grab somebody else. After we get all my people together and cleanin' themselves and doin' for themselves and respectin' themselves and quit fightin' and killin'. I want to get my people straight and clean. It don't impress me to see a lot of white hands now."

"What do you mean by straight and clean?"

"Get 'em off dope," he said. "You know the problems. Alcohol, tobacco. I want 'em to get self-respect and dignity, unity and love for self. Then I'll grab white folks' hands. Anything wrong with that? If God was here, the judge of the world, He would say, 'You right, Muhammad. There ain't a damn thing wrong with helpin' yourself first.' "

In the past, some black fighters had been talked into posing as defenders of the sport against Clay and his Muslim ways. Frazier was not one of them. He said, "I want no part of such a role. I'm no Uncle Tom, and I won't let any promoter or press agent push me into that position. I'll simply be in that ring doing as I always do. I believe I can beat anyone now, and I only want a chance to prove it."

A lot of the reporters felt Frazier could win, too.

"Clay is strictly a slap-hitter, all wrist and forearm, and his delivery is made from an up-on-the-toes ballet position from which it is impossible to generate even a modicum of power," wrote Gene Ward, veteran boxing expert for the *New York News*.

Joe Louis told Howard Cosell on ABC-TV that Cassius "lacks the killer instinct, he just doesn't have it."

Syndicated columnist Mel Durslag observed: "Muhammad Ali's quickness has diminished. The jab is missing, and, shockingly, the legs, perhaps the greatest ever belonging to a heavyweight, are not responding reliably. He can't move 15 rounds at the pace required against a puncher as persistent as Joe."

Still the veteran sports observer of the *Washington Post,* Shirley Povich, saw the match shaping up as almost a fight of the century.

"Few fights will answer more curiosities," Povich said. "Is the unbeaten Frazier that great a fighter? Can Ali stand up to him? Against a boring-in Frazier can Ali get away with those amateurish back-bends that have taken him out of trouble against other opponents? And how long will it take Ali to land a bomb on a Frazier who is given to fighting wide-open, and can he make it stick? It is the promise of an epic fight of the kind that used to be staged in the big ballparks."

The solicitude of Clay was difficult to understand. Here he was approaching the most desperate stand of his life with $2.5 million in the bank for him and a five-year prison sentence hanging over him (but which would be lifted by the Supreme Court three months later) and he found time to worry about the members of the press corps who thought Frazier could whip him.

"You fellas gonna look so bad," he told them. "You gonna feel so bad when you have to eat your words." And then he patiently explained to the poor, ignorant writers why the greatest, the fastest, the most gifted heavyweight who ever breathed could not possibly lose to an amateur like the 1964 Olympic champion when they met in Madison Square Garden.

"I had to whup Sonny Liston twice for the title and they still didn't believe it," he said. "Then I said something about Vietnam and they gave my title to Ernie Terrell and I had to whup Terrell. I was three years in exile and my title is so big they had to give it to two men, Frazier and Jimmy Ellis.

"After three years in exile and four years just about outta training, they put the two top contenders on me, Quarry and Bonavena, and I had to whup both of them. I'm sick and tired of it. I never wanted a fight so much in my life as this one. I can't sleep at night, I can't run, I'm so anxious to get to him.

"People say, that Frazier, he awful strong. Well, then, he better get some Ban® roll-on. If Joe Frazier whups me, I'm gonna get down on my knees right in the ring in Madison Square Garden and I'll crawl across and say, you are the greatest, you are the true champion..."

And on...and on...and on...

It was inevitable that astrologer Laurie Brady, President of Astro-Plan, Inc., of Chicago, had to get her two cents worth in. On the eve of the fight she wrote in the *Chicago Daily News:* "It's in the stars that Joe Frazier will beat Muhammad Ali and that the fight may be stopped in the fifth round. But this one is not easy to read. Frazier's personal chart looks very good, while Ali's does not show such good aspects.

They are both Capricorns born five days less than two years apart. That is probably part of the reason for the difficulties."

Oh.

At the weigh-in, the twenty-seven-year-old Frazier was listed at 205½ lbs., and Clay, twenty-nine, came in at an even 215.

The fight was close for the first nine rounds. Clay used his superior reach to spear the charging Frazier. Then in the 10th round, the bout began to change. Frazier won the 10th by a narrow margin but then nearly scored the 24th knockout of his career in the 11th. He hurt Clay with a smashing left hook to the head, drove him to the ropes with two more lefts and a right to the body and had him staggering around the ring. Clay was clearly in trouble as he tottered to his corner at the end of the round and the capacity crowd of 19,500 went wild.

Frazier kept up the pressure in the 12th and 13th rounds as Clay's trainer, Angelo Dundee, and his alter-ego, Bundini Brown, pleaded with him to take charge.

He did in the 14th round.

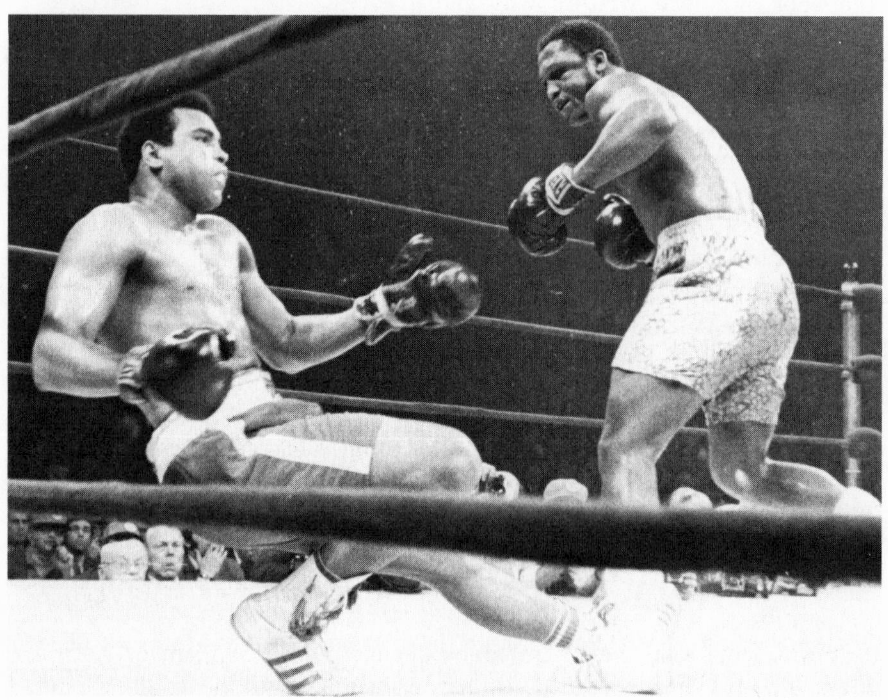

Cassius Clay finds himself in an unfamiliar position as Frazier connects to send him to the canvas and thwart Clay's attempt to win back the disputed crown in New York, on March 8, 1971. The judges awarded Joe the 15-round decision.

But then came the 15th round, the round which told the story of the fight which ended one of the most incredible comeback attempts in sports history. At the bell, Clay rushed out with a bid to end the bout. Then suddenly Frazier's hook flashed and the crowd went into a frenzy. Clay was down. He got back up at the count of four and took referee Arthur Mercante's mandatory eight count. Frazier landed several solid body and head punches as Cassius reeled around the ring until the bell ended the fight.

There was little doubt who the winner was.

The referee voted for Frazier, 8 rounds to 6 with 1 even; judge Artie Aidala had Frazier in front, 9 to 6; judge Bill Recht gave it to Frazier, 11 to 4.

For Clay, the defeat foiled his attempt to become only the second man in history to win back the heavyweight championship.

It marked the first defeat of his professional career.

Joe Frazier, still undefeated, had replaced Muhammad Ali Cassius Clay as The King.

24. George Foreman

IT was George Foreman day in Houston, Texas, his old hometown—where he used to be a juvenile delinquent. Now in February, 1973, the 6 ft. 3 in., 217-pound heavyweight was regarded as a model citizen as well as a sports hero. He rode in a chauffeured limousine with a police escort on a tour of the black ghetto where he grew up.

"The last time I saw any policemen in this neighborhood," said George, "they weren't helping me—they were chasing me."

He didn't elaborate, but his mother, who was sitting next to him in the open car, guessed that her son was referring to a street fight eight years earlier.

"The police came and took him to the station," she said. "They called me and said to bring four damn good men to get him, because no two ordinary men could handle him."

George Foreman is the first to tell you that he wasn't exactly an All-American boy when he was growing up in Houston. He is a refreshingly honest young man.

"Casting about for places to put the blame for troubles a person has is an old human trait," he said. " 'They' is an easier word to use than 'I', when things don't go right. But in getting by an obstacle, or a trouble, or a problem, the key—and I know this because I've had them all, and still have some—is to take after it, all alone if that's the only way. More times than not, battles have to be taken on alone. The messes a man gets into, they're the same. They don't hunt him up; he went looking for them, whether he always knew it or not. He has to get into them himself, even if he has company at the time. Nobody got me down in the street, for instance, held my nose and poured cheap wine down my throat when I was a kid. Not at all. I got the bottle, tipped it up and drank it. Who would believe me if I said somebody forced me to drink

George Foreman took rank with Joe Frazier by becoming only the second man in history to win both the Olympic Games and professional heavyweight title.

that stuff? I don't force that easy. The memory of that wine is so clear to me that the smell of it now makes me sick to my stomach.

"And when I was going about my first record-setting—which was how many windows I could break in a row without getting caught—I can't lay the idea on anybody else's doorstep. It was all my own, and I got all the way up to 200 before the Houston police thought it just might be me and looked me up to talk about it. It was quite a record, if one just wanted to look at the size of it, but it wasn't sensible or respectable to do it. These were the things that happened when I thought I had nothing going for me, but it was mostly my attitude toward life that made it so. There was the high school there in the bloody Fifth Ward of Houston, and I dropped out of it in the ninth grade. It was my decision, not the school's."

The ghetto has many names. In Chicago they call it The Valley. It's The Fillmore in San Francisco. In New York, the people call it Harlem. For George Foreman, it was called the Fifth Ward of Houston.

"People are always asking me if growing up in the Fifth Ward was rough," George said. "Well, it wasn't. I did it easily. Everybody's always calling it the ghetto, but to me it was home. I was 13 years old when I quit school, and for a while I hung around the streets. I took an occasional odd job to get enough money to get by. I was heading in the direction that would eventually find me in jail or dead. My decision to be a bad guy was what caused my mother—bless her for all the suffering she endured for me—to have a nervous breakdown. I had about lost faith in everything before I was even started, I guess, but Mom never lost faith in me.

"Then, one day, I finally made a right decision, and it came in an unlikely place—a pool hall in Houston. I was watching television and the program broke for one of those public service announcements. It's a part of America that when a man gets famous, becomes a celebrity, they ask him to do these commercials about all kinds of things. Some are for causes, like fighting cancer, or helping the retarded kids. This guy I was watching on TV was recruiting, and he was saying he was once a down-and-outer himself. Boy, was he on my wave length, talking my language! I listened to him, half-like at first, and then he said he had this one skill, and finally got a chance to use it and made it big. To anybody listening who needed a skill to get a job, he said, why not give The Job Corps a try?

"That's for me, I said to myself, and I put down that pool cue and picked up hope. The Job Corps took me, thank God. There was some money in it, $30 a month, and $50 to go in the bank, and they'd send some home to my mother. Did she ever need it then! It wasn't until then that it began to dawn on me what America was really all about, how there were things being done to really try to help people such as me find some way out of the jungle. Work is such a big four-letter word. I'd known a lot of the other four-letter words and they couldn't help anybody. This one meant sweat. It meant getting banged around. It meant being more tired than I had ever been in my life. And sore in more places, too.

"Don't talk down the American system to me. I know what men go through to make it run. I also know that some of its rewards can be there for anybody, if he will make up his mind, bend his back, lean hard into his chores and refuse to allow anything to defeat him. I can honestly say I worked for it. I say, worship the opportunity this country grants to those who will really try, don't knock it."

George Foreman is a first-class example of a young American who reached boxing's highest goal through talent and hard work. He accomplished his lofty dreams in an old-fashioned, unsophisticated manner, a Horatio Alger story at its best.

Donald Buchannon remembers George Foreman. He was one of the first men in the Job Corps Program to work with the boy.

"It cost Uncle Sam about $10,000 to put George through Job Corps but he was worth every penny," Mr. Buchannon said. "He's paid back every cent through his example. If just a fraction of our population could make the growth and development that George has made, just in their personal development, their personal habits and attitudes, it would be a great world.

"George was sent to us at the Fort Vannoy Job Corps Center near Grants Pass, Oregon. He was just a 16-year-old kid off the streets of Houston, but he knew exactly what he wanted. He wanted to finish his education, that was his primary goal. Then, he wanted a skill, not the common labor type, but a skill—anything that Job Corps had to offer that would give him a good trade. Vannoy was opened only two months before George arrived in October of 1965, and we had no sophisticated vocational training. After three months, George asked to be transferred to the Parks center in Pleasantville, California, so he could learn a skill. I told him I didn't think he was ready, that he needed to bring his work habits up. He was too much in a hurry.

"You could outline a timetable for him. We might say it's going to take 14 months, 18 months and George would say, 'I'll do it in eight.' His basic determination was excellent; that and his drive and his belief that he could do whatever he set his mind out to do. The good thing about it is that he never set his goals so high that he wouldn't be able to achieve them. He knew his capabilities. He would be a success at anything."

George Foreman finally earned a transfer to the Parks center in Pleasantville, California, where Nick Broadus, the recreational director, steered him into boxing. James Jackson was one of the instructors and took a big interest in George.

"I remember one day a bunch of us guys were standing around looking in the mirror striking different boxing poses," Foreman said. "Suddenly Mr. Jackson walked in. He took one look at me and said, 'Hey, George, you look just like Joe Louis standing there.' To most kids, Louis was still something of a hero to us. Mr. Jackson's comparison made me feel proud."

James Jackson had been a middleweight boxer while he was in the Army, and had fought 18 amateur bouts and five professional matches before joining the Job Corps. He weighed only 150, but used to get into the ring with the much bigger Foreman and spar with him.

"George had learned his fighting in the streets of Houston," Jackson said. "He quickly discovered that organized boxing was something else again. But he was big, about 250 pounds and out of shape, and I could tell he had an ability from just looking at him."

Under Jackson's expert guidance, Foreman had his first amateur bout in February, 1967, and 20 months later he was winning the Gold Medal at the Olympics in Mexico City. George earned world-wide fame and the lasting admiration of Americans when, after defeating Iones Cepulis of Russia in the heavyweight division final, he circled the ring waving a small American flag in his right hand. It at a time when members of his own generation were burning down buildings on American campuses in all-out revolt against The Establishment—so George became an instant hero to the silent majority back home.

A super patriot?

"I have no political aspirations and I don't support black militants," George told the press afterward. "I'm going to turn pro and will be

Foreman KO'd Russia's Iones Cepulis in the second round to win a Gold Medal at 1968 Olympics in Mexico City.

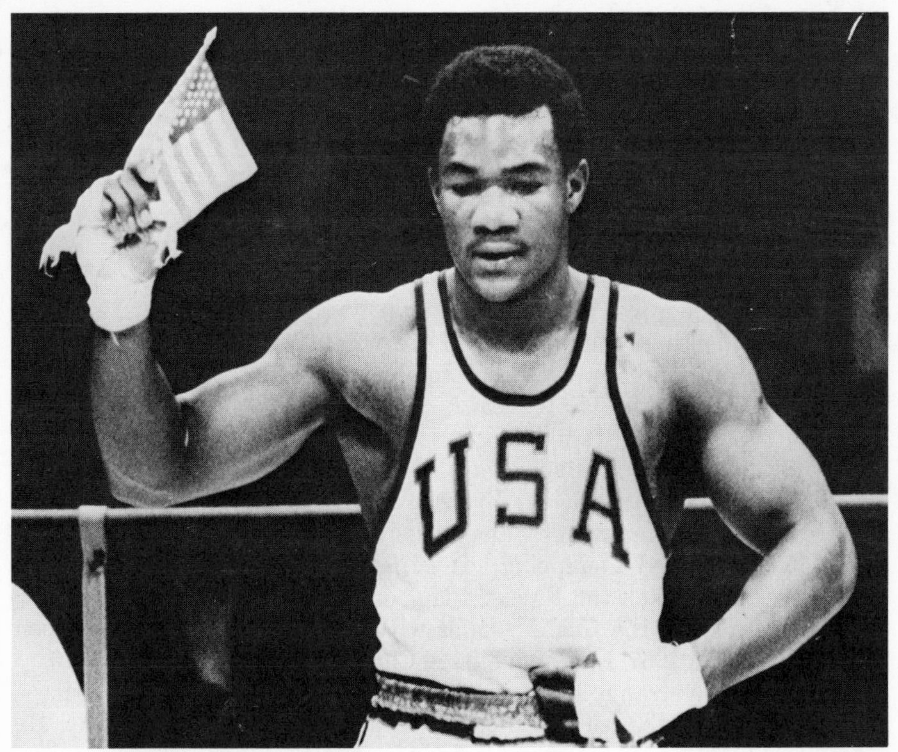

George endeared himself to millions of Americans who were watching him back home on TV, when he walked around the ring wavinq the American flag after winning the Olympic heavyweight title in Mexico City.

fighting just to earn a living, to win. There's none of that fighting for the black man or the white man. I just want to represent myself properly in my profession. I fear no man but must admit a black cat can turn me into a sniveling coward. Man, I admit it—I am probably the most superstitious man in the world. I won't walk under ladders. I'm careful with mirrors. I don't light three on a match. I spit on my thumb when I see a load of hay."

On the way to the Olympics, Foreman posted a 21-3 record, scoring 18 knockouts. This put him on the road that would eventually lead him to the heavyweight championship of the world. George and Joe Frazier are the only fighters in history to win both the Olympic and professional heavyweight crowns.

"George is an exceptional example of Job Corps," Donald Buchannon said. "An example that we're awfully proud of."

It is a mutual admiration society.

On the back of George's boxing robe are the words: "George Foreman, the fighting corpsman."

On October 1, 1968, when Foreman was finishing his training for the Olympic games, he said, "Give me 2½ years and I'd like to be heavyweight champion."

After cleaning up all heavyweight contenders in Mexico City, he launched his pro career and won 26 straight fights, 23 by KO. At the age of twenty-two, he was ranked as the No. 1 contender by the World Boxing Association and was marked by the experts as a he-can't-miss star. Dick Sadler was his manager and did a remarkable job with him.

Foreman gained confidence with every fight.

He was unimpressed by either Joe Frazier or Cassius Clay the night they fought for the championship.

"Pitiful," he said after the fight. He wasn't being arrogant. He didn't say it for publicity. "It sure wasn't the fight of any century. The skill displayed was as little as any I've ever seen in a ring."

Foreman had improved tremendously as an all-around prize fighter. He had developed a snapping left jab and power in his right hand. He had already broken the Frazier-Clay course record on George Chuvalo. The latter went the full 15 rounds with Clay in 1966. Frazier stopped him in four in 1967. Foreman blitzed Chuvalo in three rounds in 1970.

And then a strange thing happened. Foreman nearly quit the ring—only three months before he fought Frazier for the championship. He was depressed over the way his finances had been handled, feeling "so

President Lyndon B. Johnson personally congratulates fellow Texan George Foreman after the nineteen-year-old Houston youth returned from the 1968 Olympics.

many people got their hands into my money, I might just be fightin' for the title, no money."

George said he knew he could beat Frazier, but he felt too many people were living off of him. He didn't want to end up the way poor old Ezzard Charles wound up—dead broke. So George talked to an old friend of his, Barney Oldfield, a Litton Industries executive. Barney told him not to quit.

"Don't let people call you a quitter," Barney advised him. "The only thing I figure you can do is go knock Frazier out and then come back and show people you can take all of this torment and still win the fight. If you reject the match, then people in boxing will always say you were scared. I've never known you to be scared of anything. And there you'd be, back proving yourself all over again."

Foreman pulled himself together. The fight with Frazier was signed and scheduled for Kingston, Jamaica, on January 22, 1973. The bout matching two big heavyweights, both unbeaten, should have been a natural, but there were several drawbacks. In the first place, Kingston was an implausible site—a city of 600,000 on a lazy tropical island with a total population of two million. It was a poor country in which factory

George receives some technical advice from a pair of former world champions, Joe Louis, center, and Archie Moore.

Another one-time world champion, ex-featherweight king Sandy Saddler, was hired as Foreman's trainer and gets in some roadwork with George.

workers earned as little as $25 a week and common laborers even less. Impoverishment had brought an outbreak of crime, similar to that in many American cities, and visitors attending the fight were warned not to stray too far from their hotels at night.

Both Frazier and Foreman were provided bodyguards. A cordon of 700 militia and 700 Kingston policemen had been assigned to the stadium. To quiet the fears of fight fans, Douglas McFarland, Deputy Commissioner of Police, publicly announced that "with our security we can guarantee complete safety for everyone." Everyone, that was, except Joe Frazier.

It was the defending champion's misfortune to get trapped on the wrong side of the ropes. The bout was Frazier's fifth defense of the title, and he still had the shadow of Cassius Clay haunting him. The oddsmakers back in Las Vegas had made the twenty-nine-year-old champion a 3½ to 1 favorite over the twenty-four-year-old challenger, who had yet to be floored in his pro career.

Will Grimsley of the Associated Press sized up the two opponents this way:

"Frazier is a punishing, bore-in slugger, a black Rocky Marciano, who disdains personal injury to mete out punishment to his foes. Foreman is a powerful giant with none of Ali's grace and speed. He doesn't swing arms, he swings wagon tongues."

The bout was sponsored by the Jamaican government. Frazier was guaranteed $850,000 against 42½ percent of the gross, and Foreman $375,000 against 20 percent. The money was stashed away in a Canadian bank for them.

"Should Frazier lose," wrote Grimsley, "all the wind would be knocked out of the much-awaited Frazier-Ali rematch, which has promoters dreaming of a $20 million or $30 million extravaganza."

George Foreman could not have cared less.

He had a job to do, and he did it with dispatch. Details of how he performed one of the major upsets of modern boxing were contained in this newspaper account:

The boxing world woke up today with a new heavyweight champion, a 24-year-old one-time delinquent whose mild manners and tender heart belie a pair of the most devastating fists the game has seen.

George Foreman sent Joe Frazier spinning to the ice-blue canvas six times and stopped the fierce, hard-punching defending champ in 1:35 of the second round in a staggering upset.

The swiftness of the turnover of boxing's most prized crown was almost unbelievable. Frazier, a brawling ex-slaughterhouse butcher, had flailed his way through 29 opponents as a pro, knocking out 25 of them, and 22 months ago had beaten Muhammad Ali in the so-called Fight of the Century.

Foreman's triumph was heady wine for the Jamaican majority in the surprised crowd of 36,000 who almost filled the combination soccer field and cycling drome that is Kingston's National Stadium.

When the battered and bleeding Frazier was led to his corner and referee Arthur Mercante raised the right arm of the new champion, the crowd went wild. Jamaicans had made Foreman their personal hero during the last week of his training. They even cheered him when he shadow-boxed.

Frazier, a renowned aggressor, who has whipped his opponents into submission with a head-bowed, bore-in attack that resembles a berserk pile-driver, came out swinging. But Foreman didn't back up an inch. His 6-foot-3-inch frame erect in his familiar stand-up style, he lashed out with twisting left hooks. Snap. Frazier's head went back but the champion continued to move forward, swinging. Snap, snap.

Midway through the first round, Foreman caught the champion flush on his bearded chin with a thundering uppercut. Frazier crumpled to the floor but bounced up, taking the regulation eight-count. Frazier hung on gamely but moments later, a pair of thudding rights dropped him a second time. Before the end of the round, a third smashing blow sent Frazier spinning underneath the bottom strand of red rope. His eyes were glazed and his legs were like jelly when he staggered to his corner at the end of the round.

As the bell for the second round sounded, Frazier came out courageously, throwing left hooks. A crashing right to the jaw sent him to the canvas for the fourth time. Frazier rose unsteadily to his feet and then—boom, boom—two left hooks by Foreman sent the champion reeling to the floor again. Foreman glanced at Frazier's corner and pleaded with Joe's seconds to throw in the towel but there was no response. Frazier rose again and again. Then a fusillade sent him into the ropes and down to the floor. This time Yancey Durham, Frazier's manager, jumped into the ring. The time was 1:35 of the second round. It was all over. There was a new heavyweight champion of the world.

Foreman told members of the press after the fight that he could see that Frazier was badly hurt and he had hoped he wouldn't have to hit him anymore.

"I just kept throwing punches," George said. "I had to do my job. But after the third knockdown in the first round, I looked over at Yancey in Joe's corner and with my eyes begged him to stop it. He wouldn't toss in the towel. The punch that started him on the way to defeat was a right hand to the body early in the opening round. I hit him and saw him wince. A strange expression came over his face. I knew then I could beat him. It was just a matter of time. God told me I would be champion. I knew all the time that I would be some day, and now I want to publicly thank God and all the people who have supported me."

The victory over Frazier brought young Foreman's record to a perfect 37-0, with 34 knockout victims.

While in the hearts of most people George Foreman was now the man of the hour in boxing, it was Muhammad Ali Cassius Clay—who else?—who had to have the last word. He claimed he didn't even bother to stay awake for the Foreman-Frazier match. He said his business manager Gene Kilroy had to wake him up to tell him who won.

"I figured Foreman would win," he said, "although I hoped Frazier would beat him so the rematch he was asking for since 1971 would settle once and for all who is the heavyweight champion of the world. I'm still the biggest draw in the ring. All the world is waiting for me. All the promoters. All the contenders. They have to wait for me. I lost to Joe Frazier for political reasons. I lost because I'm a Muslim, because I refused to go to Vietnam. But I'll still be around when both Frazier and Foreman are gone. The cream always comes to the top, so I'm still on top. They can take my title, they can take the Frazier fight from me, but I'll be back and then they'll see a different Ali."

Joe Frazier was much more humble in defeat than Clay. In April of 1973 he fought an eight-round exhibition in Seattle against *four* opponents—two rounds per man—and during his stay in the Pacific Northwest he told Earl Luebker, Sports Editor-columnist of the *Tacoma News Tribune*, that he felt Foreman would be a "good champion."

Frazier told Luebker, "I want to get George in the ring again and get the title back where it belongs. I'm in good shape. I've been train-

All in a night's work. George Foreman becomes the 24th fully recognized heavyweight champion in history as the referee stops the fight in the second round of the Joe Frazier bout at Kingston, Jamaica, January 22, 1973.

ing and backing away from the table. I thought I was ready when I fought Foreman the first time, but things didn't work out that way. I can't change my style that much, but the next time I fight George I'm going to carry my hands higher and put a guard around my chin."

Frazier made it no secret that he was not a charter member of the Cassius Clay Fan Club.

"I'll keep calling him Clay," Joe said. "I have a little trouble pronouncing his other name. We just don't get along anymore. I remember the first time I fought him. He hit me four or five times in one flurry, and then said, 'Don't you know that I'm God?' Then I hit him a couple of times, and said, 'God, don't you know you're in the wrong place tonight?' "

"God" was also in the wrong place on the night of March 31, 1973. On that evening in San Diego, a relatively unknown ex-Marine, Ken Norton, won a 12-round split decision over Muhammad Ali Cassius Marcellus Clay.

Several days after his defeat, Muhammad held a news conference back at the Hotel Roosevelt in New York. He was forced to speak through clenched teeth—a habit that developed when Norton broke his jaw and doctors had to wire his jaw shut.

"It's a warning from God," Ali said, pointing to his fractured face. "I neglected my God during training and paid the price."

The two fighters fought again the following September 10th. This time the 31-year-old former champion tended to business. He trained down to 212 pounds and looked trim. But he also looked old, and he needed all the strength and guile he could muster up to win a 12-round split decision over Norton. The fight was so close that had Norton won the 12th round, he would have won the match.

"If I had lost," Muhammad said afterward, "the era of Ali in boxing would have ended. This victory saved me from oblivion. If you looked at movies of my early fights, you would see I haven't slowed very much. I have made my comeback. I would like to fight Frazier next."

He got his wish.

One month later, Muhammad and Smokin' Joe Frazier, who had decisioned European champion Joe Bugner in 12 rounds in London, on July 2nd, signed for a January, 1974, rematch.

And everybody knows how that one came out.

LEGENDARY PROMOTERS

25. Sunny Jim Coffroth

THE golden days in California, short-lived though they were, still thrive in the memories of ringworms.

That halcyon era had its roots in the gladiatorial mayhem of 1891 when James J. Corbett and Peter Jackson fought 61 rounds at the California Athletic Club. In those days, prize fighting was illegal in the state of California and ring battles were fought with bare knuckles or skin-tight gloves on barges anchored in midstream or in equally inaccessible places.

The California Athletic Club gave boxing its first real start toward respectability in the state.

California had two outstanding heavyweights, Jim Corbett and Joe Cheynski. The latter was the first Jewish-American to bid for ring honors as a heavyweight. Gentleman Jim and Cheynski carried on an intense rivalry and their battles focused interest on ring affairs in the Far West.

When Bob Fitzsimmons came on the scene, New Orleans came forward with offers of huge purses and the play was taken away from California. But when Fitz knocked out Jem Hall in New Orleans in 1893, winner-take-all of a $40,000 purse, the promoters only paid part of the guarantee. Once again California stepped into the spotlight—but when New York passed the Horton Law legalizing prize fighting, the money matches shifted, this time to the East.

The gambling fraternity wasted no time getting a stake in New York boxing. The climax came when Corbett knocked out Kid McCoy in five rounds, August 30, 1900. The fight was such an obvious fake that the Horton Law was rescinded and boxing in New York was finished.

Chicago was next. The Windy City had been making determined bids for name fighters. Although contests were limited to six rounds, the bouts were drawing well and the short distance appealed to fighters who had been going 20 and 25 rounds in other cities.

The Chicago Boxing Story was virtually a replica of what had happened in New York, however. The poorly-advised Joe Gans was knocked out by Terry McGovern in the second round, December 13, 1900. The match was such a flagrant "tank job" that Chicago officials barred boxing of any sort for many years.

With New Orleans, New York and Chicago in the throes of a pugilistic embargo, California was ready for a rebirth of boxing.

San Francisco, at this time, was ruled by a political czar named Abe Ruef. He was very powerful and influential. Most of the seats of city government were held by his friends.

Holding down a clerkship in the Surrogate's Court was an alert twenty-seven-year-old named James J. Coffroth. Ruef liked the young man. One day the czar asked him, "Jim, is there any particular field you are interested in?" Without hesitation the young man replied, "I'd like a permit to promote boxing matches." The wish was granted.

Coffroth took a lease on the Mechanics Pavilion, largest in San Francisco with 20,000 seats on a square block of floor space, and set out to get the big names in New York.

One of the first persons Coffroth contacted in New York was Big Jim Kennedy, the outstanding fight promoter of the day. This was typical of Coffroth. His strategy always was to go straight to the man at the top, omitting the endless sifting of underlings. Tex Rickard, who was to come along later, used a similar procedure.

Kennedy agreed to come in as Coffroth's partner. It was an ideal alliance and presaged the golden glove days in California. With Big Jim as his business sidekick, Sunshine Jim Coffroth (he got the nickname because of his uncanny luck with the weather) took over the fight game in San Francisco.

Sunny Jim had great business acumen and was instinctively a gambler. He sold himself and his promotions by offering the very best. The happy combination of big money, Coffroth's splendid reputation and the outlawing of boxing in other major cities attracted the best talent to California.

Kennedy died three years later and Coffroth took over alone.

Sunny Jim's forte was publicity. He held daily press conferences, graphically describing the abilities and idiosyncracies of his fighters. The sports writers ate it up, giving Coffroth plenty of space. Jim seldom had a losing show.

Sunny Jim held his press meetings at the Indoor Yacht Club, located in the heart of San Francisco, within only a few blocks of all newspaper offices. He saw to it that there was always plenty to eat, drink and smoke, and colorfully clad Hawaiians to do the serving. He had the grand manner and his hospitality was superb.

Coffroth was liberal almost to a fault. He handed out complimentary tickets with abandon. When this was called to his attention by a sports writer, Jim replied, "I know you'd not ask for them if you didn't need them. I know I'm going to give them to you anyway, so why not give them with a smile and have your good will?"

Terrible Terry McGovern helped Coffroth to get off to a flying start in 1901 by going West to knock out Oscar Gardner and Aurelie Herrera, the latter in an exciting battle in which the Brooklyn Machine Gun was on his knees in an early round.

Coffroth promoted a heavyweight championship fight between Jim Jeffries and Gus Ruhlin in his first year. That was on November 15, 1901, and Jeff won by a knockout in the fifth round. The following year Jeff fought for Sunny Jim again and knocked out Bob Fitzsimmons. Then, on August 14, 1903, Coffroth matched Jeff and Corbett and grossed $63,340, a new high for boxing.

One of Coffroth's greatest promotions was the second fight between Battling Nelson and Jimmy Britt. Britt had defeated Nelson in 20 rounds, December 20, 1904, in San Francisco, and Sunny Jim offered a purse of $20,000 (this for two lightweights, neither of them a champion) to them to meet outdoors in a return match, September 9, 1905. The bout was signed and Jim set about building a special outdoor arena. Coffroth wanted to make it a fight to the finish, but that wouldn't work because the law required a specific number of rounds. He asked Billy Roche, famous referee and manager, how far he thought the men could go. Roche felt that the limit was 45 rounds—thus the 45-round game was born.

Sunny Jim pulled out all the stops. He plastered the billboards of San Francisco with posters, an unprecedented type of advertising for prize fighting. Hotel lobbies and prominent windows displayed life-size cutouts of the combatants. Nothing was spared in the ballyhoo campaign and the fans flocked in. Nelson then flattened Britt in the 18th round.

Coffroth was most affable and had numerous friends, but he could be tough when annoyed. It was the gruff, bellowing tactics of Billy Nolan, manager of Nelson, that made him explode. Some claim this caused the Nelson-Gans fight to be transplanted to Goldfield, Nevada, though the real reason was that San Francisco hadn't yet recovered from the terrible earthquake of 1906. A contributing factor was that an unknown by the name of Tex Rickard, a front man for the Goldfield production, had offered Nelson a personal guarantee of $20,000. Nolan had demanded $10,000 from Coffroth when the pair had fallen out. This match started Rickard as a fight promoter.

Real opposition to Coffroth came after the earthquake shook the boxing game apart in San Francisco and the city began to rebuild. A Los Angeles laundry owner named Tom McCarey, whose son Leo was to later scale the Hollywood heights as a motion picture director, stepped into the boxing picture. Uncle Tom McCarey took over an arena in Vernon, a suburb seven miles from Los Angeles, since prize fighting was banned in the city proper. The arena had been built by a syndicate headed by Baron Long, owner of the Los Angeles Biltmore Hotel. It was a failure until McCarey took charge and began to bring in big-name fighters and important matches. He staged them well, did a thoroughly capable publicity job.

Abe Ruef, in the meantime, had been ousted from San Francisco and sent to prison. While Coffroth had little to do with Ruef's political machinations, he was put out with the rest. A city commission granted permits to three supporters of the new regime and Sunny Jim was barred from promoting within the city limits. So Coffroth took his fights to Colma, in San Mateo County, only a hop-skip-and-a-jump from San Francisco. The fighters remained loyal to him, so did the clientele, and boxing suddenly found itself booming on two fronts–Coffroth's and McCarey's.

Historians have criticized Sunny Jim for his role in luring Jim Jeffries out of a six-year retirement to be led to the slaughter in Reno in 1910 by Jack Johnson. Coffroth sent Sam Berger and Jack Gleason to Jeffries to persuade him into making a comeback. Sealed bids were then filed by promoters who wanted the bout. Coffroth's was $100,000, nearly $40,000 more than the Jeffries-Corbett fight had grossed. It was a stunning blow when the match went to Rickard with a bid of $101,000. There were some who suspected the bids had been fixed. The fight drew $270,775. Rickard and Gleason cleaned up $120,215. It was the only serious mistake that Coffroth ever made. In the end he was happy to have had nothing to do with a match that set boxing back many years.

Every topnotch fighter fought for him over a period of 14 years, from Jeffries to Willie Ritchie, either in San Francisco or just outside it when he moved to Colma and Daly City.

Coffroth, first of the great promoters, was a man of many firsts:

First to promote the 45-round fight.

First to put up a $20,000 purse–for the second Nelson-Britt fight. It gave Rickard and the Goldfield gamblers the idea for the $30,000 purse for Nelson and Gans.

First to have made successful motion pictures of a fight. He collected his first major money, $135,000, as his share of the film of the second Nelson-Britt bout.

First to sell ringside seats for as much as $20–for the mismatch that brought out Stanley Ketchel and Jack Johnson at Colma on October 16, 1909.

First to put referees in the ring dressed in tuxedos. English referees served in evening clothes outside the ring, but Coffroth put his men right in with the fighters. Such referees as Billy Roche, Eddie Graney and Jack Welch became widely known by working in Coffroth bouts.

First promoter to properly advertise a prize fight.

Sunshine Jim Coffroth was truly a man of vision who was not afraid to take a chance.

He gave boxing its greatest boost at a time when the game needed it most.

26. Tex Rickard

As the fight game grew in the early 1900s, it was only natural that a great promoter would come along. Sunny Jim Coffroth had given the sport its first real promotional impetus, but the king of them all was George Lewis Rickard, a flamboyant, mercurial little man who broke into boxing quite by accident.

Tex Rickard was raised and cultivated in the topsoil of western Texas during the pioneer days. He got his business start in Nome, Alaska, operating the town's biggest and wildest gambling house. He moved his headquarters to Goldfield, Nevada, by 1906.

Rickard soon became the No. 1 citizen of Goldfield by bidding for the finish fight between Bat Nelson and Joe Gans. The real motive behind the bid, however, was to get an attraction that would bring suckers to town, peddle them mining stock and lead them to the gaming rooms. Tex was named to run the show.

Of course, the promotion was a fantastic success, and Rickard was on his way.

People thought Tex was crazy when he dashed to New York and, backed by Montana mining tycoons, bid $101,000 for the Jeffries-Johnson bout, this one to be staged in San Francisco. He offered Jeff and Li'l Arthur $10,000 bonuses.

The bout was the brainchild of San Francisco's Jack Gleason, who formed a partnership with Tex. The pair ran into trouble immediately after winning the bid for the match. They ran short of cash, having apparently over-bid their hand.

"We've got to win our backers' confidence," said Rickard.

He then announced publicly that all advance ticket money would be deposited in a leading San Francisco bank. The bank in turn would send along to the ticket holder a stub of his deposit showing the seat location. Tops at ringside was $60.

Details were moving smoothly and a sellout house was in prospect when Governor Gillette of California suddenly banned the fight, explaining he didn't like the setup. Tex and Gleason were in real trouble. They faced public disgrace and possible imprisonment.

But Rickard found a way out. Hollywood movie magnates came to the rescue and purchased the film rights for $101,000. Those holding ducats were paid off and the match was transferred from San Francisco to Reno, Nevada.

Rickard poured on the publicity when the papers were signed. Though crude, self-made and lacking polish and finesse, he was a masterful showman instinctively. He firmly believed that money made money. He had Jeffries and Johnson photographed in New York's old Cadillac Hotel feasting their eyes on the $20,000 they received in bonuses, nicely spread out in $20 gold pieces. (Later Rickard was to hit a new high in this type of ballyhoo when he handed Gene Tunney a widely pictured check for a million dollars.)

Rickard also recognized the value of gambling concessions in Reno, and made a deal with Ole Elliott, proprietor of one of the town's most flourishing gambling dens. The move paid off beyond Rickard's wildest dreams. He devoted more time to the gambling rooms than to the Jeffries-Johnson fight.

When the movie company chipped in for the movie rights, it was agreed that the fee would be sliced three ways—between Jeffries, Johnson and the promoters. Johnson had additional ideas, however.

"We'll cut the profits three ways," Jack said, "but there'll only be two of us dividing the movie money—Jeff and I! You three white fellows might outvote me."

Rickard and Gleason received full shares of the gate receipts, but were cut out of the picture revenue.

It was Rickard's first major setback.

Tex had no equal at raising money. He never had much of his own, yet managed to somehow turn up with scads. The adventurous little Texan made his pile in that gloriously insane era after the First World War, when greenbacks blew like dust, the market boomed, speaks blossomed, and the national desire seemed to be to have one helluva good time.

"Hello, sucker," Tex sang—and people came running on the double.

Rickard's move to New York and his incredible success was largely due to Dempsey. The Manassa Mauler drew $8,600,000 in five fights promoted by Rickard. Tex never "seed" anything like it—all the finest people came to his shows. At old Madison Square Garden, he put the politicians in their places, cleaned the ringside of hoodlums and enticed high society to come in. The result was a superior level of respectability for boxing.

Tex paid his fighters fantastic purses and loved doing it. The money only poured right back into the boxoffice. He doted on "productions," printed huge tickets, embossed and gold-backed.

"Get the finest people and give 'em the best," was his credo.

Rickard's strategy precluded bothering with underlings. When he promoted a fight he went straight to the top–to the governor, the mayor, leading merchants, and newspaper publishers. Once they had pledged their cooperation, he moved in and went to work with all 16-inch guns blazing.

It was Rickard's gambling philosophy that when you have a hunch, back it with everything you own. In 1921, he decided to let all the chips ride on Dempsey and a public going sports-mad. In his New York hotel suite, he frightened his associates with the size of his thinking.

"I'm gonna stage a heavyweight champeenship fight that'll make the Dempsey-Willard deal look like nickels and dimes," he said blandly.

Rickard was a man with a rare gift for selling his dreams, and he reached outside the sports world into the highest theatrical circles for his backing–William A. Brady and C. B. Cochrane, of London. Then this master of the dream-up and steam-up, with his native understanding of mass psychology, cast around for a challenger of Dempsey. The French war hero, Georges Carpentier, was a logical choice.

Carpentier and his manager, Francois Descamps, had few illusions when they went in to make their deal with Rickard. After what Dempsey had done to Willard, it seemed as if Carpentier was being asked to take greater chances than when he had gone into combat against the Boche. The only thing that could lure him into such a match was the promise of more money than any fighter ever before had received, $200,000.

Doc Kearns, Dempsey's canny mouthpiece, said the champion was entitled to at least $100,000 more than the challenger. Not even 40 percent of the gate would satisfy the astute Doc.

Rickard, the plunger, was really over his head this time.

With two such unprecedented guarantees made before a single ticket was sold, there wasn't a house big enough for the kind of dough Tex needed to get off this half-million-dollar hook. So the enormous bubble grew and grew. Rickard, it was decided, would build an arena especially for the occasion, with the largest seating capacity in the world–100,000 seats!

Brady and Cochrane needed no psychiatrist to tell them they had involved themselves with a madman when Tex broke ground for his arena at Boyle's Thirty Acres in Jersey City. No match in boxing history had drawn more than $500,000, but Tex was sleep-walking into one that would need nearly a million dollars to break even. They were sensible showmen, not wild-eyed gamblers. They picked up their money and went home.

At this dark hour, in walked Mike Jacobs, destined to succeed Rickard as boxing's leading promoter. In a rare moment of discouragement, Tex said, "Don't bother me, there's not gonna be a fight."

"No fight!" exclaimed Mike. "There's gotta be a fight. This is the biggest thing that ever hit the fight business. It's a million easy."

"Yeah, I know," admitted the despondent Rickard, "but I wish you could convince my backers."

Jacobs asked, "Well, what do we need those guys for?"

"Who else can keep this thing going?" Tex wanted to know. "If I don't get twenty thousand to the contractor by this afternoon I've got no arena. That's just the beginning of our woes."

"I'll be back in an hour," Mike said.

When Jacobs returned he pulled out $20,000 in cash.

"Go pay the bum," he said. "This is an advance on the first five rows of ringside."

Then Uncle Mike went out to do a selling job among his fellow ticket speculators. He convinced eight brokers to put up $25,000 apiece in return for choice sections of the house, and Tex was saved.

Rickard's million-dollar daydream, which had frightened off the two outstanding showmen of the day, exceeded Tex's most lavish hunch. Even the calculating Doc Kearns missed up on this one, for his $300,000 guarantee didn't look quite so large when compared with the $720,000 Dempsey might have earned had he accepted the proffered 40 percent of the gate.

The Dempsey-Carpentier extravaganza was further in the way of evidence that the unpredictable Rickard never allowed setbacks to deter him.

It was Richard F. Hoyt of Wall Street who financed the old Madison Square Garden for Rickard. The fast-talking Tex simply dropped into Hoyt's office and the deal was closed in 15 minutes.

When Tex Rickard died, his body lay in state at the Garden as thousands passed his bier to pay last respects. He must have been nailed in the coffin. Otherwise, he would have been spinning with that mob coming in on the cuff.

27. Mike Jacobs

THE tallest Horatio Alger tale is mild stuff alongside the story of Mike Jacobs, absolute czar of boxing from 1937 to '47.

Perhaps no ring promoter in history had a tighter monopoly on the sport than the man who rose from the seamiest slums of Manhattan to multi-millionaire.

While it is probably true that no one else ever made such huge profits as Jacobs from boxing, it is also true that no promoter ever ran boxing as well. Look at the record:

In the decade following 1937, Jacobs staged 61 championship fights. He promoted upward of 1,500 boxing programs, grossed more than $10,000,000 with Joe Louis alone, staged virtually 70 percent of all the matches below the heavyweight division that grossed more than $100,000. He attracted nearly half a million people to 34 Madison Square Garden shows in a single year, and grossed in that same year $5,500,000. Over a period of 15 years, Jacobs sold tickets to approximately 10,000,000 people, a total of something like $30,000,000.

As a ticket seller, Jacobs had no peer.

"Put a ticket in his hand," remarked a long-time associate, "and Mike could squeeze three times as much money out of it as anybody else."

No one chased a buck quite as hard as Jacobs.

He once admitted, "If I made a hundred this morning, I'd be hustlin' for a quarter this afternoon. I can't help it."

Mike was a loner. He had few friends. He played all his cards close to his chest. But he knew how to fill a house. And the more money he made for himself, the more he made for his fighters. Once he said a fighter had a deal, it was like money in the bank. The fighter didn't need a contract.

Jacobs cornered the market of fighting flesh by advancing thousands of dollars to big-namers. Once they were in to him for $10,000 or $15,000, they had to fight for him in order to get off the hook.

Uncle Mike, the squire of "Jacobs Beach," first scaled the heights as the box-office man for Tex Rickard. As a ballyhoo man and ticket seller, Mike's ingenuity amounted to genius.

Jacobs never missed an opportunity to pick up a spare buck. Before the First World War, he made a bundle off Caruso one season, did all right with Emmeline Pankhurst, the suffragette, and even had a Fifth Avenue fashion show going for him—with successful side forays into the stock market and real estate.

Uncle Mike's chief nemesis was Harry Grayson, veteran sports editor of NEA Service, Inc., the Scripps-Howard feature service. They battled for years. In Grayson, Uncle Mike met his match.

Unlike One-Eye Connolly, who did a highly publicized single for years, Grayson, an adroit gatecrasher also, invaded the Garden on the night of one of Jacobs' shows with a platoon of rabid but ticketless associates. He and his nondescript band had met only the stiffest opposition in the past and, familiar with Mike's reputation, devised their most ingenious method of infiltration—Operation Scatter.

The platoon formed in single file with Grayson at the end of the line. They marched smartly through the gate, pointing back to Grayson as the holder of the tickets. Once inside, the group executed Operation Scatter, losing themselves among the crowd. Grayson presented a single ticket to the attendant.

Since the ticket-taker had the temerity to inquire about the advance guard, Grayson coldly informed him that "I never saw them bums in my life."

Jacobs blew his top when he heard about it, installed extra guards on duty to block Grayson at the next fight. Grayson arrived at the Garden with virtually the entire force of the NEA composing room in tow. Operation Scatter failed, and Grayson indignantly entered the arena to search for Promoter Jacobs. He found him sitting behind the working press seats at the ringside.

"Come out in the lobby and meet my friends," Grayson said brightly. Jacobs looked at him coldly.

"How many?" he asked.

Grayson informed him that there might be as many as 15. "You've got a helluva nerve," snapped Jacobs, as they moved toward the lobby.

"And *you* have no nerve," said Grayson. "I suppose you just inherited this joint, yuh bum."

Uncle Mike looked incredulously at the Grayson entourage, still nicely formed in a single line despite the bedlam in the lobby. Although buffeted by the crowd, Grayson escorted Jacobs down the line like a guest speaker at a Kiwanis luncheon. "This is Pete, the foreman

...Tommy, the press man...Irish, the linotyper." Jacobs grew visibly shaken as the introductions continued. The last man, a stout linotype operator from Brooklyn, finally had his turn. "And this is Eddie, the printer," announced Grayson.

Eddie blinked, thrust out his hand and said: "I didn't get yer name, Mac."

Jacobs' shoulders sagged.

"Bring the stiffs in," he said to Grayson.

Michael Strauss Jacobs was born at 651 Washington Street, New York City, March 10, 1880. In the next half century he rang the bell in at least three different fields—excursion-boat concessions, ticket speculation and the beak-busting business.

Jacobs had an amazing capacity for success. With no schooling, no knowledge of a trade, no one to help him, he hustled himself a $1,000 stake doing odd jobs before he was sixteen years old. After sixteen he was never broke again.

Max Baer was the only fighter who could bamboozle and charm the sulk out of Uncle Mike. Once, early in his career, Baer swaggered into Mike's inner sanctum, lifted him out of the chair and, with a flourish, seated himself where none but the Jacobs posterior had ever rested. Max waved a hand at Uncle Mike and put his feet on the desk.

"You're looking at the man who's going to save the fight game!" he declared.

From memory—having once done it many years before—the cantankerous Jacobs grinned.

Some ringworms called Uncle Mike greedy, nicknamed him Monopoly Mike, and perhaps they were right. Going after the buck, he pulled out all the stops. The little wheels in his brain never stopped whirring. He was the first one to sell a boxing series to a radio sponsor (1937), the first to cash in on television (1944).

In 1942, with everybody going off to war, Mike thought it would be a great idea if his pet tiger, Billy Conn, joined the Navy. "But I want to join the Army," Billy said.

"Join the Navy," Mike insisted.

"But why should I join the Navy?" Billy asked.

" 'Cause Louis joined the Army," Mike said. "He done like I told him he should." Mike was a schemer. "See?" he said. "Louis in the Army, you in the Navy. It looks very good. When the war is over, maybe before, we have another fight. You get even with Louis. The champion of the Army and the champion of the Navy."

Billy was unimpressed.

"What difference does it make?" he said. "Who wants to be in the Navy? Suppose I should get seasick?"

"Join the Navy," Mike said. Mike was Billy's meal-ticket.

"All right," he agreed finally. "Where do I go to sign up?"

Mike told him and he started for the door. Two hours later, Billy was back in Jacobs's office. "I joined the Army," he announced. Mike leaped from his chair like he'd been stuck by a fork. "What!" he shouted. "The Army! I said the Navy! Louis is in the *Army!*"

"So am I now," Billy said. Mike sat down. He closed his eyes, suppressing a strong desire to strangle Conn. Then: "Go ahead," he said, "tell me what happened."

Billy said he had carried out Mike's instructions. He went down to the Navy, there were a lot of guys milling around and he didn't know which way to go. There was an old guy there and he was hollering at everybody. He was wearing a sailor suit—well, not exactly a sailor suit, Billy said. "He's got on a uniform," Billy explained. "He's got a cap on and a lot of gold stripes on his sleeves. I go up to him and ask him which way do you go to join the Navy and he starts yelling at me."

"Get over there!" he roared at Billy. "Get in that line over there!"

Billy didn't like this big bloke roaring at him like a lion. He wanted to bust him in the mouth but he didn't because he was an old geezer. Instead, he asked, "Are you in the Navy?"

The old salt was fit to be tied. Was *he* in the Navy?

"All right," Billy said to him, "on account of you're in the Navy, I am going to join the Army because I don't like bums like you and if you are my age, I will put the slug on you."

"So," Billy told Uncle Mike, "that's how I come to join the Army."

Uncle Mike put his face in his hands and had a good cry.

Promoter Jacobs was charged by some experts with being bad for boxing. Others, however, lined up on his side. Red Smith once wrote of him, "If anyone in the world has run fights on the level, Mike has."

Uncle Mike Jacobs died of a heart attack in 1952.

At the funeral, one irreverent oldtimer gazed at Uncle Mike's bier and said, "If he gets to Heaven, 10 to 1 he finagles the choice tickets from St. Peter and makes a bundle scalping 'em outside the pearly gates."

Rest in peace.

APPENDICES

HEAVYWEIGHT CHAMPIONSHIP RECORDS

Name	Nationality	Fighting years	Total bouts	Knockouts	Won on decision	Lost on decision	Draws	Won on foul	Lost on foul	No. of times knocked out	No-decision bouts	No contest	Year born	Year died
John L. Sullivan	USA	1878-05	75	16	15	0	3	0	0	1	40	0	1858	1918
James J. Corbett	USA	1886-03	33	9	11	1	6	0	1	3	2	0	1866	1933
*Bob Fitzsimmons	USA	1889-14	41	23	5	0	1	0	1	6	5	0	1862	1917
Jim Jeffries	USA	1896-10	23	16	4	0	2	0	0	1	0	0	1875	1953
Tommy Burns	Can.	1900-20	60	36	10	4	8	0	0	1	1	0	1881	1955
Jack Johnson	USA	1897-28	113	44	30	1	14	4	1	5	14	0	1878	1946
Jess Willard	USA	1911-23	36	20	4	3	1	0	1	2	5	0	1881	1968
Jack Dempsey	USA	1914-40	81	49	10	6	8	1	0	1	6	0	1895	–
Gene Tunney	USA	1915-28	76	41	14	1	1	1	0	0	17	1	1898	–
Max Schmeling	Ger.	1924-48	71	39	14	5	5	3	0	5	0	0	1905	–
Jack Sharkey	USA	1924-36	55	15	20	8	3	3	1	4	1	0	1902	–
Primo Carnera	Italy	1928-45	99	66	18	5	0	2	1	6	0	1	1906	1967
Max Baer	USA	1929-41	79	50	15	9	0	0	1	3	1	0	1909	1959
Jim Braddock	USA	1926-38	85	26	25	20	3	0	0	2	7	2	1905	–
Joe Louis	USA	1934-51	71	54	13	1	0	1	0	2	0	0	1914	–
Ezzard Charles	USA	1937-59	122	58	38	17	1	0	1	7	0	0	1921	–
Jersey Joe Walcott	USA	1930-53	67	30	18	11	1	1	0	6	0	0	1914	–
Rocky Marciano	USA	1947-55	49	43	6	0	0	0	0	0	0	0	1923	1969
Floyd Patterson	USA	1952-	(still fighting)										1935	–
Ingemar Johansson	Swed.	1952-63	28	17	8	0	0	1	0	2	0	0	1932	–
Floyd Patterson	USA	1952-	(regained title from Johansson, still fighting)										1935	–
Sonny Liston	USA	1953-70	54	39	11	1	0	0	0	3	0	0	1932	1971
Cassius Clay	USA	1960-	(still fighting)										1942	–
Joe Frazier	USA	1965-	(still fighting)										1944	–
George Foreman	USA	1969-	(still fighting)										1949	–

Note: Records do not include exhibition bouts.

**Born at Helston, Cornwall, England, but became U.S. citizen.*

Heavyweight Title Bouts

1889–July 8–John L. Sullivan beat Jake Kilrain, 75 rounds. Richburg, Miss. (Last championship bare-knuckle bout.)

*1892–Sept. 7–James J. Corbett defeated John L. Sullivan, 21 rounds, New Orleans. (Used big gloves.)

1894–Jan. 25–James J. Corbett knocked out Charley Mitchell, 3 rounds, Jacksonville, Fla.

*1897–March 17–Bob Fitzsimmons defeated James J. Corbett, 14 rounds, Carson City, Nev.

*1899–June 9–James J. Jeffries beat Bob Fitzsimmons, 11 rounds, Coney Island, N. Y.

1899–Nov. 3–James J. Jeffries beat Tom Sharkey, 25 rounds, Coney Island, N. Y.

1900–May 11–James J. Jeffries knocked out James J. Corbett, 23 rounds, Coney Island, N. Y.

1902–July 25–James J. Jeffries knocked out Bob Fitzsimmons, 8 rounds, San Francisco.

1903–Aug. 14–James J. Jeffries knocked out James J. Corbett, 10 rounds, San Francisco.

1904–Aug. 26–James J. Jeffries knocked out Jack Monroe, 2 rounds, San Francisco.

*1905–James J. Jeffries retired. July 3–Marvin Hart knocked out Jack Root, 12 rounds, Reno, Nev. Jeffries refereed and presented the title to the victor. Jack O'Brien also claimed the title.

*1906–Feb. 23–Tommy Burns defeated Marvin Hart, 20 rounds, Los Angeles.

1906–Nov. 28–Jack O'Brien and Tommy Burns, 20 rounds, draw, Los Angeles.

1907–May 8–Tommy Burns defeated Jack O'Brien, 20 rounds, Los Angeles.

1907–July 4–Tommy Burns knocked out Bill Squires, 1 round, Colma, Cal.

1907–Dec. 2–Tommy Burns knocked out Gunner Moir, 10 rounds, London.

1908–Feb. 10–Tommy Burns knocked out Jack Palmer, 4 rounds, London.

1908–March 17–Tommy Burns knocked out Jem Roche, 1 round, Dublin.

1908–April 18–Tommy Burns knocked out Jewey Smith, 5 rounds, Paris

1908–June 13–Tommy Burns knocked out Bill Squires, 8 rounds, Paris.

1908–Aug. 24–Tommy Burns knocked out Bill Squires, 13 rounds, Sydney, New South Wales.

1908–Sept. 2–Tommy Burns knocked out Bill Lang, 2 rounds, Melbourne, Australia.

*1908–Dec. 26–Jack Johnson stopped Tommy Burns, 14 rounds, Sydney, Australia. Police halted contest.

1909–May 19–Jack Johnson and Jack O'Brien, 6 rounds, draw, Philadelphia.

1909–June 30–Jack Johnson and Tony Ross, 6 rounds, draw, Pittsburgh.

1909–Sept. 9–Jack Johnson and Al Kaufman, 10 rounds, no decision, San Francisco.

1909–Oct. 16–Jack Johnson knocked out Stanley Ketchell, 12 rounds, Colma, Cal.

1910–July 4–Jack Johnson knocked out Jim Jeffries, 15 rounds, Reno, Nev. (Jeffries came back from retirement.)
1912–July 4–Jack Johnson won on points from Jim Flynn, 9 rounds, Las Vegas, N. M. (Contest stopped by police.)
1913–Nov. 28–Jack Johnson knocked out Andre Spaul, 2 rounds, Paris.
1913–Dec. 9–Jack Johnson and Jim Johnson, 10 rounds, draw, Paris.
1914–June 27–Jack Johnson won from Frank Moran, 20 rounds, Paris.
*1915–April 5–Jess Willard knocked out Jack Johnson, 26 rounds, Havana, Cuba.
1916–March 25–Jess Willard and Frank Moran, 10 rounds (no decision), New York City
*1919–July 4–Jack Dempsey knocked out Jess Willard, Toledo, O. (Willard failed to answer bell for fourth round.)
1920–Sept. 6–Jack Dempsey knocked out Billy Miske, 3 rounds, Benton Harbor, Mich.
1920–Dec. 14–Jack Dempsey knocked out Bill Brennan, 12 rounds, New York City.
1921–July 2–Jack Dempsey knocked out Georges Carpentier, 4 rounds, Boyle's Thirty Acres, Jersey City, N. J.
1923–July 4–Jack Dempsey won on points from Tom Gibbons, 15 rounds, Shelby, Mont.
1923–Sept. 14–Jack Dempsey knocked out Luis Firpo, 2 rounds, New York City.
*1926–Sept. 23–Gene Tunney beat Jack Dempsey, 10 rounds, decision, Philadelphia.
1927–Sept. 22–Gene Tunney beat Jack Dempsey, 10 rounds, decision, Chicago.
1928–July 26–Gene Tunney knocked out Tom Heeney, 11 rounds, Yankee Stadium, New York; soon afterward he announced his retirement.
*1930–June 12–Max Schmeling of Germany defeated Jack Sharkey in fourth round when Sharkey fouled Schmeling in a bout which was generally considered to have resulted in the election of a successor to Gene Tunney, New York City.
1931–July 3–Max Schmeling knocked out W. L. Stribling, another contender for the title, in 15 rounds in Cleveland.
*1932–June 21–Jack Sharkey defeated Max Schmeling, 15 rounds, decision, New York City.
*1933–June 29–Primo Carnera knocked out Jack Sharkey, six rounds, New York City.
1933–Oct. 22–Primo Carnera defeated Paulino Uzcudun, heavyweight challenger, 15 rounds, in Rome.
1934–March 1–Primo Carnera defeated Tommy Loughran in 15 rounds in Miami.
*1934–June 14–Max Baer knocked out Primo Carnera, 11 rounds, New York City.
*1935–June 13–James J. Braddock defeated Max Baer, 15 rounds, New York City. (Judges' decision.)
*1937–June 22–Joe Louis knocked out James J. Braddock, 8 rounds, Chicago.
1937–Aug. 30–Joe Louis defeated Tommy Farr, 15 rounds, decision, New York City.
1938–Feb. 23–Joe Louis knocked out Nathan Mann, 3 rounds, New York City.
1938–April 1–Joe Louis knocked out Harry Thomas, 5 rounds, New York City.
1938–June 22–Joe Louis knocked out Max Schmeling, 1 round, New York City.
1939–Jan. 25–Joe Louis knocked out John H. Lewis, 1 round, New York City.
1939–April 17–Joe Louis knocked out Jack Roper, 1 round, Los Angeles.
1939–June 28–Joe Louis knocked out Tony Galento, 4 rounds, New York City.
1939–Sept. 20–Joe Louis knocked out Bob Pastor, 11 rounds, Detroit.
1940–Feb. 9–Joe Louis defeated Arturo Godoy, 15 rounds, decision, New York City.
1940–March 29–Joe Louis knocked out Johnny Paychek, 2 rounds, New York City.
1940–June 20–Joe Louis knocked out Arturo Godoy, 8 rounds, New York City.
1940–Dec. 16–Joe Louis knocked out Al McCoy, 6 rounds, Boston.
1941–Jan. 31–Joe Louis knocked out Red Burman, 5 rounds, New York City.
1941–Feb. 17–Joe Louis knocked out Gus Dorazio, 2 rounds, Philadelphia.
1941–March 21–Joe Louis knocked out Abe Simon, 13 rounds, Detroit.
1941–April 8–Joe Louis knocked out Tony Musto, 9 rounds, St. Louis.
1941–May 23–Joe Louis beat Buddy Baer, 7 rounds, Washington, D. C., on a disqualification.

1941–June 18–Joe Louis knocked out Billy Conn, 13 rounds, New York City.
1941–Sept. 29–Joe Louis knocked out Lou Nova, 6 rounds, New York City.
1942–Jan. 9–Joe Louis knocked out Buddy Baer, 1 round, New York City.
1942–March 27–Joe Louis knocked out Abe Simon, 6 rounds, New York City.
1946–June 19–Joe Louis knocked out Billy Conn, 8 rounds, New York City.
1946–Sept. 18–Joe Louis knocked out Tami Mauriello, 1 round, New York City.
1947–Dec. 5–Joe Louis defeated Joe Walcott in a 15-round bout by a split decision, New York City.
1948–June 25–Joe Louis knocked out Joe Walcott, 11 rounds, New York City.
*1949–June 22–Following Joe Louis' retirement Ezzard Charles defeated Joe Walcott by a unanimous decision, 15 rounds, Chicago. (NBA recognition only.)
1950–Sept. 27–Ezzard Charles defeated Joe Louis in latter's attempted comeback, 15 rounds, New York City (Universal recognition).
1950–Dec. 5–Ezzard Charles knocked out Nick Barone, 11 rounds, Cincinnati.
1951–Jan. 12–Ezzard Charles knocked out Lee Oma, 10 rounds, New York City.
1951–March 7–Ezzard Charles outpointed Joe Walcott, 15 rounds, Detroit.
1951–May 30–Ezzard Charles outpointed Joey Maxim, light-heavyweight champion and challenger for heavyweight title, 15 rounds, Chicago.
*1951–July 18–Joe Walcott knocked out Ezzard Charles, 7 rounds, Pittsburgh.
1952–June 5–Joe Walcott outpointed Ezzard Charles, 15 rounds, Philadelphia.
*1952–Sept. 23–Rocky Marciano knocked out Joe Walcott, 13 rounds, Philadelphia.
1953–May 15–Rocky Marciano knocked out Joe Walcott, 1 round, Chicago.
1953–Sept. 24–Rocky Marciano knocked out Roland LaStarza, 11 rounds, Polo Grounds, New York.
1954–June 17–Rocky Marciano outpointed Ezzard Charles, 15 rounds, Yankee Stadium, New York.
1954–Sept. 17–Rocky Marciano knocked out Ezzard Charles, 8 rounds, Yankee Stadium, New York.
1955–May 16–Rocky Marciano knocked out Don Cockell, 9 rounds, Kezar Stadium, San Francisco.
1955–Sept. 21–Rocky Marciano knocked out Archie Moore, 9 rounds, Yankee Stadium, New York. Marciano retired undefeated, Apr. 27, 1956.
*1956–Nov. 30–Floyd Patterson, a contender, knocked out Archie Moore, 5 rounds, Chicago, gaining the championship.
1957–July 29–Floyd Patterson knocked out Hurricane Jackson, 10 rounds, Polo Grounds, New York.
1957–Aug. 22–Floyd Patterson knocked out Pete Rademacher, 6 rounds, Seattle.
1958–Aug. 18–Floyd Patterson knocked out Roy Harris, 12 rounds, Los Angeles.
*1959–June 26–Ingemar Johansson, Sweden, knocked out Floyd Patterson, 3 rounds, Yankee Stadium, New York.
*1960–June 20–Floyd Patterson knocked out Ingemar Johansson, 5 rounds, to become first man to regain heavyweight title, New York.
1961–March 13–Floyd Patterson knocked out Ingemar Johansson, 6 rounds, Miami Beach.
1961–Dec. 4–Floyd Patterson knocked out Tom McNeeley, 4 rounds, Toronto, Canada.
*1962–Sept. 25–Sonny Liston knocked out Floyd Patterson, 1 round, in Chicago to become new champion.
1963–July 22–Sonny Liston knocked out Floyd Patterson, Las Vegas, Nev., for second 1st-round KO in a row.
*1964–Feb. 25–Cassius Clay became new champion with TKO, 7 rounds, over Sonny Liston at Miami Beach.
1965–May 25–In return title match, Cassius Clay KO'd Sonny Liston, 1 round, Lewiston, Maine.
1965–Nov. 22–Cassius Clay TKO'd Floyd Patterson, 12 rounds, Las Vegas, Nev.

1966–March 29–Cassius Clay decisioned George Chuvalo, 15 rounds, Toronto.

1966–May 21–Cassius Clay stopped Henry Cooper, 6 rounds, London.

1966–Aug. 6–Cassius Clay knocked out Brian London, 3 rounds, London.

1966–Sept. 10–Cassius Clay knocked out Karl Mildenberger, 12 rounds, Frankfurt, Germany.

1966–Nov. 14–Cassius Clay KO'd Cleveland Williams, 3 rounds, Houston.

1967–Feb. 6–Cassius Clay decisioned Ernie Terrell, 15 rounds, Philadelphia.

1967–March 22–Cassius Clay knocked out Zora Folley, 7 rounds, New York City.

1967–May 9–Cassius Clay kayoed by World Boxing Association. Title taken away from him for refusing to accept Army draft. Clay was banned in all of U.S. and heavyweight title was vacated, thus opening way for elimination tournament to determine successor.

*1970–Feb. 16–Joe Frazier knocked out Jimmy Ellis, 5 rounds, to win the vacant title, New York City.

1970–Nov. 18–Joe Frazier knocked out Bob Foster, 2 rounds, Detroit.

1971–March 8–Joe Frazier decisioned Cassius Clay, 15 rounds, in New York as Cassius tried to become second heavyweight in history to regain crown.

1972–Jan. 15–Joe Frazier knocked out Terry Daniels, 4 rounds, New Orleans.

1972– –Joe Frazier stopped Ron Stander, 4 rounds, Omaha, Neb.

*1973–Jan. 22–George Foreman, a 3½ to 1 underdog, scored a sensational 2nd-round KO over defending champion Joe Frazier, at Kingston, Jamaica.

1973–Sept. 1–George Foreman knocked out Joe "King" Roman at the two-minute mark of the first round in what referee Jay Edson called a "one hundred percent mismatch." The bout was held in Tokyo and was Foreman's first defense of the crown. His end of the purse was $1 million.

1974–Mar. 26-George Foreman TKO'd Ken Norton, 2 rounds, Caracas, Venezuela.

**Title changed hands.*

PHOTO CREDITS

For the photos on the pages indicated, the author would like to thank the following organizations and individuals:

Page 5, UPI; page 13, photographer unknown; pages 23, 27, 31, 33, 36, 38, 41, 43, 48, 52, 63, 66, UPI; page 71, photographer unknown; page 73, UPI; page 74, photographer unknown; given to author by the late John B. Kelly; pages 75-78, UPI; page 79, courtesy of the late Dan Morgan; pages 82, 84, 85, 87 and 90, UPI; page 91, from the late Grantland Rice; pages 92-93, UPI; page 95, Acme (now UPI); page 96, UPI; page 99, UPI; page 101, UPI; page 102, courtesy of the late John B. Kelly; page 105, UPI; page 107, photo from UPI; ticket courtesy of Dr. Charles P. Larson; pages 108, 112, 114, and 118, UPI; page 124, Acme; page 126, UPI; pages 129-130, Acme; page 132, International News Photo; page 133, Acme; page 134, Pacific & Atlantic Photo; page 135, Acme; pages 136, 138 and 139, UPI; page 141, International News Photo; pages 144 and 146, UPI; page 151, International News Photo; pages 153 and 157, UPI; page 159, Acme; pages 163, 165, 170, 171, 174, 175 and 182, UPI; pages 184 and 185, Acme; page 187, UPI; page 189, from James J. Braddock's scrapbook; page 191 and 195, UPI; pages 197 and 199, Acme; pages 203, 204, 205, 206, 208 and 210, UPI; pages 211 and 219, Acme; pages 224 and 227, UPI; page 229, from Pat McMurtry's scrapbook, lent to author for this book; pages 232, 235, 239, 240, 241, 244, 247, 249, 251 and 252, UPI; page 253, courtesy of the late Harry Grayson; pages 255, 256, 258, 260, 261, 264, 265, 267, 268 and 269, UPI; pages 271, 273, UPI; page 275, Ken Ollar; page 276, UPI; page 279, Ken Ollar; pages 281, 283, 285, 289, 290, 295, 296, 297, 298, 300, UPI; page 302, Ken Ollar; pages 306, 307, 309, 312, 319, 320, 323 and 324, UPI; page 325, from Morley Brotman; page 330, Lyle M. Lathrop; pages 334, 338, 341, 342, 344, 350, 353, 356, 357, 358, 359, 360 and 363, UPI.

Index